MW01230483

The History of the Sierra Club

1892–1970

The History of the Sierra Club 1892–1970

MICHAEL P. COHEN

SIERRA CLUB BOOKS   SAN FRANCISCO

The Sierra Club, founded in 1892 by John Muir, has devoted itself to the study and protection of the earth's scenic and ecological resources—mountains, wetlands, woodlands, wild shores and rivers, deserts and plains. The publishing program of the Sierra Club offers books to the public as a non-profit educational service in the hope that they may enlarge the public's understanding of the Club's basic concerns. The point of view expressed in each book, however, does not necessarily represent that of the Club. The Sierra Club has some sixty chapters coast to coast, in Canada, Hawaii, and Alaska. For information about how you may participate in its programs to preserve wilderness and the quality of life, please address inquiries to Sierra Club, 730 Polk Street, San Francisco, CA 94109.

Copyright © 1988 by Michael P. Cohen

All rights reserved under International and Pan-American copyright Conventions. No part of this book may be reproduced in any form or by any electronic or mechanical means, including information storage and retrieval systems, without permission in writing from the publisher.

LIBRARY OF CONGRESS CATALOGING-IN-PUBLICATION DATA

Cohen, Michael P., 1944–
   The history of the Sierra Club, 1892–1970.

   Bibliography: p.
   Includes index.
   1. Sierra Club—History. I. Title.
QH6.C64 1988 333. 95'16'0973   88-42550
ISBN 0-87156-732-6

Production by Susan Ristow
Jacket design by Paul Bacon
Book design by Wilsted & Taylor
Printed in the United States of America
10 9 8 7 6 5 4 3 2 1

Contents

Preface

This narrative history of the Sierra Club follows the evolving purposes, activities, campaigns, and controversies of the conservation organization from its origin in 1892 through the tumultuous events of the 1960s, and concludes at the beginning of the more complex environmental decade of the 1970s. When Holway Jones began his history of the early Sierra Club in 1963, he hoped "those who follow us may have the advantage of lessons learned and mistakes endured. That is why history is written." In taking up his task, I have tried to follow his aims.

For that reason I have attempted an "inside narrative" and a view from the top, from the perspective of the board of directors. I borrow the term "inside narrative" from Herman Melville, who used it as a subtitle for his novella *Billy Budd*. I mean that this history focuses on the views of those on board the ship; it is not balanced by the perspective of other conservation organizations to any great extent or by the perspectives of federal agencies or private corporations. When I began to write this history, I did not attempt a picture of objective reality taken from some distant planet. I did not do research in Park Service or Forest Service archives. This history concerns itself with what individual directors and the board as a whole thought, believed, and guessed. I relied on the information available to the board when it made its policy decisions. Sometimes that information was limited. I did not concern myself with facts alone, but also with inferences, and the way they were used within the Club; I did not ask whether policies were right or wrong, but only tried to give the prevailing reasons and logic that carried the board. No doubt individuals sometimes misperceived the facts, as, perhaps, when many Club members believed in the early 1950s that the United States Forest Service had changed from a custodial agency to an exploitive one. Sometimes the board of directors depended on reports which in retrospect were flawed. I tried to convey the consensus and atmosphere, the analysis and emotion which led to the Club's policies. When I could, I documented private views which motivated individuals and swayed the board. Did the board contradict itself? Often. I often indicated these contradictions by ironic juxtaposition.

As a consequence of its method, this history is meant to reveal the history of American conservation as it unfolded from the perspective of what has been described as the "amateur tradition in conservation." An amateur is a person who engages in an activity for the love of it—not an amateur because he is unpaid, but by virtue of his motives. Any history must engage itself not simply with acts but with intentions. As much as possible, events and the motives behind them are seen by the participants themselves, who have reflected on their own roles. To accomplish this, I have often used oral histories. This was necessary because the Sierra Club as an amateur organization often did not leave a complete trail of official documents and correspondence in the way that federal agencies like the National Park Service or United States Forest Service have. As single sources, oral histories present the historian with problems. They are dependent on the questions selected by interviewers. The memories of narrators of oral histories can be faulty and self-serving. Their remarks are not checked for accuracy by their interviewers or editors. The perspectives of oral histories are often developed after the events they recount, sometimes fifteen or twenty years after. I have been careful to indicate views which were expressed after events, and have attempted to counterpoint the views of several narrators when I have used oral histories. I have used the minutes, publications, and correspondence of the Club first, but have used oral histories a great deal. Some critics will no doubt find the balance of materials I have used has limited this narrative's objectivity. Nevertheless, by the process of selection and juxtaposition, I have tried to accurately portray what happened, what participants believed at the time, and what participants believed in retrospect.

Any historian who attempts to write about live humans faces the problem of objectivity. Many of the chief participants in this narrative are still active conservationists. Many have not completed their careers and consequently it behooves a historian not to be too sure of judgment. Yet it is unavoidable that the acts of these people will be judged, and when this narrative judges their acts, let the reader understand that it judges acts, not persons.

I have often allowed participants to respond to their critics. I have also allowed many to respond to this history. Some have disagreed with my characterization of events. Such a process can develop into an endless dialogue about intentions; when writing about acts that the participants have themselves judged, one has to stop somewhere, and often the place where one stops is a matter of discretion rather than completeness. I have attempted to stop at that point where inquiry ceases to focus on the act and shifts to the nature of the actor. Nevertheless, I have allowed many of the participants in this history to judge each other as persons, not in order to suggest that conflicts were personal, or to perpetuate gossip, or to certify these judgments, but to indicate the human context in which many policy decisions were reached. I hope the reader will not find these personal responses of participants to each other gratuitous; I can only point out that I have included them only when I believed them relevant to understanding the flow of ideas and acts in this history.

The years encompassed by this book have been described as the epoch that includes the rise and fall of modernism, with the amateur tradition being a response, reaction, or romantic revolt against the modern world, modern technology, or even the ideology of modernism. I leave the reader to judge this issue, since this narrative has attempted to engage itself in a flow of ideas and attitudes which are sufficiently complex and disparate to preclude me from making such a categorical judgment. The questions one asks determine to a great extent the judgments one can make. I have not asked the kinds of questions which might have made this history a compilation of the Club's campaigns; as a result this is not a "Fight to Save . . ." narrative. Nor has my intention been to write a narrative in order to give the Club or individuals credit for conservation victories. As a result, the structure of this narrative reflects the flow of ideas and policy in the Club more than it reflects the progress of its campaigns. For instance, I break the major campaigns of the 1960s on the redwoods, North Cascades, and Grand Canyon into several phases which fall within the 1950s, from 1960 to 1965, and from 1965 to 1968. Over these years the Club changed radically, as did the conduct of its conservation campaigns. Focusing on what the Club attempted and why, how ideas flowed to the board of directors, how they were discussed, and how acted upon, this history follows the way policy evolved and how changes in policy led to reevaluation of conservation strategies and allowed the Club to evolve.

During the first wave of conservation (1892–1914), up until

the death of its first president, John Muir, the Club was active primarily in the creation, development, and protection of Yosemite National Park and in the fate of the wilderness of the Sierra Nevada. The Club developed an ambitious outings program during this period; it was engaged in the *aesthetic* side of conservation, and commited itself to the development of California's scenic resources. During the years 1915 to 1934, characterized by the leadership of Will Colby and Francis Farquhar, and by close personal relations with the administrators of the infant National Park Service, Club officials supported the newly created national park system and recommended expansion of national parks in California. In addition, Club members actively explored and mapped the Sierra Nevada. This period ended wth the beginning of Franklin Delano Roosevelt's New Deal, sometimes known as the second wave of conservation.

The first chapter of this history summarizes those eras, including more than forty years of the Club's history. It is meant to introduce general trends in the Club and important early figures. I have relied on secondary sources for this chapter and have provided this material primarily as background for the more thoroughly researched and more detailed narrative that follows. I must give the greatest credit for this early material to Holway Jones, whose published and unpublished work on the early Club informs my perspective. I also include three portraits in the early part of this narrative, entitled "John Muir," "Walter Huber," and "Norman Clyde." These character sketches are meant to provide some human depth in the early sections. They are sketches, not meant to be biographically complete.

By the early 1930s a new generation of Club members had become proficient in technical skills of mountaineering and skiing, eventually using those skills to develop mountain troops for the United States Army during World War II. These members began to absorb modern ideas about *recrea-*

tion in the wilderness, ideas first articulated by Robert Marshall of The Wilderness Society. Further, these members began to reevaluate the recreational purposes of the national parks. This generation included Ansel Adams, David Brower, Richard Leonard, and Bestor Robinson, who play prominent roles in the rest of this narrative. Reconsidering Club policies in the light of *ecological* ideas about wilderness—ideas espoused by Aldo Leopold and introduced to the Club by Harold Bradley and Lowell Sumner—reconsidering the concepts of recreation and parks, the Club eventually changed its own purposes, particularly the one which called for "rendering accessible" the mountains of California.

The Club began to act upon its new ideas in the 1950s. So began a period of meteoric growth, as the Club's board directed it toward national prominence to defend the integrity of the national parks on a national scale and to mobilize over the controversy surrounding Dinosaur National Monument. The Club became a major force in what was called the wilderness movement. During these years the Club became more militant as it lobbied for the wilderness bill to preserve undedicated wilderness.

Hoping for support from the Kennedy presidential administration (1961), the Club escalated its campaign for the wilderness bill, and upon passage in 1964, devoted much of its energy to implementation of the Wilderness Act. It attempted to take advantage of the third wave of conservation, embodied by the policies of Stewart Udall, and embarked upon vigorous national campaigns for the preservation of the North Cascades, redwoods, and Grand Canyon. This period ended in the late 1960s with an internal crisis for the now large national Club, and with the advent of a larger and more encompassing movement called environmentalism.

This history ends with the Club's transition into an environmental decade—a transition which began in the 1950s with the Club's exhibit "This is the American Earth." The

Club advanced into the 1970s with more comprehensive environmental policies. But that is the subject for another volume in the Club's history.

Because the Club's growth parallels the growth of the division of forestry in the United States department of agriculture, created in 1881 and renamed the United States Forest Service in 1905, and the growth of the National Park Service, created in 1916, any history must of necessity be tied to the fate of those two agencies. The Club's policies closely followed and sometimes anticipated, because they advocated, the growth of federal bureaucracies.

Though the story of the Club in its first fifty years, from 1892 to World War II, is important, the focus of this history is on the growth of the Club into national prominence, following one group of members who became visible in Club affairs during the 1930s and who emerged after the war to direct the Club through the 1950s and 1960s. These members represented one generation of Californians who watched their state grow from a province to a center of power and the most populous state in the union. That same generation would see the rise of California political figures to national prominence. It would also see the Calfornia life-style become fashionable across the continent. Remarkably, it is only a slight simplification to say that one generation of Club activists was responsible for the evolution of the modern Sierra Club.

The research for this history was done during the years 1984 and 1985, and the history was written between 1985 and early 1987.

Acknowledgments

If I have learned anything in studying the Sierra Club, it is this: history, that great river, is neither made nor understood by individuals alone. I could never have navigated these wild waters without help.

First of all, this history owes its substance to librarians: Lorraine Warren at the Southern Utah State College Library, Marie Byrne at the Bancroft Library, Barbara Lekisch at the Sierra Club Library, and Lee Kosso at the University of Nevada Reno Library. In addition, I received copies of important correspondence and other materials from Nathan Clark, Ann Lage, Richard Cellarius, Thomas Jukes, Ruth Dyar Mendenhall, and Martin Litton.

Many men who appear in this narrative helped me scout the rapids. David Brower was, as always, generous with his time and good advice. Richard Leonard read the manuscript for accuracy and offered encouragement. Martin Litton not only supplied a great deal of information, but willingly stood on the bank and discussed issues in his usual candid way. Michael McCloskey read the whole manuscript thoroughly, and read several sections more than once.

In particular, three people of the Club facilitated my adventure and kept up my morale. James Cohee of Sierra Club

Books, Ann Lage of the Club History Committee, and Michael McCloskey, Chairman, saw this book through many hard times. Without them, I might well have walked out of these canyons after my boat flipped the first time.

I conferred with many colleagues, sometimes indoors and often outdoors. James Aton, Robert G. Young, Peter Givler, Alfred Runte, and Charles F. Wilkinson discussed this project from its early stages. A great many people exercised their patience with me, particularly while I learned to run real rivers of the American West, the Green, Yampa, Colorado, and Snake. More than one friend towed my kayak to shore, and helped me bail it out.

As part of the process specified by the Sierra Club Publications Committee, many readers offered critiques. Betsy Barnett, Susan L. Flader, Dave Foreman, Roderick Nash, Harold K. Steen, and William A. Turnage corrected inaccuracies, provided perspective, and suggested solutions to the author's problems. Nevertheless, the errors committed in these passages are my own.

In addition to reading manuscript, Marvin Baker defended the autonomy of this project when a defense was crucial.

Richard Hart of the Institute of the American West provided a forum where I discussed ideas with colleagues, the National Endowment for the Humanities provided a Travel to Collections fellowship, and Southern Utah State College provided a sabbatical leave.

Unfortunately, the Ansel Adams Publishing Rights Trust refused direct quotation of any letters or memoranda written by Ansel Adams, even those donated by Adams to the Sierra Club Archives and those written as part of his official capacity as a member of the Sierra Club board of directors.

I am in the debt of two judicious editors. Jim Cohee entrusted me with this work, saw me through the writing, and helped separate the essential from the superfluous. Sam Allen kept me honest.

This book is dedicated to Valerie Cohen, my mate. She did not have to type it, but read countless versions. For many months, Valerie returned with me to the turmoil of the 1960s, and while living also in the 1980s learned along with me the dialectic of theory and practice in environmental politics. Her sharp eye for ethical behavior and personal integrity kept our little boat away from more than one sharp rock.

The History of the Sierra Club

1892–1970

CHAPTER ONE

Make the Mountains Glad

John Muir in California, 1868–1890

It is a truth universally acknowledged that John Muir, a single man in possession of a vision, founded the Sierra Club. The historian finds no such simple truth. Further, as the Club's purposes have changed over nearly a century, so have the interpretations of Muir's vision. Ever constant, the icon has remained Muir the visionary, the Club's—and perhaps the conservation movement's—"saint and messiah."[1] Muir the man remains more elusive. Recent work by biographers and historians has developed a more complete picture of the man.[2] The ideological leader of the Sierra Club, president from 1892 to his death in 1914, Muir differed in many ways from the citizens of San Francisco, Palo Alto, and Oakland who would charter the Club.

John Muir was born April 21, 1838, in Dunbar, Scotland, the third in a family that included eight children. He came to Wisconsin in 1849, at the age of eleven, where his father kept him engaged clearing land and farming until he left home in 1860. He attended the University of Wisconsin (1861–1863), traveled, and worked various jobs until he was temporarily blinded in an industrial accident in the spring of 1867. This critical event led him to reconsider the direction of his life and pursue the botanical studies he loved. That year he began

1

his 1,000-mile walk to the Gulf of Mexico, a journey which eventually took him on to California.

Thirty years old when he first came to California, he hurried through San Francisco on his way to the mountains he sought. Unlike the professors at the University of California and Stanford who helped organize the Club, Muir had not finished his formal college education; he later decided not to become a college professor if it meant leaving the wilds. But by the early 1870s Muir had determined to be a professional nature writer, and soon this occupation required him to spend his winters in Oakland, where he turned his journals into articles.

There were other paradoxes in Muir's career. The man who was to spend his life decrying the destruction of the mountains by "hoofed locusts" spent his first summer in the Sierra as a shepherd. The man who published his first essays in *Overland Monthly*, the journal "Devoted to the Development of the Country," would become the foremost exponent of California's wild beauty, and would lead an organization which would one day devote itself to opposing the blind development of the country. Further, the man who would come to embody what was called the out-of-doors gospel of wildness earned his living raising hybrid fruits on a farm in Martinez, California. There were indeed many Muirs, most prominently the rebellious wilderness devotee living in Yosemite in the early 1870s, and another writing twenty years later for the eastern press: the publicizer, booster of parks. Muir's complexity was reflected in the Sierra Club, just as the Club took its purpose, and its members their personal commitment, from the Californian landscape. To see what that personal commitment was or would be, one must ask what kind of life Muir sought in California.

When Muir arrived in California in 1868 his goals were ambitious and intensely personal. What he sought was aesthetic, religious, scientific, ethical, and perhaps finally individual: to know himself as a whole and harmonious human being in the natural world. Though he began the rediscovery of California in 1868 as a botanist, and reveled in the wealth of her flora, he soon directed his attention to the geology, geography, and ecology of the Sierra. He followed the watersheds of the Yosemite High Sierra and then the Kings Canyon region, tracing the paths of glaciers. The essential Muir, camping above Yosemite Valley during an early autumn storm, wrote: "I spring to my feet crying: 'Heavens and earth! Rock is not light, not heavy, not transparent, not opaque, but every pore gushes, glows like a thought with immortal life!'"[3] Wildlife guided the pattern of his life in the mountains, as he came to admire the harmonious lives of the bears, deer, mountain sheep, squirrels, and water ouzels. He ascended major unclimbed summits, explored unknown canyons, climbed trees in wind storms, and ran through the meadows of Yosemite during flood and earthquake, rejoicing in the wildness of nature. He wrote copiously in his journal, and sketched the mountains in which he dwelt. His personal experience was the best testament for the new consciousness that California needed if it was to grow beyond the exploitive mentality of the gold rush.

A new consciousness had been asked for by Thomas Starr King when he lamented in 1860 that Californians "may make an outward visit to the Sierras, but there are no Yosemites in the soul."[4] In 1864 Congress granted the State of California a tract of land, including Yosemite Valley and the Mariposa Big Trees, stating that it "shall be held for public use, resort and recreation, shall be held inalienable for all time." The Yosemite grant was congressionally decreed, but administered by the state through an appointed commission. Though Muir knew that "not one can sing like the Merced [River] . . . of sublime Yosemite she is the voice," Muir himself became the voice of Yosemite, sang the Yosemite of the soul.[5]

For a world that required science of an explorer, Muir completed his *Studies in the Sierra* by the mid 1870s. Though his devotion to nature was religious at root, aesthetic in expression, and ecological in intellectual conception, Muir also spoke the language of mechanistic science, and his ability to speak this language was crucial to his future role. And though Muir vigorously opposed the contemporary theories which purported to explain the evolution of the Sierra, he made lasting friends among some of those whose theories he refuted. One such theorist was Joseph LeConte (1823–1901), a charter member of the Club, who came to the state in 1869 as a professor of geology and natural history at the University of California. Generally conceded to be California's most influential teacher, LeConte spent much of his career attempting to reconcile his personal theism with his professional commitment to the theory of evolution.[6] Not only did Muir's theory about the glacial history of the Sierra differ from LeConte's, but the way they reconciled their scientific thought and personal values differed. While LeConte finally separated his evolutionary scientific views from his personal Christian values, subjected, as he said, the "lower" animal part of himself to the "higher" divine part, Muir tried to integrate the animal and spiritual parts of himself and refused to separate his religious and scientific insights.

LeConte frequently came to the Sierra with his students and enjoyed the social aspects of an excursion to the wilds. Muir usually explored the Sierra in solitude. Yet the two sat together one evening in 1870 above Tenaya Lake and communed. LeConte later remembered "the deep stillness of the night; the silvery light and deep shadows of the mountains . . . all these seemed exquisitely harmonized with one another and the grand harmony made answering music in our hearts."[7] They agreed that the beauty of the Sierra should be shared, and twenty years later, when they joined in the organization of the Sierra Club, it was to institutionalize such communion.

Thirty-seven years old in 1875, Muir was beginning to ask, "What is the human part of the mountain's destiny?"[8] Muir's *question*, phrased with such care, was better than the more traditional American *assumption*, which required that the mountain play its part in human destiny. Such an inquiry may well be taken as the intellectual origin of the American conservation movement. Muir's answers would inspire those who shared a more than utilitarian and mechanistic vision of America's future. When Muir began to think about what men would do with the mountains he did so while he was in the mountains, and he began with an understanding of the spiritual and intellectual value of nature, next to which a man or his creations were nothing. As he wrote in the fall of 1874, "Civilization and fever and all the morbidness that has been hooted at me has not dimmed my glacial eye, and I care to live only to entice people to look at nature's loveliness. My own special self is nothing."[9] Muir's ideas about conservation were rooted in a non-anthropocentric, or egoless, experience of the mountains. And most of this experience was gained during the late 1860s and early 1870s, spent almost entirely in the mountains. He learned what was good for nature and what was good for culture, or so he believed. He could report that "Nature may have other uses even for *rich* soil besides the feeding of human beings," and when the prayers of prospectors sinned against science, "like prayers of any kind not in harmony with nature, they are unanswered."[10]

By the late 1880s his conservation goals were more specific. And fortuitously, in June of 1889 he formed a close and lasting relationship with Robert Underwood Johnson.[11] An editor for *Century Magazine*, the successor to *Scribners* (which had published much of Muir's earlier work), Johnson badgered Muir to return to writing as early as 1884, while Muir toiled on his ranch. In 1889 Johnson came to California and asked Muir to say yet another word for California's natural resources. Together in the Sierra, while they visited Muir's favorite haunts in the Yosemite grant, they planned a campaign for a large Yosemite national park surrounding the small state park which had been set aside in 1864. A conception sophisticated beyond any which would appear over the next half century, Muir's idea of a Yosemite national park was essentially ecological, since it began with the preservation of the complete watersheds of the Merced and Tuolumne rivers. It was also an ingenious recreational plan, since it offered a dual park, the watershed of the Merced developed for intensive tourism and the watershed of the Tuolumne left wild for a higher, more primitive kind of recreation. Though Muir abhorred the idea of tourism as a search for "wonders and curiosities," the essays he would write for Johnson, entitled "Treasures of Yosemite" and "Features of Yosemite," would set a precedent in the rhetoric of park boosters. Piercing through the clichéd conventions of tour-guide writing, he lectured his readers on the wholeness and harmony of the larger landscape—"things frail and fleeting and types of endurance meeting here and blending in countless forms, as if into this one mountain mansion Nature had gathered her choicest treasures."[12] Further, the coordination of Muir's literary contributions with Johnson's abilities as a publicizer and congressional lobbyist would set a pattern for the conservation campaigns of the future. In 1890 Yosemite National Park was created by Congress as a result of the effort of two men.

The success of Johnson's and Muir's first campaign for Yosemite was followed by failure when they proposed a national park for the Kings River watershed to the south—a region of even wilder country extending from the crest of the Sierra and Mount Whitney and encompassing the headwaters of many major Sierran streams, rugged glacial valleys, and the western forest belt, including a good many Sequoia groves. Their successes and failures, their strategies and tactics, the kinds of compromises they were willing to make, and the consequences, foretold the kinds of problems future conservationists would inherit.

The major problem Muir and Johnson faced was the limited range of arguments which could be advanced for national parks. As historian Alfred Runte has noted, in conception and in the arguments for their passage, national parks had to be justified by predetermining criteria of monumentalism and economic worthlessness.[13] For the American aesthetic, not the things frail and fleeting, but only types of endurance were interesting. Typically, the United States Congress would preserve as parks only lands whose resources could not otherwise be developed. On the other hand, Muir recognized early and insisted with increasing vehemence as the century drew to a close that mountain parks which included only rocks and which were denuded of trees, flowers, and other wildlife were sterile monuments. In the event, the parks movement would be tied to an almost purely aesthetic justification for much of its history. Muir chafed against the political realities of monumentalism and economic worthlessness, yet he was a realist. If he wrote to Johnson saying, "As I have urged over and over again, the Yosemite Reservation ought to include all the Yosemite fountains," he also conceded in his proposals for parks that the mountains were "not valuable for any other use than the use of beauty" and that "no interests would suffer."[14]

Muir once told Johnson, "The love of Nature among Californians is desperately moderate; consuming enthusiasm almost wholly unknown."[15] With Yosemite, this meant that the state simply did not care about the fate of the valley itself. Consequently, Johnson and Muir directed their rhetoric almost entirely to the urban East, rather than to rural or western audiences, for whom the aesthetic argument carried little interest in comparison to arguments based on economic development. From the very beginning, parks were presented through ornate descriptive prose, elaborate drawings, paint-ings, photographs, and engravings, which Johnson distributed to Congress. The parks movement, as represented by Muir and Johnson, advocated federal control rather than state management, not simply because they feared local neglect, but because California had demonstrably failed to manage Yosemite satisfactorily.

If the argument for national parks was directed toward the aesthetic-minded eastern audience, the development of parks would have to allow that clientele to enjoy the parks' treasures. In 1891 Muir proposed access by way of roads to the wild Kings Canyon country. He and his ideological heirs conceded the need for accommodations in national parks sufficiently luxurious to house the lovers of beauty. The Muir who deplored the overdevelopment of Yosemite State Park would advocate development of wild lands in order to preserve them as national parks.[16]

So it was that the public Muir of the 1890s presented a "genteel wilderness" in his writings, and sometimes compromised the integrity of the wild lands he loved to establish them as parks and protect them from sheepmen, hoofed locusts, lumbermen, and miners. This Muir would have a powerful influence on the conservation movement and on the Sierra Club. Like this Muir the early Club took up aesthetic arguments. Only much later would the conservation movement rediscover the younger Muir who disparaged mass tourism.

Birth of the Sierra Club 1892   Late in 1889 Muir met in San Francisco with his artist friend William Keith, with Warren Olney, a lawyer who was to become mayor of Oakland, and with a group of professors from the University of California and Stanford, including Joseph LeConte, J. Henry Senger, William D. Armes, Cornelius B. Bradley, and Stanford president David Starr Jordan.[1] The idea for the meetings was probably Robert Underwood Johnson's, and a part of the

Johnson–Muir strategy for establishing a Yosemite national park. "Why don't you start an association," wrote Johnson in November 1889, while he pushed Muir to finish the essays which *Century* would publish; "it would have a good influence if you guarded carefully the membership."[2] At the University of California there were already ideas for an Alpine Club, and the name Sierra Club came from there.

Whether the meetings in San Francisco were at the impetus of Muir and Johnson, who wanted to form an organization for the defense of the Yosemite national park they were about to propose, or whether they were at first about a mountaineering organization proposed by Senger and Olney and agreed to by Muir, the ranks of those interested had grown to 27 individuals by late May of 1892, and Warren Olney drew up the Club's articles of incorporation for a meeting held on June 4, 1892. Muir, who hoped "we will be able to do something for wilderness and make the mountains glad," was the unanimous choice for president.[3] There were other officers, and 283 charter members enrolled by the following winter, including many prominent Bay Area professors, scientists, politicians, and business leaders.[4]

The articles of incorporation for the Club stipulated nine directors, to carry out a hierarchy of recreational, educational, and political purposes:

> To explore, enjoy, and render accessible the mountain regions of the Pacific Coast;
>
> To publish authentic information concerning them;
>
> To enlist the support and coöperation of the people and the government in preserving the forests and other natural features of the Sierra Nevada Mountains.[5]

This combination of scientific, educational, developmental, and recreational aims was not unusual, just as the Sierra Club was not the first organization interested in preserving wild landscape.[6] According to Joseph N. LeConte—called Little Joe to distinguish him from his father, Dr. Joe—the first purpose of the Club, including the words "render accessible," was Senger's, and the third purpose was Olney's.[7] In January of 1893 the Club began to publish its *Bulletin*.

The purposes of the Club accurately reflect the values of its founders. As an organization it would find its own aims expressed in Muir's published works over the next two decades, when he returned vigorously to his writing career after an absence of nearly ten years. *The Mountains of California* (1894), dedicated to his wife, would become a new testament from the California wilderness; *Our National Parks* (1901), compiled from writings from 1897 on and dedicated to Charles Sprague Sargent, eminent botanist and lover of trees, would attempt to balance the recreational and utilitarian uses of western wild lands; *My First Summer in the Sierra* (1911), dedicated to the Sierra Club, set out a personal narrative dramatizing the spiritual and recreational benefits of Yosemite; and *The Yosemite* (1912), dedicated to Robert Underwood Johnson, would be a guidebook and defense of the integrity of Yosemite National Park. Following Muir, their most articulate spokesman, the men and women of the Sierra Club gave formal expression to a distinctly Californian relationship to the outdoors, and responded to what Kevin Starr calls "a deep California hope: that a regional heritage could be defined and preserved."[8] For them, the Sierra was a cultural resource which needed to be known, shared, protected for the future.

The time was opportune. If political corruption in San Francisco had reached one of its frequent climaxes in 1891, there were signs of change in the next year, leading to an era of reform during the period 1892–1901, particularly during the administration of Mayor James D. Phelan.[9] The kind of men who chartered the Club welcomed reform, yet would soon have to choose between the welfare of the city and their beloved Sierra. As prominent but not wealthy Californians—for the Sierra Club was predominantly a middle-class organization—they were the kind of Californians who would be called progressives by later historians. As the historian describes him the California progressive was middle class, urban, and religious; he had a northern European name, hoped that politics might be a moral exercise, but found himself a citizen of a city famous for its political corruption.[10] Envisioning a spiritual future for California, he found himself caught between two materialist forces. First, the life of his state was dominated by one corporation, the Southern Pacific Railroad. Second, the industrial life of his cities was characterized by well-organized labor unions who dramatized class conflict, sometimes in violent ways. As far as the progressive was concerned, the problems of California were rooted in class consciousness. He hoped for a period when classes and political parties would be abolished. The progressive movement in California was a microcosm of national political change.[11] Warren Olney, for instance, ran successfully for mayor of Oakland only after he received both Democratic and Republican nominations. The progressive's rhetoric, like Muir's, would always suggest that political issues were not partisan but moral, fought between the forces of right and wrong.

In a state where politics were usually issue-dominated, where political parties received relatively less loyalty, and which saw the economy racked with land booms and land busts, the Sierra Club would play its role in the dialogue about the possibilities for California. In the early 1890s the country had been told by its census bureau that it had no more frontier, and was told by a junior progressive historian, Frederick Jackson Turner, that its character had been determined by interaction with wilderness along the frontier; there seemed to be several possible but conflicting visions of the future. California was potentially a garden "wherein we may assemble for play, or where we may sit in seclusion for work," as Charles Keeler, a charter Club member, argued.[12] Keeler's garden was derived from an Oriental or Mediterranean model. Or California was a desert, stern, harsh, and at first repellent, where the poetic chaos of sublime but lonely desolation might dominate the human soul. As Kevin Starr points out, these separate literary visions—Mary Austin's Californian as desert dweller, John Muir's Californian as mountain dweller, or later Robinson Jeffers' Californian as dweller by the sea—suggested possibilities for a pastoral or rural life, possibilities that played in the Californian mind against the other possibility of an urban future, essentially cultured, artistic, European, tame.[13]

Just as Muir's proposal for a Yosemite national park depicted a partly wild and partly tame Sierra, so the member of the Sierra Club wished for his state to be partly developed and partly wild. Unlike the hypothetical American who searched for a middle-ground landscape, the Sierra Club member wanted to retain the wild mountains while he developed his own cities. Over the next few years he would discover the inherent conflicts in his aspirations. Muir himself would have a long and hard struggle of conscience as he attempted to protect the moral and spiritual ideals he found in nature while he faced political and economic forces which would be necessary for developing the Californian and American culture he desired.

During its early years the Club shaped and was shaped by the rise of the national movement called conservation. Through its vigilant policy of protection, it began to act in the interests of Yosemite, and learned how to deal with dissent within its ranks. It discovered the need to create programs such as outings to assure its own continuance. It had to choose between provincial and national interest in the fate of Yosemite Valley, and then to form political alliances for the power that would make its policies influential. Not least, it experienced its first major crisis and its first major public campaign when it argued in a controversy heard nationally over the disposition of Hetch Hetchy Valley in Yosemite National Park.

What has come to be called conservation was a fluid and incompletely formed idea in 1891. In 1892 the Forest Reserve Act, as Muir called it, had given the United States president the right to set aside forest reserves, and the following year several were created in three states. Muir considered these to be not simply *re*serves, but *pre*serves; what a reserve was, or what its future might be, was in no sense clear.

The early history of Yosemite dramatized in microcosm the problems of reservations. The Yosemite Valley and Mariposa Big Trees had been granted to California by Congress in 1864, "for public use, resort and recreation . . . inalienable for all time."[14] Many in the Club believed Yosemite Valley constituted America's first national park.[15] Muir had never been happy about California's administration of Yosemite Valley, but advised by Johnson, he attempted the cautious use of understatement in dealing with the state commission. Muir was particularly disturbed to see and smell the hog pens in the valley, and he objected to the use of meadows as pastures. The Club could not approve unrestricted and unplanned development by private entrepreneurs. It seemed better to consult than protest too vigorously. On the other hand, one of the charter members of the Club, an artist named Charles D. Robinson, was so deeply offended by the condition of the valley that he pressured both Muir and the Club to confront the state. By 1893 the members of the Club had reason to take action against the state commission that managed this land. As Warren Olney wrote to Muir, the depredations in the valley were serious, and the Club could not avoid involvement, in part because of the vigor of Robinson's complaints. In October 1892, only a few months after the Club was formed, Robinson began to argue that the "Sierra Club . . . has a mere existence for its own pleasure—that is all. . . . In short the

Club, like the state, is nerveless and dead regarding Yosemite, as I see things."[16] Muir was sympathetic to Robinson's view that the valley should be managed by federal, not state, means. But some Californians like Warren Olney feared the state would lose prestige if it relinquished the valley to the federal government, and the Club would lose prestige if it seemed to resist California's aspirations.[17] The differences between Robinson's and Olney's perspectives suggest a conflict which would recur. Robinson was alarmed with the condition of Yosemite and was committed to whatever strategy might help; he wanted immediate action and was not afraid of confrontation. Olney was more interested in preserving the viability of the Club so that it could continue to join in the growth of California, and he was willing to negotiate even if the process was slower, even if the gains might be less dramatic.

Federal policy for managing the public domain had not yet been established. Though Muir advocated as early as 1890 the reservation of the "whole roof of the Sierra" and Johnson had approved such a plan, taking it up while he lobbied for the Yosemite National Park Bill of 1890, the means of management were still unclear.[18] Linked to federal control, which Muir would champion for Yosemite Valley openly from 1895 on, and which he would also advocate for much of the western wildlands in the late 1890s, was the question of permanence for reservations. In 1892, in an era when the status of the public domain was uncertain, the boundaries of Yosemite National Park, surrounding the Yosemite Grant, were under constant threat of diminution, as they were again in 1905 when the park's boundaries were significantly altered. The act of 1890 put Yosemite National Park under the exclusive control of the secretary of the interior, who was duty bound to make rules and regulations "to provide for the preservation from injury of all timber, mineral deposits, natural curiosities, or wonders within such reservation, and their retention in their natural condition."[19] But it was not until 1916, when the National Park Service was created, that there came into being a distinct and autonomous agency to protect national parks and adequate regulations to direct their management. So with Yosemite the Club attempted to defend two separately administered parks, whose problems differed and whose status was in no sense secure.[20] Further, the Club lacked solidarity on the subject.

Late in 1895, at its annual meeting, the Club began to deliberate on the preservation and management of national parks and forest reservations. By this time Yosemite National Park had been patrolled for five years by the United States Army.

Speaking consecutively, Muir and Professor William Russell Dudley of Stanford University praised the army's work in the national park. As Dudley argued, "To pass from the trampled meadows of the reservation to the protected meadows of the National Park was a lesson in patriotism."[21] Like Muir, Dudley believed that forestry might become a province of the army, taught at West Point. Like Dudley, Muir argued that "forest management must be put on a rational, permanent, scientific basis, as in every other civilized country."[22] This sounds so little like the kind of statement natural to Muir that it is hard not to see it as a concession to utilitarian considerations. Muir agreed when the elder Joseph LeConte announced, "Now, I am perfectly satisfied that nothing can save our timber land except complete reservation by the Government."[23] Thus the Club would advocate reservation, strong federal control, and utilitarian management of the nation's forests by scientific principles. Dudley would continue in 1900 to ask that the Club "throw the weight of its little influence in favor of reserving all the forest lands surrounding the great valleys of California" forever in the hands of federal control.[24] At this meeting in 1896 speakers for the Club advocated exactly the principle of progressive conservation

which would be advocated by Gifford Pinchot and Theodore
Roosevelt in the next fifteen years. As far as Muir was concerned, "I think I said truly that this part of the work of the
Club dependent on the action of Congress was in great part
lawyers' work, and that Mr. Olney, our Vice-President, ought
to do it."[25]

As the decade wore on, however, it became clear that Muir
did not define scientific management as the more utilitarian
conservationists did. He believed that forests should be managed for themselves, not for maximum possible economic
benefit. When he began to see what was called scientific
management in practice, he was appalled, just as Aldo Leopold would be forty years later.[26] Most historians date Muir's
split from Pinchot and scientific management from 1897,
when Muir discovered that Pinchot advocated sheep-grazing
in the forest reserves. Hoofed locusts. According to Will
Colby, who informed Muir's first biographer, Muir told Pinchot, "I don't want anything more to do with you."[27] By 1897
Muir was saying of trees, "They cannot run away; and even if
they could, they would still be destroyed—chased and
hunted down as long as fun or a dollar could be got out of
their bark hides."[28] He never returned to the Pinchot fold.

After 1895 there were clear factions in the Club and clear
differences over the meaning of conservation. Forest reserves
would be transferred in 1905 from the department of the interior to the department of agriculture; factions within the
Club would split over local versus federal control of the public
domain, over utilization versus preservation of forest preserves. At bottom, members wanted both the cultural, material growth of California and the preservation of its natural
beauty, wanted to keep their regional pride, with the security
of federal control, wanted scientific management of forests,
but wished to accrue spiritual benefits from their wild lands.
They did not want to choose sides between bears and men,
between trees and men, between God's nature and man's sci-

ence.²⁹ When the Club began to ask what it could contribute to the social fate of California, how it could help to preserve the natural environment, and how it could balance use and preservation, idealistic members believed that these were not conflicting aspirations, but that with careful federal management, nature and culture could be balanced and reconciled.

When John Muir compiled the articles he had writ- *Colby's* ten between 1875 and 1882, publishing the collection *Strategies* in 1894 as *The Mountains of California*, his focus, like that of the Club, was upon the state's crowning jewel, 1892–1905 the Sierra Nevada—its natural history, peaks, lakes, forests, and wildlife. Muir was 54 years old when he helped organize the Club in 1892, and by that time in his life was becoming the genteel writer who would be celebrated in the eastern urban centers as a kind of "John the Baptist" of the out-of-doors gospel, the publicizer who engaged himself in "calling everybody to come and enjoy the thousand blessings" of the wilderness. When Muir reminisced in *The Mountains of California* about the time when all California was wild and deplored "the wide-spread deterioration and destruction of every kind already effected," still he celebrated her scenery in the Sierra as "the most attractive that has yet been discovered in the mountain ranges of the world" and "her incomparable climate and flora" as "the best of all."³⁰ Most of his best writing in the years that followed, like the best efforts of the Club itself during its first fifty years, would be devoted to choice parts of the Sierra—particularly Yosemite—which he and the Club helped protect as national parks.

A popular view of the Club as attempting to carry the gospel of the mature, more genteel Muir into the modern world is born out by a summary of its conservation activities in the years culminated by the National Park Service Act of 1916. The ideas of a younger and more radical Muir were not rediscovered until the Club was a half century old. The Club's own tally of its early conservation victories indicates that it took a primary interest in the creation and maintenance of national parks. Yosemite alone, with the complex affairs surrounding its boundaries and management, has been worthy of more than one book and is likely to produce more. Though the Club did express views favoring the creation of Grand Canyon, Mount Rainier, and Glacier national parks, it focused almost entirely on the mountains and forests of California, paying particular attention to the areas that became Yosemite, Sequoia, and Kings Canyon national parks.

This period marked what has been called the first wave of American conservation, the birth of the Progressive Conservation movement, which attempted, in the words of one historian, "the transformation of a decentralized nontechnical, loosely organized society, where waste and inefficiency ran rampant, into a highly organized, technical, and centrally planned and directed social organization which could meet a complex world with efficiency and purpose."[31] During this period, characterized by the classification and reservation of public lands and the origins of the agencies to manage them, the Club established its role as a consultant and supporter, hoping to maintain a balance between two sides of conservation—aesthetic and economic—corresponding to two kinds of reserved lands. The Club's *Bulletin* quoted with approval the words of J. Horace McFarland of the American Civic Association, who said, "The primary function of the national forests is to supply lumber. The primary function of the national parks is to maintain in healthful efficiency the lives of the people who must use that lumber."[32]

Muir began in the late 1890s to write expansively about tourism as an antidote to the "vice of over-industry" and to the utilitarian emphasis of the Pinchot conservationists. "The tendency nowadays to wander in wilderness is delightful to see," he had written for *Atlantic*; "thousands of tired, nerve-shaken, over-civilized people are beginning to find out that going to the mountains is going home; that wilderness is a necessity; and that mountain parks and reservations are useful not only as fountains of timber and irrigating rivers, but as fountains of life."[33]

Most active members of the Club had joined not because they were interested in the economic uses of nature but because they were drawn to the healthful aspects of recreation. Some of Muir's best confederates were not the charter members of the Club, but a group of members who constituted a younger second generation of the Club. They included, in addition to Little Joe LeConte, who was a charter member and served on the board of directors for 42 years (1898–1940), Edward Taylor Parsons and his wife Marion Randall Parsons, who between them served for 34 years, she succeeding him when he passed away (1904–1914/1914–1938), William Frederick Badè, who served 29 years (1907–1936), and, most important, William Colby, who served on the Club's board for 49 years, 47 of them as secretary and 2 as president (1900–1949). These younger members were particularly active in the outdoors and in the first Club campaigns.

Will Colby visited the Sierra for the first time in 1894, at the age of nineteen, with a group of students and teachers from the University of California. They had all been reading the descriptions of the Sierra by Muir; that summer Colby acquired "a very wonderful insight into the beauties of the Sierra and the magnificence of the range," realized that travel of this strenuous sort would be a lifetime activity, and met a number of men who were active in the Sierra Club. As he remembered, "Most of the people who went to the Sierra belonged to the Sierra Club."[34] Naturally he was drawn into the Club ranks.

Orphaned at the age of six, Colby was a self-made man, with tremendous drive. While supporting himself by teaching, he graduated from the Hastings Law School in 1898 and was to become an eminent mining attorney. During the sum-

mer after he graduated, when the Club decided to provide
tourist information in Yosemite at a small cottage, Colby was
chosen to be Club representative there.³⁵ By 1900 he was appointed Club secretary, and as a result became very close to
Muir.

Colby's first major contribution to the Club was a proposal
for an annual outing. Because he believed national forest reservations would be established soon and that major goal of
the Club attained, he feared in late 1900 that without a goal
the Club might fade away.³⁶ Following the strategy Muir had
used on Robert Underwood Johnson, and even the motive
which had drawn Colby to the Club—"if people in general
could be got into the woods, even for once, to hear the trees
speak for themselves, all difficulties in the way of forest preservation would vanish"—Colby and Muir worked out a proposal for the first Sierra Club outing, in 1901.³⁷ An outings
program would not only awaken people to nature, but reju-
venate the organization by providing good fellowship. A
Sierra Club outing might be a far cry from the lonely journeys
of Muir thirty years earlier and closer to the university outings of the senior Joseph LeConte, emphasizing community
rather than solitude. Nevertheless, it would be an integral
part of the Club's role in the future. During the first outing,
when 96 Club members journeyed to Tuolumne Meadows in
Yosemite National Park, the elder Joseph LeConte, while
touring in Yosemite Valley, died of a sudden illness. News of
this event struck sorrow into the group, who had read Le-
Conte's *Journal of Ramblings Through the High Sierra* in anticipation of the adventure; nevertheless, a new community was
formed that summer.

The outing was a huge success and became a yearly event;
one can see the joy outings brought to members by reading
the narratives published yearly in the *Bulletin*. Over the years
the outings program would bring many of the most active
Club members into the fold. The Sierra Club's future policies

would be based on first-hand experience, and would be directed toward the spiritual, aesthetic, and communal benefits which could be acquired in the wilds. It was for this reason that Muir's *My First Summer in the Sierra* (1911), about his baptism into Yosemite's wilderness, was dedicated "To the Sierra Club of California, Faithful Defender of the People's Playgrounds."

Like members of the Sierra Club outings, President Theodore Roosevelt, on a visit to California in 1903, was guided in Yosemite by Muir. Roosevelt praised the Club for its role in conservation.[38] But unlike members of the outings, the president had other and more pressing political obligations. Roosevelt's arrival in California, in the same year that the first automobile crossed the continent, was at the behest of San Francisco politicians.[39] In the next two years the controversy within the Club which led to a campaign for the recession of Yosemite Valley to the federal government called out California provincialism. That provincialism would lead James D. Phelan, as mayor of San Francisco, to say of Muir in 1909 that he would "sacrifice his own family for the preservation of beauty."[40]

As Colby remembered, William Randolph Hearst's *Examiner* had asked about Yosemite, "Do you want to have this taken away from the residents of California and practically moved back to Washington?"[41] Colby responded by framing an argument about the gains to California from national tourism. In the political campaign that followed, Colby realized that Muir's friendship with E. H. Harriman, president of the Southern Pacific Railroad since 1901, could be used to the Club's advantage. The Club lobbied the California legislature, relying heavily on the railroad's influence in Sacramento. This was not a safe course, since the railroad, and its chief counsel William Herrin, were well hated by the San Francisco Progressives, and Herrin himself was known to brag that the railroad had kept California shackled for so long "because of its control of the reform movements."[42] In the campaign of 1905, thirty-year-old Colby and sixty-seven-year-old Muir lobbied and exhorted in Sacramento. As Colby said, "I learned more about politics and the state legislature in those few weeks than I have in all the rest of my life put together."[43] Muir himself, actively involved in the campaign, wrote to Robert Underwood Johnson in 1905 that his political education was complete: "Now that the fight is finished and my education as a politician and lobbyist is finished, I am almost finished myself." In fact he was only beginning. In the next decade the Club would find itself opposing not only the Progressive Conservation movement, as represented by Pinchot, but the plans of its home city, San Francisco.

Hetch Hetchy   While Colby and Muir were engaged by the
1906–1913   campaign for the recession of Yosemite Valley to
                     federal control, San Francisco was engaged in
gaining federal support for its application to develop the water of the Tuolumne River for domestic use. By mid 1906 the city had gained the support of Gifford Pinchot for its application, and the prospect of a dam and reservoir within a national park was imminent. Colby was aware of the deeply troubling situation from early 1905.[44] Beyond that, after the great earthquake San Francisco engaged in a program of rebuilding to be bigger and better. This new impetus for growth threatened to unbalance the two sides of conservation by allowing economic development to destroy an area which had been reserved for the spiritual health of Americans. Supporters of the water development project, including many in the Club, saw the proposed dam as necessary to the development of the West, an antidote to water monopolies and to the growth of the Pacific Gas and Electric Company within the State of California. The secretary of the interior, James Garfield, held hearings in San Francisco on the dam during the

summer of 1907, while the Club was on its summer outing. Nobody testified against the project.[45]

Involved in the campaign to prevent a dam at Hetch Hetchy were both political and philosophical allegiances. The question was most clearly put to California by the philosopher George Santayana. "When you escape, as you love to do, to your forests and your Sierras," he told Californians, "I am sure that you do not feel you made them, or that they were made for you. . . . In their non-human beauty and peace they stir the sub-human depths and the superhuman possibilities of your own spirit."[46] But for Pinchot, at this stage of the game the aesthetic side of conservation could not go ahead of the economic and moral aspects.[47] The dam must be built because the Sierra was made for man. As Santayana knew, Pinchot had simplified a subtle and complex issue.

By 1907 Pinchot had consolidated his control of the national forests and had also gained the confidence of Roosevelt. After 1905 the forest reserves were controlled by the department of agriculture. As forester, Pinchot renamed the Bureau of Forestry the Forest Service to reflect the agency's commitment. The forest reserves were now called national forests, and Pinchot made clear that they were not to be held inviolate.[48] He prepared a three-point program of conservation, which included use and development, prevention of waste, and "benefit of the many, not merely profit of the few."[49] He had issued the first version of what was called the Use Book. As the little red Use Book indicated, resources were not "locked up," but available to the home-seeker, the prospector and miner, the user of timber, the user of the range, and the user of water. The forests were available and waiting to be filled by power plants, mills, roads, trails, canals, reservoirs, telephone and power lines. "On a National Forest," Pinchot reported, "the present and future *local* demand is always considered first."[50]

In this light, the Club began to wonder about the permanence of any federal reservation. Unlike the national forests, the national parks at this time lacked a separate agency for administration, and as a result lacked a policy of protection. The Club had supported federal control of Yosemite, and saw California cede Yosemite Valley to the federal Yosemite National Park in 1905. Soon it was watching the federal government side with San Francisco against the interests of Yosemite National Park. How could philosophical, aesthetic, or spiritual arguments compete with mechanistic or material arguments for the nation's strength in the future? Muir's original proposal for a Yosemite national park included a wild watershed, and the very wildness of that watershed made it vulnerable to economic exploitation. What kind of compromises could the Club attempt? In a contest between the city and the river, the victor seemed assured. Muir had argued in 1897 that only Uncle Sam could preserve the defenseless trees. On a more cosmic scale, as Muir's language declared, the great treelike watershed of the Tuolumne River, with its branching canyons and magnificent Hetch Hetchy Yosemite, could not run away. And the advocates of the city, Holway Jones has pointed out, had the legislative precedent for their right-of-way. Early in 1908 they had the approval of the secretary of the interior.[51]

Muir and Colby began a vigorous campaign opposing the Hetch Hetchy dam as an invasion of Yosemite National Park and a desecration of the canyon of the Tuolumne River, at the risk of alienating many of the progressives in the Club and finally confronting Gifford Pinchot, to whom Roosevelt had given so much authority. Leaders of the Club found early a strategic difficulty: though they wished to be friendly to the larger aims of the progressive government, and though they considered the Club a reformist but not radical group, they would be perceived as "a certain class of citizens . . . who may be called chronic opponents. They never originate ANYTHING and they always oppose EVERYTHING."[52] Such was clearly not the case, yet it was a consequence of the role the Club chose as "faithful defender" of a kind of progress that had already been made in the national parks, which was being constantly threatened. Perception of the Club as a blind opponent has never completely gone away. More than fifty years later the Club took up the slogan coined by David Brower—Not blind opposition to progress, but opposition to blind progress—in order to combat this false impression.[53]

By 1908 the severity of the split between the Pinchot-style conservationists and the "preservationists," as they were called by their critics, became clear—at least to preservationists—when Muir was not invited to Roosevelt's Governors' Conference for Conservation. Absent, the Club's board of directors wrote a letter to the members of the conference, counteracting the utilitarian version of conservation with its own expression that "the moral and physical welfare of a nation is not dependent alone on bread and water. Comprehending these primary necessities is the deeper need for recreation and that which satisfies also the esthetic sense."[54] In this letter the board argued that tourism was economically valuable, and that even from an economic point of view "scenic resources," as the Club began to call them, needed to be preserved. Such an argument was congruent with the Club's more specific statements about Hetch Hetchy the previous year. In line with its argument about tourism, a committee made up of Muir, Will Colby, Little Joe LeConte, William Frederick Badè, and Edward Taylor Parsons had advocated several new trails out of Yosemite Valley, leading to the watershed of the Tuolumne River, and a road into Hetch Hetchy Valley. Muir, Colby, and their confederates were willing to "improve" access to Hetch Hetchy. So, too, the same group had argued in September 1907, Hetch Hetchy should not be used as a reservoir, giving reasons which ranged from the concrete value of the place in itself, as a scenic resource, as a camping ground, and as a point of access to the wilderness, to the abstract principle of the park and the rule of law that created it. In addition, a committee of the Club's board argued in a letter to the secretary of the interior, in what was later to appear rather mild language, that San Francisco wanted this reservoir in a national park only because "the cost would be less," and that consequently "we do not believe that the vital interests of the nation at large should be sacrificed and so important a part of its National Park destroyed to save a few dollars for local interests."[55]

However, as Club historian Holway Jones has observed, there was to be a "Battle Within the Battle."[56] As early as 1907 Will Colby found it necessary to explain the decision of the committee of the board of directors which had written these letters on Yosemite and Hetch Hetchy, because the Club was not unanimously opposed to the utilization of Hetch Hetchy. So he framed arguments to those within the Club.[57] The most articulate member of the opposition was Warren Olney, who had recently lost his bid for reelection as director of the Club. Olney believed that San Francisco's needs were more important than those of the park. He was not just for development, and certainly did not advocate private interests; he believed he was fighting for good government, for public water and power supplies, for the public interest as he saw it.[58] Olney said that a lake would enhance the beauty of Hetch Hetchy, the scenery would not be changed in the lifetimes of most people interested in camping there, and the region upstream would still be available.[59] Though Colby answered these arguments, dissent would not go away, and finally the division became so serious and so crippling to the Club's ability to act that Muir threatened to resign. Colby met this crisis with a whole series of stratagems which would set precedents for the Club.

Colby established a separate organization called the Society for the Preservation of National Parks, with Muir as president, and a network of council members from all over the country. This organization made the Hetch Hetchy campaign national and relieved pressure from the members in San Francisco. Colby himself was employed by a law firm which was one of the leading proponents of the Hetch Hetchy water scheme, so he had to pull strings from the background. But he wrote to Pinchot, "We are going to keep up the good fight without fear or favor, 'if it shall take until doomsday.'"[60] The society issued pamphlets, using Muir's stirring rhetoric and Colby's careful technical arguments. Nevertheless, dissension within the Club was so embarrassing by the end of 1909 that Colby and the board submitted their decision on Hetch Hetchy to the membership in the form of a referendum.

Despite practical problems with framing the initiative ballot, the response was 589 in favor of retaining Hetch Hetchy in its natural state to 161 opposed, out of a total membership of about 1,000. The ballot was followed by a special meeting, requested before the election by the dissenting minority. Muir and Colby packed that meeting, which became a hopeless tangle and concluded nothing.[61] Though the controversy ended within the Club, about fifty members resigned; Warren Olney was one of them. As his daughter remembered, the subject was so painful after his twenty years of friendship and service that Hetch Hetchy was never again a permissible subject for conversation in the Olney household.[62] Such a divisive and emotional issue lost the Club some of its appearance of solidarity, at least in the eyes of San Francisco.

Internal problems were a crucible that transformed the Club, separated—some might say—the pure at heart from those who could be swayed by local interests. But more to the point, these problems opened up a vigorous dialogue, identified the real leaders in the ranks, tested organizational structure, and made the Sierra Club known nationally. During this campaign Muir remained the moral leader of the Club, but Will Colby emerged as the political and organizational leader. Muir was not the man who forged the Sierra Club's campaigns, though he served as president from 1892 to 1914. It was Will Colby who took in his hands the responsibility for conducting the battles, as they were called, for Yosemite National Park and especially for Hetch Hetchy. It was Colby too who would later take the lead in the campaign to create a Kings Canyon national park. And it was Colby to whom Muir wrote the most personal and confiding letters. He was the one who shaped the Club into an advocate and faithful defender of parks, state and national, or "people's playgrounds" as Muir called them. He was the one Muir would praise as "the only one of all the club who stood by me in downright fighting."[63]

Colby's strategies were various. Certainly he depended on Muir's rhetoric, as published by the Society for Preservation of National Parks, by the Sierra Club, and by Johnson. As Muir countered the "bad arguments," used by schemers "to prove that the only righteous thing to do with the people's parks is to destroy them," he also exploded the idea that the "sham lake" at Hetch Hetchy would be anything other than "an open sepulcher" for most months of the year.[64] His rhetoric was appropriate for an age that tended to see political issues in moral terms. It was also heartfelt; Muir *knew* that Hetch Hetchy was a sacred place and that the proposers of dams were "temple destroyers" who worshiped the dollar. In letters to the East, Muir referred to the "mad God-forgetting Progressive days."[65] If the time was not right for Good, Wild, and Sacred to replace the eternal verities of the Good, True, and Beautiful in the American consciousness, then the religious argument might still work. But as Roderick Nash has shown, even a conservationist who was sympathetic to the Sierra Club perspective, like Congressman William Kent of California, would find Muir "without the social instincts of the average man." As Kent wrote to a colleague, "with him it is me and God and the rock where God put it, and that is the end of the story."[66] Given the popularity of conservation among the progressives, and given the precedence of efficiency in that gospel, as Holway Jones points out, the issue of cost *was* a determining factor, for those who placed their faith in engineers. As a mining lawyer, Colby was prepared to control Muir's zeal and to deal with the technical problems a Hetch Hetchy dam would create in Yosemite National Park.

Further, Colby acquired the backing of a national coalition, and particularly the support of Horace McFarland's American Civic Association.[67] He arranged with McFarland that Walter Fisher, President Taft's secretary of the interior, be taken to Hetch Hetchy Valley. With McFarland, Colby organized two massive public letter-writing campaigns. Most important, he began to advocate alternate sites for reservoirs within Yosemite National Park, which the Club would approve if San Francisco renounced its rights to the site in Hetch Hetchy.[68]

In the end nothing could stop the concerted plans of San Francisco, supported by Pinchot and the progressive conservationists. Congress approved the Hetch Hetchy dam, and President Wilson signed the act on December 19, 1913. Yet the Hetch Hetchy controversy became a precedent in the Club's history and in national history, because Muir, Colby, Johnson, and their allies were able to make it a national issue.

The most important precedent for the future was *The Legacy of* that a national park was not inviolate. Hetch *Hetch Hetchy* Hetchy was lost to Yosemite. On the other hand, Muir wrote to Johnson after the final loss, "the conscience of the whole country has been aroused from sleep."[69] Also important for the future was the meaning to the conscience of the Club itself of the so-called Battle for Yosemite. Hetch Hetchy was a precedent-setting campaign, and Remember Hetch Hetchy would become a battle cry for the Club for another century. As Colby wrote in the first *Sierra Club Handbook* thirty years later, "While this particular battle was lost . . . it has deterred others from attempting similar inroads. The prestige of the club was enhanced immeasurably."[70]

The immediate lessons of the campaign, as applied to conservation organizations, might be summarized as follows. First, the Club learned that solidarity would always be a problem when a regional conservation organization tried to support national interest at the expense of local economic growth. Second, the Club's lack of solidarity could be quite detrimental to its ability to act in the public interest. This became clear in San Francisco and in the hearings in Washington, D.C.[71] And third, the effort of carrying on such an arduous campaign was itself extremely difficult for an amateur organization. As Badè wrote to Horace McFarland four years before the campaign ended, "Both Colby and I are hoping that this Hetch Hetchy fight will be soon over, or we shall not only be bankrupt but shall have to give up our professions."[72] For Badè, a college professor, and Colby, a lawyer, this was not simply a question of time but of personal pressure. As public men, they both endangered their careers by advocating such an unpopular cause. Badè even gave up a sabbatical leave in Europe so he could testify in Washington.

A more subtle but more pervasive and long-lasting legacy of Hetch Hetchy would plague the subsequent history of conservation in America. Not only did the Hetch Hetchy campaign alienate Muir from Pinchot, but it "severed relations between the preservationists and the utilitarian conservationists," as Holway Jones has argued.[73]

Harold Bradley, the son of a charter member and a later president of the Club, was in 1913 a young professor at the University of Wisconsin. He wrote in despair that the battle put him in a position of "sentimentalist" and "inexact dreamer," as against the Pinchot men of "cold analytical temperament." Such a polarity would not allow any reasonable decision, but instead created a travesty, put forth as a "proper weighing of the economic value of playground areas over against the economic value of their conversion into municipal assets."[74] This polarity hardened, so that David Brower would characterize it in 1947 as "the campaign between men of vision and the cash-register men."[75] In the future, those advocating economic use would be "the enemy." By the mid 1950s Grant McConnell, a political scientist who influenced Club policy in the post-World War II era, had characterized the profound differences between the two streams of conservation this way: the scientific, professional ideas of Pinchot emphasized use and material values while the Muir tradition, which "elevates nonmaterial as above material values as a matter of principle," is at bottom religious and led by a small but dedicated group. The political result, McConnell concluded, "is confusion and uncertainty as to the meaning of conservation."[76] Just as Muir could no longer advocate the policy of wise use after 1897, so too the Hetch Hetchy battle irrevocably defined the Sierra Club's role as dissenting, in opposition to economic development, not everywhere but certainly in national parks.

Muir's defeat on Hetch Hetchy at the end of 1913 was perceived almost universally as a personal martyrdom when he died a year later. Colby believed "Muir was tremendously exercised to think that a great part of his work would be undone." In other words, defiling Yosemite National Park was "a tremendous blow," tantamount to breaking Muir's heart and killing him: "I'm quite sure that this loss of Hetch Hetchy Valley had a great deal to do with Mr. Muir's subsequent illness and ultimate death."[77] This view has come down in the lore of the Club. For the religious stream of conservation, a personal commitment to a sacred landscape and principled commitment to the public good would be so closely interrelated that men and women would defend their wild lands as if they were defending their lives.[78]

Critique of the campaign itself would influence the conduct of future conservation campaigns. It has been argued that the furor over Hetch Hetchy created an appreciation for the importance of parks in America, and perhaps for wilderness, and conversely that "Muir, Johnson, and their colleagues were able to create a protest because the American people were ready to be aroused."[79] Roderick Nash believes that Muir and his colleagues paid insufficient attention to the wilderness quality of Hetch Hetchy, instead depending on a rhetoric focused on the need for aesthetic "scenic wonders" or recreational "public playgrounds."

Richard Leonard, who as president led the Club into its next major national campaign, opposing dams in Dinosaur National Monument forty years later, drew the following lessons from Hetch Hetchy. First of all, the campaign showed the need for an organization national in scope. Second, it demonstrated the need for a national park service to protect the interest of the parks, and also demonstrated the importance of arousing the conscience of the country. Third, it dramatized the dangers of organizational factions, a problem that would recur infrequently but dramatically in the Club's history.[80] In the campaign the Club set a precedent by offering alternate sites for economic development, and the campaign further suggested, in the roles of Muir and Colby, the two-sided aspect—moral and practical—of future conservation campaigns.[81] Yet Muir and Colby, as leaders, had been forced to set up the separate Society for the Preservation of National Parks to carry out Club policy in 1909. And even fifty years after the Club had lost its campaign at Hetch Hetchy and had published its own history of the campaign, members of factions quoted their own history while debating the possibility that the Club might repeat its mistakes, might fail to carry out its own policies because of internal dissent.[82] The final, most important lesson, according to Leonard, was that Muir fought the battle of Hetch Hetchy every year for thirteen

years, "and he only lost it once. That is the tragedy of conservation or environmental battles."[83] As one activist of the
1960s would argue in more militant terms and with more urgency, such potential for tragedy required no equivocation:
"The extractors of the earth don't ever give up, because it's always there for them to take. Whatever's saved is still there to
be taken later. And you never get anything back."[84]

When John Muir died on Christmas Eve, 1914, he left *Muir's*
more than the legacy of the Hetch Hetchy campaign. *Legacy*
He left a vacuum in Club ranks and left many strands
of his dream unbraided, but his writings set out a pro- *1914*
gram for those who would make his ideas live in the
twentieth century. *The Mountains of California* was a reminder
that he had always wished to see the whole roof of the Sierra
reserved. *Our National Parks* indicated how much Muir loved
trees, and led the way for an organized, comprehensive federal program for national parks. *My First Summer in the Sierra*
was a guide to the kind of personal initiation to the wilderness he felt was vital for the health of individuals, an initiation that the Club pursued through the outings program. *The
Yosemite* was his reminder not only of the tragedy of Hetch
Hetchy, but of the Club's special responsibility to Yosemite
National Park. Because many felt that Muir was not properly
valued as a scientist, the *Bulletin* began to reprint his early
geological research, *Studies in the Sierra*. Muir had been working on a book called *Travels in Alaska* when he died, and his
vital interest in Alaska would one day claim the attention of
the Club.

Muir's most important legacy to the Club may have been a
cadre of devoted members who would pursue his goals.
Many Club members expressed their own devotion to Muir
in the *Bulletin* over the years 1916 to 1919. For Colby, as for
Robert Underwood Johnson, Muir was the enemy of philis-
tinism and commercialism; Muir represented the kind of

man "who will never be fully appreciated by those whose minds are filled with money getting and the sordid things of modern every-day life."[85] Colby remembered in particular Muir's hope that a national park in the southern Sierra would render accessible the Kings River region. "Every possible aid and encouragement should be given by the Club for the preservation, road and trail building," Muir wrote, "but unjust one-sided comparisons [between Yosemite and the Kings River Canyon] seeking to build up one and glorify one region at the expense of lowering the other is useless work and should be left to real estate agents, promoters, rival hotel and stage owners, etc. Certainly the Club has nothing to do with such stuff."[86] Muir had wanted a Kings Canyon park because he felt that the whole Sierra was worthy of park status; he found the Sequoia forests, the wildlife, the meadows, and the grand yosemite-like valleys particularly vulnerable to destruction, and worried less about the high peaks and passes, which were economically worthless. Since 1912, legislation had been periodically introduced to enlarge the small Sequoia National Park to include the south fork of the Kings River, the Kern River Canyon, Tehipite Valley, and the crest of the Sierra—especially the crest of the range from Mount Humphreys down to Kern Peak.[87] It was enough for Colby in 1916 that "John Muir during his lifetime heartily endorsed this plan," in fact proposed it.[88] After 1912 Colby expended substantial energy on this campaign, reaching limited success in 1926, and then continuing to lobby for a larger park over the next fourteen years. Creating a national park in the southern Sierra constituted the main goal of the Club's conservation efforts until 1940, when Kings Canyon National Park was established.

Many believed that of all the objects in nature, trees appealed to Muir most strongly, and were the living beings he most wished to preserve. Indeed William Kent, an opponent of Muir on Hetch Hetchy, had donated a tract of coast red-

woods north of San Francisco to the federal government in
1908, under the name Muir Woods. Henry Fairfield Osborn,
one of the originators of the Save the Redwoods League, remembered of Muir, "To him a tree was something not only to
be loved, but to be respected and revered."[89] Other notable
scientists, like C. Hart Merriam and Charles Sprague Sargent,
concurred with this view of Muir as predominantly a lover of
trees. They could point to Muir's writings for evidence.

In 1875, Muir had set out to survey the extent of the sequoia in the Sierra, and discovered a more extensive and
healthier range than anyone had suspected. He had refused
to accept the verdict of other botanists who thought the coast
redwood was too useful to last long. Those who followed the
tree-loving Muir would seek to preserve the coast redwood
(*Sequoia sempervirons*) and the giant sequoia (*Sequoia gigantea*) which grew on the west slope of the Sierra. As his writings make clear, Muir's favorite pine was the sugar pine (*Pi-
nus Lambertiana*), and the Club would also seek to protect
this tree, much sought for lumber where it grew most beautifully on the western boundary of Yosemite National Park.

Two Club members in particular would complete Muir's
literary work. Marion Randall, who consistently joined Club
outings and was a friend of Muir's daughter Wanda, had
married one of Muir's loyal supporters, Edward Taylor Parsons. When Randall's husband died in 1914, Will Colby suggested that she help Muir with his Alaska book.[90] This activity was congenial to both, and she edited *Travels in Alaska*
after Muir's death, also edited the book reviews in the *Bulletin*
for many years, and was the first official Club lobbyist in
Washington, D.C., going there in 1920 to speak for enlarging
Sequoia National Park. Marion Randall Parsons was the first
woman who was truly a Club activist. A novelist and painter,
she was energetic and articulate. As a member of the Club's
board after her husband died, she served in that position for
more than twenty years.[91]

The bulk of Muir's literary legacy was organized, edited, and published by William Frederick Badè (1871–1936). Badè, who joined the Club in 1903, was a close friend of Warren Olney, but a staunch worker on the Hetch Hetchy campaign. To Badè, Muir's "gentleness and humaneness toward all creatures that shared the world with him was one of the finest attributes of his character."[92] From the first, Badè was taken with Muir's favorite bird, the water ouzel, and Muir's religious side interested him particularly, since Badè was a teacher at the Pacific Theological Seminary. Muir did not think of his writings as one long autobiography, but as Muir's literary executor Badè edited Muir's collected works as a biographical series, beginning with *A Thousand-Mile Walk to the Gulf* and concluding with a two-volume *Life and Letters of John Muir*. Badè also edited the *Bulletin* for many years, and in addition to serving on the board for nearly thirty years, was president of the Club for three years (1919–1922).

As the Club grew, it embarked on projects for exploring and rendering accessible lands in the Sierra, often in the name of Muir. The legacy of Muir was promulgated in 1913 when the Club bought property at Soda Springs, Muir's favorite camping spot in Tuolumne Meadows. The Club obtained this property partly to preserve it as a central starting point for outings on the east side of Yosemite, and planned to conduct outings there every three years. Though Muir was not an advocate of improvements in parks, in 1915 the Club erected a lodge on the Soda Springs property, designed by the well-known Bay Area architect Bernard Maybeck, and named for Edward Taylor Parsons. This property would frequently be the base camp for future outings, as it was in 1915, and would remain in Club hands for more than fifty years, managed as a public campground until it was deeded to Yosemite National Park. Later, the Club bought other properties in the Sierra.

A system of trails which would make the High Sierra more

accessible was soon being advocated in Muir's name. The John Muir Trail, connecting Yosemite with Mount Whitney, affording a route for traveling with pack animals along or near the crest of the Sierra, would be planned primarily by the Club, and the route for it would be explored by Club members. Muir had excelled in off-trail excursions along the glacial pathways, and had believed that pack animals were an encumbrance; nevertheless, Colby thought the trail "a most appropriate memorial to John Muir, who spent many of the best years of his life exploring the region which it will make accessible."[93] The Club lobbied for state appropriations over the years, and the John Muir Trail was completed in 1930. Soon after the Club published *Starr's Guide to the John Muir Trail* (1934), kept in print continuously thereafter.

Exploration in the name of Muir continued over the years, as parties of Club members sought new routes in the High Sierra, published maps, and suggested new trails. In 1919 an elaborate trail including a cable and a stairway was placed on Half Dome, under auspices of the Club, the gift of a Club member. Muir's comment on the idea of making the summit of Half Dome accessible had been, "For my part I should prefer leaving it in pure wildness, though, after all, no great damage could be done in tramping over it."[94]

Colby announced in 1915 that the Club board had chosen its second president, the senior Joseph N. LeConte. It would become an unwritten law after Muir that an individual could serve only two years as president, and throughout the Club's history this law would only twice be broken. In 1916 Colby, as Club secretary, marked the Club's 25-year anniversary, reminding members that "the club's prime object is service," taking members to the mountains, publishing information. The Club advocated "the great principle that national parks should be inviolate"; it spread the gospel of out-of-doors. Colby inspired the Club with Muir's message: "As we journey to the mountains year after year, his spirit is there to give us renewed courage to meet the problems and carry on the great work that has fallen to our lot."[95] In the coming years, following the spirit of Muir, the Club would also establish its own strategies, reminded by Robert Underwood Johnson that Muir was "not a 'dreamer,' but a practical man, a faithful citizen," and by another activist that Muir "had the outward bearing of an unsophisticated farmer but was at home with the most polished men of the world."[96]

National Park Service 1916

The times demanded a more worldly leadership, as in 1916 the advent of the National Park Service demonstrated. The post-World War I era in which the park service grew was a time of rapid change and rampant commercialism. The period that followed the war brought not only massive land speculation in California, but the energy industry to the West, including petroleum exploration and development, hydroelectric power projects, and most important to the parks, the automobile.[97] It also brought vast economic growth in the West. Western commercial banks grew quickly, first entering the real estate market and soon providing capital for energy exploitation. It was a period of tremendous economic prosperity, and produced a generation of men who had the leisure, money, social connections, and power to support the idea of a national park system in America. It was a period of amazing social contrasts and incongruities, the age when the robber barons began to feel philanthropic and to feel a duty to preserve the beauty of the United States, sometimes by buying up great tracts of land and donating them for public recreation. It was also the period when a rising mobile middle class began to make itself felt in national politics and consequently in conservation. It was the age of modernism, avant-garde poetry, and also of Prohibition. These contrasts and contradictions would have a major impact on the national parks, and on the role of the Sierra Club.

The idea of a national park service had grown slowly. Muir had hoped that the recession of Yosemite in 1905 would be followed by "righteous management" of the parks; by 1910, in the face of the Hetch Hetchy threat, the Club was actively advocating a bureau to run them.[98] In 1912 the Club *Bulletin* expressed high hopes that a centralized park administration would be established.[99] With the election of Woodrow Wilson, chances seemed good.

In May of 1913, while working his way through law school at the University of California, twenty-three-year-old Horace Albright was invited to Washington by his economics professor, Adolph C. Miller, when Miller became an assistant to Secretary of the Interior Franklin K. Lane.[100] Albright (1890–1987) discussed the invitation with his good friend and law professor William Colby, who encouraged him to go. One of Albright's first and most heartbreaking tasks was to sign Secretary Lane's name to thousands of letters answering citizens who protested the Hetch Hetchy dam. During the summer of 1913, Lane, Miller, and Albright toured the national parks. The next year Albright received his law degree, and while he remained in Washington considering his future, Colby offered him a position in the Colby law firm. Meanwhile, Miller, who was perhaps a perfect example of a new professionalism buttressed by political progressivism, moved on to other responsibilities in the Wilson administration. He was replaced by an entirely different kind of man, Stephen Mather.

Mather (1877–1930) was another graduate of the University of California, though a resident of Chicago.[101] As a borax industry executive and publicist, he conceived the brand name Twenty Mule Team Borax. Soon after, he left his employer, became a successful entrepreneur with his own borax business, and was a rich man by the age of 47 when he retired from business. A mountaineering buff after he had climbed Mount Rainier on a Sierra Club outing in 1905, Mather sought recreation in the wilds as a way of avoiding overwork and the nervous breakdowns which followed periods of intense effort throughout his life. According to his biographer, the first Sierra Club trip had changed Mather's life. He was, in personality, the exact opposite of Muir, an outgoing, vigorous, sociable, charismatic fellow, a fraternity man, a Rotarian, a back-slapping restless sort, alternately enthusiastic and despairing, uncomfortable with solitude, and full of ideas. He was half Babbitt, half something else, the very model of the American salesman.[102] In 1912 Mather met Muir while traveling in the Kern River Sierra. Two years later Mather was incited to write an irate letter to Franklin Lane about the condition of the thirteen parks and more than twenty monuments, the depredations in and around them, and the sloppy way they were being run. Lane responded by asking Mather to come to Washington and "run them yourself."[103] Lane said he was looking for "a new kind of public official, one who will go out and sell the public on conservation, then work with Congress to get laws passed to protect the national parks."[104] He was, he said, offering to a man of vision the possibility for public service. Mather accepted, and convinced Albright to stay on to help run the parks. Mather would personally supplement the small salary available to Albright from the department of the interior.

Mather was an outgoing idea man; Albright was the hardworking, diligent, organizational expert who could build a federal bureau into something permanent. Though he would remain in the background until Mather's retirement, he would do the groundwork, would build the infant park service into a powerful administrative system, a complex bureaucracy, with a growing array of parks and monuments. But at first, the parks were plagued by unsatisfactory appropriations, and Mather's solution was often to make up the deficits through personal contributions. (Colby used the same method, on a much smaller scale, to support the Club's outings, which lost money year after year.) As Mather's biographer puts it, "The Mather achievement was necessarily the achievement of a wealthy man. The big gesture, the princely gift, that was the rich soil out of which the National Park Service grew."[105] Mather's first gesture, in 1915, was to buy personally the old Tioga mining road—with contributions by the Sierra Club and by his wealthy friends. The road was in bad repair but provided a means of transportation from Yosemite Valley to the east side of the Sierra, through Tuolumne Meadows.[106] It would be necessary to improve the road, and in that process the Club would have a role to play.

By 1916 Mather was submitting personal reports to the Sierra Club on the national parks.[107] He wanted a national park service and an extended system of national parks and monuments. To get these, he needed to demonstrate for Congress that parks were needed by people, that people could get to the parks, and that people would appreciate the parks they visited. As a publicizer of the out-of-doors gospel he was willing to sell his ideas by providing a good deal more than wilderness. He would build roads, as he began to think of tourism in automotive terms. Indeed, one historian shows that some national parks were created by Congress only when Mather could show they were accessible.[108] But Mather went further than that; he began to conceive a grand automotive tour of America.

Muir's approval of autos in Yosemite has been much discussed in Sierra Club circles. He wrote in 1913, grudgingly and with heavy irony, that there was no keeping the "useful, progressive, blunt nosed mechanical beetles" out; yet such an event would scarcely matter for mountaineers.[109] Mather, however, began to see that parks were good for auto tours and monuments useful as way stations between grandiose parks. That was to invert the means and ends of Muir's views and the Club's purposes. Consequently, Mather followed the Club policy of "rendering accessible" the mountains with an enthusiasm which went beyond Club aims and would some day give the Club reason to worry—but not for several decades. His first priorities for Yosemite were improving the Tioga Road, purchasing many private toll roads, and developing facilities, including new hotels and trails. While he worked closely with Joseph N. LeConte and William Colby on these ideas, he outlined plans of a similar nature for other parks.[110] This was in line with Mather's policy of good roads, good beds, and good food in the parks. There was little doubt that an act establishing a national park service would soon be passed by Congress. Though the Club supported park service legislation, Horace McFarland and his American Civic Association lobbied harder.[111]

Mather organized conferences, where superintendents met with the public. One was held in Berkeley in 1915, and the Club participated.[112] He took influential men, including legislators, editors, writers, and representatives from the railroads, to the country which would one day be Sequoia–Kings Canyon National Park. He courted chambers of commerce and automobile societies. And he got results. In 1916 *National Geographic* devoted an entire issue to the national parks.[113] Mather brought Robert Sterling Yard, an eminent journalist, to Washington, D.C., made him head of the National Parks Information Office, and paid out of his own pocket. Soon Yard placed a *National Parks Portfolio* on the desk of every congressman.[114]

All of this was part of the program necessary, Mather believed, to pass the Park Service Act over the opposition of the ten-year-old Forest Service, and to guarantee that the parks were being used. No doubt the program gained the parks friends. The congressmen who submitted and supported park service legislation were Reed Smoot of Utah, John E. Raker of California (who was also the sponsor of the bill to build Hetch Hetchy dam), and William Kent (also a Hetch Hetchy dam advocate). The bill which finally succeeded was strongly influenced by Frederick Law Olmsted, Jr., son of the man who wrote the first management plan for Yosemite and planned Central Park in New York City. Olmsted, Jr., conceived and described the purpose of the National Park Service: ". . . to conserve the scenery and the natural and historic objects and the wild life therein and to provide for the enjoyment of the same in such manner and by such means as will leave them unimpaired for the enjoyment of future generations."[115]

Advocates of the service debated many details of the legislation, especially sheep-grazing within the parks, an idea advocated by Kent and opposed strongly by Mather. Because Mather was of the opinion that even a compromised bill was better than none, he did not insist upon "pure" parks. Later the Park Service could get rid of the grazing provisions. This, Albright remembers, was to be a consistent strategy of Mather's: pass the act first, clean up the act later.[116]

While Mather was on a junket to the Sierra, Albright did the grinding legislative work in Washington, D.C., and attempted to get some appropriations for the service. He used the connections he had made with western conservationists and with his old colleagues from the University of California. The National Park Service Act was finally signed in August 1916. Its first-year budget was $19,500, including salary for five permanent employees. As Albright knew, until the service could get significant appropriations it would not really exist.[117]

In 1917, on the eve of American involvement in World War I, Mather suffered one of his periodic "nervous collapses," and twenty-seven-year-old Albright, in charge of the Park Service, found that Benjamin Ide Wheeler, president of the University of California, was asking Secretary of the Interior

Franklin Lane to allow 50,000 sheep to graze in Yosemite. As he remembers, Lane gave permission, and commanded Albright not to tell the Sierra Club.[118] The fledgling National Park Service was hard pressed to stop intrusions into the parks everywhere. Working with Duncan McDuffie, an old friend from California and later a Sierra Club president, Albright was able to stop most grazing in the parks. He was aided by a strong response from the Club.

By this time—1917—the Park Service was manned almost entirely by Californians, all of whom had close connctions to leaders in the Club. One more connection was made when a young Club member, Francis Farquhar, came to Washington during the war in the course of his duties in the navy. Farquhar (1888–1974) had graduated from Harvard in 1909 and joined the Club two years later.

Mather dabbled in mountaineering; Farquhar was a serious climber. He went on his first Club outing in 1911, and made a first ascent of a Sierra peak with Will Colby. He pursued mountaineering through his life as a pioneer of new routes, as a rigorous student and editor of mountaineering literature, as a writer of mountaineering history. He became editor of the *Sierra Club Bulletin* in 1926, and during his twenty years in this position turned it into the most highly respected mountaineering journal in America. Introduced to Mather by Albright while he was in Washington in 1918, he would soon join the ranks of the Park Service, first as an employee, using his training as an accountant, and finally—and throughout his life—as a public advocate.

Meanwhile, Albright stayed in Washington, working to expand the parks to include larger Sequoia and Yellowstone parks, a Teton park, and a Grand Canyon National Park. He also sought to establish a firm policy for managing the parks. Much of the work credited to Mather over the years was done in a quiet way by Albright. For instance, Albright claims he and Robert S. Yard drafted a park management policy in

1917, sending it to Farquhar, Colby, Badè, and Joseph Le-Conte of the Club.[119] The Club was consulted in those days through close and direct individual contact between the administrators of the Park Service and prominent Club members. After Albright received comments, he remembers forwarding his policy on to Mather, who was recovering from a breakdown but gave it his seal of approval. This influential statement of policy was formalized as a letter from Secretary Lane to Mather, dated May 13, 1918.

The famous Lane letter, published in the 1918 Club *Bulletin*, announced three broad principles:

> First, that the national parks must be maintained in absolutely unimpaired form for the use of future generations as well as those of our time; second, that they are set apart for the use, observation, health, and pleasure of the people; and third that the national interest must dictate all decisions affecting public or private interest in the parks.[120]

Later commentators would observe that the first two instructions were probably contradictory, and the third a pious hope.[121] The service would permit grazing of cattle in all parks except Yellowstone. The parks would lease lands for hotels, camps, and transportation facilities. They would eliminate private holdings and prohibit commercial cutting of trees, but they would construct roads, trails, and buildings, harmonizing such improvements with the landscape. As the letter indicated, "Every opportunity should be afforded the public, whenever possible, to enjoy the national parks in the manner that best satisfies the individual taste." Thus, with the exception of hunting, all outdoor sports including mountain climbing, swimming, boating, fishing, walking, horseback riding, and motoring would be heartily endorsed. The letter went on to encourage the cooperation of the Park Service with railroad associations, chambers of commerce, tourist bureaus, and automobile highway associations.[122]

This document suggested not only what the parks would become, but what the Sierra Club would stand for in the decade of the 1920s as a supporter of the Park Service.

On the
Road with
Stephen
Mather
1920–1925

By 1919 Stephen Mather had recovered from his nervous collapse of 1917 and invited Farquhar to join the Park Service. Mather's charisma was irresistible. As Farquhar remembered, "his fire was indescribable and absolutely unique. . . . If he was out to make a convert, the subject never knew what hit him."[123] Farquhar was a convert. This was fortuitous, since Mather's highest priority, like that of the Club, was to expand Sequoia National Park as Muir had wished so many years earlier.[124]

Through the 1920s the Club was completely engaged in supporting and supplementing the policy of the Park Service. People like Farquhar and Colby began to use the language of Mather, distinguishing places of "national park caliber" from areas which were not worthy to be "crown jewels." From the beginning, Farquhar was involved in Mather's automotive jaunts around the country, first to Sequoia with influential men, including politicians like Chester Rowell of Fresno, publishers like Harry Chandler of the *Los Angeles Times*, and others. It was, Farquhar remembered, a way to educate people with influence and "indoctrinate them with our ideas."[125] Later Farquhar served a short stint in the Park Service as a field auditor, and became the unofficial San Francisco agent for Mather.[126] He also visited the southwest with Mather in 1923 and 1924, trying out the grand auto tour between the parks and monuments in Utah and Arizona.

When Theodore Roosevelt died, Mather men tried to work for an addition to Sequoia National Park that would be named for Roosevelt. The Club took up the idea. Later, additions to Sequoia would be proposed to Congress under the name of Muir. Farquhar testified on the Sequoia enlargement for the Sierra Club.

It was not always true that the Mather men agreed on the quantity of development in the parks. For instance, around 1919 there was serious thought of running a cable car across the Grand Canyon. Albright reported to Mather that Farquhar, who had just been to the canyon, was greatly in favor of the plan and was supported by Lane, Yard, and himself. Mather, however, found the idea quite unacceptable.[127] Thus it appears that Albright and Farquhar, to perhaps a greater extent than Mather, would advocate maximum park access.[128] So too, with regard to roads, the Sierra Club would in 1927 advocate more roads in Yosemite than even Mather asked for—not only roads surrounding both rims of the valley, with spurs to scenic viewpoints on the summits of El Capitan, Taft Point, and Yosemite Point, but even a road up Tenaya Canyon, and many more.[129] These were friendly disagreements; everyone agreed upon a need to develop the parks, and differed only on the degree of development necessary.

By 1920 the parks were suffering a crisis. The Federal Water Power Act of 1920 opened up large portions of the public domain, including the national parks, to entry for water projects.[130] Immediately the City of Los Angeles filed applications for several areas in Yosemite and six sites within the Kings Canyon region.[131] There was also a proposal before Congress to allow a reservoir in Yellowstone National Park. Though the 1920 act was amended the next year to exclude existing national parks, it would be a major block to getting the full Kings Canyon region added to Sequoia National Park.

The enlargement of Sequoia was resisted strongly not only by sheepmen, mining interests, and timbermen, but by the Forest Service, which did not want to cede lands it administered to the Park Service.[132] Henry Graves, who had been chief of the Forest Service since 1910, had been publicly stating for years that parks should only be created in areas having no merchantable timber. He had also opposed creation of a separate park bureau, hoping the parks could be administered by the Forest Service.

In 1920, when he left the Forest Service, Graves published a strong statement in *American Forestry*.[133] Complaining that the nation did not have a clear-cut recreational policy, he conceded a vast increase in public use of wild lands for recreation, but continued to beg the question of National Park Service policy by asking whether economic resources in the parks could be used for "industrial purposes." He claimed that the public could not distinguish between forests and parks, insisted that the physical differences between them were slight, and believed that segregating great areas of mountain land would lock up natural resources needed by American industry. "Some persons have even gone so far as to advocate that practically the entire crest of the Sierra Nevada and Cascade mountains and other extensive areas be incorporated in National Parks," he reported. Even local residents, he argued, were split into factions when new parks were suggested, some mistakenly believing that a park would bring more income from tourism than a forest, through scenic highways and development, while others wanted to see resources "utilized under proper restrictions." So Graves offered a compromise, parks "with provision for the utilization of the economic resources where this does not conspicuously deface the country." As he continued, he had other suggestions, including the placement of the National Park Service in the department of agriculture. The general message was this: with many legislative proposals afoot to commercialize the resources of parks, the Forest Service was in a strong position to argue that the forests were just as safe as the parks, and that the Forest Service was not going to concede recreation to the Park Service.

Farquhar thought that the compromise Graves suggested, which would allow power development in future parks, was "very satisfactory to all save a few ultra-enthusiasts."[134] When Graves resigned in 1920, the Club began making peace with his successor, Chief William Greeley. It was standard procedure to elect the chief of the Forest Service as an honorary vice president of the Club. On the occasion, Badè suggested that there could be a reconciliation between the Park Service and the Forest Service.[135] Farquhar, writing to Mather a month later on the right kind of strategy for the Roosevelt-Sequoia bill, agreed, saying that "in the first place we must come to an agreement with the Forest Service if possible."[136] The Club found itself acting as an intermediary between the Forest Service and Park Service in negotiations over the extension of Sequoia.[137] Editorials in the *Bulletin* would become accommodating to Forest Service views, to the point that Farquhar eventually hoped that the Club would find itself "drawn into closer and closer relationship with the two branches of our government that administer the national forests and national parks."[138]

In this context one can define what would come to be called purism. Conservationists might disagree about the kinds of recreational activities appropriate in the parks, but at bottom purism was a stand which required that there be no compromise of the integrity of a park.[139] Mather was not a purist. Though sensitive to scenic intrusions like the cable car in the Grand Canyon, he would rather see a compromised park established than none at all. His policy was followed by Farquhar, who was now the Club's chief lobbyist in Washington. Farquhar believed that it would be impossible to achieve any extension of Sequoia if park advocates continued to insist on a "power-proof" bill. But Badè and the Club's board remembered Hetch Hetchy, perhaps because they, unlike Farquhar, had been through that heartbreaking campaign. So, as wires were exchanged, Farquhar found that the Club did not wish him to act on his own discretion and insisted that he not compromise.

Badè's communications in the fall of 1921 became stronger

and stronger, indicating that the Club would not support a compromise, and did not believe in soft-pedaling on the issue. "The sooner there is a showdown the better," Badè finally wrote to Farquhar.[140] Farquhar chafed at the board's unwillingness to let him act on his own discretion. He was hard beset when he found Robert Sterling Yard of the National Parks Association also vehemently opposed to a park which could be developed for hydroelectric power. Farquhar's solution was to negotiate with a vice president of Southern California Edison, and get a personal promise that the Edison Company would support the park bill and would promise not to file claims for power in the area. This, he thought, "sort of pulled the rug out from under Mr. Yard."[141]

The conflict between Yard and the other Mather men went deep.[142] As early as 1917 Albright had perceived Yard as a threat to his own authority in the Park Service.[143] When federal law prohibited Mather from using private funds to pay for Yard as the official Park Service publicist, Yard set up the National Parks Association, with Mather's financial support, "to defend the National Parks and National Monuments fearlessly against the assaults of private interests and aggressive commercialism."[144] Yard, in turn, always felt that Mather needed such an association, because the man was "naturally incoherent."[145] Among Club members views of Yard conflicted. Some, like Marion Randall Parsons, thought of him as an eastern urban type, "with us, but not yet of us."[146] Later Club members too would find Yard insufficiently informed on the western lands, especially with regard to Kings Canyon.[147] Some would find his unwillingness to compromise "stiff-necked" and harmful to the parks movement.[148] Some have even referred to him as a fanatic.[149] Albright, for one, apparently thought that Yard was an inept administrator and a zealot. Other purists like Yard would criticize the conciliating and diplomatic policy of Mather, Albright, and Farquhar.[150] But the natural inheritor of Yard's purism within the Sierra

Club would be Martin Litton, who would not arrive on the Club scene for another twenty-five years.[151]

In 1926 the Club succeeded in obtaining some of the park Muir conceived as Kings Canyon National Park. Ironically, two important parts of the Kings River itself—Tehipite Valley and the South Fork Canyon—were left out of the park because of great pressure applied by local irrigationists. As Colby remembered, "We finally agreed that we had better take what we could before the opposition arose. So the headwaters of the Kern River, including Mount Whitney and that area, was added to Sequoia National Park."[152] In the *Bulletin* Colby explained why some canyons of the Kings were left out, and expressed hope that Congress would add them.[153] Fourteen years later it did.

The movement that Stephen Fox has called the amateur tradition in conservation was characterized in the 1920s by a triangle of close personal connections among the leaders of service organizations like the Sierra Club, the administrators of federal agencies like the Park Service, and businessmen. Albright, for instance, was known for his ability to work quietly with businessmen and conservationists behind the scenes. Members of the Club were optimists, in the tradition of Mather; they welcomed the growth of their state—for Club membership was still confined to California. They believed in the progressive tradition they had inherited and were willing to wield political power. They were men of the world, or aspired to be. There were few college professors among Club leaders of the 1920s. Instead, engineers (Walter Huber), accountants (Francis Farquhar), businessmen (Duncan McDuffie), and lawyers (Will Colby) became prominent. These men were immersed professionally and personally in the economic growth of California, not wealthy yet, but the prime movers in what one might call the philanthropic tradition of conser-

Fellow Travelers
1925–1930

vation, where business provided the individuals, progressi-visim provided the ideology, and American industrial growth provided the economic power. In 1908, at the Governor's Conference on Conservation, Roosevelt had said "the conservation of our national resources is but part of another and greater problem . . . the problem of national efficiency, the patriotic duty of insuring the safety and continuance of the nation." When Badè quoted Roosevelt's statement approvingly for the 1919 *Bulletin*, he reached a sympathetic audience in the Club.[154]

Kent's gift of the Muir Woods was an example of good things to come. When Mather decided to sell national parks to America, when he spoke of the standards, dignity, and prestige of the park system, he was appealing to middle-class values in an economically mobile public, but also to the rich public-spirited men who might make contributions to the national welfare. There was little federal money for preserving parks or even for utilitarian conservation. There was a good deal of private wealth in the 1920s. Yet the gifts of the rich would create some scandalous abuses of the lands which, by their very worthiness to be national parks, rightfully belonged to the public. Even as the association of businesses and public servants would spell disaster for Secretary of the Interior Fall at Teapot Dome, so there would be analogous problems in the parks. As Robert Caro has shown in his monumental history of parks in New York, the rich and the very rich—the Mathers who made their fortunes by mining, the Rockefellers who made theirs by pumping oil—were preservation-oriented but elitist when it came to recreation.[155] Even more than Mather, for instance, John D. Rockefeller, Jr. was ignorant of the ecological ideas necessary to true preservation but interested in dictating management policy for natural ecosystems. The results of following Mather's instincts on the north rim of the Grand Canyon, or Rockefeller's in the game preserves he donated to the Grand Tetons, were distressing to men who knew something about ecology.[156] Personal contributions were welcome, but the advice of the contributors sometimes wrongheaded. However clumsy as the first efforts at philanthropic conservation might have been, they spelled a new beginning.

In California, in the redwood groves along the coast, anyone could see the worst and most obvious results of exploitation of resources. Consequently, a California manifestation of the philanthropic tradition grew with the Save-the-Redwoods League. Created in 1919 by nature lovers and tree lovers, buttressed by men like Mather, including a group of philanthropists, entrepreneurs in petroleum and hydroelectric power, and wealthy eastern patricians, the Redwoods League drafted its bylaws in 1920.[157] It went to work to establish a California state park system. It also created new personal connections. Secretary of the Interior Lane was its first president; Newton Drury, an advertising man, became its first executive secretary. Drury was to be the fourth director of the National Park Service, holding the post from 1940 until 1951. As a professional fund raiser, his job at the League was to encourage private contributions for buying as many of the coast redwoods as possible. He encouraged people to give memorial groves, and planned dedication ceremonies, including memorial plaques. His techniques were modeled after those that Mather used in selling the parks and those Drury's brother used in advertising for the Southern Pacific Railroad. Drury needed to make the League appear decorous, moderate, civilized, and politically conservative, or he could not attract the kind of money he needed. He carefully avoided offending any future benefactors. The whole idea of philanthropy was, for men like William Kent, connected to showing that the American system was superior to Russian communism. There would be no Muir-like rhetoric condemning commercialism from the League.

The Club welcomed the Redwoods League with great enthusiasm. The 1920 *Bulletin* opened with a recently discovered and unpublished statement by Muir, entitled "Save the Redwoods."[158] Badè editorialized that Muir himself had advocated private philanthropy in the saving of redwoods. With such a precedent, the *Bulletin* suggested, the board had voted to support the League and urged its members join to assist in the good work.[159] Many leaders of the Club would also serve in the Redwood League.

A most important Club member in the Redwoods League was Duncan McDuffie (1877–1951), a Bay Area subdivider and real estate speculator.[160] McDuffie personified the social ideals of the Redwoods League. He sometimes wrote in religious terms about the redwoods as forest temples. He was a mountaineer of some distinction, and as part of a Club party helped open up the route for the John Muir Trail across Muir Pass in 1908, and later participated in the first ascent of the treacherous Black Kahweah. He became a Club director in 1922 and a director of the Save-the-Redwoods League in 1925. He would be president of the Club from 1928 to 1931 and president of the League from 1944 until his death in 1951. In addition, he was a business partner of Governor C. C. Young of California, and helped Young organize a California state park commission.[161]

McDuffie's powerful influence would bring the presence of the Club to bear on the state park system of California. By 1925, the Redwoods League had begun a major campaign to establish state parks in California, and place them under a commission separate from the state forestry board. Thus, on a state level, the league was advocating exactly the position that Mather was on a national level. And on the state level the utilitarian wing of conservation responded, as did the U.S. Forest Service, that one agency could manage both economic and recreational use of forests.[162] The League's plan for California parks, which Colby helped draft, included three bills, one for a state park commission, one for a six-million-dollar budget to purchase state parks, and one for a statewide park survey. The bills were passed by the California legislature, and in 1926 Frederick Law Olmsted, Jr. was hired by the league to study and make recommendations for the administration of Californian parks. That same year, Governor Young and the progressive Republicans swept the elections. Now McDuffie and Drury began to organize what one historian calls the largest publicity campaign in California's history, for a bond election that would fund a state park system.[163] Before this bond appeared on the ballot, Young appointed a park commission and, through the influence of McDuffie, Colby became a member and was elected first chairman of the board.[164] Why Colby, who felt that he could do more good from the outside as Sierra Club secretary? McDuffie was the logical candidate, but felt that he could not serve because his professional real estate activity might be seen as constituting a conflict of interest. Drafted, Colby could not refuse service, and remained on the state commission until 1936. With Colby's lead, the Club threw itself into the campaign for a bond issue, which passed in 1928. League donations for the purchase of state parks would now be matched by state money.

The Club might well be pleased with the progress made in the 1920s, knowing that the National Park Service was well established under the leadership of men who were closely connected to Club leaders, knowing that it had achieved much of its plan for an enlarged Sequoia National Park, with the prospect for greater enlargement in the future. The encouraging progress of the California state parks allayed some fears for the future of California forests; California lands which were not up to national parks standards might be included in the growing state park system. The League would insure preservation of redwoods, and Colby was a powerful force on the state board. Though the Club might remain ambivalent about utilitarian conservation, editorials in the *Bulletin* by Francis Farquhar suggested that the Club was making its peace with the U.S. Forest Service, now that the Park Service seemed secure.[165] At the close of the 1920s the Club could turn away from political activity toward its purposes "to explore, enjoy, and render accessible."

CHAPTER TWO

Climb the Mountains

Walter Huber, 1883–1960

What of the people whose lives were shaped by the Club that Colby forged? There were many, and some, like Walter Huber, rose to prominence in Club affairs.

Walter Huber was born in San Francisco and educated at the University of California, in Berkeley, where he graduated in 1905 as a civil engineer. He joined the Club in 1907 and went on his first High Trip in 1908, the year Club membership reached one thousand. On High Trips Walter Huber became a climber of Sierra Nevada summits, eventually leading first-ascent parties to the summits of Mount Haeckel, Mount Powell, and the South Guard of Mount Brewer, leaving on several of these a small tag bearing the emblem of the American Society of Civil Engineers, with dates and names of the parties scratched upon it. He was not one of the Club's great mountaineers, but he certainly enjoyed his climbing, and frequently wrote up his ascents for the *Bulletin*. He also established lifelong friendships with fellow High Trippers Frances Farquhar, young Ansel Adams, Will Colby, and others, and eventually with the first two directors of the National Park Service, Stephen Mather and Horace Albright. He was one of the fortunate few who could tell of meeting John Muir in the mountains. On the 1908 trip, as a hurried youth of twenty-five, he was noticed by Muir, who called out, "Young man, what is your great hurry? If you travel that fast, you are going to miss a glorious chance to see some of the best in nature. You have to saunter along and let this rare beauty soak in."[1]

Huber met his second wife, the woman he would marry in 1941, on a High Trip many years earlier. Alberta Mann Reed attended as many as ten of these excursions. A good part of their personal life was fostered by the Sierra Club, even as Walter Huber's professional life was fostered by the American Society for Civil Engineers. He served as president of both organizations during his productive life.

In the many articles he wrote for the *Sierra Club Bulletin*, Huber gave testimony to the personal importance of the High Trips. Not only did they provide a wonderful experience at the time, but they also provided memories, to be relived whenever participants met. When he could not attend the annual High Trip of 1927, and wrote of a private excursion in the Colorado Rockies, he spoke of himself as an exile.[2]

Walter Huber grew influential in the conservation affairs of California and the Sierra Club. As regional engineer for the U.S. Forest Service from 1910 to 1913, he supervised applications for the construction of dams and hydroelectric power plants in the national forests. This allowed him to spend a good portion of his time traveling in the Owens Valley, on the east side of the Sierra, where Los Angeles was developing its water resources. Later this valley would provide access to the highest peaks and wildest regions of the Sierra. Huber's work frequently took him to Lake Sabrina, a reservoir at the head of the middle fork of Bishop Creek. He was able to visit the Palisades Glacier in 1910, traveling by buckboard and pack-train from the town of Big Pine. He encouraged more travel into this area, writing for the *Bulletin*, "As this wonderland at the head of Big Pine Creek becomes better known, it will have many admiring visitors."[3] As a result of his position with the Forest Service he became aware of a proposed reservoir that threatened Devil's Postpile and Rainbow Falls, was able to mediate between the Club and the chief forester, and planned for a Devil's Postpile national monument. He personally surveyed the area for the monument, and the Club gave him much of the credit for its creation. After 1913 he went into private practice as a structural and hydraulic engineer, often working for the federal government. During World War I he was assigned to survey the Little Colorado River for possible power development.

In 1915 he was elected a director of the Club, an office he held for more than thirty years. He was active in the Club's campaign to create a national park in the Kings Canyon region. He served as vice president of the Club for several terms, as president from 1925–1927, and became an honorary vice president in 1948. At the same time, his professional influence grew in government circles; he served on the Yosemite Advisory Board in the early 1930s, and helped approve the improved Tioga Road, which would bring admiring visitors to the wonderland at the head of the Tuolumne River.[4] He was appointed to the secretary of the interior's Advisory Board on National Parks and Monuments in 1953. He became chairman of that board three years later, and held his position until a year before his death in 1960.

No doubt Walter Huber's progress through the affairs of the world provided him with many a crisis of conscience, yet he never seemed to find conflict among his roles as professional, Sierra Club director, and public servant. When in 1955 Robert Sproul awarded him an honorary Doctor of Laws degree on behalf of the University of California, Sproul defined very well the role Huber had taken for himself as a director of the Sierra Club and as an engineer: "Your unique contribution to the State and Nation has been to combine the private practice of your profession with a high sense of public responsibility and thus to help preserve the works of God while serving the needs of Man."[5] This was indeed the ideal role for a Club member of his generation, but it was an ideal increasingly difficult to preserve at the time Huber received his award.

Yet how could Huber know when he surveyed the Little Colorado River that the whole river system would be the object of a scheme as vast as the Colorado River Storage Project? That the Club would expend great energy opposing dams on the Colorado, and eventually make a principled stand opposing most hydroelectric power as unnecessary?[6] He could not know that the Club would confront the Forest Service in the late 1950s over multiple use, the possibility of preserving the works of nature while using them for the needs of man, or know in the 1930s when he served on the Yosemite Advisory Board and approved the Tioga Road project that the Club would change its view of the road in the 1950s. How could he foresee the growth of the Club or its transformation into a dynamic grass-roots organization?

How, when reviewing the career of a man like Huber, does the historian honor his service while recognizing that his life's work—indeed, the technological aims of his generation, shared by fellow members of the Sierra Club—led to many of the environmental problems of the late twentieth century, that his views on public service and on the very nature of the Club became less tenable in the post-World War II world?

In 1947 Huber had argued that the Sierra Club should never contradict its previous statements on Park Service policies,[7] and in 1956 he had sat at a meeting where the Club directors discussed Mission 66—Conrad Wirth's project for improving Park Service facilities, including the Tioga Road—and where the Club's directors wondered how to respond to park improvements. Joel Hildebrand, one of Huber's contemporaries who was also a past president of the Club and an honorary vice president, pointed out that "the Sierra Club plays two roles: [as] a public spokesman for the protection of the wilderness and natural scenic values, and as expert consultant on park matters resulting from the many years of experience that our members and leaders have had."[8] Neither Huber nor Hildebrand could foresee that those two roles might ever conflict, as they did eventually over Mission 66, the Tioga Road, and the general development and management of the national parks.

Certainly these men were troubled when they discovered that their roles as public spokesmen and expert consultants could conflict or cause dissension within the Club itself. For their generation, the ideal Sierra Club was impartial and respected, and it showed the world a consolidated viewpoint. Its board of directors remained a little aristocratic and its members were nearly perpetual. They were invited to serve because they were the honorable kind of men, said Hildebrand, who held honorary degrees.[9] Huber was concerned that the rotation of directors would create confusion. He said that it took a board member years to become conversant with the background and thinking of the board. He claimed it had taken him nine years before he became an effective director.[10]

In 1972, Marshall Kuhn, chairman of the Sierra Club History Committee, sent a lengthy questionnaire to selected longtime members of the Club. Walter Huber had been dead for more than ten years, but his wife Alberta Reed Huber replied promptly. She indicated that she had joined the Club for hiking and recreation. That her two children were not members. That she belonged to several other conservation groups. That she particularly enjoyed her High Trips. That she knew many of the old members. However, she attached a cover note saying, "I doubt if my answers will be of any value to you. I am one of the 'oldtimers' who still belong but do not go along with it." At the end of the form she wrote, "I have not been in sympathy with the Sierra Club for a number of years."[11]

Certainly she spoke well for the views she shared with her husband. But the hiking and recreational organization that she had joined half a century earlier had become something quite different. As a conservation group too the Club had changed many of its policies, also its methods, and most important, the nature of its organization. Indeed the world had changed. For the Hubers' generation, the earth would abide forever, the rivers would run into the sea. There was no question of the possibility of preserving the works of God while serving the needs of man. But younger people were becoming fearful, and matters of conservation had become problematic, in theory and practice.

Recreation   The High Trip, initiated by Will Colby in 1901, was an
1901–1950s   annual summer affair, the idea copied from the outings of the Mazamas, an outdoor organization in the Pacific Northwest. Colby planned the annual outing as a strengthening feature for the Club, "awakening the proper kind of interests in the forests and other natural features of our mountains," with the added benefit that it would "tend to create a spirit of good fellowship among our members."[1] The High Trips were major expeditions. Most of the equipment and food for the campers was packed in by mule; the food was elaborate and cooked by a professional staff—for many years by Charlie Tuck, the Chinese cook. By the second year well over two hundred people had come to the High Sierra by this means, and were served by as many as fifty packers and commissary employees. The High Trip remained this size for several decades.

The High Trip could "explore, enjoy and render accessible" the mountains of California; more important, it was a way of establishing a folklore and a set of rituals which would make the Club cohesive. Every housekeeping duty came to have a new significance on these trips. Washing clothes, serving dinner, bathing, making camp, all took on established forms. It was as if society were recreated, as Colby had hoped, beside the "companionable streams" and "below the myriads of stars that no mere lowlander can ever hope to see."[2] Even the

Sierra Club cup, worn on the waist, came to have a lore of its own and became an emblem displayed with pride.

The reason for these trips came directly from Muir. "Climb the mountains and get their good tidings," he wrote in 1901 in *Our National Parks*; "Nature's peace will flow into you as sunshine flows into trees. The winds will blow their own freshness into you and the storms their energy, while care will drop off like autumn leaves."[3] Muir's purpose in encouraging the Sierra Club outings was philosophical and political: if he could say that the hundreds of people who went on High Trips were using the parks, that was an argument for creating and preserving parks. Further, the Club scheduled many trips into the Kings Canyon area during the campaign for establishing a national park there so that Club members would know the area and write knowledgeably to Congress.

The Club touted its own outings in these early years because, as the *Handbook* said, with the outings "the chance came for more than a hardy few to climb those distant, inaccessible mountains. Many who would never have been able to become acquainted with the high peaks or even to imagine setting foot upon them, found it possible."[4] When the club encouraged creation of a national or state park, or discouraged a certain kind of development in an area of particular scenic importance, it advocated the recreational philosophy that guided its own outings. Often a person who served as a Club spokesman on conservation matters also organized outings, as Colby did.

The Sierra Club was from the beginning interested in mountaineering, hiking, and camping, activities which were part and parcel with nature study or the aesthetic uses of mountains and forests. For a man like John Muir, religious, artistic, scientific, and athletic pursuits were undifferentiated activities, but as the technology of these activities led to specialized pursuits and particularly technical sports, such as rock climbing, skiing, and even backpacking, Club members often became specialists in one outdoor skill. For a while, the new experts were absorbed into traditional outings; but eventually specialization led to division. Many of these new leaders devoted themselves almost entirely to training and testing members, and found their lifelong commitment to sport sufficient involvement in the Club.

Nevertheless, the original undifferentiated Sierra Club cultural event, the High Trip, remained *the* Sierra Club outing until 1941, and was like the standard feature of many western outdoor clubs. Although High Trips visited Glacier National Park, Yellowstone, and the Canadian Rockies, they normally remained in the Sierra Nevada. At first, High Trips established a permanent camp from which side excursions were taken with packtrains or backpacks; High Trips gradually became large-scale roving pack trips, yet continued to fill the need, according to the *Sierra Club Handbook* (1947), of "getting a maximum number of campers into the mountains with the minimum number of pack animals."[5] Associated with these large excursions were many mass ascents of major peaks. In 1903 nearly one hundred and fifty people in two parties climbed Mount Whitney on a High Trip. In 1905, fifty-six people, including fifteen women, ascended Mount Rainier.

Will Colby led his last High Trip in the summer of 1929, the year when Mather retired as head of the National Park Service. The excursion followed the John Muir Trail from Florence Lake to Tuolumne Meadows. Marion Randall Parsons participated. After her husband died in 1914, after Muir died, after she edited *Travels in Alaska*, she had gone to France for the Red Cross, tended wounded soldiers, and relocated refugees. Like so many of her generation, she had kept her spirits up by thinking about the undesecrated American earth, imagining a High Trip to the John Muir Trail after the war.

Melancholy pervades her account of Colby's last High Trip; the end of the Colby High Trips seemed like the end of an era.

She wondered whether the Sierra Club was waning, whether its days of usefulness were passing or past. Considering the year—1930—her anxious mood was hardly surprising. "We banished the sheep from the national parks, it is true, and limited the herds that might browse in the forest preserves," she wrote, "yet the parking areas and vast spreading campgrounds are treading down the mountain meadows no less surely, no less devastatingly than the trampling hooves." She wondered whether the Sierra Club needed to restate its aims for a modern age:

> . . . in earlier years it was in the last degree important to make known to an indifferent and ignorant public the very existence of the fast-disappearing mountain beauty that our generation was just in time to save. But time has turned the tables on us a little disconcertingly. Our problem is no longer how to make the mountains better travelled and better known. Rather it would seem, how from the standpoint of the mountain-lover "to render accessible" may be more truly compatible with "to enjoy."[6]

The times were changing, and the meaning of the phrase "render accessible," too. Though the High Trip emphasized mountaineering, and much energy was still devoted to opening up routes, the routes were becoming more technically difficult. It may be argued that this activity was an extension of the frontier experience, which demanded "dependence on personal effort for survival," as one devotee of wilderness recreation put it.[7] Or it may be seen as a latter-day extension of the great surveys of the nineteenth century, as modern men nostalgically sought the experience of Clarence King, John Muir, and John Wesley Powell. In the mountaineering literature which Francis Farquhar knew so well, the Club primarily followed the pervasive argument that mountaineering was an aesthetic experience; the men who opened up routes on the high peaks were expressing their love for the mountains.

Early Sierra Club members were pioneers in exploring, photographing, and mapping the High Sierra, and their efforts led to strong support for a trail which would run along the crest of the Sierra from Mount Whitney to Yosemite Valley—the John Muir Trail. To render the mountains more accessible, the Club published information: in the nineteenth century, several maps; in the twentieth century, *Place Names of the High Sierra* (1926) by Francis Farquhar, then *A Guide to the John Muir Trail* (1934) by Walter A. Starr, Jr., and finally Hervey Voge's *A Climber's Guide to the High Sierra*, published serially in the *Bulletin* beginning in 1937, and in 1949 as a separate volume.[8] These were followed in later years by many other guides and handbooks, all of which were published not for Club members alone, but as a service to anyone who wished to visit the mountains. Meanwhile, many smaller Club expeditions made first ascents of major peaks on the crest of the Sierra, traversed rugged unknown country, and brought back to the *Bulletin* information on geography, routes, and technique. In one sense, the completion of the John Muir Trail in 1931 marked the end of this exploration of the Sierra Nevada, as Francis Farquhar remarks in his history of the range.[9] It also marked the end of the Club's most enthusiastic phase of trail building.

On the annual High Trip of 1931, Farquhar, along with Robert Underhill of the Appalachian Mountain Club, introduced the proper use of the climbing rope. Immediately after, Underhill and a group of select Club climbers began to apply the technique to Sierra climbing. He joined Norman Clyde, already the grand old man of the Sierra, and two younger men, Glen Dawson and Jules Eichorn, in an attempt on the great east face of Mount Whitney. Their success ushered in a new era for Californian mountaineering.[10] Most important for the Club, these advances in technique attracted a new generation of activists.

Chief among the new generation of Club outings activists was a quartet of men who would have an immense effect on the Club in the next three decades. Ansel Adams, David Brower, Richard Leonard, and Bestor Robinson became prominent in Club outings during the 1930s, and represented the new aesthetic, philosophic, analytic, and practical directions for Club thinking. When they first came to prominence they were perhaps what they would always be.

The senior member of this group was Bestor Robinson (b. 1898), a prominent attorney educated at the University of California, who had practiced law in Oakland for nearly a decade. Robinson was an enthusiastic hunter, climber, and skier. From the first he was interested in expeditions to the desert peaks of Baja California and to the alpine heights of Canada. He joined the Club outing to the Canadian Rockies in 1929. Like many Club members, he was at first willing to be guided by others, especially by Norman Clyde, who led people up many Canadian peaks that summer. When surveying El Picacho del Diablo in Baja California in 1930, Robinson was told by an Indian guide, "Es imposible, Señor." A year later he organized an expedition to El Picacho with younger rock scramblers, and made sure to include Norman Clyde. The ascent was a success. After Underhill introduced more technical climbing skills to the Club in 1931, Bestor's interest in pure rock climbing was whetted.

Robinson became a director of the Club in 1933 and continued in that position for more than thirty years, serving as president from 1946 to 1948. As a prominent Californian lawyer, he also served as a member of the secretary of the interior's Advisory Committee on Conservation and the California region's Forest Service Advisory Committee in the 1940s and 1950s. Later he would serve as an adviser for private recreational developers, such as Walt Disney at Mineral King.

In the early 1930s Robinson joined the Cragmont Climbing Club, a group of young men who practiced technique on the local rocks of Berkeley, who had been organized by Richard Leonard (b. 1908), a young law student. Leonard had grown interested in the Sierra in 1930 when he first entered the back country of Kings Canyon. In the same year, he led a group of Eagle Scouts on a two-month burro trip in Yosemite's back country, along with the famous geologist François Matthes. But pressed by his law studies Leonard found that he often had to make do with local climbing. "It was because of Underhill's example and my desire to get some short exercise that I became interested in rock climbing," he remembers. "Rock climbing takes only about three hours or less, whatever you want."[11] Leonard's analytic mind was engaged by the technical problems of serious climbing. Soon he, Robinson, and others planned strategy for themselves for serious ascents in Yosemite.

The friendship between these men was cemented by more than sport. Not only did Leonard and Robinson share a profession, they shared a common view of the role of the Club. Leonard joined the board of directors in 1938 and continued in that capacity for thirty-five years. He was chair of the Club's Outing Committee from 1936, Club secretary after Colby retired, and president from 1953 to 1955. He also became a member of the council of The Wilderness Society after 1948, and facilitated the alliance between the Club and the Society. As far as Robinson was concerned, Leonard was a real leader, representing a cross section of Club views.[12] And as far as climbing went, the practice at Cragmont had forged a team capable of the first ascent of Higher Cathedral Spire, and capable of teamwork in other realms. It was no surprise, then, that after Pearl Harbor, when army captain Leonard was about to ship out as supervisor of a work team in the Orient, Robinson would pull strings which would land the younger man in Washington, D.C. as an executive officer.[13] Though these men would disagree over a "philosophy of wilderness," as Robinson called it, they would rarely disagree over conservation practice.

The course of Ansel Adams' career was less conventional and less devoted to recreational technique. Born in San Francisco, Adams (1902–1984) early pursued a passion for music, and embarked on an education as a pianist. Indeed, he later instructed Jules Eichorn, who became a musician. But Adams' first visit to Yosemite at the age of fourteen led to a passion for the moods and light of the mountains. As he would later say, he discovered one day while climbing Mount Clark such a pointed, almost religious awareness, that "there are no words to convey the moods of those moments."[14] He became custodian of the Club's LeConte Lodge in 1919. Through the 1920s Adams rambled in the back country of the Sierra, scrambling up many peaks, often with the LeConte family. Though he started taking pictures in the wild with a brownie box camera in 1918, by the 1920s he was no longer a hobbyist, but a serious photographer. He marked his arrival as an artist on April 17, 1927, when he produced the plate for *Monolith, the Face of Half Dome*. In the late 1920s Adams began to do photographic work for Don Tresidder, the president of Yosemite Park and Curry Company. By 1929 he was taking winter back country trips and filming winter sports. He produced a photographic essay on skiing in Yosemite for the Club *Bulletin* in 1931, depicting "a world of surpassing beauty, so perfect and intense that we cannot imagine the return of summer and the fading of the crystalline splendor encompassing our gaze."[15] Adams became a director of the Club in 1934 and continued in that position for more than thirty-five years, contributing his aesthetic vision to the causes of the Club.

The youngest of the new generation was David Brower (b. 1912) of Berkeley. Though he went to college in the late 1920s, he left in 1931, "a sophomore dropout," to use his phrase.[16] He took a variety of jobs, taking leaves of absence when he was lured into another mountain trip. In 1935 he obtained a job operating a calculating machine in Yosemite for Yosemite Park and Curry Company, where he later served as publicity director. He met Adams in 1933, and later had business with him in Yosemite, since Adams' photographs were often used for company publicity; Brower learned something about photography and began to think about writing. More than anything, he wished to travel the mountains with skill, and endlessly. He was instructed in mountaineering by Norman Clyde, whom he met in the Sierra, but received his main instruction from the Club's rock climbing section of the Bay Chapter. His first *Bulletin* article, "Far From the Madding Mules" (1935), narrated a ten-week trip in the High Sierra. Brower began exploring the kind of questions Muir had meditated when he decided that going to the mountains was "going home" nearly a century before. "Was ten weeks, then, the limit? Could the Sierra offer only a transitory enjoyment, merely a temporary escape?" Brower asked. The answer he received when he returned to Berkeley was, "This person was not coming home—he had just left it."[17] In the end Brower would not spend his life in the mountains, as Norman Clyde did, just his summers. Like Muir, Brower returned regularly to the lowlands. He was appointed to his first Club committee in 1933, to the *Bulletin* editorial board in 1935, and became a member of the Club's board in 1941. There he would serve until he was appointed the Club's first executive director in 1952.

Many young Club members devoted themselves to mountain craft. Richard Leonard overcame fears within the Club that technical rock climbing was too dangerous, and established his Cragmont group as the rock climbing section of the San Francisco Bay Chapter. An active rock climbing section in Southern California soon followed. The advent of technical rock climbing opened up a whole new spectrum of recreational possibilities in the mountains. Club mountaineers, led by Leonard, developed the dynamic belay for safeguarding the leader, a technique which absorbs the force of a climber's fall by letting the rope slide around the belayer. This, in turn, led to the use of pitons, and finally expansion anchors or "bolts." Sierra Club climbers attempted new and more difficult routes, on the Cathedral Spires in Yosemite, Shiprock in New Mexico, and around the world after much technical development by Club members in the armed forces during World War II. Club members like Leonard and Brower not only established new climbing standards, but prepared to train the first group of special forces in the army, forces who could meet and do battle with the mountain troops of Germany and Italy.

Many early technical mountaineering accomplishments were achieved by Club expeditions, and there were later expeditions to Mount Waddington, Mount McKinley, Mount Saint Elias, and peaks in the Himalaya. But most of the climbs were conducted by members who ventured forth on their own in groups of two to four. These outings produced a different kind of cohesiveness than the High Trips. It was not clear to anyone that technical climbs produced conservation warriors, yet a list of the active Club rock climbers in the early 1930s doubles as a list of the men who became the Club's most energetic campaigners for conservation issues.

In a specialty such as rock climbing ethics are involved in the use of technology; there is also an ethics associated with technical climbing as a recreational tool. A climbing rope may not be much like a mule, but the use of both ropes and mules has an impact on wilderness and parks. As it turned out, the ethics of recreational rock climbing were not very different from those involved in leading High Trips. First and foremost, the use of an area—perhaps in a national park— should leave it unimpaired for future generations. Ansel Adams asked, "How can we define the delicate borders between ambition and the search for perfection and identity?" He answered, "I abhor the drilling of expansion bolt holes in the pristine flanks of El Capitan and Half Dome; it is a desecration."[18]

Adams knew that technical mountaineering, pursued only

as a sport, might not develop the important rituals which insisted on respect for the mountains themselves. It is not clear that a highly technical sport produces the same cultural restraints that are held by amateurs who are active for recreation. The typical Sierra Club member in the 1930s, a professional in "real life" and (unlike Muir) never a full-time mountaineer, might hire a climbing guide, since he considered himself an amateur. But with the advent of easy automotive transportation there grew a tremendous recreational explosion and a recreational industry, and there were more unaffiliated climbers every year. So the Club began to trouble itself about climbing ethics as an issue of public access. It is an interesting coincidence that the same issue of the *Bulletin* in which an older generation of members mourned the completion of a destructive, over-engineered access road through Yosemite—straight where it should have curved—carried an article by a younger Club climber who celebrated the first direct ascent of the northwest face of Half Dome, anticipating that "improvements in technique and equipment just keep on happening."[19]

Technical climbing produced a new set of leaders, and if the modern climber was often a solitary sort—like Norman Clyde in the 1930s or John Salathe in the 1940s—who might never enter the realm of conservation leadership, outings nevertheless continued to attract people to the Club and led to the growth of local chapters and local activism. As one leader of local rock climbing and ski-mountaineering trips put it, "You will find that a large number of people join a club like the Sierra Club because they like the out-of-doors, and they want to be with kindred spirits and share enthusiasms. Conservation comes later."[20] Four Club chapters had evolved in California by the mid 1930s: the Angeles Chapter in Los Angeles (1911), the San Francisco Bay Chapter (1924), the Riverside Chapter in Southern California (1932), and the Loma Prieta Chapter in Santa Clara County (1933). Each had budding local outings programs.

Many who became Club leaders, like Brower, Leonard, and Robinson, were drawn into Club affairs because of specific recreational programs, and later became engaged in conservation. They led the way in developing technical mountaineering and skiing, and they taught the next generation, inculcating values while teaching craft. Sometimes, as with Phil Berry, Club leaders were drawn by traditional outings like High Trips, and were influenced by leaders like David Brower. Sometimes young men like Will Siri were drawn by specialized Club activities, ski facilities, or the opportunity to learn climbing from the old hands in the Club. Such people did gravitate to conservation activities.[21] And some, like Michael McCloskey, who was active in the Boy Scouts, were introduced to the outdoors by other organizations and gravitated to the Club because of its conservation program.

High Trips, then, ceased to be the Club's only cultural center and proving ground for Club leaders, especially as mass outings such as High Trips were becoming less tenable in what seemed to be an increasingly crowded and mechanized America. Yet the Sierra Club would continue to be unique as a conservation organization precisely because of its recreational emphasis. It developed into a grass-roots organization because of a constant stream of new members attracted by its diversified outings program, conducted through the chapters.

Mountaineering 1930–1954

The Committee on Mountain Records began to compile a climbing guide to the Sierra in the mid 1930s, adapting European standards of difficulty in climbing, "not to promote competition or afford a means of grading climbers for public recognition, but, rather, to give each climber an opportunity to judge for himself what climbs he should undertake under varying conditions."[22] Applied first by Richard Leonard, who wrote the guide to the Sawtooth Ridge in northern Yosemite, and revised in 1939, the system gave a numerical rating to climbs from easy to very severe. Climbing technique had advanced sufficiently that the numerical rating was subdivided to allow for gradation of difficulty within larger classifications. This was a far cry from the cryptic notes venerable mountaineer Norman Clyde had sent to the *Bulletin*. Clyde simply transcribed his journal, noting "good rock-work . . . very fine rock-climb . . . good rock-climb, involving passing or surmounting numerous pinnacles. . . . Agassiz, from the northeast; *one of the finest rock-climbs in the Sierra.*"[23]

In the new *Climber's Guide to the High Sierra* (1954), Clyde's routes would be outlined in much greater detail, with their difficulty classified. The measure of a climb, as described by the new system, was no longer aesthetic, but technical. Consequently, aspiring young climbers saw the rating system as indicating a ladder of accomplishment in itself. The search for climbs of greater difficulty began to take on a direction encouraged by the Sierra Club Decimal Rating, the name under which it came to be known.

The climbers inspired the next evolution in Club folklore, and climbers' ironic humor was the signature of the era. The High Trip's flag had been the bandanna, described in the 1947 *Handbook* as "a square piece of cloth, usually red, used as towel, sunsuit, lunch bag, neckerchief, wash cloth, creel, headdress, apron, scarf, pot holder, terminal protection in case of torn pants, first-aid bandage." Participants composed mock epics about perilous ascents of a nontechnical nature:

> Lead on, Brave Parsons, thou who ne'er
> Has quailed before the trail
> Lead on to Ritter, may our legs
> Fail us if thee we fail.[24]

A new generation of outing members made fun of their borrowings from European terminology: "A sharp ridge is not called a ridge but an *arête* which is the French word for fish bone,—the kind that sticks in your throat and in spite of the fact that our geologist friend and companion Professor Hills of Vassar assured us that there has not been a fish on top of these mountains in at least six million years."[25] When May Pridham produced the "Little Gem Climbing and Skiing Equipment Catalog" in the 1930s for the *Mugelnoos*, a newsletter for Los Angeles rock climbers and ski-mountaineers, she included such items as the "Little Gem Suction Cups . . . for high-angle friction climbs" and the "Little Gem Ski Booster . . . Especially adapted to the use of the 'three-track' type of skier."[26] In "Adjectives for Climbers," David Brower reported: "Interesting—Describes a climb one grade higher than you'd care to lead just now."[27]

Many Club members turned their attention to equipment. Bestor Robinson, chair of the Winter Sports Committee, wrote an article for the *Bulletin* on "Equipment and Technique for Camping on Snow."[28] And developments in equipment led to significant feats in the mountains. Jules Eichorn, Richard Leonard, and Bestor Robinson made first use of pitons in the Sierra Nevada, climbing the Cathedral Spires of Yosemite Valley in 1934. Shiprock, New Mexico, was ascended with the aid of expansion anchors in 1939 by Raffi Bedayn, David Brower, John Dyer, and Bestor Robinson. On that ascent the military metaphor predominated: Leonard "served as intelligence officer" but was not on the ascent, Raffi Bedayn was quartermaster, supplying food, Robinson was the "Rock Engineer," and Brower, the friction climber.[29] Brower's "strictly military" remarks, made in the army style, seemed inappropriate to Robinson, who believed navy terminology would be more appropriate on the climb of a peak with a nautical name.

It was unintentional that the experience of these men turned out to be applicable to the conduct of war. By October of 1941 Leonard and Robinson were in Washington, D.C., working on equipment for arctic warfare. Robinson became commander of a "cold climate technical unit," while Leonard studied foodstuffs and clothing and tested fibers—a task which led to the introduction of the nylon climbing rope.[30] Soon Brower was training soldiers to be army mountain troops, as were others who had been active in Club outings—men like Einor Nilsson, who had helped Joel Hildebrand devise the Club's ski tests, and Raffi Bedayn, who was an innovative designer of climbing hardware.[31] It was not all work. Nate Clark remembers an outing in April of 1941 when Bestor Robinson, Alex and Milton Hildebrand, Charlotte Mauk, Lewis Clark, Einar Nilsson, David Brower, nine others, and he spent five days in the "wonderful wintry wilderness" of the Sierra testing equipment like the first mummy-type sleeping bags, climbing Bear Creek Spire, and having a generally good time.[32] The joy of recreation anticipated the needs for warfare, perhaps accidentally, but quite directly.

When the members of the Club came back to the postwar world they knew a lot about technique and had already written much on what they had learned. In *The Manual of Ski Mountaineering*, published by the University of California Press (1942), Robinson wrote on camping equipment; Joel Hildebrand (a University of California chemist), on waxes; and his sons Alex and Milton, on cooking, avalanches, and transportation of the injured.[33] Leonard relayed what he had learned about equipment, compass, and map. Brower was the expert on route finding, the technique of travel, and rock climbing. Stewart Kimball, a doctor who was later to direct the Club's outings program, wrote on first aid. *Belaying the Leader* (1956), published after the war, was more technical still, and included, aside from Leonard and Wexler's seminal treatise on the use of the rope, ideas from newer and younger climbers like Will Siri and Charles Wilts, who discoursed on belaying, the construction of pitons, and the use of expansion anchors.[34] As Walter Huber had used his skills while a consultant on park roads, so these men applied their skills as scientists and engineers to advance the techniques of recreation.

The consequences of these developments were all-pervasive. The military metaphor was entrenched in the Club's language, not only in speaking of climbing, but also in speaking of conservation.

Even Muir had been seduced by the idea of skiing *Skiing* when he wrote of an excursion to Lake Tahoe for the 1878–1938 *San Francisco Daily Evening Bulletin* in 1878. Skiing was a rather comic affair, he thought while witnessing the antics of a friend who "launched himself in wild abandon, bouncing and diving, his limbs and shoes in chaotic entanglement, now in the snow, now in the air, whirling over and over in giddy rolls and somersaults that would shame the most extravagant performances of a circus acrobat." His friend's descents were "most remarkable specimens of falling locomotion." When the man would "gather himself, pick out the snow from his neck and ears, and say with preternatural solemnity, 'This, Muir, is the very poetry of motion,'"[35] Muir replied disparagingly that it was probably like the poetry of Whitman, of which he apparently did not approve. Skiing permitted a recreationist to experience the Sierra in winter, so Muir's reminder that there was a great absurdity to the downhill enthusiasm hardly seemed to matter. There was no question that influential members wanted Sierra Club members to ski.

Club members had to make a complicated set of decisions about the role of the organization in promoting skiing as a sport. Certainly none of them could have forecast the growth of recreational skiing in the period after World War II, or what it would mean to the mountains near Donner Pass and Lake Tahoe. Yet they early recognized that in the realm of winter sports the issues of appropriate kinds of recreation, appropriate development of areas, and appropriate access were vitally linked.

As early as 1915 the *Sierra Club Bulletin* carried articles speaking in poetic terms of wonderful flight on the hickory wings at Tahoe, complete with photographs of up-to-date skiers lined up with their long single poles.[36] In 1930 Don Tresidder wrote that "within a very few years there will be found in the Sierra Nevada of California the outstanding winter resorts of America."[37] He did not believe that competitive skiing would be the primary interest of the Club, but expected that ski touring and ski mountaineering would have thousands of devotees. In the same year, Orland Bartholomew reported a remarkable solitary ski journey during the winter of 1928, along the Sierra Crest from Lone Pine to Yosemite Valley.[38] Francis Farquhar, editor of the *Bulletin*, thought that Bartholomew's account marked a new development in recreation. "With increased interest will come increased facilities," he wrote in 1930.[39] He applauded the establishment of a series of ski cabins in Yosemite National Park: "Through this means it is now possible to make a winter tour to Tuolumne Meadows with almost the same facility as is afforded by the Yosemite 'hikers' camps' in summer." Indeed, he expected that the Club would have regular midwinter trips all over the Sierra: "Every Sierra Peak will before long have its winter-ascent, and with these climbs will come new experiences, new triumphs over difficulties, new unfoldment of the grandeur and beauty of our High Sierra." Farquhar would be president of the Club during just those years when it would be most enthusiastic about skiing.

A Winter Sports Committee chaired by Ansel Adams, and including Bestor Robinson, Oliver Kehrlein, Orland Bartholomew, and Frederick Reinhart, recommended in late 1930 that the Club "enter into a program for the encouragement of winter trips and expeditions into the Sierra Nevada backcountry," but leave the exploitation of snow sports at resorts to others.[40] The annual number of the *Bulletin* the next year had an article on skiing by Adams, illustrated by his photographs of skier Jules Fritsch descending Lembert Dome, standing on the summit of Mount Watkins, and leaping off a corniced ridge with crisp High Sierra peaks in the background.

Unlike mountaineering, skiing had the possibility for organized competition. One of the chief advocates of competition was Joel Hildebrand, who thought the revival of skiing in California a perfect winter form of the Club's original purposes. Hildebrand was nearly fifty years old in 1930 when he began to encourage the revival. A few years later he would serve as the manager for the United States Olympic ski team. After that, he was Club president during the successful campaign for Kings Canyon National Park.

At the very inception of skiing as recreation the standards associated with competitive sport were instilled as prerequisite to competence. Racing improved the technique of the individual skier, or so the argument went. The consequences of this attention to skiing as sport and as "style" were interesting. Joel Hildebrand wrote:

> I would urge our ardent mountain climbers to restrain their ambitions to climb peaks in winter till they have learned to ski. One should be ashamed to make a long descent by "sitzmarking" at every turn when it should be possible to run down under control in a beautiful series of christianas or telemarks. To one who has learned to ski, it is this, not the mountain-peak, that is the greater glory.[41]

It was no longer sufficient to climb the mountains and get their good tidings. One also had to descend gracefully. To encourage competence and to screen Club members for difficult ski outings, Hildebrand and others designed ski tests. These were originally highly formalized, almost military in their rigidity. Further, members who passed the fourth class, third class, second class, or first class tests were awarded pins and badges of different colors.[42] Soon skiing enthusiasts were boasting about the number of Club members who had passed each category.

The advent of winter sports led to the building of lodges. The Club already owned LeConte Lodge in Yosemite Valley, had built Parsons Lodge in 1915 on property it owned in Tuolumne Meadows, and cooperated in building the Muir shelter in what later became Kings Canyon National Park. In the 1930s the Angeles Chapter of Southern California constructed the Harwood Lodge in San Antonio Canyon, and skiers in San Francisco decided that they, too, needed a winter lodge, at Donner Pass. The result, in 1934, was the Clair Tappaan Lodge, planned specifically for skiers; it was followed by smaller outlying huts for ski-tourers, and matched by two more lodges in Southern California. These ski lodges were by no means elaborate resorts, but most were not shacks either. Members planned and built them, as volunteers for the most part, and they were open only to members and guests. As a direct result of its interest in skiing, the Club was becoming—in a small way—a developer and landlord.

The Sierra Club was proud of leaving its signature on the California landscape; it had written itself into the creation of Yosemite National Park, and all the way down the Sierra Crest when it encouraged building the John Muir Trail. Its Committee on Mountain Records encouraged climbers to build cairns and leave Sierra Club registers on Sierra peaks. And the Club left its signature when it encouraged any kind of recreational activity.

Club members began to ask what kinds of activities would be good for the Club's institutional aims and for the lives of the men and women who participated. Ideally, what was good for the organization and its people was also good for the land. Many members, for instance, believed that a ski resort improved the landscape on which it was built.

Several did not, and wondered if the Club had lost sight of

the original purposes of its recreation. In 1938, David Brower encouraged members to transcend ski-resort thinking:

> Before skiing had made its relentless surge toward universal popularity, . . . skiing was the most practical means of reaching snow country, where men could pause amid the majestic winter scene to contemplate their sublime surroundings. This was the golden age of skiing . . . [but] with mechanization came a mania for speed. . . . Mountains became mere proving grounds for exhibitions of tricks and technique. Men worshipped perfection in tempo, vorlage; were consecrated to mastery of controls and schusses, corridors and flushes; talked of waxes and edges, ski-meets and records. They admired their apparel, while the peaks went unnoticed. They slashed trails in the forests, built elaborate lodges, gashed mountains with highways, wired peaks with funiculars. They conquered the wilderness. Men now ski superbly. But what have they lost?[43]

This was a warning by a twenty-six-year-old member who had belonged to the Club only five years. A ski resort, he thought, constituted a practice slope for something better, so he insisted that ski mountaineering was *the* true form of recreation that the Club ought to encourage. It is not clear that his elders or even his contemporaries wished to be preached to by this youngster.[44]

Recreationists were preached to by Adams as well, who accepted rock climbing "with the greatest enthusiasm" but also warned, "we should bear in mind that the mountains are more to us than a mere proving-ground of strength and alert skill. Rock climbing should be considered a thrilling means to a more important end."[45]

For many members who devoted themselves to outings attaining perfect technique in sport seemed a cause good in itself. But was it? Brower and Adams asked. The board had encouraged the building of winter ski trails, and winter ski huts along those trails, though none were built.[46] Was this the right direction? After the war the Club would have to decide whether it approved development of ski resorts at Mount San Gorgonio in Southern California and at Mineral King, adjacent to Sequoia National Park. These were practical examples of larger philosophical issues the Club was preparing to confront. Soon the Club would advocate national parks as nature preserves and wilderness, rather than for their recreational possibilities.

Wilderness   The idea for a Kings Canyon national park as a wil-
Parks   derness park, according to Joel Hildebrand, belonged
          to Bob Marshall of The Wilderness Society.[47] The
1935–1948   Club continued to express interest in the area, press-
          ing for additions to Sequoia National Park, resisting
California state plans for a highway into Kings Canyon, and in 1937 considering the possibility that Kings Canyon would be better protected as wilderness if administered as a Forest Service Primitive Area. Without Club support, the bills for a Kings Canyon national park in the 1937–1938 session of Congress failed. Secretary of the Interior Harold Ickes felt that the Sierra Club had been dragging its feet, and came to San Francisco in October 1938, where he and all fifteen Club directors were feted by Francis Farquhar at the Bohemian Club. The result was a compromise. Ickes promised to protect the wilderness values of Kings Canyon by provisions in a new park bill, and the Club promised to support the park.[48]

Adams sent his first book, *Sierra Nevada: The John Muir Trail*, to Ickes early in 1939; according to one Park Service official, not only did these images constitute a noble supplement to the voice of John Muir, but were a most effective voice for wilderness parks in themselves.[49] Meanwhile, Brower photographed and produced the Club's first movie,

Sky—Land Trails of the Kings, with Leonard's help during 1939 and 1940 High Trips.[50]

When a bill for a John Muir–Kings Canyon Park was introduced by Congressman B. W. Gearhart early in 1939, the Club, convinced by Ickes that this would not be another Yosemite with luxury accommodations like the Ahwahnee Hotel, was prepared to endorse the idea of a "primeval national park."[51] The proposed park would include much of the area that Muir had originally proposed for a Kings Canyon national park, land that had been left out of Sequoia National Park—unfairly, the Club thought.

What was a primeval park? The Gearhart bill contained a provision "to insure the permanent preservation of the wilderness character" of the Kings Canyon region, and placed sharp prohibitions on permanent improvements like hotels and roads. There was universal agreement about the need for primeval parks among the Club's directors. President Hildebrand explained—"without reflecting on the splendid work of the United States Forest Service"—that status as a national park was necessary so the area would be "protected by a service which did not consider these primeval areas as 'pools (of resources) for future commercial development.'" Francis Farquhar explained that the "primeval national park definition" was necessary to "aid in strengthening national park standards which are in danger of becoming less clearly defined with respect to the great scenic parks of the West."[52]

The board was willing to recognize the claims of citizens in the San Joaquin Valley upon the waters of the Kings River for flood control and irrigation. The canyons of the Tehipite and South Fork were withdrawn from the park proposal to placate irrigationists. Interestingly enough, the Gearhart bill was opposed by both The Wilderness Society and the National Parks Association because the lower canyons, including Tehipite Valley, were not included in the park proposal. The Club chose to follow the Mather strategy, believing that the high country of the Muir Trail was its first priority, and that the lower valleys might be protected later. This was what David Brower seemed to have in mind when he wrote that the Club thought these areas were of "far less wilderness importance than the High Sierra above them."[53] Half a loaf was better than none. The board indicated its own predilection for back country recreation; where the High Trip went was where the park should be.

Kings Canyon represented a significant early move toward wilderness ideas. Resorts, including elaborate ski resorts, were not in the direction of traditional Club thinking, at least according to the spokesmen of 1939. The Gearhart bill passed both houses of Congress by early 1940, and Kings Canyon National Park added 438,000 acres to the national parks in California. The creation of Kings Canyon National Park consummated the Club's most important conservation campaign of the 1930s.

During World War II the Club was relatively dormant. At the same time, members who spent their service in Europe did learn some lessons. As David Brower wrote in 1945, the mountains of Italy, Austria, Yugoslavia, and Switzerland seemed shattered remains of what once must have been beautiful wilderness. Europeans had improved and exploited their mountains too much, in the name of recreation. "Were Yosemite in Italy," Brower wrote from overseas, "there would be a hotel on the saddle between mounts Lyell and McClure, accessible by a very good and prominent tramway."[54] No members wanted a ski lift on Mount Lyell, the highest peak in Yosemite, but members would disagree on whether such a prospect was good or bad for other mountains outside national parks.

Further, the very people who were the vanguard in the recreational programs of the Club before the war—David Brower, Richard Leonard, Bestor Robinson, and Joel Hildebrand, who had skied together—found themselves after the war in sharp discussions about the direction and extent of development appropriate for the mountains of California. At issue was a perceived need for ski resorts, and the problem presented itself with Mount San Gorgonio, in Southern California, where developers had proposed a ski resort before the war.

About half the members of the board were avid skiers, and in the flush of an exciting new sport they were apt to be rash. Even Brower had advocated a ski lift from Yosemite Valley to the summit of Mount Hoffmann in 1936, until he was dissuaded by Arthur Blake.[55] Doris and Richard Leonard had started skiing around 1933, but were more moderate in their enthusiasm; they preferred going cross-country, and never used lifts.[56] Bestor Robinson had a more pluralistic view of recreation. He explained his philosophy later, in 1972: skiing and wilderness camping were both "very valuable contributions to the American way of life. . . . I had no use at all for the argument that there was something superior in the wilderness use and that the [resort] skiers should be considered a second class use."[57] Neither did Robinson see any fault in the fact that ski resorts were money-making enterprises.

Mount San Gorgonio became the focal point of disagreement. After the war there seemed to be an influx of new members who only joined for the low-cost skiing at Clair Tappaan Lodge. "We worried," Brower remembers, "about the change in club character if skiers who were more interested in building lifts and sliding down hills should outnumber the John Muir types." This was especially true because the "wilderness we had helped save was now threatened by a bunch of skiers in southern California who wanted to develop San Gorgonio."[58]

There was no question about the quality of skiing at San Gorgonio, a high, fine, open mountain with broad, beautiful slopes and the most dependable snow cover near Los Angeles. Cross-country skiers had been using it in significant

numbers for quite a while. "But that," Richard Leonard remembers someone saying, "doesn't make any money for
anybody because you are doing it on your own two feet."[59] It
was also a wild area. San Gorgonio's status could be changed
at any time by the chief of the Forest Service. The Forest Service, in turn, was subject to pressure from congressmen in
Southern California who supported a proposal to run a road
into the heart of the wild area and build a small (5- to 10-
acre) ski area. That little road, Leonard thought, would be
like a worm in an apple.[60]

The board itself was split on the subject, and members who
came from Southern California were themselves divided.
Preserve the boundaries of the primitive area to protect summer recreation, said Lewis Clark. Make a ski area, with clear
limits, said Glen Dawson.[61] With no models for appropriately
designed Californian ski resorts to use as examples of the
right kind of development, the ambivalent Francis Farquhar
acted the chorus for the board in this drama: ". . . the line
must be held unless it can be proved (with the burden of
proof resting on those who wish revision) that it is in the interest of the entire community that the proposed modifica-
tion be made. Recognizing the desirability of ski development, the directors must yet realize that this is the one
remaining Wilderness Area available to a large metropolitan
area."[62]

A month later, at the beginning of 1947, Bestor Robinson
became Club president. Preparatory to a February public
hearing on the exclusion of the ski section from the San Gorgonio Primitive Area, the *Bulletin* published both sides of the
issue, Brower writing in opposition to development and Robinson writing for it, the latter anonymously.[63]

Brower's article amplified the policy agreed upon by the
board.[64] He feared that development would set a precedent
for other lands administered by the Forest Service, especially
in the Sierra. "Can a conservation organization place the

construction of ski facilities, or any development, above wilderness?" he asked. The board had proposed that the Forest Service acquire all private inholdings before taking any action which would increase land value, that the Forest Service require a complete factual study and formulation of specific plans for the resort before holding hearings, and that preservation of the wilderness character of the area be paramount to the construction of ski facilities. Brower went further and satirized the "enthusiastic and sometimes even evangelical skiers" by telling them to look beyond their ski tips and see that "the sole value of a mountain is not just that it tips a snow slope downhill."

Robinson's anonymous article was concise, sober, and factual. As Brower still believes, it was also wrongheaded: "Robinson would have given San Gorgonio away."[65] Robinson pointed out that the value of wilderness was in its use by humans, that humans required reasonable access, and that the Club purposes included "rendering accessible." He said that there was no escaping the phenomenal growth in recreational skiing, that new plans and policies for wilderness areas would have to be created, and that they would have to be predicated on developing cooperation between winter and summer users. He believed that Sierra Club opposition based on empty principles constituted "intellectual myopia": "It may well be that human intelligence is not capable of evolving a plan which will provide reasonable winter use without destroying the wilderness. Until the making of such a plan is earnestly attempted, however, it cannot be said that it is hopelessly objectionable. The result is too important to predetermine its impossibility."[66]

Indeed, others knew that California needed skiing as good as that available in Europe; as Brower remembers, "We didn't want Sun Valley to take it all away from us."[67] For these reasons the Winter Sports Committee assigned a subcommittee to survey California's ski terrain. Along with Lowell Sumner, a pilot and influential Park Service biologist, and Dick Felter, committee chair, Brower asked, "Where, within close enough range of skiers who want to develop San Gorgonio, is there better skiing, development of which skier-conservationists can approve and advocate?"[68] Committee members agreed that many small, poor developments were more disfiguring to the landscape than a few centralized, large, well-planned resorts—a view also held by Bestor Robinson. They hoped that ski areas could be superimposed on already used summer resorts. They tried to create a survey which would "anticipate the needs of the promoters of winter sports" but also protect wild areas: "It must accumulate the data that can persuade the promoters to look elsewhere." What they turned up would be a problem in the future. In their aerial photographs, Mineral King loomed large, the caption to its photo reading, "Probably the most spectacular site for commercial development on the west slope of the Sierra. Major road realignment and costly snow removal, chargeable only to skiing, would be required for full development of the site. It is now excellent ski-mountaineering country." It was not Forest Service wilderness, was served by a road, but was an enclave in a national park.

Why were Club members doing the work of developers? Later they would oppose development of Mineral King for skiing, because such a development would perpetuate a corridor into wilderness. But in the late 1940s, the board decided only that "although the Sierra Club does not advocate the development of any particular region for skiing, the Club cannot, as a matter of principle oppose the development of Mineral King, or any other non-wilderness area."[69] Later the Club would be charged with duplicity, with waiting until San Gorgonio received wilderness status before opposing development of Mineral King.[70]

The Club's strategy to preserve the San Gorgonio area was dictated by the lack of any statutory protection for Forest

Service-administered wilderness areas. Leonard recognized the problem when Oliver Kehrlein, the head of the Club's Public Relations Committee, sent out a pamphlet "to the effect that the Forest Service had lost its mind and . . . must be 'brought to its senses.'"[71] Leonard knew how impolitic this was, since the Forest Service was judge and jury on San Gorgonio, and the regional forester had complete discretion in such decisions. Under such circumstances, the Club had to be as cooperative and useful as possible if it hoped its advice would be taken. Leonard himself produced a brief for the Club and presented it at the public hearing on the future of the San Gorgonio Primitive Area. His elaborate but respectful argument addressed not only development, but practical issues like potential avalanche hazards, and conflict among users; his essential message: *Once developed, the wilderness is gone forever. But if it be preserved, development can be rapid whenever needed.*"[72] The Club had made up its mind on recreational development, but protecting wilderness was a delicate issue. Joining other organizations, it would have to lobby for statutory wilderness protection or be fighting—to use the military metaphor—rear-guard actions everywhere, and every year.

To explore, enjoy, and render accessible the mountain regions of the Pacific Coast; to publish authentic information concerning them; to enlist the support and coöperation of the people and the government in preserving the forests and other natural features of the Sierra Nevada Mountains . . . Sierra Club Bylaws

Access: Revising the Bylaws 1947–1951

These purposes were becoming more problematic after World War II, but were linked in the following way: as an exemplary organization—its means of influence being largely educational—it was natural that the Club should publish authentic information and enlist cooperation and support. Because there was a right way, and there were many wrong ways, to do anything, the methods the Club used when it went about exploring, enjoying, and rendering accessible the mountains of the Pacific Coast were all important. Its members expected that their activities would be under close scrutiny, and welcomed the occasion to demonstrate what John Muir called the "right manners of the wilderness." Small groups and large eagerly joined outings which were closely linked to conservation activities. Since the early Club devoted itself to aesthetic conservation, it naturally directed its outings and conservation activities primarily to creating and protecting national parks, whose fundamental purpose, after all, was "to conserve the scenery and the natural and historic objects and the wild life therein and to provide for the enjoyment of the same in such manner and by such means as will leave them unimpaired for the enjoyment of future generations."[73]

When Richard Leonard became chair of the Outing Committee in 1936 he did not alter the cultural basis of the outings, but faced with many purely practical issues, he instituted a new set of diversified outings, some of which required that participants be more self-reliant. First came Burro Trips, begun by Milton Hildebrand in 1938, not only because burros created less impact than mules, but because participants were responsible for themselves and their animals. Eventually this kind of trip evolved into a leisurely outing for families with small children. On Knapsack Trips, begun by David Brower in the same year, participants carried their own food and equipment, were most independent, and easier on the mountains. Two years later, after coleading the 1939 and 1940 High Trips, Oliver Kehrlein organized the Base Camps, where participants were packed into one place for two weeks and cared for by a professional staff, in the elaborate High Trip fashion.

Some were offended by the large number of people participating in the more luxurious Base Camps and High Trips, but the High Trips in particular were rich in tradition. Brower at first was ambivalent about the changes in Club outings. Of Knapsack Trips, he remembered, young people "would get through the mountains well and enjoy them, then be off somewhere else, and not around to man the defenses when we got into the conservation battles. The High Trip was the best source of the conservation warrior."[74]

In other words, the High Trip remained the cultural center of the Club's outing program, but diversified outings met the needs of a diversified set of new members, as well as a whole new set of conservation problems. River Trips were instituted by Brower when the Club became active in preserving Dinosaur National Monument, so members could see the threatened area. Many Club trips in the 1940s and 1950s ranged out of California to embattled parks like Grand Teton National Park and proposed wilderness areas like the Wind River Mountains in Wyoming. New trips such as the Threshold Trip, initiated by Brower, were instituted to meet the needs of members who desired a different kind of recreation, while the nature of some outings was changed because of increased recreational pressure on the mountains.

During the era of the Colby High Trips it was the general view that nobody else was in the mountains. As that became less true in the 1930s and after the war, when the back country began to be heavily used, several important issues came into play. Even before the war, stock used for recreational trips was beginning to do serious damage to the back country meadows; consequently the ethics of using pack animals for Sierra Club trips was called into question. Then there was the matter of packing in and serving people who could not get to the mountains on their own, who had not "earned" the experience, and who added to overcrowding. Other users of the back country were displeased when they came upon the large Sierra Club High Trips. Even loyal Club members like

David Brower were at first put off by the mob. "It looked like quite a lot of people, and it was," he said of his first encounter with a High Trip in 1933. "If the 'horde,' so called, bumped into somebody who was overwhelmed by it, they'd invite this person to dinner to try to make him feel better."[75] Inviting guests to dinner was probably not a sufficient solution to this public relations problem. If Muir had extolled in his writings the joy of solitude in the wilds, why was the Sierra Club encouraging an experience which was anything but solitary? One might notice that this critique of large back-country outings is rooted partly in a puritan attitude, in ascetic discipline or self-reliance.[76] It also has a purely aesthetic side to it. In any case, the human experience might be dulled if the routes were too easy to follow, too well-documented in guides, too physically easy. Not only might the horde be doing unnecessary damage to the mountains, but it might be experiencing them in an inappropriate way.

Damage to the mountains was addressed by the chair of the Outing Committee himself. Before World War II the National Park Service had made studies of meadow deterioration in the Sierra, and after the war use of the parks seemed to be increasing beyond all expectations. So in 1947 Richard Leonard coauthored an article with Lowell Sumner, the Park Service biologist, in which they went to great lengths defending Sierra Club methods of packing on trips and attributed the damage being done in Sierra meadows to carelessness by others.[77] But the writing was on the wall. Large parties using many pack animals would be an increasing problem even in the large back country of the Sierra. The days of the old-fashioned High Trips as an approved form of recreation were numbered.

Now the original concept of the Club outing—to make the Club cohesive and give members firsthand knowledge of areas they wished to protect—had to be balanced against purely practical issues. In 1947 the Sierra Club was not "loving the mountains to death," yet in following a kind of "wilderness cult," so-called by Roderick Nash, it was encouraging ever-increasing use of wild areas in parks and forests, still convinced that places no one knew could not be preserved.

In 1947, then, the issue of "rendering accessible" had become more complex, waiting for attention by a board of directors trying to reorganize itself. Indeed it was over the issue of access that Will Colby's influence began to wane significantly in Club affairs. Some young members of the board, like Richard Leonard, remembered that the transition began over the question of a road into Kings Canyon, and involved some bitterness, for Colby finally said, "Nobody respects my judgment, or that of John Muir. I am getting out."[78] Others, like David Brower, believed Colby was simply growing weary, that his resignation from the board was a natural consequence of age.[79] In any case, the issue of access separated the newer generation from many of the old, and it was nowhere more clearly demonstrated than in the changing response to the improvement of the Tioga Road in Yosemite National Park.

It was natural that the Club should come to its first postwar crisis of conscience over Yosemite or Kings Canyon. Colby's Club had been the moving force in creating and defending these parks. As an organization primarily interested in non-commodity uses of the nation's land, the Club had its closest philosophical ties to the National Park Service and had established close relations with the agency's early administrators. Club members considered themselves watchdogs over the Sierra and scrutinized any actions by the Park Service to alter or develop areas within its jurisdiction.

As was typical in this period, there was an issue of internal cohesiveness in the Club as well. Some of the younger members suspected that the words of the bylaws were being misinterpreted by the public to mean that the Club advocated building more roads and accommodations, and they advocated amendment. Consequently, fifteen years after Marion Randall Parsons stated the problem, the men of the board decided she had been right. For several, the priority for the future was not to get people into the mountains, but to manage and develop parks properly. Developing the John Muir Trail was what Colby had meant when he said "render the mountains accessible." That work was finished. He now suggested that the Club might change its articles to say "to render *appropriately* accessible."[80] This did not clarify the issue.

In the most benevolent possible sense, "to render accessible" meant to provide to the public a new freedom to enjoy its own American landscape, particularly mountains. For that reason the Club was especially concerned about any regulations that would limit the ability of citizens to use their parks appropriately. Leonard and Colby were particularly distressed that Yosemite National Park had begun to regulate back-country camping and require backpackers to register for designated sites. Though Colby conceded that in Yosemite Valley restrictions were necessary because of what he called "the extreme use of 'mass man,'" like Leonard he intensely disliked regimentation.[81] But to post-World War II America, freedom of access meant primarily roads of higher standards, built for speed and comfort.

Before the board would act to change the bylaws it reconsidered decisions made back in the 1930s, when it was completing the John Muir Trail and publishing Starr's *Guide*. Then the Club had approved and consulted on the route for the Tioga Road as an "improvement" to Yosemite National Park. A decade later this road would bring many uncomfortable issues home to the Club, including allegations of "elitism" and "purism."

The Tioga Road, laid out for mining wagons in 1883, passes from the west side of the Sierra all the way up to the crest at Tioga Pass on the eastern border of Yosemite National Park. The mines failed in the panic of 1883, the road deteriorated, but the Sierra Club contributed funds in 1915 when Stephen Mather decided to purchase the road and donate it to the national park. Though his road was repaired and re-opened, its route was essentially unchanged, following the contours of the land in a manner that was fascinating to some people and frightening to others. The State of California constructed a connecting route up Lee Vining Canyon on the east side of the Sierra; as travel to the park increased from both directions, pressure developed for improvement of the route to "higher standards of travel." The National Park Service adopted a plan to reroute the road through what Club members thought was "magnificent wilderness country to the north of Mount Hoffmann among the beautiful Ten Lakes of that area."[82]

A report written in 1934 by Club directors Francis Farquhar, Ernest Dawson, William Colby, Walter Huber, and Duncan McDuffie conceded that an improved Tioga Road would "enable travelers to reach Tuolumne Meadows and the eastern portions of the park readily and with comfort." It also accepted the premise that the road would be used for trans-Sierra travel, and noted that motorists would appreciate the fine views available from the proposed "high-line" route to be cut through Ten Lakes Basin. However, the report finally argued that the Club had allegiance to the primary object underlying the creation of parks, which was to preserve something Muir had called "pure wildness." For that reason the report recommended improvement, not realignment, of the road.[83]

Since the Sierra Club was loath to see virgin country despoiled, the board believed it was choosing the lesser evil in recommending that the route remain the same. The Park Service accepted in large measure the Club's recommendations, and this was a source of pleasure to those who wanted the Club to be consulted on park matters. Much of the re-engineering and construction of the road was completed in the 1930s, before the war. The remaining and most difficult section, however, was to go through one of the most beautiful areas in Yosemite Park, through the shining granite domes surrounding Tenaya Lake. Perhaps no road could be put through such a place without seeming to be a desecration. Yet precisely in that area the Park Service would decide to relocate several miles of road, cutting across glacial polished slabs both southwest and north of Tenaya Lake. Even widening the old road in this area would produce considerable damage to the landscape.

The improvement of the Tioga Road carried implications which went far beyond Yosemite or the Sierra Club, not only because engineers threatened to alter one of the most beautiful natural landscapes in America, but because park administrators followed a policy of opening up remote portions of national parks to high-speed auto travel. By cooperating in the 1930s, the Club seemed to endorse a Park Service mission, not as caretaker of wild lands, but as developer of recreational opportunities. This problem became acute a few years later when Conrad Wirth's Mission 66 program was instituted.

Harold Bradley became aware of these implications in the late 1940s, and attempted to galvanize the Club to action. Born in 1879, son of one of the founders of the Club, he participated in the campaign over Hetch Hetchy during the years 1906 to 1913, even while far away at the University of Wisconsin, working as a physiological chemist. He retired in 1948 and returned to his family home in Berkeley, but not before a long and rewarding winter ski tour in the Tioga Pass, Tuolumne Meadows area of Yosemite National Park. The six-week excursion with his sons and their wives revitalized Bradley's interest in conservation matters. He was a vigorous 68 years old at the time. Later, in 1951, he became a Club director, serving for ten years, and was president of the Club from 1957 to 1959.

On his ski tour in 1947 Bradley was enchanted. "When

winter drapes a shining mantle of snow over Tioga and the Meadows," he wrote, "all their lost youth returns and the wilderness is restored." There was nothing to remind the traveler on skis "that man had already begun his reduction of this lovely region to just another automobile route through mountains." The whole region, he thought,

> is not inaccessible, but requires of those who would
> enter it a certain degree of faith, of hope, and of love.
> Above these, perhaps, it demands a degree of familiar-
> ity, experience, and competence in the mountains and
> in the winter. To those devotees who desire admission
> strongly enough to add personal toil to the require-
> ments already mentioned, the rewards in terms of
> beauty, inspiration, and peace are beyond calculation.[84]

His inspiration was spiritual and "elitist," and he was will-ing to make himself an expert on the engineering of modern highways. Bradley had to get his facts in order to oppose credibly progress and "improvements." In August 1947 Brad-ley put a proposal about the Tioga Road to the board of directors.

Bradley rooted his critique of the improved Tioga Road in a desire to see the park values preserved for the Tuolumne Meadows region of Yosemite.[85] He pleaded for "the preserva-tion of this section of our High Sierra in its present semi-primitive nature in summer and in its winter wildness." His basic premise was that primitive roads were a means that the Park Service should use to limit visitation to the wilder and more fragile parts of the parks. The old Tioga Road discour-aged "the mere restless driver and the speed addict"; conse-quently a poor road helped Tuolumne Meadows escape over-crowding. Bradley feared that an improved road would become an all-weather road and lead to intense development for winter and summer recreation. Not only was he con-vinced that Tuolumne had its highest winter use as a ski tour-ing area, but he thought it should be *zoned* only for that winter use. Further, he thought that the twenty-mile primitive section of the road could be improved only slightly and still remain "in consonance with a rugged mountain region."

He envisioned a bleak future for the area during summers if the high-standard highway was completed, including rapidly increasing visitation, brutal scarring of the mountain scene, and added facilities which would bring about the problems already troubling Yosemite Valley. He foresaw pressures by the trucking industry and every chamber of commerce from Salt Lake City to the coast, all pushing for more improvements. For winters, he envisaged a full ski resort, with dance hall and barroom, "jazz and all the conveniences expected at a modern ski resort." For him, the lesson was simple: "Changes of this sort have a way of breeding more changes. . . . There is indeed no obvious terminal point to the forces which destroy wilderness, once you introduce them in a region such as this ."

Why, Bradley wondered, was the Tioga highway necessary? For safety? "At fifteen miles an hour"—a maximum on the historic trans-Sierra rural road in Yosemite—"serious accidents do not occur." Speed? "It is a device and a necessity of business." Access for trailers or commercial trucking? That was what the Park Service should deter. No, he said, the mistake was possible because "we have accepted the engineer's dogma for low grades and high speeds in the mountains without questioning the validity of his premise." Such improvments only made the visitor forget "just what a National Park is, and for what purpose it was created." The visitor did not demand jazz, a bar, or speed at his public library or in his church, because he understood those places better. "The only remedy for this situation," said Bradley, "is the expressed opinion of the informed and intelligent citizen, the conservation-minded, the Park devotee, the lover of these mountain sanctuaries for what they are."

If these sentiments were elitist or purist, then Bradley thought the time had come to express them vigorously. He was supported strongly by David Brower, then editor of the *Sierra Club Bulletin*. But when in August 1947 Brower introduced Bradley's proposal to the board as an essay for publication, he encountered considerable resistance. As the minutes read, "Mr. Colby felt that to print such an article calling for a reexamination after the road had been two-thirds completed would place the Sierra Club in a very awkward position, particularly since the Club had endorsed the program and participated in present general plans when they were first formulated."[86] Though there was no vote, when Brower appealed three months later that the article be published, Bestor Robinson "pointed out what he considered a basic error in Bradley's article: that wilderness areas are for enjoyment by those with leisure and financial ability to go to them for more than week-end trips."[87] Others also expressed reluctance to see the article published, and in the end it was not. A toned-down version, coauthored by Bradley and Brower, was published by the *Bulletin* in 1949.[88]

Meanwhile, the Club dragged its feet on a Tioga Road policy for over a year. It did not wish to damage its credibility with the National Park Service. Neither did it want to appear elitist or purist to the general public. Walter Huber did not wish to inconvenience the Park Service, "making it discard work already done and start over." Francis Farquhar urged another "on-the-ground study." Colby still felt that "the more people there are who see the meadows and the high country of a National Park, the more people there will be to fight to defend the great values there."[89] He felt sure that John Muir would approve the plan completing the road. By this time, in 1948, younger directors Ansel Adams and Richard Leonard had proposed a new alternate route for the road to avoid Tenaya Lake.[90]

The board of directors attempted another strategy, to establish a Club policy about all park roads. They directed Bradley to formulate a policy for roads in national parks. Bradley's draft proposal argued, once again, that parks were becoming

overcrowded, that overcrowding led to developments "urban, permanent, and foreign to the park scene," attracting
more people "so that in the end we have a recreational resort
in place of a National Park"; that one factor which determined overcrowding and overdevelopment was the system of
roads in the parks. Richard Leonard, Club secretary, sent out
this document during the summer of 1949, asking for comments from Club directors, officers, and Conservation Committee members. "When all comments have been received,"
he said, "it should be possible to prepare a revised statement
that will include all areas of agreement and represent a
strongly unified Sierra Club opinion."[91]

Board response to the proposal was generally not favorable. One director, for instance, asked that any criticism of
trailers be eliminated, and questioned whether it would be
politic for the Club to advocate low-standard roads in order
to prevent use of the mountains: "I admit we do want to limit
use and hold the mountains inviolate only for those who will
take the time and make the effort to see them," he wrote, "but
we are being very exclusive in our attitude and we are making ourselves open to the charge of snobbishness."[92] The
board was careful to revise the words of the policy statement,
to make it sound more positive. Votes over the Tioga Road
policy were split, and the issue was tabled. Consequently the
Club did not confront the Park Service until plans for blasting
the granite around Tenaya Lake were fixed and construction
had begun.

The Club did reconsider its image, and decided to change
its statement of purposes. In 1951 the board recommended to
the membership that the Club's purposes be changed from
"explore, enjoy, and render accessible the mountain regions
of the Pacific Coast" to "explore, enjoy, and preserve the
Sierra Nevada and other scenic resources of the United
States." Soon after, this change was approved by the
membership.[93]

CHAPTER THREE

The Way to Wilderness

Norman Clyde, 1885–1972

When, in 1969, a graduate student did a sociological study of the Sierra Club, he distributed his results to some members.[1] One longtime member responded to the resulting report in the following way:

> To its leaders, *the Sierra Club is a cult.* You say something about the professions of its founders, but the point is that they put themselves under the leadership of John Muir . . . the High Priest. In the mountains he slept on the ground and lived on breadcrusts and tea. . . . The mantle of John Muir—not Muir, the leader, but Muir, the devotee of the mountains of California—descended to Norman Clyde, who dropped out of society in the 1920's to lead a solitary, hippie (but non-drug) life in the southern Sierra Nevada. The older leaders of the Club regard Norman Clyde as a Dalai Lama.[2]

Thomas Jukes, who authored this analysis of Sierra Club values, is known as a master of polite invective, and spoke with tongue in cheek.[3] He was himself a climber, and organized the Atlantic Chapter of the Sierra Club. As an eminent chemist who spent his career developing pesticides, he would have his falling out with the Club as it began to enter its environmental phase in the 1960s. His historical facts here are inaccurate on several points, and not meant as unbiased history, yet his perspective is too intriguing to ignore. Another version of the historical facts was recorded by Richard Leonard.

"Let me tell you one story," Richard Leonard told an interviewer in the 1970s, "about Norman as he was once. This is one of the unfortunate things that I think ought to be recorded for the future, since this is history." It was back in 1941. As Leonard remembers, Norman Clyde "was leading a party up the Matterhorn. It has a frightening name, but it is an easy climb."[4]

Matterhorn Peak, that wonderful mountain on the north edge of Yosemite, where one might recline on the summit under the wide light of the Sierran sky and read messages from previous climbers in the Sierra Club register, a cast aluminum box bolted to the rock. Norman Clyde, who called himself the old gaffer in later years, had left Prince Albert tins; Muir had left nothing at all. "The mountains will turn into Buddhas," Gary Snyder had written in this register. Later Jack Kerouac wrote of his hike up Matterhorn Peak in *Dharma Bums*, the novel which ushered in the so-called rucksack revolution.[5] The Norman Clyde most people knew was taciturn, but the *Sierra Club Handbook* of 1947 said: "In the course of many High Trips, he has led hundreds of members up peaks. Almost all Sierrans who have acquired the passion for climbing, acquired that passion from some other member, if not from Norman Clyde, who gave them a boost by sharing his enthusiasm and his knowledge of how to do it."[6] Clyde, then, helped usher in the Sierra Club's rucksack revolution.

Born in 1885, Norman Clyde graduated from Geneva College in the state of his birth, Pennsylvania. He came to California in 1911 or 1912, having been drawn by Muir's *The Mountains of California*. He married, but his wife died only three years later. He spent his first summer in the Sierra in

1914. He attended the University of California briefly, then he taught school, and became principal at Independence High School in the Owens Valley, from about 1920 to 1927. When he left that occupation, he spent most of the rest of his years in the Sierra, with occasional excursions to other mountain ranges. Norman Clyde died in Big Pine, California, in 1972. During his most active years, in the 1920s and 1930s, he was one of America's foremost climbers, credited with 1,500 climbs and at least 200 first ascents. A man of prodigious strength, his feats were legendary and he was known as the Old Man of the Mountains, or sometimes the Pack that Walked like a Man. Harold Gilliam compared Clyde to Thoreau, indicating that Clyde's Walden was the entire Sierra and his cabin he carried on his back.[7]

Richard Leonard did not think of Norman Clyde as a Dalai Lama or a Thoreau, but as a poor soul. Leonard's view was colored by his own role in Club affairs as he spearheaded changes in the Sierra Club during the 1940s, when he and the other men he dubbed "the young turks" succeeded in changing the bylaws from "render accessible" to "preserve." They called it purism, the turning away from human concerns to concerns for the mountains themselves. Muir had discovered his own kind of purism on his walk toward Florida. The world, he said in 1868, was not made especially for man, and man would have to accept the consequences. "Surely the Old Muir would have noticed that there were too many people in the mountains, that they were overloading them, and beginning to damage the beautiful country," Leonard recalled in 1972.[8]

"And Old Colby," Leonard went on, "the old Dear, he could never understand. He said that old Muir wanted people to enjoy the mountains, as many as possible."[9] The young turks made Colby—the Club patriarch—honorary president, Leonard said, but changed the bylaws. When Leonard named his own generation, he may not have remembered that the young turks who instigated a bloodless revolution failed to carry out promised reforms despite their supposedly liberal ideas. Leonard chaired the Club's Outings Committee from 1936 to 1952. During Leonard's reign, the Club boasted, "Many who never would have been able to become acquainted with the high peaks or ever imagine setting foot upon them, found it possible."[10]

The Club had been rendering the mountains accessible for a long time. Muir himself had guided the uninitiated. In the summer of 1875 he led a couple of young students up Mount Whitney, taking particular care that no one would be led by him through unnecessary dangers. Particularly, he said, he "remained firm in avoiding dangerous ice slopes." Yet he also wrote, late in the same summer, "No mountaineer is truly free who is trammelled with friend or servant, who has the care of more than two legs."[11] So it was that climbers like Leonard and Clyde might have inherited Muir's ambivalence.

Leonard was not very much like Norman Clyde. At the ranch where the old gaffer spent his last days, Norman Clyde lived in an abandoned house which was owned by the Los Angeles Water District. He stole a bit of Big Pine Creek for his use; he burned wood for heat, kerosene for light. He acquired his furniture at the local dump. Norman Clyde was no famous conservationist lawyer. Like Muir, he was a graduate school dropout, poor, but never an ex-climber. Like Muir, he was "hopelessly and forever a mountaineer." Like the Muir of "A Geologist's Winter Walk," Norman Clyde desired to spend all of his time in the mountains and suspected that his body became less trustworthy through intercourse with "stupid town stairs," "dead pavements," and "town fog."[12] Jules Eichorn said of him: "For me there can never be another human so completely in tune with his environment—the mountains—as Norman Clyde." David Brower remembers Clyde's advice: "'The mountain will always be there tomorrow,' meaning that we ourselves might well not be if we push too hard and long at the wrong time."[13]

"Norman must have thought he would give a thrill to the party," Leonard's story of Matterhorn Peak went on, "and took them across a steep snow bank on about a forty-five degree slope." "They were not roped," said Leonard, "because it was such an easy climb."[14] Norman Clyde was no showman, and he taught David Brower the principle of three-point suspension essential for unroped climbing—a lesson about the conduct of life on the heights: never move more than one limb at a time when on dangerous ground. The rope turned climbing from a solitary to a social skill.

Leonard was proud of the nylon rope which constituted his contribution to the safety of mountaineering, the mathematics of climbing. Unlike Clyde, who spent most of his life in the mountains, Leonard was drawn to climbing by a "desire to get some short exercise. . . . To my mind it has always been the solution to a difficult problem, or trying to accomplish something that has never been done before . . . that provided the real joy of climbing."[15] For Leonard, the most difficult problem was safety:

> One of the policies of the English [mountaineering]
> writers was that if the leader fell, since he knew that the
> other members of the party could not protect him, he
> had therefore violated his duty to the others because he
> was going to kill them, too, so they should cut the rope
> and get rid of him since he had betrayed them by falling.
> I thought that was a heck of a way to climb if you
> couldn't trust your own pals that you were with.[16]

This duty to others was no joke, though a later generation of climbers would joke about the so-called belaying knife. Brower had respected Norman Clyde and credited him with giving good mountaineering advice. Never move more than one limb at a time when on dangerous ground, Clyde had said.

"The last man was a little bit clumsy, and he broke out the final step," Leonard said, "and crashed down into the rocks." Leonard knew the mathematics: "It was like a fifty-foot fall over an overhang." On the same High Trip but off on another climb, Leonard did not witness the fall. The Club had a doctor along on those trips, and the doctor was a skillful surgeon; the doctor "took seventy six stitches in putting the poor man's scalp back on, and then he had to carry him for two days."[17] There was always a doctor along; that was part of making the mountains accessible.

"Norman was angry," Leonard told the interviewer. "He said 'To hell with him, let's go on with the climb.' He was going to go."

Brower does not remember anyone quoting Norman as saying such a thing: "What I remember is that Norman was annoyed that the victim had not properly used the footsteps Norman had punched into the snow for the party. . . . For years and years Norman had 'barleysacked' people up difficult pitches when he had to, with bemused patience. On the Matterhorn climb he was impatient when sympathy was needed, and he had chosen too dangerous a course for the novices who followed him."[18] Brower, who had also been off on another climb, remembers two accidents on successive days on the same snowfield.

The old gaffer could be full of fury. One day at a Base Camp in 1968, the trip leader—this history's author—decided to read from Muir's "Snowbanners of the California Alps" at evening campfire.[19] It was a short piece written for armchair mountaineers, genteel Muir, and much admired by the campers. "Fancy yourself dear reader," Muir had written as he depicted the banners from a "forest window" for his *Harper's* audience. "They are twenty miles away, but you would not want them

nearer." Muir could not help but say that there would be
something more surpassingly glorious if the middle ground
were obliterated, leaving only the violent and stark scene,
"the black peaks, the white banners, and the blue sky." At the
end of the reading, Norman Clyde stood up and kicked the
fire. He growled, "Muir was no real mountaineer. He spent all
his time down in Yosemite Valley." His eyes burned in their
sockets; his set teeth gleamed in the firelight above his griz-
zled jaw. The silence of the forty campers lasted until the old
gaffer had passed into the dark toward his sleeping place.

The young crew who ran that 1968 outing knew something had happened between Clyde and the Club, before
their time. In 1968, Clyde was 83, an old man who came on
the outings as naturalist, an honorary leader who spoke of
natural history, gathered wood for the campfires, and spun
yarns late in the evening. The teenage children who came
with their parents for the two-week family vacation called
him Norman. Their parents disapproved of the large fires
Norman Clyde made, but would sometimes throw a big log
on, right before retiring to bed. Clyde grew livid when he discovered a large log smoldering in the morning. "Heating up
the night air, I s'pose," he would growl. He was not overly
fond of the campers, liked some, but never hid his disgust for
others. Perhaps Norman Clyde had not changed from 1941 to
1968, but he seemed—to the young crew—an essential in-
gredient of Sierra Club outings.

Just as the author of this history could not forget Clyde's
words of 1968, so Leonard could not get over the words of
Clyde reported to him in 1941: "He was our official guide,"
Leonard remembered; "we were paying him, you see, giving
him a free trip and paying him to take people on these
climbs."[20]

Giving a free trip to a man who spent more time in the
high mountains than anyone could imagine, and who had

pioneered perhaps a thousand new routes when he was between forty and sixty years of age. A man who had spent
most of his adult life traveling solitary through the Sierra, carrying on the Muir tradition, making his home on the heights.
The old gaffer sauntered into camp alone, arrived from some
obscure direction, from some mysterious place in the mountains, always carrying his own gear in a pack of legendary
size. Many of the campers were uncomfortable with this lit-
erate man, who read Schiller in German, Sophocles in Greek,
who was so self-reliant he could spend a whole winter skiing
on the peaks, living alone in an old rock cabin, banked by
cords of firewood. He wrote, he took thousands of photographs, but campers didn't trust a man who carried a loaded
revolver for scaring bears. Norman Clyde never talked about
his contributions to safety. Safety was what? The mountains
were safest when men thought they were dangerous. He did
talk about the bodies he had found—like that of Walter Starr,
Jr.—by following the blowflies. He never talked about his
climbs. He told stories about being in the mountains. He was,
in a profound sense, the ultimate purist.

Leonard told the interviewer, ''I set up a kind of trial that
night, and I and some of the other experts went over it with
Norman, and we fired him that moment.''[21] Brower remembers agreeing that the Club could not have Norman leading
High Trip climbs any more. Norman Clyde was fifty-five years
old when he was fired.

Muir, Clyde, Leonard, Brower, even Jukes: all exceptional
men. Yet they illustrate a disjunction between the generations, perhaps a disjunction in the Club mind. One might
look back at Muir and see the loner and the leader, the anti-
social and the social, the lover of wilderness and the booster
of parks. Leonard was angered by Clyde, Jukes derisive,
Brower admiring but forced to act; the Club found Clyde's
way in the mountains enlightening, but his way with people

offensive, his wild life valuable, but his hostility impossible. The actual events on Matterhorn Peak are not clear; Brower believes that Leonard's memory, like his own, is flawed. However, the accident or accidents did occur, and Norman Clyde was an impatient if not angry man.

In the city Norman Clyde had abandoned so many years ago—where he studied literature until asked to read it in translation—that was where he would be judged. He distrusted the place, and was himself distrusted. A man ended up relinquishing authority, to something. Muir entrusted himself to the Sierra. Norman Clyde to what? Three-point suspension, to himself? To the mountains as Muir had? Tom Jukes trusted technology. Leonard, technique and analysis, based on traditional American social and economic values. What can a historian trust? The memory of men? The wisdom of time? Memory often serves self. Some men grew wise as they grew old, and some men did not. If young Muir was right, wisdom never dwelled in the city at all. Yet this is certain: many young mountaineers recognized wisdom in the unfaded eyes of Norman Clyde, a long time ago. As Brower recalls, "I knew Norman Clyde from 1933 until his death, and liked him."[22] The old gaffer had his reasons.

While the Club engaged in California matters, it was also part of a larger wilderness movement, which included The Wilderness Society, incorporated in 1935 by Robert (Bob) Marshall, Aldo Leopold, and Robert Sterling Yard.[1] Robert Sterling Yard, in particular, had broken with Mather's Park Service policies because they were too elaborate and development-oriented.[2] For the Society, Franklin Roosevelt's Civilian Conservation Corps (CCC) programs represented an emergency, not to the national parks, but to the public lands administered primarily by the Forest Service. As Yard wrote, "The craze is to build all the highways possible everywhere while billions may yet

The Wilderness Society 1935

be borrowed from the unlucky future. The fashion is to bar-
ber and manicure wild America as smartly as the modern
girl." It was against this trend that the Society's platform recognized wilderness—"the environment of solitude"—as "a
natural mental resource having the same basic relation to
man's ultimate thought and culture as coal, timber, and other
physical resources to his material needs." Leopold asked, "Of
what avail are forty freedoms without a blank spot on the
map?"³

Wilderness could even be seen in political terms. There
were wilderness advocates who thought of their "movement" as a way to save the American way of life from the Red
Menace. As one forester had put it in the early 1920s, wilderness provided moral benefits which were also politically salubrious: "If the American population can be made to feel
contented and its effort directed to useful channels, enlist-
ment in the Red organizations of this critical period of unrest
can be averted. I can conceive of no more useful purpose the
forests can be made to serve."⁴

The theory of wilderness as lotus land never carried much
strength and The Wilderness Society made no such partisan
political statements. According to its platform, a wilderness
environment was a human need, not just a luxury or play-
thing. The Society argued that "motorway and solitude together constitute a contradiction"; the Society also sub-
scribed to an ecologically based definition of wilderness:
"Since primeval succession can never return once continuity
has been severed, it is manifestly the duty of this generation
to preserve under scientific care, for the observation, study,
and appreciation of generations to come, as many, as large,
and as varied examples of the remaining primitive areas as
possible."⁵ The Society was skeptical of modern technology.
Leopold argued, "Despite the superficial advances in technique, *we do not yet understand and cannot yet control* the longtime interrelations of animals, plants, and mother earth."⁶

Because members of the Society were professional land managers, they classified wilderness in managerial terms. There were five types of wilderness, the first, called Extensive Wilderness Areas, defined in recreational terms by criteria of size and space and bearing on the quality of experience for visitors; the second, called Primeval Areas, defined in ecological terms as "the culmination of an unbroken series of natural events, stretching infinitely into the past"; the third, Superlatively Scenic Areas, of primary aesthetic interest; the fourth, Restricted Wild Areas, relatively "free from the sights and sounds of mechanization" and close to metropolitan areas; and the fifth, Wilderness Zones, compromised areas where it was still possible "to undertake long journeys under the impetus of one's own energies instead of those of a machine."[7] The first two types of wilderness became the basis for the U-Regulations, formulated through the efforts of Bob Marshall. The U-Regulations defined for Forest Service managers three designations: wilderness areas, wild areas, and roadless areas.

The *why* of the Society was stated quite clearly by Leopold. "There is a particular need for a Society now," he said, "because of the pressure of public spending for work relief." But also Leopold hoped that the organization would constitute "a disclaimer of the biotic arrogance of *homo americanus*. It is one of the focal points of a new attitude—an intelligent humility toward man's place in nature."[8]

How was The Wilderness Society different from the Sierra Club? It claimed that it did not plan a large membership or fine establishment, and that its members were men "young in spirit," including "executives of the most influential national conservation organizations." It planned to focus primarily on national forest lands, unlike the Club, which was interested in parks, and to have a national influence, as opposed to the Sierra Club's regional scope. But as it grew up, its aims influenced and then converged with those of the Sierra Club. Its prominent members, Olaus Murie, Sigurd Olsen, and especially Howard Zahniser, had constant commerce with Club members and encouraged cooperation between the two groups. Luna and Starker, the sons of Aldo Leopold, as well as George Marshall, the younger brother of Bob, would later serve well as directors of the Club. Unlike the Sierra Club, The Wilderness Society for many years did not organize outings, teach mountain skills, or provide social kinds of entertainment. It published *Living Wilderness* and tried to influence government policy.

Robert Marshall (1901–1939), the motive force of The Wilderness Society, exemplified a curious tension in wilderness thought. He was Jewish, participated in his philanthropic family's staunch advocacy of minority rights, civil rights, and particularly American Indian rights. Further, there were significant humanistic aspects of Marshall's thinking, including the influence of William James and Freud. Marshall was an existentialist, a humanist, and a full modernist, in the tradition of Joseph Wood Krutch.[9] A fervent devotee of the New Deal, he was adamant—perhaps socialist—in insisting that every acre of the country's forests should belong to the people and be administered by the government.[10] But when he conceived of wilderness as a recreational resource, he was an unabashed elitist. Marshall was not afraid to use the term "locking up" when speaking of wilderness areas, because he did not trust the business world to act as steward for these areas. He felt that wilderness provided primary values rather than economic needs, because it had "exerted such a fundamental influence in molding American character." With degrees in forestry, a doctorate in plant physiology, and a career in government service, he was no typical bureaucrat.

In "The Problem of the Wilderness" of 1930, reprinted in the *Sierra Club Bulletin* in 1947, Marshall struggled with the philosophical and policy problems concerned with man's relations to nature. His definition of wilderness—an early expression of ideas later institutionalized in the Wilderness Act of 1964—was recreational:

> . . . a region which contains no permanent inhabitants, possesses no possibility of conveyance by any mechanical means and is sufficiently spacious that a person in crossing it must have the experience of sleeping out. The dominant attributes of such an area are: first, that it requires anyone who exists in it to depend exclusively on his own effort for survival; and second, that it preserves as nearly as possible the primitive environment.[11]

Having worked as chief forester for the Indian Bureau, Marshall knew the passion with which Native American communities like the Tewan Pueblo and Taos Pueblo guarded their sacred wilderness, but what about modern European man? The benefits, Marshall was sure, were the same for primitive and modern man: physical, mental, and aesthetic. Unlike Muir or Native Americans, Marshall did not see wilderness as an expression of God. For pure aesthetic enjoyment, he thought, "there can be no extraneous thoughts—no questions about the creator of the phenomenon, its structure, what it resembles or what vanity in the beholder it gratifies." Though he clearly respected Indian ways of thinking, he was modern, not neoprimitive.

When Marshall found a tension between physical and mental benefits of experience in wilderness, he elucidated exactly the paradox of humanism that Joseph Wood Krutch explored in *The Modern Temper* (1929).[12] Krutch had argued that modern humanism was at war with itself, since civilized men wished to be both a part of nature and separate from it, did not wish to give up animal pleasures, yet realized that civilized society required a renunciation of the "bestial." Physical health was to some extent tied to the spirit of adventure, without which life would be, Marshall believed, "a dreary game, scarcely bearable in its horrible banality." On the other hand, Marshall quoted Krutch's thesis that "'if life has any value at all, then that value comes in thought,'" and Marshall tried to demonstrate further that wilderness provided the best incentive to independent cogitation. He also valued the purely primitive pleasures of the body. "One of the most profound discoveries of psychology," he said, "has been the terrific harm caused by suppressed desires." He believed that he had discovered in the wilderness experience William James's "moral equivalent of war." As he quoted approvingly from Bertrand Russell's *Essays in Skepticism*, "'many men would cease to desire war if they had opportunities to risk their lives in Alpine climbing.'"

Bob Marshall's ideas came out of a world of skepticism. His thought was that of an alienated intellectual. Behind his interest in wilderness was the disillusionment he learned in Krutch's *The Modern Temper*. Krutch's exposition of the prevailing mood in western civilization was subtitled "A Study and a Confession," and chronicled modern man's loss of illusions, loss of trust in ideology, loss of God, of love, of faith in science, of meaning in art. For Marshall, the only escape from this predicament was an escape to a world where man was not a dominant presence. Wilderness was valuable because it provided solitude and fostered individuality, as modern society did not.

Thus Marshall could be a primitivist and an elitist at the same time. He quoted with approval Willa Cather's romantic version of Indian land policy: "'The land and all that it bore they treated with consideration; not attempting to improve it, they never desecrated it.'" Using her view as a foundation, he attacked automobilists who argued that for the majority of Americans wilderness seemed inconvenient. Krutch had said, "We cannot make physical speed an end to be pursued very long after we have discovered that it does not get us anywhere."[13] Marshall found the automobilist argument for easy access "almost as irrational as contending that because more people enjoy bathing than art exhibits therefore we should change our picture galleries into swimming pools." Just as the democratic philosophies of men like Paine, Jefferson, and Mill were followed by practical administrators who funded the high cultural needs of civilization—museums, art galleries, and concerts—even at the expense of "small additional happiness to the mobility," so too wilderness areas which would be used by few, though available to all, should be supported as a cultural resource. Taste, Marshall believed, was not determined by the lowest common denominator.

Aldo Leopold (1887–1948), an original thinker and literary figure whose stature continues to grow, sought a wider audience than Marshall in his writings.[14] Like Marshall, he was interested in the value of wilderness to civilization and the history of their interaction. Unlike Marshall, he did not emphasize the recreational potential of wilderness. Instead he explored its historical value.

The historian Frederick Jackson Turner argued in his essay "The Significance of the Frontier in American History" (1893) that "American development has exhibited . . . a return to primitive conditions on a continually advancing frontier line." And on that frontier "the wilderness masters the colonist."[15] Turner believed that the American democracy "came from no theorist's dream of a German forest. It came, stark and strong and full of life, from the American forest."[16] Some modern social historians, like Richard Hofstadter, parody Turner's thesis by paraphrase and amplification: "Democracy does not yet emerge from society or ideas or from the internal dynamics of human institutions but still comes from the forest—ambling forth, one imagines, like some amiable cinnamon bear."[17] Yet Turner's thesis was perhaps America's most important contribution to the understanding of its own history, particularly in the American West. It was a thesis absorbed by the wilderness movement as an argument for preserving wilderness, and is present in the writings of Leopold.

In the early 1930s Leopold established himself as an expert on wildlife management. According to one biographer, "the year 1935 marked a reorientation in his thinking from a historical and recreational to a predominantly ecological and ethical justification for wilderness."[18] Thus, at just the moment when Leopold was helping create The Wilderness Society, he was entering a phase in his thought which led to a radical reconsideration of land management. He argued in 1934, "In the long run we shall learn that there is no such thing as forestry, no such thing as game management. The only reality is an intelligent respect for, and adjustment to, the inherent tendency of land to produce life."[19] Leopold believed, "Wilderness is the raw material out of which man has hammered the artifact called civilization"; but he also believed, like Turner, that on the American continent wilderness transformed the colonist.[20] Leopold's dialectical view of American environmental history led to a necessary dialectic in the affairs of men:

> A harmonious relation to land is more intricate, and of
> more consequence to civilization, than the historians of
> progress seem to realize. Civilization is not, as they
> often assume, the enslavement of a stable and constant
> earth. It is the state of *mutual and interdependent coopera-
> tion* between human animals, other animals, plants,
> and soils, which may be disrupted at any moment by
> the failure of any of them.[21]

This ethical imperative for wilderness management went far beyond matters of recreation. When Leopold became a leader in the wilderness movement, he tried to change America's view of its own history, first of all by reinterpreting it as environmental history, and secondly by preserving that wilder-

ness which Turner claimed had molded the American character. Like many in the Sierra Club, he may have started as a
recreationist, but he did not end there.

Leopold's major influence on the Sierra Club began after
his death in 1948. *A Sand County Almanac and Sketches Here
and There*, published posthumously in 1949, was reviewed
admiringly by Harold Bradley for the *Bulletin* in 1951.[22] Bradley, who was a close colleague of Aldo Leopold in Madison,
gave Brower a copy of the book in 1950.[23] Brower obtained
permission from its publisher to quote from it in the pages of
the *Bulletin*. The book was sold through the Club offices in
following years. Brower dates his change in outlook, from
recreational ideas of wilderness to ecological ideas of wilderness, from reading Leopold.

As historian Robin Winks has argued, we Americans are particularly obsessed with our future: "Those things which we
preserve, must be relevant and invariably relevant to some
future point. The past [to be worth preserving] must be usa-
ble, it must help define future goals for the nation."[24] So it was
that neither Robert Marshall nor Aldo Leopold was interested in wilderness only as a sign of the past, but wanted it
preserved as a resource for the future. Winks also points out
that in 1940, fifty years after Turner announced that the
American frontier was closed, substantial portions of America—particularly in the West—remained frontier by Turner's
own definition. Winks wonders, "Are deliberate recreational
and conservation preserves frontiers or not?" and concludes
that they are not, since they "are not lands of opportunity in
the sense of being open to further exploitation and entrepreneurship."[25]

For Leopold and Marshall these preserves would be lands
beyond the frontier, their highest use non-economic. The positive traits in the American character—not all of them generated by Turner's thesis—were those produced by non-

economic intercourse with the wilderness. Here was the basis
for Harold Bradley's later praise of bad roads. And here too
was a reason why the board of directors decided on February
17, 1951 that the Club, after fifty-nine years of existence,
should change its bylaws so they would read not "explore,
enjoy, and render accessible," but "explore, enjoy, and
preserve."[26]

Progress   In recent years, some writers have mounted a vigor-
Toward a   ous attack on the wilderness movement.[27] Was the
                wilderness movement, as these critics claim, really
Land Ethic   politically conservative, an attempt by an aristocratic
                elite, in the tradition of John Quincy Adams, to lock
up America's resources, to keep them away from the people?
Was it an attempt by America's haves—America's leisure
class—to withhold economic power from the have-nots?
Was Andrew Jackson, who threw open the land to the
people, the true benefactor for land-hungry Americans seeking control over their lives?

It depends on how you feel about so-called progress, and
the so-called progressives. Wilderness advocates of the 1930s
emerged from a modern world very different from that of
Pinchot and Theodore Roosevelt; their thought was tempered in the crucible of the depression, as they watched the
New Deal's strategy for alleviating the economic plight of
America. Though Leopold and Marshall were both sympathetic with the aims of the New Deal, they were critical of
several important modern ideas. They did not believe, as the
modernists did, that man created the world in the act of per-
ceiving it, or that man needed his natural environment for
only economic uses. They did not believe that man appreciated—in scientific, philosophical, or psychological terms—
his roots in his natural environment, or even understood the
relationships among the wild entities in that environment.
They did not believe that massive utilization of America's re-

sources was the best long-term solution to a social, political, economic, or perhaps moral crisis. They did not believe that America could solve its economic problems while in a state of ecological ignorance.

They *did* believe: that the wild American land was essential not only to the economic health of its human inhabitants, but also to their mental health; that Americans could learn to have a sense of place, and that they could—if they wished— come home to their primitive continent and inhabit it as an indigenous species; that Americans could learn to live in a stable and harmonious relationship with an eternal, though changing, land.

As wilderness advocates approached this biocentric ethical position, they began to pledge allegiance to the continent, as well as to the country. In the post-World War II era, the great age of loyalty oaths, such allegiances could easily be misunderstood. Though the leaders of The Wilderness Society hardly wanted to abolish centralized governmental control of resources, they began to diverge from traditional resource development, uncomfortable with the purely economic definition of conservation—in the Forest Service's slogan, The Greatest Good for the Greatest Number in the Long Run. Neither Leopold nor Marshall would be happy with the fictions called "legal wilderness" or "sociological wilderness," since wilderness was neither simply what a law claimed it was nor simply the *terra incognita* of people's minds.[28]

They believed that wilderness should be preserved not only for human benefit but for itself, yet wished to see wilderness managed by law so that people could enjoy it. Leopold, as a professional game manager, wished to see hunting privileges extended in certain areas at certain times. Marshall discussed with Sierra Club members the possible means for making Sierra wilderness more accessible for young people and low-income groups.

Both Leopold and Marshall were professional land man-

agers, but they did not pledge allegiance to specific government agencies in the way that Horace Albright or Stephen
Mather had to the National Park Service. A manager who is
truly of the agency, or committed primarily to the law which
enables it to perform, sees a different reality from that of Leopold or Marshall. He is "acculturated" by his agency and
works within its values, his duties and attitudes circum-
scribed by the agency's enabling legislation.[29] "The only reality," Leopold had said, was not forestry or land management,
but an intelligent respect for and adjustment to the fertile
earth. Marshall knew the urban world, its possible reality or
nightmare where "there will be countless souls born to live in
strangulation, countless human beings who will be crushed
under the artificial edifice raised by man."[30] Yet a manager
like Horace Albright saw the National Park Service as an
institution. His allegiance was to growth of the agency's
strength, size, and budget.[31] His predecessor, Stephen
Mather, denied the right of the Forest Service to develop recreation programs, claiming that recreation was the sole responsibility of his agency. In the extreme example, a manager
like Conrad Wirth saw a national park as the sum of facilities,
roads, and buildings built for visitors, saw a different reality
from those engaged in the wilderness movement.

Passage of the Taylor Grazing Act in 1934 marked a symbolic step in American land policy, bringing not only the closing of the public domain and the beginning of what is now a
vast system of public land classification, but also marking the
beginning of a significant transformation from traditional
public land law to modern land law.[32] Traditional public land
law dealt with private rights in conflict, but men like Leopold
and Marshall were instrumental in the evolution of modern
land law, which has increasingly attempted to deal with
these matters in the public interest. Perhaps the last steps in
this process have been the codification of the rights of non-
economic interests and introduction into the law of the biocentric rights envisioned by Leopold.[33]

The Wilderness Society was filled with men who framed many of the early land laws, as well as making administrative decisions on the management of land. Marshall's introduction of the U-Regulations and Leopold's management of wildlife constituted practical, painstaking, direct work in the area of land management. Whatever their temperaments, these men did work within government agencies, yet many of their ideas were slow in being introduced to public land law or administration. This was especially true of Leopold's Land Ethic.

Leopold had introduced his essay, "The Land Ethic," by projecting the progress in civil rights forward into the future. He believed that rights would someday be assigned progressively to non-human parts of the world, until men would recognize that "a thing is right when it tends to preserve the integrity, stability, and beauty of the biotic community. It is wrong when it tends otherwise."[34] This was Leopold's ultimate justification for wilderness. Roderick Nash sees this progressive assignment of rights to non-human parts of nature as a part of Leopold's contribution to an understanding of ecological history and to furthering the ecological ethic.[35] Yet if John Muir arrived at a biocentric outlook in 1868 while on his thousand-mile walk, and Leopold in 1935, the same transformation was much slower in coming to conservation organizations or to national institutions. A sign of the Sierra Club's evolution toward a comprehensive land ethic was the commencement of the biennial wilderness conferences.

Norman Livermore (b. 1911) had worked as a packer in the High Sierra every summer since he graduated from high school. He packed for High Trips back when they included more than 200 participants, first for other outfits, and finally as the owner and operator of Sierra Pack Trains. As he remembers, the packers often needed more than 120 head of stock—horses and mules—for those trips. That was his introduction to the

The Wilderness Conference 1949

Sierra Club. The Club, he later told an interviewer, was "led by rock climber types, and I was definitely not of that fraternity. . . . The packers always used to say, 'Why should I go up that peak? I never lost anything up there.'"[36] The Sierra Club was not his only large client. He also packed for the high-country trips of the American Forestry Association.

He was not a typical cowboy. As a future secretary for resources under California governor Ronald Reagan, he first interested himself in the economic aspects of wilderness while an undergraduate at Stanford. This led to his organizing the High Sierra Packers Association. He began to write his M.B.A. thesis while at Harvard. When he finished "The Economic Significance of California's Wilderness Areas" at Stanford in 1936, he wondered about organizations which might act as defenders of the Sierra, considered the newly organized Wilderness Society, and in the same year joined the Sierra Club. In 1941 Brower or Leonard proposed Livermore as a board member. Though he had been skiing up at Norden for several years, he was no rock climber, so he was skeptical. "'Oh,' they said. 'You'll have no trouble at all; everybody knows you from the high trip.'"[37] Because the High Trip was so intertwined with Club leadership, members knew him, and elected him director.

During the summer of 1947, Livermore was conducting a high-country pack trip for the American Forestry Association. Unable to attend a meeting of the Club's board of directors, he sent an urgent letter: "The time is already at hand," he wrote, "for the Sierra Club to take the lead in the formulation of a constructive policy for the administration of the entire High Sierra Wilderness Area." He proposed a conference, which would be attended by superintendents of Yosemite, Sequoia, and Kings Canyon national parks, supervisors of the Sierra, Sequoia, and Inyo national forests, representatives from the High Sierra Packers Association, and appropriate officials from the Forest Service, Park Service,

Sierra Club, and California State Fish and Game Commission. The subjects to be discussed, he thought, would be permits and regulations for the use of pack stock, high-country ranger districts, camp cleanup, trail maintenance, fish planting, and funding for management of the Sierra back country.[38] Livermore desired a unified and well-coordinated management policy for the entire Sierra. A committee was appointed by Francis Farquhar, Sierra Club president, to consider organizing such a conference in the spring of 1948.

The board of directors procrastinated, largely because of Farquhar's attitude to the proposal. As Bestor Robinson put it, "The president [Francis Farquhar] exercised a certain stubbornness that if he couldn't get a consolidated viewpoint on the part of the Club, calling such a conference would only disclose to those with whom we held such a conference our own inability to agree."[39] On the contrary, Livermore thought, the Club, "being impartial and respected," was the best organization to get the participants together. Brower and Leonard supported Livermore's proposal with enthusiasm.

Livermore recognized the need for meeting, because of greatly increased recreational pressure on the Sierra, and suspected that the Club would be taking a much larger role in public policy issues in the future. The 1947 Annual Number of the *Bulletin*—in its second year of Brower's editorship after Farquhar's many years of service—reflected a strong shift in emphasis. Only the year before the featured articles had been largely about outings and recreational matters. Now the pages included a piece by Norman Livermore on "Sierra Packing and Wilderness Policy," and the groundbreaking article by Richard Leonard and Lowell Sumner, "Protecting Mountain Meadows."[40] Brower took the liberty of amplifying those themes of wilderness and the problems of rangeland management by reprinting two highly influential articles of wider than Californian interest. "The West Against Itself," by Bernard DeVoto, a highly effective argument about land-use planning and the abuse of agricultural lands over the entire western United States, had appeared only a few months earlier in *Harper's*.[41] The other article was "The Problem of the Wilderness" by Bob Marshall. The Club's directors would not, in 1947, follow DeVoto's reasoning, although in the end they chose to follow Marshall's ideas.[42] They took the advice of Colby, who argued against being drawn into a controversy over grazing rights or other economic issues still perceived as far afield from the real Club interests, because such activity might weaken the Club's strength.

So the limits to Sierra Club biennial wilderness conferences were drawn. The wilderness conferences were conducted for more than twenty years; the first on April 8–9, 1949, in Berkeley. Though Livermore proposed the conference, he did not organize it. By 1949 he was increasingly engaged in his own lumber remanufacturing business, and in 1952 he began to work for the Pacific Lumber Company. Many people contributed to conference organization—chief among the early ones, Charlotte Mauk and Doris Leonard. Women played a much greater role here than they had in previous Club conservation activities. In later years, Peggy Wayburn and Maxine McCloskey, the wives of Club president and executive director, would make major contributions, organizing the programs and editing the proceedings. Not only did these meetings put the Club at the center of American thinking about wild areas, but they provided a forum for agencies engaged in managing wilderness.[43] As David Brower points out, Howard Zahniser was generous in encouraging the Sierra Club to hold these conferences, rather than insisting on leadership by his own Wilderness Society.[44]

Wilderness conferences reveal the evolution of Club thinking on wilderness. If, as Roderick Nash argues, historians should elucidate "not so much what wilderness is but what men *think* it is," then Nash's classic *Wilderness and the American Mind* is largely a result of the issues discussed at these conferences.[45] From the Forest Service point of view, the Sierra Club's perspective naturally grew out of its role as "a prime consumer of wilderness recreation."[46] Certainly the Club was thinking in recreational terms and Livermore was already thinking as a recreational resource manager when he suggested the conferences. It did not yet seem necessary to explore the philosophical basis for valuing wilderness. After all, the Club had the gospel of Muir and the example of the thinking of The Wilderness Society. Nor did the Club at first see that the conferences would lead toward new land law legislation. It already had the National Park Service Act of 1916 as the basis for most of its conservation efforts. But members of the Club had fallen into a way of talking about wilderness which contained many contradictory attitudes and severe limitations. Many ideas which had been born in the 1930s would slowly reemerge as the discussions became more complex in the 1950s and the 1960s.

By constructing a system of trails between old and new ideas, the Sierra Club wilderness conferences facilitated the flow of public perspectives into emerging federal land management policy. The early wilderness conferences brought together four major—though diverse—perspectives on wilderness, represented by (1) conservation groups, particularly the Sierra Club, The Wilderness Society, and the National Audubon Society; (2) land managers, including the National Park Service, the National Forest Service and its Division of Wildlife Management, and the Bureau of Reclamation; (3) economic users, like stockmen and the timber industry; and (4) recreational concessionaires, primarily wilderness guides and packers. None of these four groups was in any sense monolithic. There was a lack of consensus not only within the Sierra Club, but throughout the range of conservation organizations; economic users often conflicted in their desires; federal agencies which administered lands often had conflicting policies. These groups had diverse definitions of wilderness and clearly conflicting purposes or uses for the public domain, and they often dramatized in startling ways that they indeed perceived separate realities. The point of instituting conferences was to share perspectives. As an added benefit, the conferences began to break down the insularity and isolation of public agencies like the Forest Service, by making them open up decision-making processes to public scrutiny.[47]

One would suppose that the Club was prepared to take a consolidated position. Yet in 1948, when "a number of officers and conservation leaders of the Sierra Club" prepared a statement on wilderness policy in response to a questionnaire circulated by the Legislative Reference Service of the Library of Congress, the finished document by David Brower and Charlotte Mauk indicated that the Club had not established a firm policy at all.[48]

The Sierra Club statement began with Marshall's recreational criteria as an epigraph: no permanent inhabitants, no conveyance by mechanical means, sufficient spaciousness that a person crossing it must have the experience of sleeping out. The document defined wilderness as land that was *valuable* because it was, first, natural, and consequently a scientific resource; second, beautiful, thus an aesthetic resource; and third, a recreational resource. The terms recreational and educational were synonyms. Wilderness constituted an irreplaceable educational resource to teach self-reliance and adaptation to environment. But wilderness also required of citizens a social contract: learning to adapt to the environment was essential to preserving wilderness for the next visitors.

The document argued further that the National Park Service could protect no wilderness because "mass use is incompatible with wilderness as we define it." Park Service lands were devoted to mass recreation; the primitive areas under Forest Service administration—the Club regretted—did not have a fixed status. Their fates were determined by the philosophy of "the greatest good for the greatest number," and these areas which constituted the best possibility for wilderness reserves were vulnerable to a most articulate part of the public which "clamors for exploitation at any cost."

The Club's document made a plea for some kind of national wilderness policy, listing the kinds of areas it felt should be protected, areas of value for historical, scientific, aesthetic, recreational, or (because close to urban centers) social reasons. It attempted to determine when these areas should be protected, what standards for inclusion in a wilderness system might be, and how wilderness could be justified in economic terms. It listed, very sketchily, kinds of appropriate use and the amounts of use. It indicated a primarily regional interest in the subject when it announced that such issues would be discussed by users and administrators of important High Sierra wilderness areas at the High Sierra Wilderness Conference in April 1949.

There was a certain innocence and excitement in the discoveries participants made during the first conferences.[49] These discussions, which led up to the first introduction of the wilderness bill in Congress in 1957, evolved rapidly from the purely regional matter of managing the recreational impact on the Sierra wilderness—dealing with litter, overgrazing, and overuse. Soon participants found they could not talk about management until they defined wilderness precisely, not only for themselves, in a way that would allow a common basis for agreement among their perspectives, but so they would be understood by the general public. By the end of a decade, they were detailing and analyzing particular qualities of wilderness, and finally surveying the available and appropriate lands for possible classification as wilderness.

No easy understanding emerged at first. Norman Livermore paraphrased Bob Marshall: wilderness was "an area large enough so that people travelling into it have to camp out, and attractive enough so that they *want* to camp in it."[50] Some of the Sierra Club members focused entirely on human uses, as a consequence of their recreational perspective. Bestor Robinson, for instance, spoke not simply as a Sierra Club member, but as a member of the advisory committee to the secretary of the interior. He recognized two contradictory philosophies underlying wilderness preservation—philosophies that came to be called anthropocentric and biocentric.[51] For the first, "the sole function of wilderness is to contribute to the inspiration and wellbeing of people," but for the second, "wilderness itself has a personality—a soul—and should be preserved for its own sake."[52] Like Livermore, Robinson tended toward the first philosophy, perhaps not even understanding the significance of the second one.

On the other hand, members of The Wilderness Society, particularly Howard Zahniser, a most zealous follower of the Marshall-Leopold gospel, tended toward the biocentric perspective. Zahniser understood well and could clearly articulate the ethical basis for the biocentric view, as espoused by Aldo Leopold. Because he was a politic advocate, he softened Leopold's attack on human arrogance, saying, "We have an inborn tendency to make over the wilderness rather than adapt ourselves to it." This was particularly true, Lowell Sumner of the Park Service pointed out, when it came to wildlife management, which was "usually taken to mean production of a species as a crop for man's use."[53] Though restoration of an environment might be an appropriate part of wilderness management, increased production of some types of animals by suppressing others—particularly by eliminating predators—was not. This was the very thesis that Leopold had devoted a large portion of his career to establishing. Zahniser recommended the three Rs—registration, reservation, rationing—not as a way of managing wilderness *for* men, but as a way of managing *men*. Among Sierra Club members, Zahniser found the strongest advocates for this view in David Brower and Richard Leonard.

As Leonard elucidated his wilderness philosophy later, he strongly opposed the "man-made philosophy that 'A bird hath no song but a human ear to hear it—a flower no beauty but a human eye to see it.'"[54] He thought his philosophy constituted a modern version of Muir's, as opposed to Colby's. Notable among the modern members who disagreed with this view that he and Brower shared were, he thought, Stewart Kimball, a director for twelve years, who, being a trustee of the Presbyterian church, opposed the philosophy for religious reasons, and Bestor Robinson, who opposed the biocentric view for practical reasons.

Since there were bound to be conflicts not simply over the philosophy of the wilderness but about practical matters, the Club invited conference representatives to speak for resource users. A former president of the California Woolgrowers Association spoke for what he called multiple-purpose use in the lands administered by the Forest Service, which did not "lock up" its resources. He believed that "increased range-management study is more important than use of wilderness as a control to show what nature can do."[55] Norman Livermore attempted to present the view of a number of lumber operators. One believed that timber in wilderness areas could be harvested selectively, leaving "strips on the main traveled roads in their natural state." Many doubted the wisdom of having so much merchantable timber kept inaccessible in parks. Livermore himself thought too much timberland was taken out of production in the establishment of Olympic National Park.[56]

No doubt the organizers of the conferences allowed these views to be expressed in recognition of what Harold Bradley called "external threats" to wilderness and the ensuing possibility of compromise. David Brower argued that when faced with a practical man "you can malign him," but "you'd rather align him, get straight to his conscience, end the conflict, and save the wilderness."[57] Yet the perspectives of the "economic" users pointed up the inescapable differences between the anthropocentric and biocentric philosophies. John W. Spencer, formerly of the Forest Service but now associated with the Izaak Walton League, argued that it was impossible to reconcile other uses with wilderness. Wilderness was not a multiple-purpose area.[58] Some, like Richard Leonard, pursued the purist thesis that wilderness was, by definition, unmanaged.

There was always the question of the regional or national constitution of the public interest. When Starker Leopold spoke of the Alaskan public's resistance to and resentment of even federal ownership of lands, and warned of the political and educational consequences, Howard Zahniser pointed out that in all of Alaska the number of people was only as great as the population of Berkeley.[59] Zahniser's point was easier to make in San Francisco than it would be at a public hearing in Alaska.

Among land managers there were widely divergent views of the public interest. Everett A. Pesonen of the Bureau of Reclamation explained that different government agencies might appear to be opposed to each other, but the conflict was really among public demands, not among the agencies.[60] Most field managers were primarily concerned with the "internal" threat to the areas they administered. Byron B. Beattie, a forest supervisor for Sierra National Forest, recalled participants from their spiritual and philosophical reveries to "the cold realities of administration." Figures on use of Forest Service Primitive Areas between 1941 and 1952 indicated a sevenfold increase in man-days. Nevertheless, representatives of the Park Service tended to believe that recreational demand, or overuse in the back country, could be alleviated by distribution or dispersal of visitors, and almost universally argued that problems could be solved with more educational

activities conducted by naturalists and more rangers patrol-
ling the back country. Joel Hildebrand and David Brower
gave enthusiastic support for greater manpower in education
and enforcement of regulations in the back country. Carl P.
Russell, superintendent of Yosemite National Park, pointed
out that in 1949 there were only sixty naturalist interpreters
in the entire National Park Service. He preferred education to
regulation. Two years later he insisted that the need for rationing (as suggested by Zahniser's three Rs) was still half a
century away.[61]

From the perspective of The Wilderness Society, wilderness
needed not only protection through discrete management,
but protection through a wilderness system which would
classify and protect by statute the many lands in danger
of exploitation for economic purposes. The so-called U-
Regulations were insufficient protection for wild areas because individual managers were beset by so many kinds of
pressures. So it was that Howard Zahniser, as executive secretary of The Wilderness Society, had introduced in 1951 a
plan for a national wilderness system, to be enacted by Congress. His eight-point plan did not at first seem feasible. But
by 1953 Eivind T. Scoyen, superintendent of Sequoia and
Kings Canyon national parks, could observe that there had
been a change in mood since the 1949 conference, "when
pessimism about wilderness preservation seemed to prevail."[62] He meant that in 1949 *existing* wilderness could be
managed so that people could use it without damaging it. Yet
at the same conference Fred Gunsky of the Sierra Club had
doubted that conservationists would ever be able to sell the
idea of preserving pure wilderness.[63]

That was why David Brower invited William J. Losh, a
public relations expert, to contribute his skill to articulating
the wilderness idea to the public. The job seemed monumental. The first sticky issue, perhaps, was economic justification.

Though many conference participants wanted to argue that the values of wilderness were beyond dollars and beyond measure, Losh suggested that the scarcity value of a commodity like wilderness might be considered. Wilderness might be sold to the people, opinion makers, and mass media as an irreplaceable part of "vanishing America." One hurdle that Losh perceived was the charge of elitism, or discrimination in wilderness use, in the wilderness movement.[64] In this context the controversy between biocentric and anthropocentric viewpoints would only confuse the public, and the biocentric view would probably alienate most people. That major problem of strategy led Howard Zahnizer to emphasize that wilderness began and ended with man, that it was a *human* concept. Brower tried an appeal directed toward traditional American values: "Thomas Jefferson, long ago, said that one generation could not bind another; each had the right to set its own course. . . . It is the national consensus. . . ."[65] Olaus Murie, a soft-spoken wildlife biologist who commanded authority by the wealth of his field experience and the distinction of his publications, redirected the biocentric ethic in a singularly engaging and understated way at the beginning of the fifth conference in 1957. He said that "he would not deny a certain aesthetic awareness by the beaver, but felt that man has a more complex problem than the beaver—he not only wants to keep alive, but also craves certain aesthetic experiences which enrich his life. He wants quality in living, not merely existence."[66] Murie's strategy for selling wilderness embodied the biocentric and anthropocentric values, stated man's stewardship of nature on a traditional basis, yet pled that man's superior consciousness required that he act as if nature's inherent values were his own.

So the conservation groups could turn to selling their idea. The last session of the fourth conference, in 1955, was devoted to classifying types of wilderness. Harold Bradley and Howard Zahniser outlined together a system which was largely that proposed by The Wilderness Society twenty years earlier. The alliance was symbolic. The Sierra Club had moved from the idea that compromised wilderness was better than none through a consideration of zoning, and had committed itself to The Wilderness Society's idea of legislation.[67] This decision marked a significant shift in emphasis for the conferences, as well as growth in the strength of the idea. In 1957 Zahniser could report on the National Wilderness System Preservation Bill, introduced to the House and Senate. The federal agencies could no longer ignore a real possibility that the bill might pass. As a result, that same conference saw participation not just by regional representatives. The power generated by the conferences could be measured by the presence of Edward Woolsey, director of the Bureau of Land Management (BLM), Daniel H. Jansen, director of the Bureau of Sport Fisheries and Wildlife, Richard McArdle, chief of the U.S. Forest Service, and Conrad Wirth, director of the National Park Service. None of these men expressed direct support for wilderness legislation—indeed they all feared that their powers of discretion would be taken from them—but they did not dare ignore the movement. In 1951 Howard Zahniser had said of the Club, "I know of no organization that is so genuinely regional and so thoroughly national."[68] By the end of the decade, nobody could doubt the second part of his statement.

Michael McCloskey believes that the wilderness movement marked the beginning of environmentalism: "The protest in the post-World War II period in the midfifties about excessive commercialization, excessive development in violation of nature sanctuaries, was the genesis of what came to be the environmental movement by the seventies."[69] In ideological terms, during the mid 1950s the wilderness conferences clarified environmental perspectives which would grow in scope.

Some, like Richard Leonard, would segregate their views of wilderness management from their views on wider environmental issues. Leonard was a purist only about some areas, and quite willing to compromise about others. Declared wilderness was nature. Other areas could be treated with anthropocentric philosophy. To a Forest Service manager, biocentric philosophy might be appropriate for legal wilderness, but not even considered when dealing with the rest of the lands under his jurisdiction. Despite Richard Leonard's view that wilderness needed to be treated as a specialized issue in a society which depended increasingly on specialization by experts,[70] these discussions about recreation provided a forum where ecological philosophy and the ecology movement were nurtured. For many committed people, preserving wilderness was a metaphorical, perhaps symbolic act, whose meaning was preservation of the earth. Indeed, the same philosophical issues went far beyond the matter of wilderness management, to a reevaluation of the larger matters. The environmental or ecology movement would argue, as Superintendent Carl Russell of Yosemite National Park did at the first conference in 1949, "It is essential for our national life and strength that we preserve our soil and water and animal life in balance. Man is inescapably a part of this biological complex."[71] When Howard Zahniser said "We must treat wilderness so that we cannot be accused of having placed our own importance too highly above it," his statement went well beyond wilderness in its implications.

Mission 66 in Yosemite 1952–1958 What the Club discussed at the wilderness conferences had broad implications and resulted in a dramatic confrontation over development of the national parks in the 1950s. The drama came to a crisis when the National Park Service began its last phase of rerouting the Tioga Road through what was perhaps the most beautiful section of Yosemite's high country. This drama revealed the divided and changing attitudes of the Club about its philosophy, its role, its strategies, and its power. The Club had always been highly attentive to national park matters, but in the postwar years it had to meet changing conditions of recreational use in the parks, as well as a new kind of bureaucratic park manager. Because it may have overestimated its strength as a consulting organization, the Club had to reconsider what it was.

The involvement of Harold Bradley and Ansel Adams illustrates the values and difficulty created by deep personal engagement within the Club ranks. The passion of these men was difficult to control and funnel within the continuity of Club policies over the years. The response of these men was highly emotional and thus seemed to run against traditional American rationalism about land as a resource. On the other hand, their involvement was of inestimable value. Their views had the strength of intimate personal knowledge and emotion, and illustrated the truest kind of stewardship. They reminded the Club that the earth was everything, and the organization was only a means of protecting the earth. Because they were truly devoted to the cause of the earth, they were able to dramatize truths that dispassionate planners tended to discount or ignore.

During early discussions of the Tioga Road, three young members on the board were seriously apprehensive about the damage the road would do: Richard Leonard, Ansel Adams, and David Brower. Brower's position on the subject was perfectly aligned with that of Bradley. Leonard believed then, and believes to this day, that persuasion was the only reasonable means the Club could use over such an issue. Though Ansel Adams never espoused the theory that primitive roads were necessary to filter the population from the wilder parts of parks, he was fearful of overdevelopment, and became most adamant when he considered what the Tioga Road would do to Tenaya Lake.

Tenaya Lake had been named Pywiack Lake by the Indians, for the shining glacially polished rocks which seemed to flow down into the water. The polished rock was a wonder to John Muir and has been a wonder to all who have visited the area. In Muir's day, there seemed no need to worry about the rock. Even after Hetch Hetchy, many Club members felt as did Nelson Hackett, editor of the *Bulletin* in 1923 and 1924, that "in general the mountains stood there, and they seemed to be impregnable."[72] But Adams saw that man could and would mar these slopes, and others.

Adams grew more and more impatient when he saw the developments all over Yosemite National Park. He became most concerned when Conrad Wirth launched Mission 66. For Adams, the improvement of the Tioga Road was part and parcel with the plan for general development of facilities in the parks. As David Brower has noted, "The battle on Tioga Road itself, then, was really the harbinger of the main battle against Mission 66, which, again, the Sierra Club lost."[73] Finally Adams would take desperate action.

What was Mission 66? At first nobody seemed to know. Everyone did know that the national parks were in poor shape after the war. Trails had not been maintained, facilities were outdated, employees were few and underpaid. When Conrad Wirth assumed the duties of director of the National Park Service in 1952, the parks were being visited by increasing numbers of people. David Brower and Marton Litton produced a whole issue of the *Bulletin* in 1952 devoted to what Will Colby called "Yosemite's Fatal Beauty," deploring the crowded and chaotic conditions on the Valley floor.[74] Bernard DeVoto took the problem to the nation in his *Harper's* column, "The Easy Chair." He pointed out that the condition of the park ranger's life was worsening, and more important, that "the most valuable asset of the National Park Service is beginning to erode away"—not simply the facilities, but the resources themselves. DeVoto's modest proposal was simple:

"Let us, as a beginning, close Yellowstone, Yosemite, Rocky Mountain, and Grand Canyon National Parks—close them and seal them, assign the Army to patrol them, and so hold them secure till they can be reopened."[75] Wirth believed the problem was a consequence of the advent of the automobile; "moreover," he said, "the types of facilities preferred by people visiting the parks in their own cars were different from the kind formerly provided for those who travelled by train and took coach tours."[76] By 1955, he said, the conditions had become deplorable; the parks would have to be rebuilt to accommodate the automotive tourist.

Wirth planned a massive campaign, which would span the ten years beginning in 1956, to put the parks in decent shape for their golden anniversary in 1966. His "comprehensive and integrated program of use and protection," as he called it, seemed reasonable enough to conservationists at first, and began with the guideline that "Preservation of park resources is a basic requirement underlying all management," although some conservationists wondered whether it was *the* basic premise of the plan.[77] They were particularly suspicious because Wirth's best ally was the American Automobile Association. Eventually his project focused on development of facilities. His own "checklist of construction accomplishments" includes, in this order, park roads, trails, airport runways (outside the parks), parking areas, campgrounds, picnic areas, campfire circles and amphitheaters, utilities, administrative and service buildings, utility buildings, historic buildings, employee residences, comfort stations, interpretive roadside and trailside exhibits, marina improvements, entrance stations, trailer sanitation disposal systems, ranger training facilities, and visitor centers.[78] This was just the sort of development that Harold Bradley feared would follow improved roads.

If a vast project of renovation for existing facilities was so badly needed, how could it fail to be a good thing? Partly because Wirth found it so time-consuming to deal with the Club over the Tioga Road and so embarrassing to deal with it in a growing controversy over projected dams in Dinosaur National Monument, he was very slow in delivering information on Mission 66 to the Club or to any conservation organizations.

Nevertheless, the board began to discuss its appropriate response to the plan in January of 1956.[79] David Brower thought there were two concerns: that the Club might not be given sufficient information soon enough to be able to participate in the plans, and that the objectives of the project did not seem to mention protection of wilderness values in the parks. Leonard reported that other conservation organizations were voicing concern about lack of public information; he worried that the Club might be put in the position of opposing plans already formulated by the Park Service. He worried further that the use of confidential information shackled the freedom of conservation groups to comment objectively. Influenced by the views of Alex Hildebrand, Club president, and Bestor Robinson, the board decided on a cautious policy. It would request more information from Wirth and would attempt to avoid potentially harmful publicity, seeking "confidential conferences between Directors or officers of the club and the Park Service prior to release of information to the public." This had been the traditional Club strategy.

Meanwhile, the chairman of the Conservation Committee, Edgar Wayburn, and his wife, Peggy Wayburn, wrote a notice for the April 1956 *Bulletin* which began to suggest the Club's position.[80] Claiming that "the mists of governmental secrecy . . . are now beginning to lift," the Wayburns tried to dispel any fears, saying that the general objectives of Mission 66 seemed "good and sound." About new roads they wrote, "It is reassuring to learn that 90% of the proposed money would be used for *re*construction and realignment of present roads." Nevertheless, the Wayburns were concerned with the lack of information, the fact that the Park Service had "not called on its many friends outside of the Service" to participate in planning, that the projects seemed to be piecemeal, did not depend on specific "master plans" for the parks, and that "the major emphasis in the publicizing of Mission 66 has been placed on construction and development." They ended with a conciliatory plea that the Club had always been good friends with the Park Service and "as good friends, we would like our support of Mission 66 to include active participation as well as passive concurring. We hope that the Park Service will make it possible for us to work *with* them in the development of this vitally important program."

Ansel Adams, however, expressed grave fears for what Mission 66 might do to Yosemite Valley and other places. In 1950 he had written in *My Camera in the National Parks*:

> The first phase of the development of the parks has been largely controlled by the requirements of public service which in many instances (and with constructive intentions) dominated planning and interpretation. The final phase will see the complete adjustment of the material and spiritual aspects of the parks to human need, with full emphasis on the intangible moods and qualities of the natural scene. . . . This is not a philosophy of arbitrary exclusion.[81]

A half decade later he worried about the increase in developments which were destroying the values for which the parks were set aside and therefore opposed the whole Mission 66 project from the beginning.[82] His comments were harbingers of a storm of protests to follow, not only about Mission 66, the development of the parks, or the improvement of the Tioga Road, but also about the strategy which the Sierra Club used in dealing with the Park Service.

As an artist, Adams felt he was an appropriate spokesman

for the aesthetic side of conservation. Though he argued in 1950 that the necessary evolution of national parks toward wilderness parks need not result in arbitrary exclusion of sectors of the public, his private letters in 1956 suggest a growing militance. In one congenial and humorous letter to David Brower, he referred to himself as a super-purist.[83] In this letter he heaped scorn on even the well-respected architecture of the Ahwahnee Hotel and LeConte Lodge in Yosemite Valley. To Adams, these buildings—indeed all permanent buildings—were an intrusion on the natural beauty of Yosemite. Further, Adams feared the modern buildings which would come with Mission 66. A sample of structures built in the Mission 66 days vindicates Adams' accurate forecast of offenses against taste. But an absolute dictum stood below his humorous aesthetic critique. The best development in the parks was to him the least, as nearly as possible invisible, and nondestructive. Further, he felt it was time to declare a moratorium on all developments—perhaps even trails—in large sections of the national parks.

Just as Henry David Thoreau, in "An Essay on Civil Disobedience," could not ask for no government and instead asked for a better government, so too Adams was willing to make his compromise. He announced that he was willing to walk the fence between "wildness" on the one hand and "accessibility" on the other. His report on Yosemite Valley, for instance, had this objective: "To return Yosemite Valley to the maximum possible condition of 'wild' quality, yet at the same time to render it accessible and available to all who specifically seek its intrinsic values."[84] What he saw happening he considered no compromise at all.

Adams was not alone in his desire to stir opposition to what he called the "bureaucratic free-for-all" he found evident in Mission 66, and to the "general NPS attitude." By 1957 the complaints came pouring in to the conservation organizations. Olaus Murie had written to the National Parks Association when he saw the bulldozers approaching. He decided that he could not swallow the "lowest common denominator" plans for Grand Teton National Park. "Grandiose architectural structures do not build an appreciation of wild country," he wrote. Another Sierra Club member wrote with dismay about the road-building plans for Utah's Arches National Monument, Deadhorse Point State Park, and Capitol Reef National Monument. "At every turn I find development of the national parks to be synonymous with the building of roads. Is it impossible for the visitor to leave his car and enjoy a leisurely walk over three or four miles of well-graded trails?" he asked.[85]

Like these others, Adams completely lost his sense of humor when he contemplated the roadwork planned for the park he loved. The letters of Adams suggest his own strong sense of personal guilt; at the end of August 1957 he reprimanded himself and the Club.[86] He knew that he had not in the past committed himself completely to opposing the new alignment of the Tioga Road. He now knew that the Tioga Road was a symbolic issue and was closely tied to the aims of Mission 66.

Adams' deep sense of personal responsibility grew more urgent over the next few months, until it strained his relations with his fellow board members. After much soul-searching he decided that the traditional Sierra Club strategy of consultation, persuasion, and compromise had led to a disaster in Yosemite. He offered his resignation from the board of directors.[87] He did this because he had already chosen to make an even stronger statement to the secretary of the interior, secretary of commerce, and director of the National Park Service.[88] Carefully supported with facts and observations, his statement to these federal officials questioned their allegiance to the National Park Act of 1916.

Bradley wrote to the board of directors that despite Adams' resignation, such personal action would be associated with the Club: "His vigorous comments and actions have at least temporarily intensified the dislike the Service has acquired for the Sierra Club during the last ten years, when we often found it necessary to protect what we believe to be too much deviation from park principles."[89]

The Club sent Joel Hildebrand's son Alex on an advisory inspection tour, and Hildebrand assured the Club and the Park Service that he felt "everyone concerned was sincerely and diligently anxious to do the best possible job," that constructive action for the future might result.[90] He tried to smooth things over and compromise.

Adams was not impressed with Hildebrand's reasonable tone, or with the assumption that it was impossible to stop progress. The sincerity and diligence which Hildebrand found in federal officials did not excuse the stark and permanent effects of road building in the vicinity of Tenaya Lake. Where there was soil, Adams argued, the growing things could recover, but the damage to the great sweep of granite—Adams used a metaphor suggesting that granite constituted the skeleton of the earth—that was permanent. Adams could not continue friendly relations with federal agencies if they continued to mutilate the earth. Further, he believed that conservation groups shared the blame, precisely because they had tried to be genteel.[91]

In the end, the board of directors declined the resignation proffered by Adams, but the symbolic meaning of his action had achieved its effect, if not by preserving the beauty Tenaya Glacier had created, then at least by jolting the policies of the board of directors.[92] As Brower had told Conrad Wirth—perhaps prematurely—when the controversy over the road began, "it was a different Sierra Club now."[93]

Yet to understand how it was a different Sierra Club, one must realize first that it was a different America after the war, particularly in the new West. The roots of the new Club developed in theory in the biennial wilderness conferences and in practice in the campaign about dams in Dinosaur National Monument.

CHAPTER FOUR

Canyons Measureless to Man

Dinosaur and the Colorado Plateau, 1950

In July of 1950, one month after the outbreak of the Korean War, there was an emergency brewing for conservationists. Only a few days after President Truman had dispatched United States forces to Asia, his secretary of the interior, Oscar Chapman, recommended congressional authorization for the Upper Colorado River Basin Project, which included two dams and reservoirs, at Echo Park and Split Mountain, within Dinosaur National Monument in the northeast corner of Utah.[1] This project was one part of a vast reclamation plan for the entire Colorado River, called the Colorado River Storage Project, and was not a complete surprise to anyone. In the midst of World War II fervor, in 1943, the Bureau of Reclamation had gotten permission to survey a dam site within Dinosaur National Monument, on the grounds of national security and the need for power. As the man who was then director of the Bureau of Reclamation later said, "You should never allow an engineer within a national park or monument."[2] By the late 1940s it was too late to avoid that; Hoover Dam had been celebrated as a great triumph by western developers, and now dams were becoming a major issue all over the West.[3]

In 1948 the Sierra Club and others had opposed the Glacier

View Dam, which threatened Glacier National Park. This project was proposed by the Army Corps of Engineers and was strongly resisted by the National Park Service. Olaus Murie, president of The Wilderness Society, had represented his organization and the Sierra Club at public hearings in 1949. They had been successful, according to Richard Leonard, "by getting into broader conservation strategy. For the first time we supported dams in other places [outside the park] in order to block a dam in a national park."[4] There were problems closer to home as well. In 1948 Los Angeles had revived applications for hydroelectric power projects within Kings Canyon National Park. As the superintendent of the park would explain a few years later, when he pled that "every resource of the Sierra Club be used to check the reasons which may be advanced for this project," Los Angeles had not pursued its long-standing plans for these projects because it had been involved in the construction of Hoover Dam. Now the growing city was looking for new sources of power, and its plans threatened to inundate the heart of the park; it advocated reservoirs in every major canyon.[5]

That same year—1948—the Upper Basin Compact was signed, which allocated the upper basin share of the Colorado River among Colorado, Utah, Wyoming, and New Mexico. This cleared the way for diversion projects and reservoirs. At the same time, just when the Park Service had begun to advance plans for expanding the national park system, it found the Bureau of Reclamation and its projects had developed into as formidable an enemy as its traditional opponents, vested economic interests. Though the bureau, as sister of the Park Service in Interior, seemed to bear the parks no malice, its greatly increased economic power coupled with its development orientation represented a major threat, not simply on the Colorado, but all across the West. In 1950, the plans were coming off the drawing boards, not for one or two dams but ten in the Upper Colorado River Basin. Out of eighty-one possible dam sites there, twenty-seven had already been mapped by the bureau.[6]

In this case, the National Park Service was unable to enter the controversy. Apparently Oscar Chapman had ordered Newton Drury, director of the Park Service, to refrain from contributing information or any statements which might help those who opposed the dam in Dinosaur—an unfortunate situation, since, as Brower believes, "Drury was the finest director the Park Service had, by far, in what he wanted to do to preserve the parks." Yet Drury was in despair, as Brower remembered, and announced that "Dinosaur is a dead duck."[7] By the end of the year, Chapman had forced Drury's resignation as the director of the Park Service.

As it happened, Richard Leonard, secretary of the Sierra Club, had also been elected to the council of The Wilderness Society in 1948 and attended that organization's annual meeting for 1950, held at Twin Springs, Colorado, in July. Immediately after the meeting a delegation from the Society, including Leonard, Olaus and Margaret Murie, and others went on an automotive tour through the monument. They were there to see what the canyons of the Green and Yampa rivers really looked like, and they discovered that the monument contained a great deal more than dinosaur bones; further, that the area to be inundated by reservoirs was a great deal more than hot rocks, as the dam proposers were fond of saying; and last, that an excursion, even in mid summer, to the so-called desert was not hot and dusty. They were awed by Steamboat Rock, which rose 800 feet above Pat's Hole, or Echo Park as it was to be called. That golden sandstone monolith constituted the monument's symbol and landmark, as Half Dome was Yosemite's; if the dams were built it would be nearly inundated by more than 500 feet of water. The canyons themselves were grander and more full of wildlife than anyone had expected.

As Margaret Murie said, "We hadn't known it was such a big world, this world of the Green and Yampa." She mused that such a place would be needed in the future, when there was no room to squeeze any more people into Yellowstone and the Grand Canyon. She was pleased to discover that "the lover of birds, the lover of rocks, the lover of mammals, the rock climbers, the geographer, the photographer, the ethnologist, had all found thrilling satisfactions down there in Pat's Hole." Like the rest of the party, she was willing to concede that dams for irrigation might be necessary for dry western states. "But, what if it can be had in some other way than by damming the beautiful canyons of the Green and Yampa in this 'convenient' spot?"[8]

The campaign that followed marked, for Richard Leonard, a return to the magnificent battles that were fought by John Muir and William Colby. Indeed, he believed in 1974 that from 1913 to 1946 the Club had worked for the establishment of the Forest Service and Park Service and for the creation of several national parks, but "didn't fight any 'battles' . . . where the Sierra Club was on one side and half the United States was on the other."[9] Just as Colby had provided the technical arguments and Muir the leadership and moral strength when they battled for Hetch Hetchy, so would Leonard and Brower work together and return the Club to its crusading spirit.

Very few people in the Club knew anything about Dinosaur or the slickrock country to the south, the Colorado Plateau. It was a vast region including most of Utah and adjoining sections of Colorado, Arizona, and New Mexico. There was increasing interest among a few Club members who had been lured by its canyons. In June of 1950, Club president Lewis Clark walked through the narrows of the Virgin River in Zion National Park with his brother Nate and other friends. He wrote about the beauty of the canyons for the *Bulletin*'s annual number the next year. The following year Steven Bradley and his redoubtable father Harold floated through the canyons of Dinosaur, and he wrote an article for the *Bulletin* praising the beauty of the river canyons.[10]

The Colorado Plateau was a much greater entity than anyone seemed to comprehend. As the area's historian C. Gregory Crampton describes it,

> The whole is a grand masterpiece of erosion, the work of the Colorado River. The waters of this great stream and its tributaries have cut out gorges, canyons, defiles in thick beds of sandstone, leaving segmented remnants in the form of plateaus, benches, mesas, buttes, and monuments between the water courses. The closer one gets to the master stream and its major tributaries, the deeper the downward departures become. The canyon predominates. Not one canyon, but a thousand: big, little, long, short, narrow, wide, deep, shallow, all in color, mostly in shades of red that gives [*sic*] the Colorado its name.[11]

Along the margin of the plateau, small samples of the great sedimentary geology had been dedicated as national parks. There was, of course, Grand Canyon National Park (created 1908–1919). Munkuntuweap National Monument (1909) later became Zion National Park (1919). Utah National Monument (1923) became Bryce National Park (1928). There were many national monuments: Rainbow Bridge (1910), Arches (1929), Cedar Breaks (1933), Capitol Reef (1937). Most of these monuments were small, containing a few isolated geological features, but the vistas they provided stretched across the space of the plateaus, far beyond their boundaries. Many national monuments preserved archeological sites, the ancient homes of the Anasazi: Mesa Verde (1906), Natural Bridges (1908), Navajo National Monument (1912), Hovenweap (1923), Canyon De Chelley (1931), Colorado National Monument (1931). These monuments too were worthy of preservation for their beauty alone. In addition there were many unprotected areas: Monument Valley, the Aquarius Plateau, Glen Canyon, the Escalante Canyons, the San Rafael Swell, Paria Canyons, Dark Canyon and Grand Gulch, the Henry Mountains and the Manti-La Sal, to name but a few outstanding places. It was a vast and wonderful region. Yet the rivers, or the system of rivers—the Green, Yampa, Escalante, Paria, Virgin, Dirty Devil, San Juan, and Colorado—were protected only while their waters flowed through Dinosaur National Monument, Grand Canyon National Park, and Zion National Park.

Dinosaur, as established in 1915, had included only 80 acres surrounding an archeological quarry. It was expanded by 200,000 acres in 1938 by Harold Ickes, Franklin Roosevelt's secretary of the interior, to include canyons of the Green and Yampa. Ickes had also tried to establish a vast Escalante national monument during the same period, which would have dedicated the Colorado and its tributaries from well above its confluence with the Green nearly to Lee's Ferry, where the Paria entered;[12] but he had failed. The rivers were the lifeblood of the region. If, in the Sierra, the John Muir Trail constituted a means for traversing the wilderness, then the Colorado itself, first descended by John Wesley Powell, was, as David Brower called it, a "wilderness river trail" which allowed access to the marvelous scenery of the Colorado's canyons.

Whatever the actual power politics inside the department of the interior—and no matter that dinosaur, like many areas dedicated in the region, was a national monument, not a national park—conservation organizations universally agreed that the sanctity of the national park system was at the heart of the Drury resignation and that a threat to Dinosaur represented a dangerous precedent for the parks. Interested primarily in this issue, not the fate of the whole region, representatives from several conservation organizations banded together and began to issue publicity, not so much against dams as for parks. Because the vast system of parks and monuments established by Harold Ickes in the 1930s—and by his predecessors—seemed in grave danger, conservationists felt called to engage themselves in a defense of past successes, in the Colorado Plateau and at Kings Canyon, Grand Teton National Monument, and other areas.

David Brower himself was becoming increasingly interested in seeing Dinosaur. The next year—1953—when Leonard became president of the Club, he made sure that Harold Bradley and Outings Committee chair Stewart Kimball scheduled three one-week river trips down the Yampa River, taking 65 people at a time. Not only did Brower and Leonard go, with family members, but five past presidents of the Club traveled through the canyons that summer: Bestor Robinson, Alex Hildebrand, Francis Farquhar, Lewis Clark, and Nathan Clark. This was the traditional Club strategy—encouraging recreational use of a threatened area—and it began to work. While about 13,000 people had visited the monument in 1950, fewer than 50 taking the trip by raft, in 1954 nearly 71,000 visitors appeared, and more than 900 rafted through the canyons. There were changes brewing with the Club as well.

On November 26, 1952, several weeks after the election of Dwight D. Eisenhower as president of the United States, Richard Leonard as president-elect of the Club told the board, "The powerful and consistent growth of the Club in recent years of membership, general activities, and [the] national conservation program . . . had made it increasingly important to have substantially full time direction by a person of high caliber and broad experience."[13] That person could be David Brower, Leonard said, if the Club acted immediately. In fact the membership was slightly less than 7,000 and the Club's annual budget a little more than $50,000 a year. And this was perhaps the most important organizational change to be proposed in the Club's sixty-year history.

Executive Director 1952–1953

Brower had wide experience in public relations, and was well suited to the position. In addition to his stint as publicity director for Yosemite Park and Curry Company in the 1930s, by 1939 Brower was de facto editor of the Club's Annual *Bulletin*, working under the official editor, Francis Farquhar.[14] Through Farquhar, in May of 1941, he had become an editor at the University of California Press, but continued his strong involvement in Club projects as a volunteer. Not only did he edit the *Bulletin*, he instituted the *Sierra Club Handbook* in 1947, bringing out a revised edition in 1951. His expertise in publicity and publishing made him a qualified candidate. In addition, he was an extremely popular choice. He had received the largest number of votes for any director in the last Club election and had served on the board of directors of the Club for nearly twelve years.[15]

On December 15, 1952, following action taken by the board ten days earlier, President Harold Crowe announced that Brower was executive director of the Sierra Club. Leonard believed that the first five months would be a trial period, and that if Brower's services proved valuable he would occupy a permanent post. This would occur in May of 1953, when Leonard assumed presidency of the Club. The board did make the appointment permanent on the eve of the annual banquet of 1953. Thus the Club acquired a powerful team in Leonard and Brower.

In a proposed letter of agreement concerning his position, Brower listed for the board what he thought would be his duties and responsibilities, delimiting his authority. "I both regret and welcome the step the club seems about to take," he wrote; "I regret it because I hate to see good hard-earned dues money spent on something we have had without apparent cost for so long. I welcome it because it would seem to mark the passing of another milestone in the growth and progress of the club." When he outlined his tentative job description, he noted that he would exercise "general supervision over the carrying out of Board directives" and would prepare recommendations. He would keep the officers and directors informed on major problems confronting the Club, build an informed membership through Club publications, maintain administrative efficiency, and speak for the Club "within the context of Club policy." Also, subject to review by the board, he would try to strengthen Club membership, maintain liaison with other conservation organizations, and assist Club committees. He would help prepare the annual budget, and would be an ex-officio member of the board of directors.[16] (He resigned as a member of the board in May of 1953, to avoid any possible conflict of interest.)

He included his first proposed budget, for 1953–1954, totalling $54,800; in addition to his own salary, rent, and office expenses and salaries, which totaled $25,500, it included $11,000 for the *Bulletin*, $7,150 for the nine Club chapters, and $6,400 for the conservation program.[17] With this modest array of resources, he and Leonard, with the board's approval, would move the Club into the national realm, facing the conservation policies of a new and—as they perceived it—dangerous administration, manned by Secretary of Agriculture Ezra Taft Benson and Secretary of the Interior Douglas McKay, whom they soon called "Giveaway McKay." The Club would need to divide its efforts over the next few months, facing not only the threats to parks and wildernesses that Eisenhower's new administration represented, but also the threats to internal operation that Club growth was already creating.

The first problems were organizational, and Richard Leonard had a genius in that direction; he recognized further that solutions to technical organizational procedures were essential if the Club was to remain coherent. The board seemed to agree that the Club, in a critical stage of development, could expect a growth in membership in chapters. How, it pondered, could the chapters feel that their interests were not slighted by the board? This question had been dramatized a year and a half earlier when the Loma Prieta Chapter claimed that a campaign to save the Butano Forest of redwoods had failed because it was too great a project for the chapter alone and the chapter could not get needed board support. The chapter consequently insisted on board representation. It was rebuked by the board for airing its complaints in the chapter newsletter.[18] A year and a half later Leonard asked the board to seriously consider "how to develop the integrated growth of the Club as a whole without the development of splinter groups." Brower felt that the answer was regional representation on Club-wide committees. There still remained a matter of coordinating the committees, and communication among them. Brower suggested that members of the board have specific assignments to coordinate committees. As president, Leonard took primary responsibility for the committees on conservation and conservation administration, delegating most other committees to other directors. As executive director, Brower would supervise the running of committees on publications, outings, elections, and special events. In addition, Leonard issued an open invitation for chapters to submit agenda items.[19] At the October 1953 board meeting, Brower submitted a report entitled "The Sierra Club: National, Regional or State."[20] How big, he asked, should the Sierra Club be? Was a thing better if it was bigger, or was the Club in danger of spreading itself too thin in the future? He separated the several issues:

1. "Should our conservation scope have national, regional, or state limits? We have left California borders in contacts on a national scale, but priorities drop as distance increases. Should we come back?"

2. In 1950, Tom Jukes had organized the Atlantic Chapter, and the board chartered it.[21] Was that an appropriate precedent? How many chapters were appropriate?

3. Should the Club pursue out-of-state outings?

4. Was the Club in danger of competing with other conservation organizations?

5. Should the Club actively seek to increase membership? Should it do so for financial reasons, at the expense of the personal criteria of membership which seemed so important in the past? What was wrong with membership campaigns, which the board had opposed in the past?

6. Should the board set a ceiling on membership?

An animated discussion ensued. For some, like Ansel Adams, conservation problems had become national and required that the Club cooperate with other organizations. "Our interests are nationwide in scope," he emphasized; "our strength comes from public enlightenment; we need more publicity." Francis Farquhar worried that the Club was in danger of losing its democratic unity. "Be careful to avoid developing the Sierra Club into a federation of clubs," he warned. Charlotte Mauk thought that would only be a problem if out-of-state chapters lacked leadership. Several, like Leonard, thought that unity demanded better communication, through more complete minutes which captured the spirit of Club deliberations. The Club had always been a democratic organization, he believed, and it was purely by accident that the majority of the board of directors lived in the Bay Area. Yet Marjory Farquhar insisted, along with her husband, that the Club would be better off helping regional organizations in other states rather than "stepping out conspicuously to organize chapters in their territory."[22]

Behind this discussion were the issues of a proposed chapter in the Pacific Northwest and whether or not that chapter would constitute an invasion of the territory of other organizations, like the Mountaineers and the Mazamas. When the board finally decided to impose no arbitrary limitation on the geographic location of chapters and approved the Pacific Northwest Chapter, it accepted manifest destiny as a national organization.

Planning to spend a year in Europe, Marjory Farquhar resigned from the board of directors. Others on the board believed she resigned because the Sierra Club was no longer a California club, and would become a diluted national organization. Richard Leonard was one, and has recently stated, "Her Club is lost. It is now a powerful, impersonal political force. It is not a club of people gathered together, it is a political force."[23] This was the Club that Leonard and Brower forged to meet the challenge of the 1950s.

Club Strategy 1953–1955

The first priority for Leonard and Brower was Dinosaur, the place to make a stand against the dam builders. Consequently, Leonard made sure that the board disapproved of the two dams proposed at Echo Park and Split Mountain, and disapproved of any dams within national parks or monuments. Yet Bestor Robinson, acting not as a board member but as an individual and a member of the Advisory Committee on Conservation to the secretary of the interior, had written a letter to a friend in Interior suggesting a compromise, allowing construction of the Split Mountain Dam if the Echo Park Dam were abandoned. Despite their general philosophical agreement, Leonard had tried to dissuade Robinson from presenting such a compromise. He had received letters from Olaus Murie and other leaders of cooperating organizations stressing the need for firm opposition to any compromise of the Dinosaur monument. Leonard therefore encouraged the board to reiterate its firm and complete opposition to any dams within Dinosaur.[24]

A resolution by the board would be meaningless unless it were backed by an active campaign. Leonard urged that the Club conduct its campaign by defending the principle of firm congressional policy for the protection of national parks and monuments. For him, the threat to Dinosaur was the most serious since the formation of the National Park Service. It was in that sense that Dinosaur presented a situation analogous to Hetch Hetchy. According to Leonard, the final decision to dam Hetch Hetchy in 1913 had been countered by the Organic Act establishing the National Park Service in 1916. A dam in a monument would serve as the worst kind of modern precedent. Even Robinson saw the importance of a successful campaign. "This lesson [to the dam builders] might well carry over to the wilderness areas of the national forests," he said.[25]

Brower was responsible for proposing a campaign. Earlier he had suggested sending Philip Hyde, a photographer, to document the area's scenic resources.[26] Now he thought the best method for publicizing the issue was with a movie which could be distributed for television and conservation groups. In May of 1953 he proposed using the donated services of Charles Eggert, a professional photographer. The board agreed that the film should show three points: "1. The river is navigable for recreation. 2. It has great scenic beauty. 3. The conflict can be resolved by alternate dam sites."[27] Brower also worked with Martin Litton to prepare an issue of the *Bulletin* devoted entirely to Dinosaur.

Martin Litton was a Southern California journalist, born in Inglewood, California, 1917. The world where he grew up had been changing over the years, not, he thought, for the better. "In the twenties California was really wonderful, and we *knew* it. We weren't looking for something better," he remembers.[28] His father was a veterinarian, and his mother, a very religious woman, taught him to revere the God in nature and to suspect the pride in man. He spent his youth exploring the San Gabriel Mountains and the Coast Range, but remembers especially his first trip to Yosemite in 1931, where he spent a month camping in the Valley. In his mid teens, he took a twelve-day hiking trip to Mount Whitney, never seeing any other hikers. But even as a teenager he had been appalled at the rampant road-building in California.

He graduated from the University of California–Los Angeles, an English major in 1938, worked for a while as public relations officer for a dude ranch in Arizona, taught a little, and worked for the *Los Angeles Times*. When the war intervened he became a glider pilot, and flew troop planes during the 1943 invasion of Europe. After the war he returned to the *Times*, and soon found a market for Sunday travel features, with lots of pictures. Brower read Litton's repeated and heavily illustrated articles on Dinosaur in the *Times* and contacted him. That was in 1952. Litton remembers saying, "I don't see that the Sierra Club does anything. I can do more by myself than I can in there." And he remembers Brower replying, "It's all going to be different now," even suggesting, "I'm in charge."[29] So Litton began to submit his photographs to the *Bulletin*, and soon contributed text as well. Litton's *Times* article "Yosemite's Fatal Beauty," deploring the overcrowding of Yosemite Valley, whose condition had so deteriorated since his youth, was reprinted in the *Sierra Club Bulletin*.

The board approved Brower's publicist methods, with the provision that the Club not attempt "to evaluate or argue the economic feasibility of the entire Upper Colorado Project."[30] Unfortunately, what Litton had in mind was precisely a critique of the entire system. In the end, it was not published in the *Bulletin*.

Though the board had set fairly narrow limits upon its Dinosaur campaign, Brower felt it was his responsibility to explore all possible avenues of action. For one thing, Litton had his ear, arguing that dams would not be necessary for power generation if oil shale was utilized, that "the whole Upper Colorado deal is open to scrutiny. . . . It doesn't seem to be too well worked out." In fact, Litton chafed against the limitations of the campaign, as set out by the board. "I think we are giving the enemy undue advantage by sticking strictly to our bird-watching and refusing to meet him on his own ground," he wrote. "It's easy to show the park value of Dinosaur but that won't save it. Let's really knock the props from under the dammers by nullifying their 'economic necessity' palaver whenever we can."[31] As Brower was later to say of Litton, for "more years than I will ever admit, he has been my conservation conscience."[32]

Instead of attempting to deal with the Bureau of Reclamation's entire plan, and its economic feasibility, most conservationists at first accepted the view that the project was for water storage and irrigation, only later comprehending the complexity of the project, which used power generation to subsidize storage, while providing no actual irrigation at all. The bureau seemed particularly proud of its figures on water evaporation for alternative dam sites, insisting that the Dinosaur dams were better than alternatives, since they wasted less water. A number of conservationists doubted the calculations they had received. Brower wrote to Aldo's son Luna Leopold, a hydrologist working for the Water Resources Division of the U.S. Geological Survey. Leopold had been unimpressed with statements by Richard Leonard, General U. S. Grant III of the American Civic Association, and J. W. Penfold of the Izaak Walton League. Responding to Brower, he stated unequivocally that it was "the height of folly to argue with the bureau about the quantities of water that will be evaporated because they are much more likely to be right than any consultant that the Sierra group could muster."[33] Luna, along with close friends, believed that the conservationists should retreat to the bulwark of their two main points—that these sites should be preserved because of their intrinsic interest, and that construction would encroach upon established monuments. But Harold Bradley, Martin Litton, and David Brower had a growing suspicion late in 1953 that the bureau's figures were wrong, either by deliberate falsification or by mistake.

Yet more embarrassing to the bureau was a document

Brower acquired from Dale Doty, assistant secretary of the interior, who had protested the project to Oscar Chapman, the outgoing secretary. Doty saw the whole project as essentially designed for power generation. He argued, first, that "the need for all the storage proposed in the Upper Colorado River Storage Project report is open to serious question," and second, that the cost of power anticipated from the Echo Park and Split Mountain dams would be prohibitively expensive. Indeed, the large allocation of cost of the projects to irrigation was unjustified, since it was not in fact an irrigation project. On the basis of power alone, only a Glen Canyon dam seemed justifiable. Doty suggested that the bureau's report be returned, and that each unit in the plan should be made to show more benefit than cost.[34] These were not issues that conservation organizations felt they could diplomatically approach in 1953.

Nevertheless, Doty's information led Brower to pursue in private the validity of the bureau's report. Meanwhile, the film *Wilderness River Trail*, with footage by Charles Eggert, Nathan Clark, and Martin Litton, edited by Eggert and Brower, was ready for distribution. Leonard convinced the board to finance distribution, even to use permanent funds, by arguing, "We must figure on shooting up some ammunition. The battle is a most crucial one. If we lose the Dinosaur issue, we will have far more to lose in the future. If we win, we will gain great respect from those who oppose us and will strengthen our position in the future."[35]

In January of 1954, the House Interior and Insular Affairs Subcommittee on Irrigation and Reclamation held hearings on the Upper Colorado River Basin Project. The conservation organizations were ready. Representatives from all the major organizations testified, and the Club showed its film after the hearings. But the most remarkable testimony was that given by Brower.[36]

When he spoke as executive director of the Sierra Club,

and on behalf of the Federation of Western Outdoor Clubs, Brower began with the traditional arguments, attempting to counteract what he perceived as testimony consisting "in large part of a single Bureau's looking upon its own work and pronouncing it good." As he attempted to give the perspectives of people he called "the present-day Thoreaus and Leopolds and Marshalls," and characterized the Sierra Club as a "good organization, devoted to idealism," he followed the agreed-upon points—the park values of Dinosaur which the dams would destroy and the possibility of alternatives. He insisted on the need for first-hand experience of the river: "If you haven't been all the way through the canyons or haven't seen one of the four color movies now available to show the trip, you can not begin to appreciate why we are so determined in wanting to preserve it."

The dams, he argued, would inundate close-up scenes and living space, would litter the monument with refuse and havoc of construction. Fluctuating reservoir levels and silt would ruin the flora and fauna. Most important, "The river, its surge and its sound, the living sculptor of this place, would be silent forever, and all the fascination of its movement and the fun of riding it, quietly gliding through these cathedral corridors of stone—all done in for good." To those who argued that the dam would only alter Dinosaur, he offered many striking parallels: a dam from El Capitan to Bridalveil Fall would only alter Yosemite; cutting the Sequoias in Sequoia National Park would still leave the distant views. "Maybe 'alter' isn't the word," he announced. "Maybe we should just come out with it and say 'cut the heart out.'" As he clearly indicated, the river system was the lifeblood of the monument. The same argument might be made, he knew, about the entire Colorado River and Colorado Plateau, but he followed the Club's directions and insisted only that dams in Dinosaur would themselves constitute "the tragedy of our generation."

When he concluded, he ventured onto dangerous ground, turning to the bureau's figures on evaporation. He was able to quote Ralph Tudor, who had testified as McKay's undersecretary of the interior, who had said that "the most important single factor in favor of the recommended plan, as contrasted to suggested alternates, is its comparatively smaller water wastage through evaporation . . . the fundamental issue. . . ." Perhaps evaporation was not *the* issue, perhaps it was a red herring, but the bureau had made it the point of contention. Accepting the bureau's own figures, and its assumption that the system had to be discussed as a whole, Brower began to work with a blackboard, using what he called ninth-grade arithmetic on Tudor's figures, and showing that a higher Glen Canyon dam, instead of the Dinosaur dams, would save water. "It is hard to believe, I know, but if I am wrong, it must surely [be] because *he* is wrong, and he is not supposed to be wrong in engineering matters or figures." The bureau scrambled to correct its errors.

Howard Zahniser was elated. He sent a telegram to the Club: "I have not seen Goliath today but David is on his way to what should be return in triumph. Salute him well. He certainly hit the giant between the eyes with his five smooth stones. . . . We all thank the Lord for the Sierra Club."[37]

After an unexpected and dramatic triumph at the congressional hearings, the next Club goal was to obtain national publicity in pursuit of its Dinosaur campaign. Articles were beginning to appear in major magazines, such as *Sunset, Life,* and *National Geographic,* even on the *New York Times* editorial page. Yet members could hardly keep up with the rapid pace of events. The Club put out a *Special Bulletin,* and included Dinosaur material in the *Bulletin,* setting out its position, answering the arguments of the dam builders, and encouraging an ongoing letter-writing campaign. In addition, Brower recommended sending letters to editors and the publication of pamphlets for members of Congress, as well as "give-aways" to be distributed at film showings.

More important for the future, the board discussed the idea of a "higher Glen Canyon Dam" to be built instead of the Dinosaur dams. This was a knotty problem. By implication, Brower's testimony seemed to recommend such an alternative. But if the Club recommended a higher Glen Canyon dam which would compensate for stored water lost by not building the Echo Park dam, then it would have to face the problem of protecting Rainbow Bridge National Monument from the rising water. Rainbow Bridge, a great arc of Navajo sandstone tucked away on the shoulder of Navajo Mountain, in one of the most remote parts of the region, was the largest known formation of its type in the world. Worse was the problem of the advisability of a dam that would inundate canyons which only a few Club activists knew were more sublime than those in Dinosaur, though not protected by national monument or national park status. Consensus was that the Club not depart from its primary thesis of protecting the national park system. As Colby argued, that position would not commit the Club to opposing or recommending the Glen Canyon project. After much discussion, the board passed a motion by Robinson: "The Sierra Club does not oppose the construction of dam or reservoir projects presently proposed in the Upper Colorado River Basin outside of National Parks and Monuments and established Wilderness areas."[38] The board would hold to its strategy.

In the meantime, the Club was coming to recognize not only the haste demonstrated in Bureau of Reclamation figures, but its own ignorance about the larger problems which the Upper Colorado River Basin Project suggested. By spring of 1954 Alex Hildebrand had prepared a report indicating that steam power generation, if subsidized by the government to the same extent as dams, would be substantially less expensive than hydroelectric generation at Echo Park and

Split Mountain. Though the board felt it should continue to interest prominent citizens in taking river trips through Dinosaur, it would also have to know much more about technical issues such as the hydrological problems of the Lower Colorado Basin, in the Grand Canyon and below, and their relation to the Upper Colorado River Storage Project. More scientific study regarding long-term evaporation was needed.

These issues would have to wait, since Brower was due to speak for the Club in a few days, on May 3, 1954, when the Hoover Commission Task Force on Water Resources and Power would hold hearings in San Francisco. It was the consensus of the board that "Brower is deemed to be on the right track in throwing substantial doubt on the economic and engineering features of the Echo Park project, in stressing the importance of preserving the scenery of the Yampa and Green River Canyons, and in keeping a close watch on progress of proposals in Congress."[39] So Brower responded, when asked whether the Club was concerned about the unsoundness of the plan as a whole:

> We started out in the Sierra Club with this position— and it is our position officially today—that we do not oppose an Upper Colorado River Storage Project which stays out of the National Park system. It just so happens that in the course of our looking into the project . . . we found it distressingly full of errors, contradiction, and inconsistencies and very questionable arithmetic, which is slowly being admitted, item by item.[40]

By fall, the publisher Alfred Knopf, also a member of the secretary of the interior's Advisory Board on National Parks and Monuments, had agreed to publish a book on Dinosaur, to be called *This Is Dinosaur*. Brower told the Club's board he hoped Bernard DeVoto and Horace Albright could serve as authors.[41] The book would not come out until 1956, and would be written by other men. But the Club had more seri-

ous problems to consider as a result of recent legislation and
a landmark decision by the United States Supreme Court on
lobbying.

Attempts to influence such potentially lucrative *Lobbying*
schemes as the Upper Colorado River Storage Project 1954–1955
would soon brand the Club as an "interest group," a
part of the conservation lobby, open to the same legislative
pressures as other groups whose interest in the public good
might seem less obvious, like the National Association of
Manufacturers, grain associations, and cotton brokers, who
also wished to influence legislation of significant financial
importance. Already, the Federal Regulation of Lobbying Act
of 1946 attempted to safeguard the public by requiring disclosure of lobbyists and the nature of their financial support, so
that the public would know how and to what extent Congress was moved by those who spent money to influence the
laws of the land. When, in June of 1954, the Supreme Court
decided that the Federal Lobbying Act did not violate the
First Amendment of the Constitution, holding that persons
or organizations which qualified as lobbyists and failed to
register could be held criminally responsible, it presented a
crisis to conservation organizations. According to the law,
when a substantial part of the funds or activities of an organization were devoted to influencing legislation, the organization might qualify as a lobbyist. If the organization did
qualify as a lobbyist, its tax-deductible status would change.

For the Sierra Club, examined four times by the Internal
Revenue Service, most recently in 1950, to lose tax-
deductible status would mean considerable financial hard-
ship. If its status were to change, its income would still be tax-
exempt. Donors could still deduct gifts to it from their own
taxes, since it had successfully argued that it was a scientific,
literary, and educational institution, the majority of its funds
and activities dedicated to these purposes and the enjoyment

of mountains rather than attempts to influence legislation. But as Leonard pointed out at a special meeting called in November 1954, though the Club had no appreciable net income, it could be vulnerable to estate taxes and stood to lose a substantial amount of money which might come to it through bequests. It was simply a fact that people shopped around for tax bargains when they wrote their wills. Even though people like Howard Zahniser thought the situation was unfair and somewhat indecent, Leonard, as a tax lawyer, understood the predicament in pragmatic terms. Nobody wanted to waste the benefits his money might provide.[42]

The Supreme Court's decision, not the Dinosaur campaign, clouded the Club's tax status. Although testifying could be justified as "giving facts" if the testimony was invited by a member of the House or Senate, when the Club encouraged letter-writing campaigns to affect congressional action it certainly was lobbying. Now, Leonard thought, the Club would have to reconsider its goals and rights, and in particular "what is and should be the status of the Executive Director of the Club? Can he in appearing before Congress or in contacting legislators represent non-tax-exempt organizations as well as the Sierra Club, and if so, under what circumstances?"[43] The Club had several possible alternatives. It could register itself or its executive director as a lobbyist, it could cease all efforts which might be interpreted as influencing legislation, or it could, as Robinson suggested, "adopt a doctrine of calculated risk."

The Sierra Club's relation to other organizations was not a moot point. The Council of Conservationists had decided to register as a lobbyist. Along with representatives like Howard Zahniser of The Wilderness Society, David Brower was a member of its executive committee. In addition, Brower was vice chairman of the Natural Resources Council of America, which would help coordinate lobbying activity for the Dinosaur fight in the eighty-fourth Congress. If the Club did not pay his expenses, Brower could not personally afford to attend many organizational meetings.

Yet if the Club registered as a lobbyist, the board could not predict its own members' response. Though Leonard believed that "to many the Club was figuratively a knight in shining armor defending the integrity of the national park system," others might object to explicit identification of the Club with lobbying work, since the term had acquired unsavory connotations.[44]

Brower believed the Club should accept its new political role, register as a lobbying organization, and establish a Sierra Club Foundation—a non-lobbying group dependent on large grants. As Brower said later, "Let the Sierra Club itself, with its membership dues, its publishing program, its outings, and the rapidly increasing amount of revenue coming in from that, support the lobbying program."[45] On the other hand, Leonard wanted to preserve the pure image of the Club, and on Brower's suggestion incorporated Trustees for Conservation, which would raise funds, to be available to The Wilderness Society and the Sierra Club, for lobbying about Dinosaur and the wilderness bill. As Leonard remembers, "Zahniser of The Wilderness Society and Brower of the Sierra Club, who were doing the actual work, felt that the public could not understand why The Wilderness Society and the Sierra Club were so cowardly that they would never speak out on matters like Dinosaur. . . . They felt that The Wilderness Society and the Sierra Club had to be free to campaign vigorously themselves."[46]

The board followed Leonard's course, deciding unanimously that "(1) the Sierra Club shall not solicit, receive or collect any funds for the purpose of influencing legislation; (2) that all club and chapter officers and employees shall be instructed to comply with this regulation." This meant, as Robinson put it, that "the status of the Executive Director shall be carefully and continuously scrutinized to see that he does not at any time do what might be ruled as 'lobbying' while being compensated by the Club for his time and travel expenses."[47]

Leonard finished the paperwork for Trustees for Conservation, an organization completely separate from the Sierra Club, five days later. It would fund and coordinate lobbying efforts. Following the desires of several directors who stressed the need for explaining to Club members that the Club was not "quitting the fight," he wrote an article for the *Bulletin*, distinguishing the respective roles of the Sierra Club and Trustees. In "We Defend the Parks: A New Ally, Trustees for Conservation, Steps Up to the Firing Line; the Sierra Club Continues to Present the Facts," Leonard laid out the situation, explained the tax laws, the conclusions of the board, and the purposes of Trustees.[48] Though Trustees would be a nonprofit organization, contributions would not be tax deductible. Its broad conservation purposes included working for the establishment, protection, and preservation of national parks, monuments, wildlife refuges, and wilderness areas; "with no privileged status to protect," it could "take the message of conservationists directly and vigorously to Congress, with no fear of violating the tax laws." The board of Trustees included several ex-presidents of the Club—Walter Huber, Francis Farquhar, and Will Colby. It involved many of the Club's most active conservationists, as well as some new names, like Wallace Stegner and Edward Mallinckrodt, Jr., who would figure as major contibutors to the rhetoric and financial support of the continuing Dinosaur campaign.

A Film, a Book, an Advertisement   Although the Sierra Club was growing in membership and stature day by day, its total financial resources were by no means as great as those of its allies in the Dinosaur campaign. Also, unlike the National Parks Association, the National Audubon Society, or The Wilderness Society, which were centered in the East, the Club was still perceived as a western regional organization. Though San Francisco had arrived as a major national corporate center after World War II, it was still not perceived by easterners as a cultural center. So it was that the Club had neither the financial means nor national stature to do battle alone. Further, when the board of directors of the Club prohibited Brower from direct lobbying, he could thereafter only make general public statements. Letters and specific appeals to congressmen would go out, the board agreed, under the name of the Council of Conservationists or the Trustees for Conservation.[49] Consequently the Club found itself acting as part of a confederation of organizations, a situation which imposed further limits.

By late 1955, the campaign to protect Dinosaur from dams seemed close to success. Though the Upper Colorado River Basin Project had passed the Senate, the House Interior Affairs Committee had attempted to remove the Echo Park and Split Mountain dams from the bill. A poll of congressmen had indicated that an unrevised bill which included Dinosaur dams could not pass the House. Even if everyone agreed Glen Canyon ought to be a national park, the present issue was Dinosaur. Zahniser believed it would be a mistake to complicate the effort by talking about Glen Canyon, or indeed to mount an attack on the whole Upper Colorado River project, which would only confuse legislators. However, Brower warned the board in October 1955 that it should not "give away" Glen Canyon; he pointed out that some thought it was of national park caliber and indicated that a Glen Canyon dam, once built, might suggest such attractive profit possibilities that proposals for dams in Dinosaur would be renewed.[50] As expressed by the board, "the conservationists' price of peace on the upper Colorado River Bill in Congress is the addition of a proviso, vis. 'No dam or reservoir constructed under this Act shall be situated in whole or in part in any National Park or Monument.'"[51] This was the wording suggested and pursued by Howard Zahniser as an amendment to the congressional bill.

As the board of directors had decreed, Brower concentrated on publicity, educational in nature, directed at the House. One project, already published in the *Bulletin*, was a photographic essay showing Hetch Hetchy Valley before and after the dam, juxtaposed to "before" photographs of Dinosaur National Monument. Brower concluded the essay by suggesting a plaque for Hetch Hetchy Dam:

HERE, NEEDLESSLY BURIED FOREVER
LIES THE HETCH HETCHY YOSEMITE
FOR HERE PROGRESS STUMBLED

If we heed the lesson learned from the tragedy of the misplaced dam in Hetch Hetchy, we can prevent a far more disastrous stumble in Dinosaur National Monument.[52]

Brower adapted his material into an eleven-minute film, called *Two Yosemites*, which he thought was the lowest-budget film on record at $500.[53] He showed it in a good many places. Zahniser got a little mobile trailer from the House Office Building, installed a projector in it, and wheeled his show to congressmen.

A more ambitious project was Brower's first attempt at an out-and-out conservation book, *This Is Dinosaur: Echo Park Country and Its Magic Rivers*, for which he persuaded Alfred Knopf to write the concluding chapter, "The National Park Idea." He persuaded experts to contribute essays. Robert Lister, an anthropologist, wrote "The Ancients of the Canyons," Eliot Blackwelder, "Geological Exhibit," Olaus Murie and Joseph W. Penfold, "The Natural World of Dinosaur." Otis ("Dock") Marston, a venerable river guide, wrote "Fast Water," and Martin Litton, unable to publish under his own name because of his ties to *Sunset* magazine, helped write David Bradley's "A Short Look at Eden."[54] Brower put together a thirty-six-page portfolio of black and white and color photographs, contributed by Harold Bradley, Martin

Litton, and Philip Hyde—the latter a past student of Ansel Adams who had done a whole series on Dinosaur.

Brower's most significant coup was to enlist Wallace Stegner to edit the book and contribute its introduction, "The Marks of Human Passage." Originally he had hoped to get Bernard DeVoto to edit the book, but DeVoto had died in November of 1955. It is interesting to conjecture what Devoto might have written, since his own acerbic view of western developers was so provocative, his view of the West as its own worst enemy so damning. To DeVoto, westerners, especially in the Rocky Mountain region, desired to have federal projects subsidized by eastern money, while at the same time they conducted an assault on their own resources with the simple objective of liquidating them.[55]

Like DeVoto, Wallace Stegner had grown up in Utah. In the early 1950s while Stegner was directing the writing program at Stanford University, DeVoto began to bend his arm to write partisan conservation material. Stegner was already a noted novelist and an expert on the Colorado Plateau. His *Mormon Country*, published in 1942, incuded chapters on the canyon country and one chapter specifically about Dinosaur. His *Beyond the Hundredth Meridian: John Wesley Powell and the Second Opening of the West*, published in 1953, was not only a groundbreaking analysis of the career of Powell, the Muir of the Colorado Plateau, but also a pioneering environmental history, demonstrating Stegner's thorough knowledge of the complex geography of the area. It has served for many as a guide to the human history of the Colorado River Basin. As natural heir to DeVoto, Stegner had dedicated his Powell book to the older man, and would later write DeVoto's biography. More important for the Sierra Club, Stegner would become a Club spokesman, in *This Is Dinosaur* and in later influential essays, "The War Between the Rough Riders and the Bird Watchers" (1959), and "Wilderness Letter" (1960), where he coined the term "the geography of hope."[56] Benny

DeVoto started Stegner writing partisan material; Brower kept him at it.

The purpose of *This Is Dinosaur* was to survey the monument's possibilities for human rest and recreation and inspiration, to dramatize the area's rich cultural resources, "one of the last almost 'unspoiled' wildernesses." In "The Marks of Human Passage," Stegner explored the human meaning of wilderness: "Describing a place, we inevitably describe the marks humans have made upon a place, the uses they have put it to, the things they have been taught by it."[57] So he summarized Dinosaur's history, and the changing tastes which first protected the bone quarry and finally the canyons themselves. Stegner most of all wrote a history of shifting perceptions. As he insisted, "A place is nothing in itself. It has no meaning, it can hardly be said to exist, except in terms of human perception, use, and response."[58] The *human* message of the book was:

> We live in the Antibiotic Age, and Antibiotic means literally 'against life.' We had better not be against
> life. . . . We are the most dangerous species of life on
> the planet, and every other species, even the earth itself,
> has cause to fear our power to exterminate. But we are
> also the only species which, when it chooses to do so,
> will go to great effort to save what it might destroy. . . .
> If we preserved as parks only those places that have no
> economic possibilities, we would have no parks.[59]

The book was hastily produced, but was a workmanlike job. The prose does not read as if it were hastily written. Though the quality of the photography is uneven, and not well reproduced, it documents Dinosaur's scenic value. It wasn't a popular book and ran to only 5,000 copies, but there was one on the desk of every member of Congress, along with a hardhitting brochure that Brower put together.

Knopf was willing to finance a book, and Edward Mallinckrodt, Jr. of Mallinckrodt Chemicals, a longtime member of the Club, approached Francis Farquhar and Joel Hilde-brand, offering funds for a public relations campaign. His money went to the Council of Conservationists, which was composed of Brower, Zahniser, Joseph Penfold, Ira Gabriel-son, and Fred Smith, its organizer. Smith wrote a full page ad, to appear in the *Denver Post* on the eve of a meeting of the Upper Colorado River Basin development groups. This was the first full-page conservation ad placed in a major metropolitan newspaper.

The ad served notice to backers of the project that conser-vation groups intended to fight the entire project if that was the only way to kill the Echo Park dam. With a Fifth Avenue, New York, address, the council felt it was in a position to an-nounce that it was a political force to be reckoned with. In the ad, entitled "An Open letter: To the 'Strategy Committee' of the Upper Colorado Project," it quoted the statement by Sen-ator Watkins of Utah that the project would not work with-out Echo Park dam, scoffed at the Bureau of Reclamation's claim that Echo Park dam was "the piston in the engine," but insisted that "conservationists who have been leading this battle are NOT anti-reclamationists, and are NOT fighting the principle of water use in the west." It warned that the posi-tion of conservationists was stronger than ever since deficien-cies and economic weaknesses of the project had been widely exposed, that parts of the project, like Echo Park dam, were "obviously extravagant" and "serve far more local political purposes than national economic purposes." The ad threat-ened further that in an election year congressmen would have to explain why they were spending their constituents' tax dollars on "a controversial project far away," and particu-larly would have to explain "the exorbitant irrigation costs which will bring into production more farm land, at a time when farmers are already suffering acutely from an over-abundance of crops." It placed the blame for a stalled Upper Colorado bill on those who insisted on including Echo Park, who "heeded those who were more interested in local politics than in national economics or other important, pertinent, public-interest considerations."[60]

That ad constituted the most dramatic attack on the project yet, and it had the desired effect. Two days later the congressional Upper Basin Strategy Committee agreed to drop Echo Park from the Upper Colorado bill. By the end of the month Secretary of the Interior McKay agreed to drop Echo Park from the project. On March 9, 1956, Zahniser's sentence was inserted in the bill: ". . . no dam or reservoir constructed under the authorization of this act shall be within any national park or monument." On the same day, Douglas McKay resigned his post as secretary of the interior. As Roderick Nash put it, "On April 11, 1956, the new bill became law, and the American wilderness movement had its finest hour to date."[61] Six months later, on October 15, 1956, President Eisenhower detonated a charge which had been buried in the monumental Navajo sandstone wall of Glen Canyon, breaking the ground for Glen Canyon Dam.

The Price of Victory
1956

If we hadn't believed in ourselves, we never would have stopped the Dinosaur thing. If we had believed in ourselves enough, we would have stopped Glen Canyon Dam on the Colorado River.
Martin Litton

There was much to be pleased about. Dinosaur National Monument had been rescued, the principle of the sanctity of national parks and monuments reaffirmed. Secretary of the Interior McKay, who appeared odious to all the conservationists, had been forced to resign. Through a variety of media, public attention had been focused on the importance of wilderness for America. Yet one historian argues that the status quo in resource management had scarcely been disturbed:

> In retrospect the alarms over the national park principle were no more profound in their impact than political expediency permitted. . . . The leaders and publicists of

those years addressed themselves only to the immediate issues. When Americans were confronted by a total ecological crisis less than a decade after . . . they had nothing more to draw upon to cope with that threat than the economic materialism, the bureaucratic inertia, and the political gamesmanship practiced by the men of the Truman-Eisenhower era.[62]

It is standard practice after a rescue operation to draw up a critique, so that innovative methods can be utilized in the future and so that any errors will not be repeated. The members of the Club's board, and of course David Brower—with ample time to reconsider the events of the early 1950s in the light of later events—have not been silent about the club's assessment of the problem, its own aims in entering the Dinosaur campaign, the means it chose to fight this campaign, and the specific techniques chosen by the board and its executive director. Further, this campaign had great personal significance to many Club members, and not only brought new activists into Club affairs, but profoundly shaped the lives of men like David Brower and Richard Leonard. It also constituted a crucial turning point in the nature of the Club's organizational structure and aims.

What was the "real" problem that the Club perceived when it entered the Dinosaur campaign? This might be reviewed in a hierarchical way. Was the "enemy" simply misguided local interests, or was it something larger, having to do with the power of federal agencies, corporations, or the banking institutions of America?

The local interests in the Dinosaur matter were personified by Arthur V. Watkins, the senator from Utah and leading proponent for the Upper Colorado River Project. Watkins was concerned that the forces in California and the East "would like to hamstring economic development in the west, leaving this vast area as . . . an undisturbed playground." Wallace Stegner responded to Watkins directly: "I love ex-Senator's state, but not his state of mind. He speaks narrowly and parochially and irritably; he suffers from a characteristic Utah xenophobia; he suspects eastern slickers of manipulating his state's interests, just as he suspects that villains in California fought the Echo Park Dam because they wanted to steal Utah's water. Unhappily, his state of mind is not uncommon in the Rockies."[63] Like Bernard DeVoto, Stegner believes that the West has always expected local interests to take precedence over national public interest:

> What the West has always done—what states like Utah, at least, have always done—is to cry like hell about the absentee landlords and the soulless bureaucrats in Washington and fight them every bit of the way. But when a Dust Bowl comes on, when a cyclic drought comes on, when a depression comes on, when resources run out, when water is needed, they cry for help to the same old Feds that they've been knocking. It's a wildly schizophrenic position they assume, and they irritate me when they do it. All right, be independent if you want, but don't be independent with your hand out.[64]

People in places like Vernal, Utah, wanted jobs, economic development that was likely to come with big construction projects. Bankers in Salt Lake had tasted the benefits of reclamation projects during the construction of Hoover Dam. They liked the flow of money. Local agricultural interests harbored impossible dreams, as they had since the days of John Wesley Powell. Certainly it had by now been well established that the Upper Colorado River Project could not be justified by its economic benefits as an irrigation project. As a water project, Club leaders then had reason to believe, it represented a massive—and unwarranted—federal subsidy to western agriculture.[65]

Others felt that the real problem was the Bureau of Reclamation, the power it had established within Interior after World War II. Leonard believes that "Giveaway" McKay wanted to "give away the national parks" to the bureau. The bureau itself "had to have a billion dollars' worth of new dams every year in order to stay alive" and was willing to give false arguments, or even lie about its figures, to assure its continuing health as an agency.[66] Almost everyone, even Bestor Robinson, suspected that the bureau deliberately falsified figures on the Dinosaur dams, and on the whole project. Like Bernard DeVoto, the members of the Club's board believed that the entire concept of reclamation needed overhauling. That is why they began to suggest alternative methods of producing power, like coal burning or even nuclear energy.

More recently, Club leaders such as Raymond Sherwin have argued that the real villains were the large corporations, which were beginning to exercise massive political and economic power.[67] The rise of what some have called "resource-based western capitalism," including such corporations as Bechtel and Kaiser, was the real threat to the western environment. Stegner believes that not all of the West thought like Watkins: "It's what you might call the Republican economic West, the development-minded corporate West."[68] Indeed, the lobbying act which created so many difficulties for the conservation organizations after 1954 was an attempt to limit the political influence of certain corporate interests. As Robert Gottlieb and Peter Wiley convincingly argue in *Empires in the Sun: The Rise of the New West* (1982), California was the center for many of these new growth-oriented institutions, which also provided the means for a powerful banking empire. In 1945, San Francisco's Bank of America became the largest bank in the world. By the 1970s, Bechtel, builder of Glen Canyon Dam, was the largest privately held corporation in the world. Gottlieb and Wiley point out that "for Kaiser, Bank of America, Bechtel, Utah Mining and Construction, and others, San Francisco was the financial and strategic capital."[69] If the development-minded corporate West was the enemy of the wild lands of the arid West, its center of operations was just down the hill from the Sierra Club's offices, in the financial district of the Club's home city.

Unable to attack directly all the forces threatening Dinosaur or the Colorado Plateau, the Club experienced some uneasy alignments, the most difficult with Southern California water interests, who wanted all the water of the Colorado River to flow to that region. Then there were people who simply did not want to support any public projects if that meant higher taxes. They were the same people, or groups, who would oppose appropriations for maintenance or improvement of the national park system. There were people who were getting energy from coal or corporations who planned to make money that way. As Brower has commented, with some embarrassment, "We would join anyone [laughter] who could help us save Dinosaur."[70] The Club tried to maintain its independence from any political engagements, particularly disassociating itself from liberal Democrats like Wayne Morse and Richard Neuberger, who advocated public power projects but thought Glen Canyon Dam was an unsatisfactory public power project. Many members of the Club were not in complete agreement with their allies. Yet Club members were hardly blind to forces arrayed on the side of western resource development. It was neither possible nor appropriate for the Club to confront them all. In this context one yet might ask whether David had slain Goliath or had only bit him on the shin. When the Club chose not to confront the whole Upper Colorado project or the powerful corporate forces behind it, this was partly because many Club members were not opposed to developing the West, were not even opposed to federal subsidies providing water for the arid West; but this was also a strategic decision, given the Club's limited means.

Why did the Club spend so much energy on Dinosaur in

particular? From Richard Leonard's perspective, Dinosaur constituted a particular kind of national monument, one which had been enlarged as a result of the political persuasiveness of Harold Ickes. Protecting Dinosaur meant setting a precedent for protecting Grand Teton National Monument and all the other gains in the national park system which had preceded the Truman-Eisenhower era.[71] There was also a virtue in creating the national movement Leonard called a "national park conscience." In 1957, Leonard argues, Los Angeles gave up its claims to power from Kings Canyon National Park—claims it had held since the 1920s—in order to gain public good will. Thus "the victory in Dinosaur, over a thousand miles away, saved Kings Canyon from dams and later saved the Grand Canyon from dams."[72] Like Ansel Adams, Leonard believed that all resource issues were national issues, and that the public interest had to be defended from local or vested interests. As a lawyer, he thought in institutional terms. The Club's aim was to concentrate on precedent-setting campaigns and public conscience. From this perspective, then, by creating a positive movement for positive principles, rather than attacking vested interests, the Club could establish the means which would defend the entire national park system. A victory for Dinosaur, in the end, would be more successful than a chancy campaign against the entire Upper Colorado River Basin Project, even if it mean sacrificing Glen Canyon.

What about Glen Canyon? Immediately after the success in Congress, David Brower, who was still in Washington, spoke on the telephone to a group of board members, urging the Club to take up the fight against a Glen Canyon dam before it was too late. Bestor Robinson felt that such a purist stand would result in defeat, since the Club had made a compromise, saying in effect that the Bureau of Reclamation could have Glen Canyon. Robinson later said that "if you didn't have the Grand Canyon then Glen Canyon should be preserved"; but, he argued, the trade-off was necessary.[73] Leonard believed in retrospect that the compromise had to be kept if the Club was to preserve its credibility. "Congress would have been convinced that the preservationists were unreasonable and were urging that the entire Colorado River be unused and just allowed to flood away into the Gulf of California."[74] Furthermore, he believed that the Club would not have been able to keep dams out of Grand Canyon if the Glen Canyon Dam had not been built. Like him, Alex Hildebrand, Club president in 1956, opposed extending the campaign to Glen Canyon. Nearly thirty years later, Hildebrand defended the compromise:

> You have to compromise. The merit is rarely all on one side even though some people like to pretend it is. The case for building Glen was much better than the case for building Dinosaur. The case against Glen didn't involve existing national parks or monuments or likely ones other than—what do you call that little monument that has the stone arch in it?"[75]

The monument with the stone arch was Rainbow Bridge National Monument, which was supposed to be protected by a check dam. Since funds were never appropriated for that dam, the waters of Lake Powell come very close to the base of Rainbow Bridge, and may someday undermine its base. That was troubling to Brower, but more troubling to him was that the Club had written off Glen Canyon without having been there. Wallace Stegner remembers, "Nobody knew Glen Canyon then except me; I'd been down it a couple of times, and I told [Brower] it was better than Echo Park. He didn't believe it and I didn't push it."[76]

For the Navajos the whole Glen Canyon region, with Navajo Mountain rising to the east, was sacred land: "The Head of Earth [Navajo Mountain] and Rainbow Bridge belong together. The sacred springs of the area—the one on Head of Earth, the one remaining near Rainbow Bridge, and lesser ones—work together and pool their blessings."[77] This strikingly different kind of knowledge demanded a different basis for land management:

> Colorado River is female; San Juan River is male. At the place where the two used to come together, where the San Juan mounted the Colorado. . . . great uncertainty now surrounds . . . this sacred place. The waters of White man's Lake Powell have been sent—prudishly, it seems—to cover the nuptial bed of two of the Southwest's greatest divinities. The exact place where these two Rivers used to come together, in one bed, is covered now. Navajo offerings can no longer be placed at the correct spot.[78]

For Brower, "'My own bitter lesson there was that you don't give away something that you haven't seen; you don't suggest alternatives until you've been there.'"[79] In retrospect, Litton too believes that sacrificing Glen Canyon was "giving up the bigger value in return for the lesser."[80] In terms of the wilderness protected versus the wilderness irretrievably lost, there can be no doubt. Glen Canyon held within it numerous side canyons which were more than the equivalent of Dinosaur, and constituted the most magnificent system of monumental sandstone canyons on earth. Brower himself has always believed that the Sierra Club could have been the keystone to a successful campaign against the entire Upper Colorado River Project, and has always felt that he personally was in a better position than anyone to stop the destruction of Glen Canyon. During those years Brower began to spend time in that country, going to what he called the University of the Colorado River.

There was no consensus among Club members about compromise, and feelings are still mixed. Unlike Martin Litton, who believes in no trade-offs and advocates the extreme position in almost every case, Brower believes in negotiation.

Even though he has reason to regret his own support for a higher Glen Canyon dam and regrets suggesting coal-fired or nuclear power plants as alternatives for dams, he still believes that conservationists can wisely help select alternatives. It is simply that their errors come too frequently from ignorance.[81]

John Muir had known Hetch Hetchy in the sacred sense that some Navajos knew Glen Canyon. The Club did not know the land of the Colorado Plateau, its history, or its spiritual significance as well as it knew its own Sierra. As a result, it acted imperfectly and with incomplete knowledge. Knowing more about principles than about the land itself, it acted in the interest of the national park system. Yet even from the view of purists, the gains of the Dinosaur campaign were substantial.

Tactical Precedents 1956–1957   During the Truman-Eisenhower era the debate about the Colorado River Storage Project was rarely conducted on the basis of principles or the rational use of science for making public policy decisions. The motives of most participants were simply political, based on economic gain, on personal or interagency conflicts within the department of the interior, on the often appalling ignorance of the general public, and on elected officials' need for votes. Nevertheless, the Sierra Club's greatest victory may have been to open these public policy decisions to public scrutiny. Dispersion of publicity, including not only facts but arguments and the expression of feelings, had become the traditional Club tactic.

Brower and Leonard reminded themselves that the campaign for Hetch Hetchy Valley was the model for Dinosaur, because there were many parallels. Both conflicts, according to the defenders of the parks, were a matter of local versus national interest. Both seemed to pit reclamation against the parks. Those who wanted the dams suggested, in both instances, that economic growth had to go ahead of scenic or aesthetic preservation, and further argued that secret water interests were behind the resistance to these public projects. The proponents of dams argued in the 1950s, as they had at the turn of the century, that the areas to be affected were only used by a group of wealthy elitist recreationists, and that reservoirs would bring a much wider recreational use.

Just as the Hetch Hetchy battle split the ranks of conservationists at the turn of the century, so Dinosaur did fifty years later. This conflict occurred within the Club as it had before; many saw defection in Bestor Robinson's role as an overly willing compromiser. As Brower has said, "He made my life more interesting than I wanted it to be throughout my career as executive director.[82] When John Muir, as a result of Hetch Hetchy, had been conspicuously missing from Theodore Roosevelt's 1908 Governor's Conference on Conservation, his absence had symbolized the final wedge between his views and those of Gifford Pinchot. When, at the instigation of Horace Albright, president-elect Eisenhower decided it was "high time the Conservation Conference of 1908 should be reborn in a mid-century setting," his close advisers managed to delay and finally distance his administration from the conference, fearing that it would merely be "a sounding board for 'zealous do goods.'"[83]

Just as Muir and Colby had planned their strategy to include outings to the Hetch Hetchy area, articles in major magazines, and a coalition of eastern and western conservation organizations, and just as Muir expressed moral outrage on the one hand and Colby attempted to deal with the engineering reports on the other, so would the future Club campaigns be organized. Muir had needed Robert Underwood Johnson to lobby Congress and provide access to the eastern press; so Brower and Leonard needed Zahniser for his knowledge of congressional affairs and Alfred Knopf for publishing. In the modern world, the Club found it necessary to extend its own financial resources through groups like Trustees for Conservation. When Mather campaigned for the National Park Service Act, he hired the fiery Robert Sterling Yard as publicity expert, held a conference on national parks at the University of California at Berkeley, assembled a distinguished group of legislators, writers, publishers, and lecturers to go camping in the High Sierra, published a *National Parks Portfolio*, which appeared on the desk of every congressman, and enlisted the support of as many organizations as he could find, including the Sierra Club and the American Civic Association, as well as automobile clubs and railroads. When Leonard suggested that Brower become executive director of the Club, the Sierra Club got a publicist, but also much more.

So it was that the Club conducted the Dinosaur campaign by extending its traditional tactics, publishing books, writing and distributing pamphlets, creating movies, encouraging letter-writing by the public, and lobbying as much as it could within legal limitations. Yet its primary innovation was to hire a permanent executive director who expressed moral outrage as Muir had. Muir had said, "The proponents of the dam scheme bring forward a lot of bad arguments to prove that the only righteous thing to do with the people's parks is to destroy them bit by bit as they are able"; Brower expressed "grave apprehension at finding that federal department officials charged by law with protecting our parks show such poor appreciation of them as to call this destruction 'altering.'"[84] Muir had grown self-righteous in his perorations, writing, "Dam Hetch Hetchy! As well dam for water-tanks for people's cathedrals and churches, for no holier temple has ever been consecrated by the heart of man."[85] Brower carried the same message to Congress, but in a more restrained and sober tone: "The axiom for protecting the Park System is to consider that it is dedicated country, hallowed ground to leave as beautiful as we have found it, and not country in which man should be so impressed with himself that he tries to improve God's handiwork."[86]

Richard Leonard has said, "Dave changed the whole course of the political effectiveness of the Sierra Club in this campaign." Not only was Brower a practical necessity for a national campaign, he also was able to capture just the right tone for the 1950s. According to Leonard, "Dave's tactics in this battle were accurate, fair, and courteous."[87] Even with Arthur Watkins, Brower remained cordial and firm. He never ridiculed his opponent. Indeed Brower respected Watkins and even admired him, especially for his role in a later campaign to discredit Senator Joseph McCarthy.[88] Brower did not curse the dam builders as Muir had. He did not attack commercial interests, as Muir did when he wrote that "these temple destroyers, devotees of ravaging commercialism, seem to have a perfect contempt for Nature, and, instead of lifting their eyes to the God of the mountains, lift them to the Almighty Dollar."[89]

As a result of the Dinosaur campaign, Leonard thought Brower a superb executive, and in a modern, restrained context, an evangelist of great persuasive powers, reminiscent of Muir. Brower was able to show that the dams in Dinosaur were not needed, without accusing the Bureau of Reclamation of incompetence or falsehood. He acted with perfect discretion, not even seeming to state that the bureau was wrong. He wrote well, was a fine editor, and was, of course, absolutely committed to the cause.[90]

Brower understood and followed the arguments that the Club had chosen, yet because he was the one using them, he recognized their limits most acutely. This caused him considerable personal frustration, and resulted in no small amount of guilt, when he wondered about the losses which the Club had accepted along the way.[91] Brower's strength came from his ability to wage a conservation campaign with personal intensity; his ability to act in a concerted way upon the dictates of conscience would also prove to be his weakness. Nevertheless, he did not attempt to usurp power from the volunteers, who—everyone agreed—constituted the strength of the

Club. Neither did he neglect their help. As Leonard remembers, "He stated many times that he had two thousand volunteers on the committees of the Sierra Club to do his work for him."[92] In the future Brower would remain eminently capable of taking and using advice—not from everyone, but from sources he trusted. Yet Brower also discovered that as executive director he could exercise a freedom not available to many of the expert volunteers in the Club. Walter Huber, for instance, supported Brower throughout the campaign, despite his early estimate that Dinosaur was just canyons and sagebrush; according to Brower, Huber was willing to check figures and provide information, but did not want his name used in the campaign because he was president of the American Society of Civil Engineers. "That happened again and again," Brower remembers; "it was sort of part of my education I guess: that you go where you can for expertise; you try to get the information you can, realizing that there are magnificent inhibitions hanging over the heads of a lot of people who should talk and can't."[93] Brower also worried about the usefulness of having members like Bestor Robinson on federal agency advisory boards: "I saw them [advisory boards] as a device, through flattery, to take key conservation people, feed them a little private information, tell them not to spread it around, and make them support the agency rather than the organization they were drawn from."[94] In other words, as Brower accepted the limitations of his role in serving the volunteers of the Club, he also decided that one chief advantage of his job lay in its independence, in full commitment to Club principles, which, he thought, went beyond that possible for many volunteers.

In the spring of 1957, Brower gave his annual report to the board of directors at the annual organization meeting.[95] The report indicated how indispensable an executive director had become. He detailed his extensive travels, necessary because the Club's executive director had become "the only comparably backed professional conservationist west of Chicago, the only one from the part of the country that has the nation's primary scenic resources, and he will find a unique opportunity to be listened to, even if not always sympathetically." What Brower meant by "comparably backed" was the Club's structure of volunteer leadership: "If a Sierra Club executive director should ever make Who's Who, it would be because these volunteers had carried him on their shoulders, and he couldn't help himself." Brower forecast many future priorities for the Club. Though "the enemy," as Brower called it, was not so clearly defined as it had been in the Dinosaur campaign, he exhorted the board to a never-ceasing effort to keep the cooperators cooperating and expand the conservation force.

He thought the most important issues of the moment were the proposals for a national wilderness preservation system, a campaign to influence Forest Service multiple-use policies, and a Club policy on pollution abatement. His agenda was organized as follows:

Though the board had unanimously approved a policy declaring that important scenic resources should not be impaired by hydroelectric generation, it was faced with at least nine major projected dams. The national park system confronted increased visitor use: "My own feeling has been that we must be careful not to seem to be against people, careful not to confuse wilderness preservation with preserving wildland setting in heavy-use areas." In the national forests, where "'multiple use' to many foresters probably means 'logging plus something else,'" there was need for better protection of forest recreation. The problem was acute and confronted the Club on every hand—in the North Cascades, in Alaska, on the McKenzie River in Oregon, the Kern Plateau, and at Deadman Summit, near Mammoth on the east side of the Sierra. This was a matter not only of large wilderness, but of protecting small scenic areas, which Brower called "every-man's wilderness experience, where indoctrination for big wilderness can take place." The Club needed to take specific action for these areas, in addition to establishing firm policy on multiple use. It also needed to press the Forest Service to establish a role for the public in multiple-use management.

In addition to the need for expanded activity for wilderness preservation, including testifying for the wilderness bill, Brower felt the Club needed a wildlife policy—which Starker Leopold had already drafted. On pollution, he thought, the Club had been "embarrassingly silent when help was needed." He called the board's attention to a policy formulated by the National Wildlife Federation.

Such an agenda suggested that the Club would continue to operate in the realm it had entered during the Dinosaur campaign; that is, it would campaign for areas outside California, support national legislation, and work with other organizations.

CHAPTER FIVE

Sawlog Semantics

The Forest Service, 1920–1956

Even while it was devoting its energies to the Dinosaur Battle—as it was called—the Club was gearing up to confront Forest Service policies up and down the Pacific Coast. The Forest Service prided itself upon professional administration, characterized by scientific objectivity, a perspective above political matters, and a utilitarian philosophy. It aspired to run its affairs as a business would. The pre-World War II Sierra Club saw no conflict between preservation and entrepreneurship; further, many of the prominent men in the Club were involved in essentially utilitarian professions.[1] Walter Huber, a civil engineer involved in surveying dam sites for the Forest Service, Will Colby, a mining engineer, Duncan McDuffie, a subdivider, and Alex Hildebrand, a petroleum engineer, provided continuous influence of the utilitarian perspective on the board of directors. For them, as for many others, the Forest Service lived up to its reputation as the agency with the most efficient managers.[2] Bestor Robinson influenced Club policy as a prominent board member for more than thirty years (1935–1966). Pleased with the professionalism of the Forest Service, and with the way it made its decisions, he was glad that so much of the public land was managed through the service's discretion.

187

He thought it was probably the finest bureau in the federal government.[3]

Under the administration of William B. Greeley in the 1920s, the Forest Service, as one historian indicates, grew "more interested in recreation, and soon developed a considerable interest in wilderness preservation, spurred to it by the aggressive efforts of Mather to take . . . National Forests for new National Parks and additions to parks."[4] The conflict over disposition of Forest Service lands intensified during the New Deal, when Harold Ickes, as secretary of the interior, not only carried on an ambitious policy of park acquisition, but attempted to have the Forest Service transferred to his department.

The Park Service rose in stature during the Mather/Albright administrations, while the Forest Service lost ground after Pinchot was fired in 1910. Many conservationists thought of the parks as besieged in the mid 1920s by special interests who wished to exploit America's priceless natural resources. Meanwhile, the Club supported the Forest Service when its mission was challenged by those who wanted to exploit forest resources in an unprofessional way. The Forest Service idea of wilderness areas, promoted by Aldo Leopold and instituted with the Gila Wilderness in 1924, was a step in the right direction, and the work of Bob Marshall in the Forest Service was much admired by Club members. Forest Service interest in wilderness may have smoothed the way for, or inspired the Park Service to pursue, an idea of Kings Canyon as a wilderness park. Because primarily interested in recreation, the Club began to express growing respect for more than the practical side of the Forest Service's mission. The Club expressed its sympathy toward the Forest Service by electing Gifford Pinchot, Henry S. Graves, and William B. Greeley to lifetime posts as honorary vice presidents, along with the chief administrators of the Park Service. From a Club point of view, the major enemies of both the Park Service and Forest Service were selfish interests opposed by all good conservationists.

Brower told Conrad Wirth that there was a different Sierra Club by the 1950s. There were also a different National Park Service and different Forest Service, not only because of changing economic and social conditions in the country, but because of a changing of the guard in federal agencies. Conrad Wirth saw himself as the first to become director of the Park Service after the service ran out of Mather men; so too Richard McArdle represented a new breed of chief foresters, among the first to serve after the service ran out of Pinchot men.[5] The Eisenhower administration marked significant changes in the personnel and policies of both agencies, and the Club found it necessary to reconsider its strategies.

It may be true, as one historian argues, that "the Eisenhower Administration has been marked by a serious lack of fidelity to the general cause of conservation."[6] But the Forest Service was not standing still. As it approached its golden anniversary in 1955, it had in McArdle a chief with much experience in the agency, acutely aware of economic realities, yet also an academic, a true professional, with a Ph.D. from the University of Michigan and a background in research. He was prepared to put the forests under modern scientific management, making the phrase "the greatest good for the greatest number in the long run" mean something more precise, in terms of careful planning, sustained yield of forests, and a balance among an increasing number of uses of the forests. McArdle accented traditional Forest Service themes, advocating economic uses of forest resources by private enterprise at maximum sustainable levels. As a bureau chief under a Republican administration, he was prepared to cooperate with private enterprise. He prepared for vastly increased timber production in a growing economy by mobilizing the service. McArdle's program included, from its inception, getting the Forest Service into the black by "upping the cut" on Forest

Service lands, building more roads for logging access, and conducting a timber resources review, which would facilitate turning as much of the Forest Service's land as possible to production.[7] McArdle's Forest Service would open the doors, dust off the inventory, and put a great deal of it up for sale.

As it did with the Park Service's Mission 66, the Club attempted to determine exactly what the Forest Service was planning. Through friendly and confidential discussions, the Club wanted to test the policies of these new administrations and test especially the resolve of their directors. The process of testing did not make friends.

In the campaign to protect Dinosaur, the Club had perceived the Bureau of Reclamation as not simply following a different policy from the Club's, but actually invading the national parks. It was easy to see who the enemy was and there was no question of defending an old ally and traditional friend, the Park Service, even with Drury gone. Soon after, cordial relations with the Park Service suffered a breach when negotiations over Mission 66 and the Tioga Road failed.

Conrad Wirth characterized the Club as an organization looking for a fight, an organization which turned against the Park Service when its leadership changed.[8] So too the Forest Service was soon alienated, and would remember an organization looking for a fight. By the late 1950s, in Forest Service circles, it appeared—in the words of one historian—that "although the Forest Service was not involved with the Dinosaur issue, it became identified with the whole 'giveaway-landgrab' image that Bernard DeVoto and Brower had fastened onto public resource agencies."[9]

Perhaps, as Martin Litton has said, any effective organization will be known by the enemies it makes.[10] Before the war, nobody in the Club would have said such a thing. Even in the early 1950s neither the Club nor Brower, its most prominent spokesman, set out to make enemies in the Forest Service.

Nor did the Club react to the service as an agency, at least in the beginning. It began, as it had with the Park Service, to question the wisdom of certain policy decisions applied to particular lands. In this process it found that unfortunately it could not maintain friendly relations, except at the expense of real issues. On the other hand, in the 1950s, when Mc-Carthyism cast suspicion on everyone's patriotism, public servants were particularly and understandably sensitive; they resented being tested. Nevertheless, the Club did regret the willingness of the Forest Service to decrease its already dwindling wilderness. The Club began to act more aggressively in its defense of forests threatened with cutting.

Because it wanted to meet the "Big Program" of McArdle's Forest Service, the Club advanced toward its own Forest Service policy, advocating a Scenic Resources Review to counteract the Forest Service's Timber Resources Review, and expending increasing effort on a wilderness bill. It became involved in the protection of newly appreciated areas such as the North Cascades in Washington state and the Three Sisters in Oregon. It became involved not simply in local issues in areas where its members, still most familiar with the Sierra, knew the country, but increasingly in areas across the nation, hoping to deal with as many issues as possible on the level of policy. But every place worth protecting had its own individual needs. The Dinosaur controversy, conducted on the level of policy, was not the full victory it might have been had the Club known the country better; so in the future the Club would have to reach out beyond itself, allying itself with local people and organizations, developing a grass-roots constituency across the country, particularly in the Pacific Northwest. An infusion of newly active members who came from beyond the San Francisco Bay Area, people like Michael McCloskey, Grant McConnell, and Dave Simons, were drawn to the Club because of its new militancy at Dinosaur. Some new activists, like Edgar Wayburn, discovered they now had a role to play in the Club, though they had joined many years previously.

Three
Sisters
1951–1955

As Michael McCloskey remembers, when Richard McArdle became chief of the Forest Service the first thing he set out to do was to review all of the Forest Service Primitive Areas, beginning with Three Sisters, in Oregon. Could this review mean the end of Forest Service wilderness? Trying to predict the future from the past, conservationists remembered that the Forest Service, which had always been commodity oriented, was reluctant even in the 1920s to make irreversible decisions for wilderness that might prevent users from drawing upon resources.[11] Nevertheless, beginning with the Gila Wilderness in 1924, it had administratively reserved millions of acres of wilderness under the bureaucratic categories of Research Reserves, Primitive Areas, and Wilderness. Established under the Forest Service's L-20 Regulation, a Primitive Area could be decreed by the chief of the Forest Service "for purposes of public education and recreation." A Primitive Area could, unfortunately, have its designation changed at any time. Even while retaining its designation, it could be logged.[12]

Actually, the Forest Service plan for upping the cut at the Three Sisters preceded McArdle's appointment as chief on July 1, 1952. In 1951 the Forest Service was trying to decide how much area it would withdraw in the lower-altitude sections of Three Sisters Primitive Area, and where to draw the new boundary. The first word to the Sierra Club came from Olaus Murie of The Wilderness Society, who argued, after a visit in the summer of 1951, that one entire drainage, called Horse Creek, not be withdrawn from the Primitive Area on the grounds of its scientific and aesthetic value.[13] The Forest Service considered making the creek itself a boundary for the area, logging one side of the valley and leaving the other "pristine." Since a natural boundary in this area, as in almost all mountainous watersheds, would be at the ridgeline, the only reason for such a strange decision could be economic gain. Further word came, in September of 1951, that the Forest Service would eliminate a substantial portion—about a fifth—of the Three Sisters Primitive Area, but promised to add approximately equivalent other Primitive Areas in Oregon.[14]

For Michael McCloskey (b. 1934), Three Sisters, where he learned to hike and climb, was like his own back yard.[15] McCloskey was to play a prominent role in Sierra Club affairs, first in the Northwest, then serving as conservation director, and finally becoming executive director after Brower's resignation in 1969. In 1951, while studying at Harvard, he also followed events back West through local publications sent from Oregon. The Forest Service's actions at Three Sisters and elsewhere led McCloskey to conclude that the new graduates of forestry schools had "an overwhelming commitment to manipulation and management, and had this stubborn streak of self-confidence. . . . They really lacked much sensitivity to environmental values."[16] As McCloskey remembers, the term "wilderness on the rocks," meaning wilderness for rocks only, got coined during reclassification of the Three Sisters.[17]

McCloskey climbed mountains but was not a rock climber. He had learned the true spiritual value of an old-growth forest while reveling in the forests, being swallowed up in the green wilderness. As he said, he "went away to college in the early 1950s feeling secure in the knowledge that all this would endure," but "the Forest Service had become a timber sales agency. . . . Recreationists could have the high country—that portion of it that was not good for pulping, grazing, or pumice mining; in other words, whatever part of it that was not good for anything else."[18] He saw the rise of "industrial foresters," and something deeper. "Beneath a windy self-righteousness," he later wrote, "I then discovered the bitter

truth about Pinchot: from the beginning forestry meant logging, and Pinchot's essential quest was 'how to make it
pay.'"[19] In the 1950s it was beginning to pay for timber men
who turned from their own lands to the national forests.
McCloskey believed that the Forest Service planned to serve
the timber interests, that the only kind of wilderness it was
interested in preserving was that part with no economic potential; its management policy constituted a decisive event
for his own developing conservation conscience.[20] Interested
in a career in politics, McCloskey would decide instead to
pursue a career in conservation.

For Edgar Wayburn (b. 1906), the reclassification of Three
Sisters had an equally major personal impact. Although he
had been a member of the Club since 1939, active in the Club
Conservation Committee and in the Bay Area Conservation
Committee, he had not yet devoted large amounts of his energy to conservation. Nor had the Club, at that time. Wayburn marks the decision to enter a national campaign over
Dinosaur as the "turning of the hinge."[21] After doing aviation
medicine research for the Air Force during the war and publishing several articles on his research, he had a promising career as a teacher, researcher, and medical practitioner. Yet he
gradually got "hooked into the conservation game," and
found himself devoting energy to it at the expense of his medical career.[22]

In 1951 he was sent as a Sierra Club representative to the
Federation of Western Outdoor Clubs. The federation was
composed of about thirty small outdoor clubs, mostly in the
Northwest. The Sierra Club's Conservation Committee
thought the federation should be a conservation organization, and believed Wayburn, a natural diplomat with his soft
southern accent, should transform it.

So the Sierra Club farmed him out, and he stuck his head
in the door, not intending to leave it in. "The delegates were
quarrelling—violently, I remember—about a place I knew
nothing about, the Three Sisters Primitive Area," he recalls.[23]

In 1952, at the federation's annual meeting, Wayburn was asked to serve as vice president and to investigate the pressing problem of the Primitive Area's boundaries. The next summer he and his wife Peggy—herself a writer and conservationist of distinction—went to Oregon. They walked around the Three Sisters Primitive Area, argued at night with the local Forest Service people, and came back convinced of the need to protect the entire Horse Creek watershed, to the ridgelines. That became the federation's stand as Wayburn assumed its presidency in 1953.

Edgar Wayburn had great respect for the Forest Service when he was young; he remembered trees the service had planted in his native Georgia during the era of reclamation. He was "brought up in conservation, if you will, partly by the Forest Service."[24] Now he believed that the service had changed from the custodial agency of his youth to a logging outfit in the 1950s.[25] He also noticed that, as an official of the federation, he was treated very cordially by Forest Service personnel as they escorted him on "show-me" trips, showing him only what they wanted him to see. He admired many foresters, he understood their point of view, he disagreed with them wholeheartedly; they were good individuals, but when they worked in the service, he "unfortunately found that the result collectively was pernicious."[26] In 1953, Assistant Chief Clare Hendee told him, over lunch, that "roading of the national forests was necessary to get their long-term timber management plan underway. Without it, things would be haphazard. It could be done in an orderly fashion once they got the roads through." What did this emphasis on roads mean? It "was evidence that even in 1953 the Forest Service had made up its mind pretty well on what it wanted as wilderness, and it was far less than we citizen conservationists wanted."[27]

In 1952 the Club was devoting the major part of its energy to the campaign for Dinosaur and had few members in Ore-

gon; it decided to support the federation's campaign to protect the section of Three Sisters which the Forest Service
wanted to log. The path toward such protection was confusing and littered with new terminology. The 53,000 acres west
of Horse Creek would be a Limited Area for the present,
which meant that the Forest Service was still preparing its
management plan. The Sierra Club board "urged that the
'limited' status be converted as soon as feasible to that designation which has the greatest stability, offers strongest protection against lumbering road-building, dams or commercial use or development and best assures that the area will
continue to be available for recreational and scientific purposes."[28] This was to advocate an opposite course from action
already taken by the Forest Service. The Forest Service had
no designation that could guarantee these things—and desired none.

Even under increasing disillusionment, the Club acted diplomatically. Charlotte Mauk, a twelve-year veteran on the
board, spoke to the federation in 1954. She hoped to take
advantage of the thirtieth anniversary of the first dedicated
Forest Service Wilderness—the Gila. Her tone was conciliatory toward the service. Because "we depend on the United
States Forest Service for custodianship of some of our
choicest primeval lands," and because "what has grown out
of [its] work has benefitted us more than we can measure,"
she suggested, "we should commend the Forest Service for
the wilderness policies it has established, and support it
strongly in every move whereby it can continue to administer
the lands under its jurisdiction so as to assure spiritual resources as well as material resources for the future." Perhaps
by reminding the Forest Service that "the wilderness we have
now is all we will ever have, and it has to last us forever," conservationists could emphasize the doctrine of "reciprocal irrevocability": developing economic resources within a wilderness is irrevocable; conversely, if "a certain area is

established as a wilderness, or a park, that ought to be an equally irreversible moral commitment to one particular use."[29]

Commending, pleading, reciprocating: this was the tone she—and the Club—would take for protecting the entire Horse Creek drainage at Three Sisters. She also suggested a case for the area in terms of natural boundaries, watershed units, serious loss of wilderness resource versus the minimal economic gain. Richard Leonard was enthusiastic about the commending, pleading, and reciprocating strategy. The next week, in mid September 1954, he traveled to a special thirty-year anniversary "show-me" tour of the Gila, where he, Howard Zahniser, and other conservationist celebrities discussed wilderness policy with the Forest Service. The Gila was a tribute to Aldo Leopold—his wilderness—and so they hoped the Forest Service would act upon Leopold's ideas. Leonard was encouraged by "the very progressive thinking of the Forest Service when you explain things to them."[30] As he remembered thirty years later, after cordial discussions with McArdle and regional foresters he came home with renewed faith in the "research forester," convinced "they will protect an area from an ecological point of view when they realize that newer and more modern thinking leads to that conclusion."[31] Leonard was not overly trusting; he also encouraged the Club's new Pacific Northwest Chapter to make itself felt at Forest Service hearings.[32] Still, many Club members apprehended an unavoidable philosophical conflict between lay or citizen conservationists and the Forest Service.

Any discussion of Forest Service management plans at Three Sisters led inexorably to a discussion on wilderness policy generally. Such a discussion ensued through the mails between David Brower and Richard McArdle.[33] Though an official correspondence, it was conducted on a "Dear Dick/ Dear Dave" basis. Brower had begun to distrust the Forest Service in 1940, convinced that bureaus had a tendency to

protect themselves rather than the resource they were supposed to protect; yet he began with the commending strategy.[34] He remembered attending a Forest Service conference
on wilderness on March 13, 1953, where McArdle had given
"the strongest statement on wilderness I have ever heard
from a public official."[35] But when Brower received in August
of 1955 the Forest Service's statement, "National Forest Wilderness Areas," he took issue with a paragraph which said
wilderness "represents the type of country which is suitable
for Wilderness and in which commercial values are slight.
This is in line with Forest Service policy of putting lands to
their highest use. . . ." Not only did such a statement contain
what Brower termed an "escape clause," but "this paragraph
forces the inference that wilderness is secure only so long as
its commercial values are slight." Brower thought the Forest
Service might be influenced by a "local perspective—of the
tendency of the region depending upon a timber economy to
see largely the dollar value of the trees, whereas the nation
must look at transcending nondollar values of the wilderness
forests." He reminded McArdle, "I don't think either Bob
Marshall or Aldo Leopold had any such escape clause in
mind or that the policy-making people of the Service have it
in mind either." So he pled, "Doesn't the Service feel the time
ripe for a stronger, more clearly delineated policy of wilderness that looks to the really long-range values of wilderness
as such?"[36] But no statement was forthcoming from the service that future decisions on wildnerness would be irrevocable.

Not only did McArdle consider such irrevocable decisions
contrary to the national welfare—"It was the policy in Marshall's and Leopold's time and there has been no change in
it"—but he said wilderness constituted only one form of recreational use, a "highly restrictive use, enjoyed by a comparatively small number of people." McArdle told Brower, "I
cannot agree with the implications which I read in your let-

ter, that wilderness areas should be set aside without first giving full consideration to other uses of the national forests. I
hardly think that you meant that."[37] So much for the concept
of "reciprocal irrevocability." The reclassification process
would continue, under the U-Regulations, and only when
wilderness represented "the highest form of public use"
would such regulations be applied.

Though Brower tried to reiterate the "areas of agreement
between the Chief Forester and our group of lay conservationists," nevertheless he expressed surprise at McArdle's adamance in "defining wilderness in terms of the *slightness of its
commercial value*."[38] He reported that the Club continued to
urge a more positive statement. Yet the chief forester's intent
to pursue a policy of "wilderness on the rocks," if really used
by the Forest Service, would be difficult to face with civility or
humor. There was to be no compromise on this issue for the
chief forester. Was the Sierra Club willing to compromise?
The question could only be answered with regard to a particular forest which grew at a place called Deadman Summit.

A few miles north of Mammoth Lakes, California *Deadman*
highway 395 winds through a volcanic area named 1952–1956
Deadman Summit or sometimes Mammoth Summit,
in the vicinity of Deadman Creek and Glass Creek. Growing
on this high plateau was a stand of Jeffrey pines, a small forest—perhaps 3,000 acres—yet one of the few virgin stands of
Jeffrey pines remaining in the West, and a part of Inyo National Forest. Because of the pumice soil and weather conditions prevailing on the east side of the range, this was an extremely slow-growing forest, and the trees stood in unique
parklike groves, ideally suited to picknicking, camping, and
other outdoor activities. A tourist driving north during the
summer from Los Angeles, after traversing more than three
hundred miles through the lower elevations, entered here his
first cool forest.

During the summer of 1952 John Haddaway, a resident of Mammoth Lakes, observed that the Forest Service had begun to cut timber in stands of Jeffrey pine, contrary to the previous practice of saving strips of forest along the highways. When he protested to the regional forester, he received a strange answer. The Forest Service, reconsidering its multiple-use plans for the area, which had in the 1920s named watershed protection and timbering as priorities, now believed that recreation would be the ultimate primary use of this forest.[39] However, a process called sanitary cutting was necessary to control rust and beetle infestations. By this time considerable timber had been cut at Glass Creek, and the same kind of operation was planned for Deadman Creek. The value of the timber itself was small, the lumber being useful only for packing boxes.

Investigating further, this local resident began to receive contradictory reports. One official said that the area was simply being managed with standard timber sales, and that preserving the pines would constitute a drastic change in approved plans for the area. A Forest Service entomologist, who was not aware of the controversy, reported that the forest was not diseased at all. When Haddaway discovered what the service had done to the Jeffrey pines at Glass Creek, he began to organize resistance by local residents to any future cutting in the area.

That October in San Francisco, a member of the Forest Service regional office delineated for the Club's Conservation Committee those areas in Inyo National Forest which would be used for sustained yield and would include timber sales, as opposed to areas which were being managed for recreation and would only have sanitary cutting of hazardous, dead, or diseased trees. Nevertheless, local residents of the Glass Creek area did not believe the service had established a clear or consistent policy for the area, and sent a representative to a meeting with Forest Service officials the next year. Brower attended, observed photographs of the lumbering already accomplished at Glass Creek and suspected that the Forest Service policy for the area was badly confused. He was thinking not only of the value of the Jeffrey pine forests and the devastation at Glass Creek, but of the precedent for policies in other forests, like those at Three Sisters.[40] Unofficially, as he remembers, he commented to Regional Forester Hendee that the problem could be solved if the service would stress first its own emphasis on recreation, would only remove trees hazardous to homes and campsites, would dispose of slash properly, and would leave virgin strips of forest 300 yards deep along the highway. Brower was assured not only that the Forest Service agreed, but that the service itself was unhappy with the cutting at Glass Creek, and would not allow a repetition of the errors there.

A few days later the Executive Committee of the board decided to send Brower to Deadman.[41] On this show-me trip, Brower remembers, his disillusionment with the Forest Service began in earnest. Not only was he appalled by the newsspeak of the service, which he later named "sawlog semantics"—a confusing, contradictory, or meaningless shifting of such terms as sanitary logging, recreational logging, heavy cut, or light cut—but he also suspected that justifications for logging, whether they were based on infestation, over maturity of a forest, or on economic considerations, were all specious. He noticed further that he got different reports on the Forest Service's plans, depending on which manager he talked to.

He was indignant at the way he was manipulated by the service on his trip because it tried to deceive him, and acted as if he could be deceived. In caution, he had arrived a day early and explored the area with John Haddaway. Then, he remembers, "the Forest Service on the following day showed me some very modest little piles [of cut timber], very carefully worked over, and said, 'this is what John Haddaway is complaining about.' Of course it wasn't. It was something they had tidied up for the little show-me tour."[42] On that day he learned that the same destructive lumbering would be done not only at Deadman Creek, but in Reds Meadow, outside of Devil's Postpile National Monument.

On December 20, 1954, Richard McArdle issued a policy statement indicating continued cutting for the area.[43] Soon after, Brower received an article on Deadman for the *Annual*, by Club member Hal Roth, which might constitute, in revised form, a response to McArdle. He proceeded to set Roth's piece in page proof and send copies to supporting organizations, including the American Forestry Association.[44] After reviewing all the contradictory statements and actions by the service, using the names of the officials involved, the article stated:

> Unless there is intrigue involved, the trouble arises from complete misunderstanding of recreational needs. . . . the Forest Service should set up a land use category in which certain areas set aside for recreation are completely excluded from timber production. . . . If the Forest Service cannot or will not formally commit itself to such a restriction in a recreational area, and should it not be possible for the Forest Service to eliminate power development and mining in these regions [big statement!], then the Sierra Club will seek necessary protection for such recreational areas from National Monument, National Parks, or state park status.[45]

At a time when conservationists supported the service in struggles with other interests, it was disappointing to have to protect recreational areas from the service itself. Though the article claimed that "we are not against legitimate lumber practices," it also endorsed the view of Hal. A. Herbert, who insisted at the American Forestry Congress in 1953 that conflict among uses under a multiple-use policy required priori-

ties, and probably some kind of zoning principle. This professor of forestry at Michigan State University found policies of
the service single-minded, and lamented that "foresters are
now trained to produce wood."

Included in Roth's article was a strongly worded draft appeal to Secretary of Agriculture Ezra Taft Benson to set aside
McArdle's policy decision on continued cutting. The appeal
spoke of a "history of misinformation and uncertain policy"
concerning the forests of Mammoth. It asked for a moratorium on logging of any kind at Deadman Creek, doubting the
ability of foresters to make decisions about recreation: "We
urge that you appoint an impartial umpire—outside of the
Forest Service—to investigate completely the whole Mammoth lakes lumbering and recreation situation."[46]

Brower claims he never intended to publish an article
stronger than he believed appropriate for the *Sierra Club Annual Bulletin*. He wanted to see some reaction inside and outside of the Club, and desired some personal accountability for
what he believed was an ethical issue. As planned, his distribution of page proofs stirred discussion within the Club, and
within allies like The Wilderness Society. He sent a copy of
the proofs to the American Forestry Association and he believes it ended up on the Forest Service's desk immediately.[47]

Why was such a turn of events significant? Brower felt that
the Forest Service wanted to discredit him, believed that immediately after his trip to Mammoth the Forest Service
people had told several Sierra Club directors that "Dave
Brower doesn't want any trees cut at all," though he never
said any such thing.[48] So he designed the distribution of
proofs as a test not only to determine the strength of Mc-
Ardle's resolve, but to find out which side the Forestry Association was on. He may even have liked the idea of an un-
stated, secret threat being passed to the Forest Service.
Determining who was a friend and who an enemy and passing secret information was not unusual during that year

when he was also busy providing and receiving secret information for the campaign to discredit the Bureau of Reclamation's plans in Dinosaur. But was the Forest Service also an
enemy, or more important, should Club policy assume that it
was? Should there be a battle between Brower and McArdle?

Relations between conservation organizations and the Forest
Service were particularly sensitive not only because the
Sierra Club and The Wilderness Society were beginning the
long campaign for a wilderness bill, but because multiple use
was coming under increasing scrutiny by conservationists.
Meanwhile the Forest Service continued to believe recreation to be compatible with timber management through the
use of sanitation logging.[49] When Edgar Wayburn later visited Mammoth Summit he saw "tree after tree marked" for
cutting, with more and more marked the further into the forest he walked. This, as he remembered, "firmed up in my
mind that condoning the apparent protection of a forest
along the road should always be avoided. It is the conservationist's job to expose the public to the worst right away."
When he returned, after the logging had been done, he was
"saddened to look at it."[50]

Richard Leonard agreed that the Mammoth area was of
great scenic value and knew that it would not recover, but
like Wayburn made allowances for Forest Service policy, "according to its lights," and never impugned the motives of its
personnel. As he remembered the situation, it was institutional, not local; "because the Forest Service in Washington
ordered every forest to cut a percentage of the total timber,
the Inyo National Forest had to cut that particular amount."[51]
McArdle said as much when he announced in December
1954 that business would continue as usual: "The Deadman
Creek drainage contains about one-fifth of the timber area of
the Owens River Working Circle which is operable under average market conditions."[52]

Brower wanted to light a fire, but others feared more than the Forest Service would be burned. Wayburn did not object to Roth's article if it remained a pamphlet, "an unpublished expression of strong feeling on the part of many conservationists." In the notes to his own copy of the confidential draft he wrote, however, "I believe that the publication of this brochure in its present form could do lasting harm to the relations of the Sierra Club and U.S.F.S. and thus prove most damaging to the course of conservation it desires to uphold." He felt that the article suggested "deliberate deception on the part of various F.S. employees," which he never believed. Particularly worried that "personalities as well as principles have become issues," he wrote, "I feel that the battles in the Three Sisters and other reclassification areas are endangered if the Sierra Club establishes itself as an 'outsider' in this controversy."[53] The Club could continue to negotiate with the regional managers, since no more logging would be done before the early summer of 1955. Wayburn's view was taken by the board of directors as a whole, which requested Brower to "discuss it further" with the Forest Service.[54]

Leonard's response to Roth's draft article—as he remembers it—was a good deal more vigorous. He believed that the local people, led by Haddaway and encouraged by Brower, impugned the integrity of the local forest ranger, the forest supervisor, the regional forester, and even the chief of the Forest Service, accusing them of accepting bribes to log the area.[55] Leonard believed that the accusations were libelous and advised Brower not to publish or distribute them. He further believed that the distribution of the article was a manifestation of Brower's distrust, an increasing belief that "the enemy," in this case the Forest Service, would get him by turning the board of directors against him.[56]

Leonard's response was rooted partly in his general assessment of the Forest Service, which "has done an excellent job and has been completely sincere in leadership in trying to provide good wilderness policy and good grazing and good timber policies."⁵⁷ His sharpest criticism has been that the Forest Service was sometimes "short sighted" in its view of recreational matters.⁵⁸ If he seemed to be defending the Forest Service against the Sierra Club, it was because he preferred traditional close personal relationships with Forest Service personnel and saw Brower as threatening those relationships. It was a point of pride with Leonard that he had known the two men who served as chiefs of the Forest Service since 1943. Even though he knew that "any forester can make an excuse for logging any tree he wants," he felt that accusing foresters of making such excuses was damaging to all concerned.⁵⁹ Most of all, it was damaging to what Brower called "the Bohemian Club Diplomacy" which the Club had always used.⁶⁰

Leonard preferred a personal and conversational style of negotiation with the heads of federal agencies. Leonard was not above passing confidential information about the directors of agencies to other conservationists, but he thought that public accusations were another thing altogether. Like Bestor Robinson, he did not object to the "basic philosophy of the greatest good for the greatest number with fairly strong governmental control" when he found it held by such people as McArdle or Marion Clawson, director of the Bureau of Land Management.⁶¹ Indeed, he continued to believe that the Club's strength depended on the friends it could keep in agencies, even if that required accommodating philosophies unlike or even conflicting with those of the Club. Leonard remained particularly sympathetic to the situation of public servants: "As I told Dave, and maybe I shouldn't have told him, public bodies normally cannot afford to challenge matters of this kind because if you start fighting with a skunk pretty soon you start smelling like a skunk."⁶² To extend his own metaphor, Leonard feared that Brower's big stink would taint not only the Forest Service and its administrators, but also the public image of individuals on the Club's board.

Precisely because he was capable of making a big stink, Brower's ascendent power in the Club troubled Leonard. One history of the Forest Service written in 1976 states that "McArdle and Brower assumed the top positions in their respective organizations at about the same time."[63] That was not an impression which Leonard—or any of the board—was pleased to anticipate, since the board, not Brower, made Club policy. As Brower himself stated more than once, the board occupied the top position in the Club. Nevertheless, Alex Hildebrand notes that in the early 1950s, while Brower was growing to be a "thorn in the side" for personnel in the Forest Service, he was also to a great extent the one officer involved in close relationships with the government officials.[64] Other Club officers receded into the background.

Brower was not alone in his view of the Forest Service. When Hal Roth finally wrote an extended letter to Secretary Benson, Martin Litton labeled his copy of the Roth letter "My Forest Service indictment file."[65]

The board took up the Mammoth forests not only because of the importance of the area, but for the sake of relations between the Club and the Forest Service. Wayburn, Bradley, and Hildebrand participated in show-me tours of the area. Roth and Brower enlisted Horace Albright to write directly to Richard McArdle.

As past director of the National Park Service, and as a local resident from the east side of the Sierra, Horace Albright carried credentials that made him more than a concerned citizen. When he wrote to McArdle on March 9, 1955 about the December 20, 1954 policy statement, he was diplomatic. In return, McArdle lectured him on "the fundamental difference in our thinking."[66] Albright replied, "I have, of course, great admiration for the Forest Service and its personnel and policies, and I know that basically every move you make you intend to be in the broad public interest. . . . But still you are going to let them do some chopping in part of my boyhood country!"[67] Though national parks might include virgin timber as a proper setting for public recreation areas, this could not be the case for the Forest Service, which needed to manage the area for more than one use. The Forest Service would be providing for "mass recreational use," McArdle insisted. "I know that this, too, may not please some few people, but our obligation is to the larger number."[68]

Further, McArdle argued in the same letter, "the extravagant statements made about this area have materially weakened the force of arguments to protect areas with more outstanding scenic and similar values." McArdle spoke with equanimity of the challenge to his decision by the Hal Roth article. He did not know whether it would be published; "however, it did cause us to again review the decision very carefully, and I have discussed it with Dave Brower."

A month later, in May 1955, the regional forester for California reported to Edgar Wayburn on management plans for the Deadman Creek Recreation Area. As chair of the Club's Conservation Committee, Wayburn passed on the letter, indicating that he interpreted the statement to mean that the area would be managed as a recreational resource, that the Forest Service intended "to survey the area specifically from the long range recreational point of view," and "to consult with conservation organizations on the ground before further action is taken."[69]

While Club members consulted with the Forest Service, the area around Deadman Creek was logged. Still, through its silence, the Club suggested that a compromise had been reached. If the virgin forest had been lost, a new Forest Service policy, on paper, had been gained. It appeared to Wayburn that making a stink had brought results, since the Club received from McArdle's office a tentative policy on Timber Stand Management in Recreation Areas, "a major victory in the recognition of the importance of recreation in overall F.S. policy. I don't believe any one of us can be unhappy with the explicit details as well as the general statements expressed. And this is probably the result of the Deadman Creek contro-

versy!"[70] The board formally commended the Forest Service
on its new recreational policy.[71]

Alex Hildebrand, Harold Bradley, and Edgar Wayburn visited Deadman Summit during the next year and were convinced that the Forest Service was finally on the right track.
Brower read their reports with dissatisfaction, and wrote, "I
hope the club will oppose the Forest Service plan." He wished
to force the Forest Service not only to administer lands for
recreation, but to preserve them as wilderness. The forest at
Deadman constituted "the finest sample in virgin state of the
finest Jeffrey pine forest anywhere," though he conceded that
"it won't be big wilderness by the definition we use. But small
wilderness needs protection and the Forest Service has not
yet developed a policy to protect it. It should do so." Brower
continued his argument in ecological terms, pointing out
that sanitary logging interfered with natural succession in
the forest. He concluded that the Forest Service administrators "have only modified their timber management instructions. A gain, yes, but not if it stops our effort toward seeking
the real and essential cure."[72]

A year later, in July 1956, the Executive Committee of the
board, with the advice of Martin Litton, Edgar Wayburn, and
David Brower, reconsidered what the Forest Service meant
by recreation at Deadman. Brower pointed out that the Forest Service was still planning to cut as much as ever, 25 to 30
percent of the trees. He read a letter from Charlotte Mauk,
who feared compromise. Litton "vigorously contended that
[the service's] kind of 'intensive' recreational use would
harm the area scenically and would impair its emotional appeal to the very visitors who are being planned for." He and
Brower still hoped that the remnant forest could be left, at
least in back areas, as old growth, virgin. The Executive Committee agreed. But for areas designated as recreational, Leonard argued, there was no escaping reality, which included
roads and facilities; recreational management was inevitable.
Leonard therefore endorsed sanitary logging in "intensive

use areas," since failure to distinguish between recreation and wilderness would only harm the wilderness concept. The Executive Committee agreed.[73]

The Hal Roth article was never published; an article on Deadman appeared in the October 1956 *Bulletin*, written by Edgar and Peggy Wayburn.[74] It was, like Peggy Wayburn's article on Butano Forest that year, a postmortem examination, a requiem for "an exquisite island of near-wilderness," now gone. Peggy Wayburn argued that at Butano "we did not go 'all out' in our efforts . . . . We did not follow through on our efforts, . . . We assumed too much . . . left the fate of Butano in the hands of others."[75] The same could be said for Deadman. When Edgar and Peggy Wayburn tried to answer the question, What is the stand of the Sierra Club? they could only state that after much thought, soul-searching, and intensive on-the-scene study, the Club approved zoning Deadman Creek for recreational use, approved the Forest Service timber management plan "for 'preparation' of the *heavily used areas* in a recreational zone" (Wayburns' italics), yet still questioned the same plan if applied in areas of less intense use. A "doubt clause" stated that "the Sierra Club Board has serious doubts as to the wisdom or necessity of the degree of cutting of the Forest Service, at least at this time."[76] But doubts, coming so late, were yet a shadow of Brower's plea to seek "a real and essential cure." The Wayburns' unanswered questions—"Did we actually make proper disposition of the area? Should the pattern set here be followed extensively?"—pointed not merely at the Forest Service, but at the policies of the Club itself.

As they reviewed the situation and tried to justify the Club's compromising position, the Wayburns insisted that "the fate of Deadman Creek is important not only in itself, but for the pattern it is setting [because] in considering the fate of Deadman Creek, it is necessary to understand what the Forest Service is." The Forest Service, charged with the custody of much of the wilderness in America and besieged "by increasing demands of economic and recreational growth," was now making plans for the disposition of many of its remaining undeveloped areas. The Wayburns pointed out that "much of the Forest Service land which we enjoy so much in its primitive state is already in a 'timber working circle,' or may fall within one some time in the near future, and so is subject to be cut eventually." The Forest Service was "far more than a timber-managing bureau," yet "according to its policy of 'multiple use,' the timber management of a Recreational Area was entirely proper." Under its own policy, in an area zoned for recreation, "sooner or later, every tree growing on it will be harvested for the sawmill."

This prospect for Forest Service recreational lands was a consequence of the structure and function of the agency. When Wayburn, Hildebrand, and Bradley visited Deadman during June of 1956, they were "convinced that the trees [to be cut] had been marked with conscientious care." Yet, the Wayburns asked, "Is it really our privilege to make *all* the irrevocable decisions now? Just what kind of wilderness heritage are we leaving for our children—and theirs?" The Club would soon challenge the mission and philosophy of the Forest Service, and the very basis of its institutional being.

Suspicions about the Forest Service were confirmed *Scenic* by James P. Gilligan's doctoral dissertation, written *Resources* for the University of Michigan in 1954.[77] Gilligan, as Brower remembers, indicated that "the Forest Service *1956–1957* looked upon wilderness as a temporary designation, to keep forests out of other hands . . . until they were ready to log."[78] Administrative protection was designedly temporary.

Early in 1956, when Brower proposed to the board a Scenic Resources Review as a way of counteracting the Forest Service's commitment to its utilitarian Timber Resources Review, he believed that by the year 2000, in light of population trends, automation, increasing leisure time, and improved transportation, "there will be more and more people to share less and less recreation area."[79] The Scenic Resources Review was a positive step, Brower thought; it suggested that conservationists wanted to make something, not just attack utilitarian doctrines. Even Robinson was enthusiastic about the idea. As he noted, the government was busy with all kinds of reports and reviews, and the Club ought to be able to slide this one in. Brower's idea would evolve over the next five years, and would finally be realized in the Outdoor Recreation Resources Review Commission (ORRRC) created by Congress in 1958. James Gilligan would direct an ORRRC study on wilderness and recreation, and would be active at the Club wilderness conferences in 1963 and 1965, chairing the 1967 conference.

For the 1956 *Annual* Brower wrote a lead article, "Scenic Resources for the Future."[80] The inventory of our recreational resources, he thought, should consist of five steps, answering five questions: 1. What do we have? 2. How much space will we need? 3. Who else needs space? 4. What are the conflicts for space? 5. Who needs the space most? To conduct the inventory, he suggested a presidential or congressional commission, a federal review, free of local or state interests. Brower's *Annual* turned toward conservation matters, orchestrated with photographs by Philip Hyde, an article by Hyde which lamented the condition of western lands not protected in parks and preserves, and a broadside by Grant McConnell, political scientist from the University of Chicago. McConnell wrote of "The Cascades Wilderness."[81] Although he did not know what administrative status—park or wilderness— could best protect the North Cascades, nevertheless Mc- Connell concluded with a critique of the Forest Service's policy of multiple use: "There is no question here of the good will of the Forest Service, many of whose officers have been drawn to their profession by a spirit of dedication. However, they are torn by the need for economic development and the demands of politically minded entrepreneurs." Though McConnell called the multiple-use policy "one of the genuine glories in the management of natural resources set forth by any nation"—a phrase which might make Brower blanch—he also argued that it was simply outdated. A place like the North Cascades needed to be zoned for its highest purpose, exploitation firmly excluded. Such places were not even playgrounds, McConnell argued, but sanctuaries. As for multiple use, it "can be made relevant for the needs of today only if it is refounded on a determination to preserve the values that are essential to a healthy civilization and on a recognition that all values cannot be mixed without the extinction of some by others." Clearly, the coordinated arguments of McConnell, Hyde, and Brower were directed toward administrative discretion in the disposition of wilderness.

The next Sierra Club *Annual* appeared only six months later, and was devoted almost entirely to material drawn from the fifth Biennial Wilderness Conference of 1957, held in March.[82] With the Dinosaur campaign off his desk, Brower brought the thinking of the conferences into the mainline purview of the Club. George Marshall, the younger brother of Robert Marshall and editor of The Wilderness Society's *Living Wilderness*, reviewed the changing concerns of the biennial conferences.[83] He believed that significant progressive steps had been taken. The first conference in 1949 simply laid groundwork; the second, in 1951, recognized that "whatever threatens a wilderness in the Sierra is essentially the same as what threatens unaltered lands in any other part of the world." The third conference, in 1953, was "characterized by a search for ways to express the value of wilderness in noncommercial terms [so that] the aesthetic and spiritual worth of wild country is recognized." This conference also began to discuss the use of urban parks for starting wilderness education. The fourth, in 1955, began to press for administrative policy on managing wilderness and discussed ways of writing up appropriate legislation to preserve it. The fifth, in March 1957, had tried to link the ideas of a recreational resources review and a wilderness system, since the first draft of legislation creating a National Wilderness Preservation System had been introduced in 1956 to the Eighty-fourth Congress, by Hubert Humphrey and John P. Saylor.

It had been tradition to conduct a voice vote on recommendations at the end of a wilderness conference. Though the meaning of this vote was ambiguous and the representatives from federal agencies were not required to commit themselves, these resolutions reflected Club priorities for the rest of the decade.[84] It was no surprise that the 1957 conference recommended a recreational review, and expressed explicit support for the 1956 wilderness bill's main points: that its application be continental in scope, that lands appropriate for wilderness be protected until the bill became effective, that the bill provide clear legislative bases for protection, and that the bill articulate a national wilderness policy and the meaning of wilderness values, and provide maximum protection. Other resolutions called for protection for what would later be called de facto wilderness; mining, roads, and air access should be denied for areas which might be designated as wilderness as a result of new legislation.

For someone who was not watching the progress and direction of the Club, the rest of the recommendations might be surprising. Most concerned wilderness in Alaska, Oregon (Three Sisters), and Washington (North Cascades and the Olympics). Most of these lands were administered by the Forest Service and Bureau of Land Management. All of these lands were outside California. The board and Brower were not dilatory in recognizing these new priorities.

Priorities   When, at the 1957 Wilderness Conference, A. Starker
1957   Leopold tried to account for the changing relation-
               ships between American culture and wilderness, he
found the unlikely progress of the wilderness idea surprising, and perhaps inexplicable. "One would have supposed that appreciation of wild country would have emerged first in some overpopulated region where wilderness was at a pre-

mium." The situation was quite the opposite. As ideas about national parks evolved, he found, first geological features were valued, then native animal life of "good" species, with the idea that parks were outdoor zoos. "In short, the national parks as preserves of unmanaged nature did not spring forth in full bloom." The idea of wilderness parks came long after the parks were created. Yet the movement seemed to be maturing. America needed wilderness not solely for recreation or even education and science, but out of "the moral conviction that it is right—that we owe it to ourselves and to the good earth that supports us to curb our avarice to the extent of leaving a few spots untouched and unexploited."[85]

That was the positive side of the movement. On the negative side there were growing reports of doom if wilderness was not preserved. Already William Vogt's *The Road to Survival* (1948) and Fairfield Osborn's *Our Plundered Planet* (1948), the first modern books on the danger of population growth, had been published and read.[86] More were coming. Perhaps the most important event of the decade was a June 1956 conference, "Man's Role in Changing the Face of the Earth," attended by the world's most eminent geographers and biologists. As if their findings warranted haste, the University of Chicago published the proceedings by the end of the year.[87] Lowell Sumner—the career Park Service biologist whose knowledge of ecology would have an increasing influence on Club policy—noted, "They produced 1200 pages of staggering evidence that the results of man's activities are now comparable in magnitude to those of major climatic, ecological, and geographical forces."[88] The cochairmen of the conference were Carl Sauer, Marston Bates, and Lewis Mumford. For geographers and humanists, Lewis Mumford found the scientific content suggested a moral when he concluded the proceedings: "Only when love takes the lead will the earth, and life on earth, be safe again. And not until then."[89]

Lowell Sumner began to express the findings of modern ecology at the 1957 Wilderness Conference. In his talk "Are

Beavers Too Busy?" he spoke of population pressure and the condition of modern man: *"more people, more complications, more stress."*[90] These conditions underlined the urgency of protecting relatively wild areas, he thought, not only for the therapeutic value of wilderness in preventing stress, but for human health generally. He referred to pollution and population dynamics. At the same conference A. Starker Leopold restated the philosophy of his father, Aldo, and Grant McConnell began to apply these ideas to a political critique of the Forest Service. What they had to say would lead the Club toward an ideology which could be distilled into two slogans. "The wilderness holds answers to more questions than we yet know how to ask," written by Nancy Newhall, came directly from the "This Is the American Earth" exhibit of 1955 and led to the resolution for Basic Wilderness Protection passed at the 1957 Wilderness Conference.[91] The other slogan spoke to the negative effects of growth and progress: "Not blind opposition to progress, but opposition to blind progress." This one was Brower's.[92] The negative slogan not only expressed lack of faith in agencies, but at bottom asserted that bureaus like the Forest Service had been captured by economic interests.

By devoting more than 90 percent of the 1957 *Annual* to the proceedings of the Wilderness Conference, Brower drew the Club into the mainstream of conservation. No more did the philosophy of wilderness get discussed at board meetings; in 1957, at least, it was debated in a public meeting, with 400 people attending. Ideas were being generated by a broad constituency. Who spoke for the Club in the 1957 *Annual*? Certainly loyal and long-standing members like Lowell Sumner, David Brower, and A. Starker Leopold. But the strength of their ideas rather than their position on the board gave them the right to speak. In many cases they had professional authority. In that context, in an age of ecology, the influence of Aldo Leopold would overshadow that of Will Colby, or perhaps even John Muir.

By publishing the resolutions of the conference, was

Brower, in essence, allowing the Wilderness Conference to make policy for the Club? Perhaps. He was prepared not only to publish the results of the 1957 conference, he was also prepared to take the message where it would do the most good, to the Northwest, and to the Forest Service, against whom these policies were directed.

If, as he hoped, recent decisions of the board and the Wilderness Conference gave him a mandate, then first of all the Club would center its attention on the Northwest, where logging was the greatest immediate threat; it would take a stand against the road building which preceded logging, resist mining interests in the forests, and try to prevent the use of administrative discretion in the disposal of wilderness by the Forest Service. Brower had proposed the Scenic Resources Review not only to give voice for recreational use of public land, but also to provide temporary protected status for any lands of "probably high scenic, recreational, and scientific potential." As the 1957 conference resolutions made clear, the Scenic Resources Review was not to be misinterpreted as a substitute for a wilderness bill or any legislation to protect wilderness, but was to be a holding action until a wilderness bill could be passed, a survey to guarantee that no worthy wilderness would be passed over. This was in line with Brower's personal feeling that Glen Canyon was being lost because nobody knew what it was. If the conservationists got a wilderness act and Scenic Resources Review, the Club's argument suggested, then there would be no resistance to multiple use and administrative discretion on other lands. One can see in this the old principle of Muir: let the "improved" lands—like Yosemite Valley—be managed by managers, but let the wild lands—like Hetch Hetchy—remain unmanaged. Conservationists supposed that such an arrangement would have worked sixty years earlier in Yosemite National Park if the institutional protection of Hetch Hetchy had been strong enough and more people had known the place.

Armed with the resolutions of the 1957 Wilderness Conference and decisions of the board to wage a campaign over the North Cascades and the Three Sisters, armed with the consensus that the Club was going to devote itself to a two-pronged effort for Scenic Resources Review and a wilderness bill, Brower would not simply give out general releases explaining the resolutions of the Wilderness Conference.[93] Feeling that McArdle and Regional Forester J. Herbert Stone in the Northwest were obdurate, he would take his message higher, to Ervin L. Peterson, an assistant secretary of agriculture who had appeared interested in wilderness, and would also take his message down the bureaucratic line, to the mid-level Forest Service supervisors.

Brower's letter to Peterson insisted that irreversible action by the Forest Service to destroy wilderness in the Three Sisters was premature, given the uncompleted studies on recreation commissioned by the Forest Service, given the lack of knowledge about present needs (carrying capacity) of wilderness, and given the lack of knowledge about the amount of wilderness needed in the future.[94] All of this was keyed to a public statement Peterson had made on managing the boundaries between wilderness and commercial interests. Brower assumed that Peterson had already heard from McArdle on the subject, McArdle having "contributed skillfully" to the 1957 Wilderness Conference.

In that same week in April 1957 Brower spoke to a forest supervisors' meeting in Portland, Oregon, on open-mindedness.[95] After reading several statements on the value of wilderness, he indicated that he did not know how much the group might be willing to agree with, and that he had been told that McArdle expected them not to agree with everything he would say, but that probably all foresters in the Forest Service did not agree with each other. Then he identified his statements as belonging to foresters working for the Forest Service ten years previously. Clearly Brower wanted to break up the monolithic ideological unanimity of the Forest

Service. Like Wayburn, he believed that the Sierra Club's message was most likely to be heard by the lower echelon, younger employees who had not yet been fully indoctrinated, and who had perhaps joined the service because they loved forests. What he had to say to these men amounted to a history lesson, revisionist though it may have been. When he concluded his speech with a discourse on the Sierra Club's conservationist role, multiple use, and wilderness, he revealed his own hopes for the Club's future role.

According to Brower, the Sierra Club had been practicing conservation for sixteen years before the word became popular. The Club had never been directly concerned with the economics of resource conservation, its specialty being the preservation of scenery in national parks, national forests, and wilderness, even state and local parks, with a deep interest in the wildlife that made those places complete. What followed was a most surprising statement: "Whether justifiably or not, those who work for conservation of natural scenery and wildlife have come to be known as conservationists, a term which excludes people who have a role in managing a resource for profit, even though they may conserve it in doing so." He took care to portray the Club as no hiking organization, given a "pronounced rise in the number who support the club solely to further its public-service program." The Club had placed "special emphasis on wilderness preservation in the last quarter century" because wilderness was "the most precious of our scenic possessions . . . if nature does something, there is a good reason for it, and it is ecologically right." He added that wilderness preservation "is least likely to get support from the branch of conservation devoted to resource management. And it can never be replaced if the resource managers covet it successfully."

Characterizing a certain kind of forester who believed that "nature never does anything right," Brower characterized himself as a "mere urban conservationist" who was "aware enough of resource-management needs to preserve wilderness from management." He was using the same strategy of argument that he had used with the Bureau of Reclamation, offering up a kind of ninth-grade forestry which caught the professionals in contradictions.

In that light he had several questions about Forest Service policy, the chief one being, "Hasn't the phrase 'in the long run' been omitted from quite a few publications lately?" This was especially significant in view of the age of the Forest Service (52 years) in relation to the time needed to determine the results of its actions (250–350 years). Wilderness was about the long run, so was conservation, and that was what the Sierra Club had always stood for.

According to his own press release—which Brower wrote before he left San Francisco—his appearance in Oregon was prompted by an attack the year before by W. F. McCulloch, the dean of forestry at Oregon State College, who spoke of "urban bird-watchers, the daffodil wing of nature-lovers," the "conservation-shouters," "fanatic 'preservers,'" "single-track recreationists," and "urban conservation do-gooders."[96] The title of Brower's press release, "Sierra Club Official Urges New Look At National Forest Uses," indicated that the Club was prepared to look up the coast and involve itself in matters pertaining to the Northwest.

When Senator Wayne Morse of Oregon placed Brower's talk in the *Congressional Record* on May 17, 1957, saying that like Brower he preferred the term "coordinate use" to "multiple use," Morse made the critique of multiple use a part of the campaign for the wilderness bill.

Simons and McConnell Brower was establishing a network of people who were prepared to do something, a "brain trust" made up of historians, political scientists, ecologists, men like Grant McConnell, A. Starker Leopold, James Gilligan. In addition to this team of academic consultants, he also attracted a group of new young people. By September of 1957 he would acquire an administrative assistant, Bob Golden. Later he would surround himself with more young professionals, including Hugh Nash, who came to edit the *Bulletin*. Most interesting among the new young men was Dave Simons, who represented what the new Club might become.

For Simons, the Club had a new set of opportunities as a result of developments in the Northwest. Though they lasted only until his premature death in 1960, his contributions earned him the right to judge the Club. To a great extent, policy regarding the North Cascades and to a lesser extent policy on the Three Sisters was developed through a constant four-cornered discussion among Brower (director of campaigns), who was interested in the Cascades and Forest Service matters; Wayburn (diplomat), chair of the Conservation Committee, who was also interested in the North Cascades but was worried that confrontation with the Forest Service would jeopardize the wilderness bill; Simons (lover of Northwest forests), who knew the country of the North Cascades and Three Sisters well; and McConnell (political scientist), who was from the Northwest and knew the politics and policies of the Forest Service.

Although the Club had created a Northwest Chapter in 1954, the task had been difficult; only 91 Club members lived in Washington and Oregon in 1953.[97] At first, the board probably thought that the chapter would simply carry its policy into the provinces, as when Richard Leonard wrote to Pat Goldsworthy in January of 1955 that the Pacific Northwest Chapter could be valuable at public hearings on the Three Sisters.[98] When the board discussed the North Cascades at the end of 1955, Brower and Wayburn recommended that the Sierra Club "should start now to become acquainted with the local situation and organize facts and views in support of the preservation of the maximum wilderness area."[99]

The Club made its first trips to Glacier Peak in 1956, in the

North Cascades. There the Wayburns met Jane and Grant McConnell.[100] Later that summer Brower came out on another trip. Immediately convinced of the value of the North Cascades wilderness, Brower and the Wayburns commissioned Philip Hyde to take a series of photographs of the Glacier Peak area. There was no time to wait for a Scenic Resources Review in the North Cascades. Brower and McConnell raised a small amount of money to support some work by nineteen-year-old Dave Simons, a native of Springfield, Oregon. Simons would spend his twentieth summer backpacking and photographing in the North Cascades, using the McConnell cabin as a base. He had much to learn as a photographer, and picked up what he could from Hyde. At the end of 1956, McConnell wrote a piece for the annual *Bulletin* on "the nation's finest alpine area and one of its most untouched primeval regions," illustrated with Hyde photographs of the North Cascades.[101]

But the area itself was so vast and so complex that the real work would be done by Simons over the next few years. Between summers, while at school in Berkeley, Simons began to consider the possibilities for preserving the North Cascades. What kind of scenic resource protection would be best? he wondered. He wrote to Zahniser, suggesting a national park, but Zahniser replied that the wilderness bill offered the best chance for preserving Forest Service land in the North Cascades.[102] Simons wrote to Olaus Murie and Murie wrote a careful letter detailing his disillusionment with National Park Service administration of wilderness.[103] Yet McConnell, ever pragmatic, warned Simons that the wilderness bill was an unknown quantity; nobody could guarantee its passage, its final wording, or what it would mean in practice.[104]

By the beginning of 1957 McConnell was presenting to academic circles his views on the weaknesses of multiple use as a Forest Service policy. By the spring of 1957 Simons had a drawn map, recommending scenic resource protection for an area of the North Cascades encompassing more than 1,300,000 acres. It would be published by Brower in the *Sierra Club Bulletin*[105] and by George Marshall in *Living Wilderness*.

In an interesting turn of events, Simons became active in the same year that Brower's conservation mentor, Arthur Blake, died. When Brower wrote Blake's memorial and spoke of being enrolled in Blake's "unscheduled conservation class" twenty years earlier, so too he might have projected his relationship to Dave Simons.[106] Brower remembered that Blake had been instrumental in silencing opposition among "purist" conservationists to a possibly compromised Kings Canyon National Park. So too, in this North Cascades campaign, Brower would set an example for Simons, returning the Sierra Club to support of the Park Service, despite widespread criticism of Park Service schemes for overdevelopment.

But in early 1957 the best policy for the North Cascades seemed to be the one the Club had adopted in January, asking the chief of the Forest Service to do a comprehensive study of the area while keeping it primitive until the study was completed.[107] As Brower wrote to a group which would become the North Cascades Conservation Council, "I look upon the club's motion as a challenge to the Forest Service to come up with concepts of park planning for the area, so much of which deserves nothing less. . . . Otherwise, and soon, it seems to me we'll have to go all out for the next step."[108] Soon Brower was arguing to this same group that the area needed the equal of national park planning, whatever agency or agencies provided it, and he suggested thinking of the North Cascades through analogy to Yosemite.[109] Soon Brower would begin to use the language of Simons.

When, in April, Simons submitted his proposal for the North Cascades to J. Herbert Stone, regional forester for the Northwest, he was surely helped by Brower.[110] When Simons wrote confidently to Stone, his letter indicated remarkable maturity in a man not yet twenty-one years old, but also writing to Stone demonstrated remarkable innocence. Stone had established a reputation among conservationists as a hearty opponent of wilderness in any form.[111]

Nevertheless, the Simons plan insisted that "national significance of the region makes it imperative that it be considered as an integral whole. Piecemeal planning cannot do justice to the Northern Cascades." The Simons plan was based on qualitative rather than quantitative values, for, as he told Stone, the Forest Service made serious mistakes when it emphasized the number of visitors using certain roads and trails, rather than the reasons people frequented these routes. Simons insisted that an integral whole park could not be planned by applying only two classes of land use, wilderness or full resource utilization for economic purposes. It seemed to him absurd to eliminate highly scenic areas from the recreational plan simply because of speculation over possible mineral values. No doubt Stone choked at the size of Simons' whole, which was perhaps four times larger than the Forest Service's Glacier Peak wilderness proposal of February 1957.

In May 1957 the Simons letter became officially a part of Club policy on the North Cascades.[112] That summer, when Martin Litton came north to Washington to work on a Cascades article, Simons learned what a militant conservationist was like. They got along famously. Brower had already filmed the *Wilderness Alps of Stehikin*; it would be released in 1958. The Club, however, had committed its major efforts to pushing policy issues, a wilderness bill, and Scenic Resources Review.

By the spring of 1958 Simons was lobbying Brower and Wayburn. First of all he wanted Brower to get Justice William O. Douglas to attend an outing in the Cascades; Brower, at the same time, pressed Grant McConnell to write a book about the area, preferably with an introduction by Douglas.[113] As far as Simons was concerned, the Club needed to run as many outings as possible into the Cascades. He lec-

tured Brower on provincialism—sending a copy of his letter
to Wayburn—complained that conservation was weakened
by a policy of fighting numerous brush fires; the Club needed
to think big, needed to think of the entire picture in the North
Cascades, whose wilderness was maybe 3,000,000 acres—
three Yellowstones. Too many people had a fixation on Glacier Peak alone, Simons believed, and were ignorant of the
whole region. The Club had responsibility not to principles,
nor policy, nor to a few sections of the North Cascades: it had
to take responsibility for preserving the region.[114]

Meanwhile, Simons was pressing Wayburn as chair of the
Conservation Committee, warning him of the danger of over-
simplifying the complex issues involved and lecturing him on
the strategies of the Forest Service. Apparently, Wayburn
tried to convince Simons that the Forest Service had a legitimate position with regard to the region, but as far as Simons
was concerned the service was not interested in considering
both recreational and wilderness values.[115] "Instead it has
considered only sections at a time in order to 'divide and conquer'—to keep this from becoming the national issue which
it should be." As far as the Forest Service's Glacier Peak Wilderness Area proposal went, "It is an 'upland rockpile.' We
are left the peaks and glaciers to view above the prospective
sea of stumps. . . . That is, they are giving us our 'upland
rockpile' *as long as it contains no minerals.*" Only an adequate
national park proposal, Simons thought, could protect gate-
ways to the areas, defend forests, and protect against mining.
Only an all-out effort like that waged for Dinosaur could accomplish the gains the Club wanted. Even if a wilderness bill
were passed—and it might take years—it could not protect
the entire area. Simons believed that the Forest Service was
"using the greatest alpine wilderness in the nation, the North
Cascades, as a hostage to let them get what they want in the
Wilderness Bill."[116] He put his hopes in the Park Service, as
Brower had.

The next month—May 1958—McConnell wrote a long,

dispassionate, and balanced appraisal of the situation, concluding that park status was best.[117] Brower used it to try to
convince the members of the North Cascades Conservation
Council. But an impatient Simons, believing he had committed himself to the big-thinking Sierra Club rather than to provincial, small-thinking local organizations, was beginning to
have doubts about his allies. He was also beginning to take a
liking to some Club dignitaries and a dislike to others. He did
not like the Clarks, and expressed stronger views with regard
to Robinson.[118] Even Wayburn was beginning to trouble him.
"Call me David R. Frustration," he wrote to McConnell. Not
only did he think that Wayburn was willing to drop the
North Cascades: "When Wayburn forms an opinion, it is almost impossible to dislodge him, it seems. He again, privately, expressed his fears of rocking the boat on the Wilderness Bill. No doubt, despite assertions to the contrary, his real
worry is the developmental aspect of the national park. On
the Wilderness Bill, he wants to fight only one thing at a
time. As I have noted before, Wayburn is a real roadblock. He
seems as solidly set in his views as a ton of concrete."[119] As Simons saw it, with Wayburn's "preoccupation with 'strategy'
on the Wilderness Bill vs. N. Cascades Park," nobody seemed
to care about the land itself. So it was that Simons prepared
what came to be called "The Brief": a short essay called "The
Need for Scenic Resource Conservation in the Northern-
Cascades of Washington."

McConnell too believed that the Cascades were being put
aside for empty ideas. Not only did he find the "improved"
wilderness bill of 1958 a "bad shock," but he was worried because he knew that Brower had invested much energy in it:

> . . . the Wilderness Bill is primarily a menace. It has to
> pass or wilderness as a policy is repudiated; if it does
> pass, however, we have very little that we don't have
> now. The bill contains a reaffirmation of 'multiple use'

and provides machinery in the advisory council for the
cooption of conservationists by bureaucrats. Moreover,
and this I did not say to Dave [Brower], the Bill will
actually make it more difficult to get a decent GPWA
[Glacier Peak Wilderness Area]. Insofar as anything in
the bill is effective, it will work both ways and in our
case, against the GPWA. I am completely appalled.
So—it just has to be a Park.[120]

But Simons was convinced by Brower that the wilderness bill
offered substantial gains, and tried to convince McConnell.[121]
In return Brower began to support Simons' park plans with
more energy. Soon Brower would be lobbying the North Cascades Conservation Council on the subject, pointing out that
no one had incurred more Park Service wrath than he: "In
my opinion the pendulum in some parks has swung too far
from preservation and too far toward mass recreation. But
bear in mind that this wrath comes from honest difference of
opinion between groups of people working for the same
goal."[122] Finally, despite Wayburn's resistance, the Conservation Committee accepted Simons' brief and resolved for a national park.[123]

As Simons told McConnell, this was only the beginning.
Simons had plans for publicity; he encouraged McConnell to
work hard on the North Cascades book; he was developing
arguments which could be made to various organizations.
More important, his work on the North Cascades convinced
him to make a life's work of conservation. For him this meant
studying political science, but included lots of English, some
journalism, and history. "I hope to go directly to work for
some conservationist organization if I can and if my qualifications measure up to what is required."

Simons represented a new breed. Not an establishment
boy from California, but a disciple of Brower; eclectic or in-
decisive in his education, but absolutely committed to con-

servation; young, poor, impatient, but willing to work on a project for years and see it through a committee; a wild character, but well versed in argumentation—perhaps he was becoming the sort of secular prophet that Brower had been to him.

By mid summer, Brower and the Wayburns had Adams taking pictures in the North Cascades for a display in New York City, Litton had published a big article in *Sunset*, and John Oakes of the *New York Times* had advocated a park in the North Cascades. Simons began to propose to the Club an Oregon national park surrounding the Three Sisters. His proposal for the Three Sisters Park would be juxtaposed to McConnell's article on multiple use in the next year's *Annual*. But there was something Simons did not tell McConnell that summer. He had worked so hard on conservation matters that his grades at school had suffered. As of September 4, 1958, he was eligible for the military draft.

Multiple Use and Escalating Rhetoric 1958   Saving the North Cascades would require more than passage of the wilderness bill; coordination among several agencies would probably be required. Therefore the Club continued to worry about its relations with the Forest Service. In terms of strategy, relations with the agency might dictate whether the Club would attack the policy of multiple use, boost the wilderness bill, or do both.

As long as the Forest Service continued to think of wilderness as merely recreation, as long as it continued to listen to representatives of industry who griped, "Never before in the history of the United States . . . has the government had on its payroll so many persons whose job it is to see that people have fun," then there was not much dialogue possible on the subject.[124]

The Park Service argued that the recreation it already provided was wilderness recreation. If the Club was willing, for a while, to vigorously criticize policies of overdevelopment, of mass recreation in the parks, was it willing also to criticize the policy of utilitarian development, of multiple use, in the forests?

The Forest Service was certainly willing to oppose the idea of wilderness with familiar talk about locking up resources and wilderness as single use. Conservationists knew that wilderness protection was compatible with at least five other uses—watershed protection, fish and game habitat, science, education, and conservation reserves.[125] But they did not want to confuse the issue, which was muddied whenever the Park Service launched an attack on multiple use, not based on any principle, but as a weapon in interagency empire-building competition.[126] Brower thought the board should indicate that wilderness classification was compatible with other uses, insist that multiple use need not apply to every acre of forest, and demand a reasonable time for public comment on management plans.[127]

The entire January 1958 *Bulletin* circled around the subject, though the actual term was scarcely mentioned. "Where Should Management Stop?" asked the Wayburns in the lead article. "Are present concepts of management consistent with the fundamental patterns of nature?" "How long does it take to judge the total effect of our management methods?" These questions received no explicit answers. This article actually lauded the "theory of 'multiple use'" which had "guided the Forest Service in its efforts to develop yardsticks for its tremendous job of management." In another article, Fred Eissler decried the use of machines in the back country of Yosemite. Although Brower's contribution spoke of wilderness as a "symbol of restraint," his prose was equally restrained: "unmanaged, unmanipulated, unmanicured trees—good old-growth, overmature, decadent, high risk snags that they may be to a silviculturist, but not to God."[128]

Olaus Murie remembered that the discussion on management was as old as his experience in the Olympic Mountains. He found the following in his journal for 1934:

> The other day I was conversing with some people about game problems.
>
> "The deep woods, all this timber," I was told, "is not good game range. There are no mountain beavers, no birds. They don't like that kind of country. Go into the logged-off places, where there is lots of brush, where the sun shines. There you will find the birds, and the feed."
>
> Yes, here it was again—mass production. The forest must produce a "crop."[129]

Murie noted that "in Nature's economy there were no 'mature' trees to be gotten rid of." He wondered whether a new outlook was needed. "We need areas all over our earth which we 'manage' with hardly any human management at all."

By April 1958 Brower was writing, "Beware of Multiple-Usermanship!" As far as he was concerned, the term was being used as a "substitute for thinking" by opponents of the wilderness bill: "If 'multiple-use' is just a euphemism—just an attention diverting device on the part of some interest bent upon exploiting some raw material for the greatest financial good of the greatest number of stockholders for the immediate present—then you are being exposed to multiple usermanship."[130]

The sudden escalation in rhetoric had to do with the fate of the wilderness bill. This was the new version, revised after the negative reactions of Horace Albright, Fred Smith, and Conrad Wirth. In June of 1957 Brower and Zahniser had testified and looked for congressional support for the earlier version. In 1958 the "improved wilderness bill" still met opposition from timber, mining, and grazing interests, and from their friends in various bureaus. At least that's how it appeared to Brower. When he remembered Arthur Blake, he

remembered "no occasion when he failed to recognize a
spade for what it was and to call it just that."[131] Why should
he not do the same? As Roderick Nash has observed, "Congress lavished more time and effort on the wilderness bill
than on any other measure in American conservation history."[132] Between June of 1957 and May of 1964 there were
nine hearings, yielding more than six thousand pages of testimony, and the bill was rewritten sixty-six times.[133]

More important, the Forest Service had begun to lobby for
its own new Multiple Use–Sustained Yield Act, which was,
according to McArdle, a Forest Service substitute for a wilderness bill. Brower and others contended it was "a shibbo-
leth to obstruct wilderness preservation."[134] Although the
Forest Service put forth many arguments for its own legislation, conservationists perceived only an effort to protect administrative discretion in the face of increasing public pressure for wilderness.

The Club's board expressed support for the wilderness bill
but had no policy on multiple use at all. It did not have a policy because it was not sure it wanted to attack the Forest Service. Brower helped Harold Bradley draft a plan—that is,
Brower thought it up and Bradley signed the letter—called
the Great Exchange Program, which would transfer timber-
and forage-producing lands from the Bureau of Land Management in Interior to the Department of Agriculture, in return for lands deeded, presumably for national parks, in the
North Cascades, Three Sisters, Kern Plateau, Wind Rivers,
and Idaho Sawtooths.[135] As Brower remembers, the Great
Exchange was doomed from the start; neither agency wanted
to lose lands to parks. The Forest Service called the proposal
a "land grab." But Brower continued a blistering attack on
the Forest Service. In the same issue of the *Bulletin* which announced the Great Exchange Program, Brower wrote, "The
[Forest] Service proposes to establish a Glacier Peak Wilderness Area of so vulnerable an outline that one observer has

said it looks like 'a Rorschach blotch designed to bring out the worst in a highly guilty subconscious.'"[136]

Brower was impugning the motives of public agencies, and from the point of view of more conservative members of the board, he was trying to make policy. And he had an increasingly effective medium. The *Bulletin*, as of 1959, was larger, used color on occasion, and came out ten times a year. Soon Brower's use of this medium became a sore issue, particularly during the presidency of Nathan Clark. Clark remembers that Brower not only began "impugning the motives of public officials," but also "publishing articles on subjects which at that time we thought were not proper for Sierra Club discussion."[137] Population, for instance.

Where did population come up, especially in the midst of campaigns on wilderness matters? And why at a wilderness conference, which Richard Leonard had so hoped would not involve itself in matters outside its own specialization? At the Wilderness Conference of 1959, Resolution 7, introduced by Raymond Cowles, said that there was no point in talking about wilderness, which would only be an incidental victim of the coming malignant population explosion. Indeed, three ecologists at the meeting persuasively confronted the population problem as related to economic growth and as a major issue to which wilderness was only a corollary.[138] Population had everything to do with wilderness. The Forest Service was saying that the use of public lands had to be escalated to keep up with expanding markets. It was time, then, to cut population growth, as A. Starker Leopold believed: "The resources of the world should be used to raise the living standards of individuals, rather than to support more individuals."[139] In fact, after giving his paper at the conference Cowles opened a Malthusian discussion which revealed that the physician Wayburn, the attorney Leonard, and even A. Starker Leopold were uncomfortable. Conservationists were already branded as Malthusian pessimists.

The deep problem was once again ideological. It was not the specific issue of population, but the growing sense of the meaning of ecology. The first speaker at the conference quoted Paul Sears, an ecologist, who said, "The whole history of the conservation movement has been an evolution away from concern with single resources to realizations of their interdependence, and of the need for viewing the problem in its entirety."[140] Indeed the 1959 Wilderness Conference was filled with speakers who presented an ecological view of nature, one which might lead the Club to take up the words of Muir: "When we try to pick out anything by itself, we find it hitched to everything else in the universe."[141]

Several years would pass before Club literature began to acknowledge those words, almost as if Muir did not write them until the Club became conscious of ecology. It would be more than a decade before those words appeared at the bottom of Club stationery, and five years before the board would decide to study the relationship between population and wilderness. Nevertheless, members of the Wilderness Conference began to remind themselves that wilderness had ecological integrity, as Muir had learned nearly ninety years earlier. The program for the 1959 conference was notable for its lack of government speakers.

Constructive Criticism 1959

When Brower reported to the board in June 1959, he called attention to a report by the National Lumber Manufacturers Association: Agriculture Secretary Ezra Taft Benson had announced the commencement of a National Forest Recreation Resources Review.[142] Brower observed, "It is interesting to see the lumbermen speak of the Outdoor Recreation Review as an 'industry-government' affair. You will note that the parent organization (us) seems to be left out of this concept."[143] Brower told the story of Frank Craighead's experience. As a wildlife biologist who had been hired by the Forest Service to set up a program of recreational research with particular emphasis on wildlife, Craighead found that he had been blocked at every avenue and given neither administrative support nor a budget. All multiple-use decisions were made by men trained in timber. Nor was Craighead slated for advancement, since he was not a trained forester. People like Frank Craighead, who would make his reputation studying grizzly bear management in Yellowstone, realized already that the issue of recreation was not just about people having fun, but about a complex of relations between human use and the ecological integrity of wilderness. His experience seemed to disclose the Forest Service's real attitudes about wilderness. Brower noted in conclusion that Joe Penfold, conservation director of the Izaak Walton League and member of the Outdoor Recreation Resources Review Commission, worried the review was in danger of becoming "no more than an inventory of fish ponds and picnic tables."

The Club's board was less concerned with the problems of the Forest Service than with its own. At the July 4, 1959, board meeting, in Tuolumne Meadows, Nate Clark presided. At that meeting there was considerable discussion, and a resolution was passed calling for Sierra Club representatives to protect the independence of the Club by cooperating with public officers in the initial stages of planning, and using only objective and constructive criticism of public policies, whether in public or private.[144]

Correspondence between Brower and Clark followed. Although Brower was speaking of relations with Wirth and the Park Service, and never mentioned explicitly the July 4 resolution, what he had to say applied to any federal agency: "If our policy should come along as one in which getting along takes precedence over protection," he said, "the club can be sure of avoiding arguments with the Service." It was precisely because the Club had emphasized agreement with the Park

Service, and let other things slip by, that it had such a pleas-
ant relationship with the Park Service. For Brower, the moral
taught by the growth of the Club during the 1950s—"it isn't
the comfortable little organization that it used to be"—and
the changes in the agencies it once could unqualifiedly support, could be summarized as follows: "Diplomacy, perfection of techniques for getting along, will accomplish a great
deal. It will not, however, save what can only be saved by
fighting."[145]

Clark was worried because, as he remembers, Brower
tended to be at the same time aggressive and secretive, because Brower, though a great conservationist, did not want to
be hindered, and because, as he wrote at the time, "the Sierra
Club could appear to be becoming a one-man organization."[146] Just as Nate Clark saw his own role as presiding over,
not speaking for, the Club, so he hoped that Brower could
understand his anxiety that "most directors have no idea
where the Executive Director is, or what he has said in the
name of the Club." Though Clark insisted that his administration's chief role was not to improve relations with the Park
Service or any government agency, he did believe his administration's chief goal should be to maximize its position of
influence:

> We cannot command anyone but ourselves, and must
> therefore use every means we can devise to increase our
> influence, even to reevaluating very often our relations
> with the Park Service, Forest Service, and any other
> organization or individual who is in a possible position
> to take action or make decisions related to our
> interests.[147]

It was Brower's move, and he made it in the traditional
way. If the Club was an "educational" organization, then he
need not publish his own views. Already he had enlisted an
arsenal of writers, and he was about to use it. First came an
essay by Grant McConnell on multiple use.

McConnell's article appeared alongside Dave Simons' article proposing an Oregon Cascades national park, in the 1959 *Annual*.[148] McConnell's historical argument demonstrated that multiple use had always meant "using the public domain for private purposes"; meant—in the words of Pinchot—that "local questions will be decided upon local grounds; the dominant industry will be considered first . . . ." McConnell believed that "in a simple sense it is true to say that multiple-use *is* Forest Service Policy." The end of World War II seemed to portend a new era in the Forest Service, when it would no longer be a custodial agency and the term *management* meant multiple use, at least to McArdle; nevertheless, McConnell argued, the service stood by the rigid principles of Pinchot. While these outdated progressive notions remained gospel to the service, they left it singularly ill-equipped to deal with its increasingly powerful policy of administrative discretion. The problem is related to the growth of modern technology. With modern technology the service had the power to do more, yet a modern forester knew more and more about less and less, and was educated mostly for industry. The old Pinchot slogan about the greatest good for the greatest number in the long run carried a bias for decisions measurable in quantitative economic terms. "It is the more insidious for being disguised," McConnell wrote. To sum up, McConnell found that the technically oriented and decentralized system of Forest Service administration favored special interests against the national interest and left the Forest Service lacking a set of values which could be used to solve conflicts in land use in the future. This analysis could be stretched and modified to fit Park Service policies as well—particularly reliance on the ideas of Mather and Albright in the modern era.

The Simons article, after a long, poetic section, quoted the Gilligan doctoral dissertation: that "not enough Forest Service men [are] sufficiently concerned about forest recreation to carry out such work enthusiastically, is substantiated by Forest Service recreation administration." Until Forest Service policies changed, Simons argued, conservationists had no choice but to turn to the Park Service for protection.

For the same *Annual* Brower produced the captions to "The Silent Procession," a collection of twenty-one photographs of the Three Sisters area. "The chainsaws roar ever closer," Brower wrote, going on:

> Here the life force has gone on, uninterrupted by man and his technology, ever since life began. This is a special place, and saving it unspoiled is little to ask. But the answer has been no; this must be added to the inventory of operable forests, even while the mills stand glutted. So much to be taken away from so many; so little added for so few.[149]

Did such a parody of the Forest Service slogan constitute objective and constructive criticism of public policies? The board thought not. Whether it was responding to these words or others by Brower did not matter. In December the board passed a policy which it called Relations with Public Agencies, but which Brower called the Gag Rule. Enlarging the resolution enacted in July 1959, the board determined in December that

> a. No statement should be used that expressly, impliedly, or by reasonable inference criticizes the motives, integrity, or competence of an official or bureau.
>
> b. In publication, objectivity can best be achieved by presentation of both sides of a controversy.[150]

Copies of this warning were sent not only to other conservation organizations, but to federal agencies as well, presumably so people like McArdle could complain if Brower or any of his allies got out of line. Coming so closely on the heels of publication of the *Annual*, the resolution applied to Brower's, Simons', and McConnell's contributions. Brower had been

aggressive and secretive because he believed the Forest Service was out to get him. The Gag Rule, introduced by Richard
Leonard, Bestor Robinson, and Elmer Aldrich—the men
Brower believed represented Forest Service interests on the
board—confirmed his suspicions.

From the board's point of view Brower was exhibiting
paranoia. In setting its policy, the board was concerned about
the tax status of the Club. Explicit lobbying against the Forest
Service's multiple-use bill could be disastrous to the Club's financial status. Though some, like Edgar Wayburn and
George Marshall, balked at a resolution which prohibited
Club publications from advocating "action" on legislative
matters, others, like Leonard and Adams, considered the financial situation serious.[151]

*The
Foundation
1960*

In retrospect, many recognized that the Club had run
into organizational problems. As Wayburn remembers, when the Club had created Trustees for Conservation, an organization that would not have to worry
about its tax status and could lobby freely, "the problem was, that the average person who was going to donate for
environmental causes didn't know what Trustees was, despite our efforts to identify this with the legislative programs
of the Sierra Club."[152] Brower continued to pull the Club into
an arena it had avoided in the past, lobbying *against* legislation proposed by the Forest Service. Later, Brower too perceived an organizational problem: "One of the reasons that
time moves on and people come and go is that some people
get a little too set in their ways and should be relieved of having to make the same decisions they've always made."[153] Just
as the Park Service had demonstrated the danger of acting on
traditional ideas about its mission when those policies would
no longer work in a changing world, and just as the Forest
Service held to principles articulated by Pinchot, so too the
Sierra Club was in danger of "making the same decisions
they've always made" when facing new challenges. Brower

wanted the Club to face squarely the possibility of losing its
tax status, and thought it should create a tax-exempt foundation which would be free from such problems. "No member would care whether his dues . . . were deductible or not,"
he said.[154] As he remembers, the conservative members of the
board "argued vociferously against it." But just as Brower
used Dave Simons as a resource for vigorous new ideas for
the North Cascades, so he had another young protégé, Phil
Berry, who could pursue the tax angle.

Phillip Berry, born in 1937, was the same age as Simons
and had become involved in the Club through the usual avenue, though at an unusually young age, joining High Trips at
thirteen and growing enthusiastic about moutaineering. Just
as Muir had been the hero when Huber first attended High
Trips and Colby had been the hero when Marion Randall
Parsons attended them, so, for Berry, Brower was *the* leader.
Brower had what people would later refer to as charisma. He
was a great climber, wore the climber's clothes, could tell war
stories from the mountain troops. Like many others, Berry
learned conservation from Brower. "Dave, at campfires,
would talk . . . about the need to preserve, and how through
enjoying these things we acquired an obligation to fight for
them if threatened. . . . Dave's campfire talks came so much
from the heart you believed every word of it. It was emotional. It was romantic. It was utterly moving."[155] From the
age of fifteen Berry spent a lot of time at Brower's home, for
he was a Berkeley kid, and Brower was fatherly. Berry also
started going to Conservation Committee meetings run by
Wayburn, who worked closely and well with Brower.

Soon Berry studied law at Stanford. Sometime late in 1959
or early in 1960, Brower began talking to him about the
Club's tax problems. Though Berry, unlike Leonard, found
tax law boring—to the point of cutting his tax class—he grew
interested and discussed the problem with some professors.[156] They thought there was a way to set up a separate tax
deductible foundation. As Brower remembers, Berry and his

professor, Phil C. Neal, worked out the language. Since Leonard and Robinson "had been trying to use some law arguments against it, and since the head of the Stanford Law School said that was nonsense, they gave up and passed the resolution that the Sierra Club had no objection to Dick Leonard's forming a Sierra Club Foundation."[157]

Though Nate Clark remembers the situation differently, and believes the idea grew up among himself, Leonard, Robinson, Harold Bradley, and Alexander Hildebrand, the resolution was introduced formally by Wayburn.[158] And though the Foundation would not be needed until 1968, when the Club had lost its tax status, there was no longer a formal reason to prevent Brower from lobbying. Leonard wrote up the articles of incorporation, and Brower began a campaign to fund the Foundation.[159]

In the long run, Berry's personal involvement in the issue would set an important precedent. Environmental law would bloom in the 1960s, and Berry would become a major force in that realm. Two years later, joining a suit brought by the National Parks Association, the Club would enter its first legal suit, over the protection of Rainbow Bridge from the rising waters behind Glen Canyon Dam.[160] Berry remembers discussing the issue with Brower, who advocated the action strongly to the board. It was, as Berry remembers, an unusual action given the outlook of the board, for it stepped up the degree to which the Club was willing to directly confront government officials.[161] Though Berry himself did not play a role in that suit, he was soon to be a key organizer of Club legal activities.

In May of 1960 the board wanted to compromise with the Forest Service, and it had a chance. As one historian of the Forest Service puts it, "to help allay Sierra Club fears about multiple use" Assistant Chief Crafts was sent to San Francisco.[162] The atmosphere could not have been less than

strained. The Club had published Stegner's DeVoto-like po-
lemic, "The War Between the Rough Riders and the Bird
Watchers," the previous May, as well as the articles by Mc-
Connell and Simons. Brower had continued to publish articles about "the big 'multiple-use' threats to the North Cascades."[163] Horace Albright contributed an article for April–
May 1960, whose title said it all: "More Park or All Forest:
Highest Use vs. Multiple Use."[164] And it was on this ground
that the Club met Crafts.

Wayburn led the attack. He was concerned about Forest
Service opposition to the wilderness bill and the Forest Service's use of the multiple-use bill to block further park acquisition. Crafts implied that the Forest Service might lessen its
resistance to the wilderness bill if conservationists would stop
attacking the Forest Service, which was also beset by timber
interests opposing multiple use. Yet Crafts would not promise
more public hearings. When asked if the Forest Service
would consider a moratorium on certain lands pending a
Scenic Resources Review, Crafts answered a flat no. Crafts
was unmoving on administrative discretion, and he was supported by Elmer Aldrich of the board, who thought the public ought not to be involved in administrative decisions.
When Wayburn pushed, Crafts pushed back.[165]

As Associate Secretary Holway Jones reported promptly in
the June *Bulletin*, the board had compromised in the end,
urging that the Multiple Use–Sustained Yield Bill include
land-use classifications that would prohibit activities that
might destroy the highest or best use of an area, and that the
bill make clear that such legislation would not contravene
further additions to the national park system.[166] The Club
minutes did not show that the Club was willing to act on
what Jones reported as "serious concern about excessive administrative discretion in the relegating to logging of most of
the remaining uncut federal forest lands." Jones reported that
the board expressed gratitude to Crafts for "his fine presenta-

tion of the Forest Service viewpoint." Brower reported on the facing page, where his column appeared under the title "The Uneasy Chair," that president Nate Clark had also fired off a strong letter to Senator James E. Murray challenging the right of the Forest Service to irreversibly change an unexploited forest reserve through multiple use without holding a public hearing.[167] Brower attempted what turned out to be an abortive campaign to request field hearings, since, as Clark argued to Murray, "Congressional action on the Multiple Use Bill at this time would be premature."[168] The Club did not testify in Washington about the multiple-use bill, and this was taken to mean that it was "accepting for the time being inclusion of the statement that wilderness was 'consistent' with multiple use."[169] It meant, in fact, that Brower was enjoined not to testify. The act passed into law on June 12, 1960.

For most of the rest of the year the board would be embroiled in discussion of Forest Service policy, particularly with regard to the land-use classifications it had suggested as a result of the meeting with Craft.[170] Clark doggedly requested from Robinson a legal analysis of the Club's plan for establishing a comprehensive land-use classification system. Robinson found, in an eight-page analysis, that such a system would not only be legal but indispensible; that zoning only after public meetings was "the preferred method."[171] Clark forwarded the policy and Robinson's analysis to McArdle. It was at first ignored and then rejected. Meanwhile Brower would act.

Outdoor Newsletter no. 6 1960

By mid 1960 Brower was freed from constraints on lobbying, and the Club could advocate letter-writing campaigns freely, in its own name.[172] In any case, Brower could no longer be accused of lobbying against the multiple-use bill, which was history. He made plans for taking what Wayburn had called the Club's philosophical, educational, and scientific ideals not to the Forest Service, but directly to the public.[173] Even while the Club was having a hard time making its budget stretch to meet its needs, the budget itself was growing, from $120,000 in 1959 to $208,000 in 1960; now, as a result of Brower's ambitious publishing plans, a great deal of it—$107,000— would be devoted to publications.[174] The new *Bulletin* was expensive, and its size and elaborateness would have to be limited.[175]

But it was 1960. A presidential election was in full bloom. Brower's job was to make the Club, as Clark had said, as influential as possible. By the end of the year the Club would have acted on several fronts. It would confront the Forest Service in the Northwest and advocate national parks. It would use media, not only the new *Bulletin*, which was directed toward a wider readership than Club members, but a whole new publishing program. It would involve itself increasingly in the legal battle over the wilderness bill. By the middle of the following year, Michael McCloskey would be retained as the Club's Northwest representative. By the end of the year John F. Kennedy was president-elect, and his secretaries of agriculture and the interior, Orville Freeman and Stewart Udall, were already selected—Udall perhaps through the influence of Brower.[176] Club influence in national affairs would leap forward. McCloskey himself would write a decisive critical analysis of the Multiple-Use–Sustained Yield Act in December of 1961. He would also involve himself heavily in lobbying for the wilderness bill. McArdle would retire in July 1961 and Wirth in 1964, the year when the Wilderness Act would be passed.

Club strategy leading to these events was not carefully orchestrated. Instead, it appears the Club was galvanized by a crisis. The crisis was the publication of *Outdoor Newsletter no. 6*, on August 22, 1960, and its subsequent distribution at the World Forestry Congress.[177]

The Club's outdoor newsletters were collections of materials issued previously in the *Bulletin* and sometimes in mimeographed form. Early issues dealt with park and forestry topics. Number 3 advertised *This Is The American Earth*, the first *Exhibit Format* book. Number 4 and later issues were focused on Rainbow Bridge, the proposed Mammoth Pass highway, and power boats on Yellowstone lake.[178]

Newsletter number 6 included a letter of transmittal addressed "To Western Editors." Signed by Brower, the letter called attention to Oregon's last chance for considering a new national park in the volcanic Cascades—a park being blocked, Brower said, by the Forest Service. Brower explained that the newsletter had been made necessary by the effectiveness of the Forest Service, an organization thirteen years younger than the Sierra Club, in manipulating the news media. The service had status as a major federal bureau and had the loyalty of its personnel, as documented in the Resources for the Future book by Herbert Kaufman, *The Forest Ranger: A Study in Administrative Behavior* (1960). It carried on a "preponderantly single-use trained and directed" program in its desire to preserve its "extraordinary freedom of discretion" and its "181,000,000-acre empire"; it wielded great political power, gained by an ability to "freely assign its personnel at public expense to the task of staving off threats to the bureau and its domain."

This was strong stuff. The material for the newsletter came mainly from Simons' article on the Oregon Cascades and Club publications on the North Cascades, but included articles and excerpts taken primarily from the *Bulletin*, especially from the June 1960 issue, which reacted to the passage of the Multiple Use–Sustained Yield Act. There was information on Forest Service plans for the Kern Plateau in the southern Sierra, on the need for reforestation, on multiple use, and on the economic virtues of tourism as opposed to logging, all in a slightly sensational format.

Reaction to the newsletter might have been small had it not been distributed at the forestry congress, where McArdle, acting as president, had arranged a program to tout his new Multiple Use–Sustained Yield Act as America's answer to the

worldwide need for forest management.[179] When McArdle
saw the newsletter, he was outraged and wrote a blistering
letter to Nate Clark. He protested the Club's "recent propaganda sheet," resented its distribution at the World Forestry
Congress, interpreted the Club's action as "an effort to em-
barrass foresters of the United States, and the Forest Service
as an agency, before the foresters of other nations," said "the
statements contained therein are replete with untruths, half
truths, slurs, innuendos and erroneous inferences . . . the use
of photographs is deliberately slanted"; he found the letter of
transmittal contained serious charges, insisted the Forest Service had taken "no position on the Club's proposed Oregon
Cascades National Park," said that the program "Operation
Multiple Use" [McArdle's term] had been widely acclaimed,
that road building was not just for timber access but for multiple purposes, and all "necessary to proper management of
forest lands"; he pointed out that "the statement that the Forest Service program will obliterate American wilderness is
completely incompatible with the facts," denied that Forest
Service employees were single-use oriented, trained to timber, but instead were "oriented toward multiple use," announced that the Club "vigorously opposed passage of the
Multiple Use–Sustained Yield bill, and was the *only outdoor
organization* to do so" [italics mine], argued that the Club's
stand on the Forest Service role in advising private growers
"how surely to obtain sustained-yield objectives" was contradictory to its own opposition to multiple-use legislation, and
concluded that although "public officials are inured to criticism, both just and unjust," such "vicious propaganda" was
too much to bear.[180]

Although Brower acknowledged the letter, pointing out
briefly that the Club did not oppose the multiple-use act and
did not advocate an Oregon Cascades national park, but only
requested a study, he indicated that Nate Clark would reply
fully when he returned from vacation.[181] Meanwhile, Brower
knew what would be coming—indeed was already arriving.

An organizer of the congress had already sent a letter of protest to individual directors, not through the Club.[182] Brower saw this as part of the effort of the Forest Service to "divide and conquer," to produce dissension and conflicting responses from the Club. Soon, as Brower might have expected, Robinson wrote to Clark, "critical of the judgment, but not the intentions and motives of Dave Brower."[183] Distributing "any material which is critical of American action" was "highly improper," Robinson said, and "as Americans we should stand together in all matters involving foreign organizations, whether they be political or non-political." Robinson also reminded Clark of the resolution made in Tuolumne Meadows about relations with government agencies, and in so doing undoubtedly suggested to Brower that the distribution of that policy to federal agencies put in McArdle's hand the sword he needed to "get Brower." In confidence, Clark told Robinson that he had not approved the newsletter.[184]

Brower notified the board that he had been told that "the Forest Service was out to get Brower by any means necessary."[185] He knew there would have to be one decisive answer for the Club. He could not write it, but he could prepare for its writing. Conferring with Grant McConnell, he received advice on political strategy. "Warm isn't it?" McConnell wrote; "Probably all to the good. Shows things struck home."[186] McConnell thought the "big threat" would come from Brower's own directors. "I certainly don't want these people caving in under this sort of attack." Brower would have to mend fences, "make a display of sweet reasonableness with them— but without promising to do the same with McArdle." McConnell felt that whether McArdle "over-responded" or "may feel hurt more than we appreciate . . . the logic of the situation now is that we are after his job." Since McArdle was now in an uncompromising position, McConnell suggested the Club "stir things up." Why not suggest that the Forest Service be transferred to Interior? (That usually made the Service mad as could be.) In any case, the idea was to keep things from quieting down for the next few crucial months, keep two ideas in the public eye, that Forest Service policy was controversial and that McArdle was arrogant and combative. If the Club could do that, then "McArdle becomes a controversial figure and the one who has got FS into this mess." McConnell hoped for a Kennedy election and said, "I really wish that we could make the point that this has been a Republican FS administration—but that can't be made in the SC name."

In a sensitive mood, McConnell went on to say that "We are not talking about recreation as they really seem to believe. What we are trying to fight for is something a good deal closer to religion. It would be good if they tried to understand this." Religious crusade, Byzantine or Machiavellian scheme, or practical politics, McConnell's kind of strategy was necessary only if the values which underlay the Forest Service as an agency made any reconciliation impossible. As later scholars have pointed out, though the Forest Service had always been a model of efficiency, its very perfection in that realm had made it mechanistic and narrow in outlook. Even within the agency critics had been calling, for more than fifteen years, for more breadth of view, imagination, and concern for resource management in relation to social objectives and criteria. As an analysis in 1966 put it, "By concentrating on techniques of scientific management, foresters had neglected to ask fundamental questions about their mission. They assumed that social needs would be related to forest management without their making any effort to ascertain those needs and develop appropriate policies."[187] Under the circumstances, McConnell's strategy was borne out, and it certainly did not lack cunning.

In a December letter to Nate Clark, McConnell expressed more completely the principles he had not discussed with Brower, given their assumed agreement. He was worried that the Club was not meeting its crisis, and there was not time. Already president-elect Kennedy had named Stewart Udall and Orville Freeman as secretaries of interior and agriculture. But the Club had become "dangerously passive" just at the time when "much attention was being paid to the state of public opinion." McConnell said that McArdle's response to "certain criticisms of current policy" had been both scurrilous and irresponsible: "I greatly fear that the McArdle letter to you and the other directors has been most cynically conceived, despite its show of heat." The design was to "persuade conservation leaders to go slow for a time." Why? McConnell minced no words: "Nothing from their [Forest Service] standpoint, given their ideological orientation and their political associations with the leaders of the lumbering industry, is more important than the maintenance of the appearance of a situation of peace in their areas of concern during the next six months." But if members of the Club were to "stand fast on our principles and rededicate ourselves to effective action," McConnell argued, "there are men of principle in the new administration."[188]

Clark distributed this letter to the board, promising discussion at the board meeting on January 21, 1961; he meanwhile put together a reply to Richard McArdle. It was a complete and decisive statement. Not only did he answer McArdle point by point, but he took up an issue which McConnell had broached with Brower. "Since when," McConnell had asked, "has it been improper to criticize the government of America?" So Clark concluded his letter by dealing directly with this issue of the Club's loyalty:

> We feel we have not criticized the Forest Service unjustly. We have been exceedingly patient and yielding. We have a fifty year history of supporting the Forest Service. . . . But we will continue to support the noncommercial public interest and to criticize the Forest Service when it deviates from what we believe is for the public good.[189]

Clark's words were directed not simply to McArdle, but to critics of the Club, within and without. It was no coincidence that a member of the Angeles Chapter had recently proposed a loyalty oath for membership in the Club, appalling even the most conservative board members.[190]

To dispel any doubts about the Club's loyalty—some undoubtedly spread by the dispersion of the McArdle attack—Clark not only wrote his letter, but distributed his answer widely, and included not only his own rebuttal but a review of events leading to the controversy. "We did not say that 'the Forest Service program will obliterate American wilderness.' We do fear—and our fear is widely shared—that the Forest Service is nevertheless in the act of obliterating it."[191] How? By impeding wilderness legislation. By refusing to hold public hearings. By using the term multiple use when it meant logging. By confusing terminology and twisting logic about such issues as *wilderness, recreation, use,* and *resources.* Finally, Clark insisted, the last paragraph of the newsletter remained unanswered: "It should not be the objective of the Forest Service to deny another great agency, the National Park Service, the opportunity to present to the nation the necessary facts about new national parks for America's future."[192] Clark could ask why McArdle expressed support for the national and state park systems of the country, while John Oakes of the *New York Times* reported that in regard to Oregon Dunes National Seashore, Great Basin National Park, and the North Cascades, "in each of these three cases, Forest Service opposition has been clear and explicit."[193]

The Club had once desired good relations with the *Policy* Forest Service because the agency's power and discre- 1960 tion forced conservationists to operate on a friendly level. Because the method of commending, pleading, and reciprocating seemed the only means of saving wilderness. Some like Leonard and Robinson valued, for personal reasons, their friendly relations with Forest Service people and supported the bureau's aims. Yet an increasing number in the Club believed it could no longer afford close relations with the Forest Service because the Forest Service itself had changed from a custodial to an exploitive organization, because the Club was supporting the wilderness bill which the Forest Service resisted, because the conservation community and the public were experiencing a growing distrust, because new young members would find the old conciliatory methods of the Club frustrating, because the Forest Service would not yield on the North Cascades or Three Sisters, and perhaps because Brower's activities made conciliation no longer possible.

In pragmatic terms, success of the wilderness bill would mean that the public would not have to plead with the Forest Service, or so people like Brower and Zahniser thought. But that success seemed far in the future. There were two routes toward establishing the wilderness bill. One was conciliation: try to persuade Forest Service administrators, don't resist the principle of multiple use, ask them to manage places like the North Cascades for recreation, hope they would agree to wilderness ideas. Or there was confrontation: don't even try to persuade them, but expose them to the public in the worst light. Attack multiple use as "timber cutting plus something else," hoping for a public outcry. Then advocate national park status for all wilderness. Since the Forest Service did not wish to lose this land, perhaps it would accept some kind of wilderness legislation. Conservationists could hope that a new presidential administration would listen to the public outcry.

In the event, the Club practiced both conciliation and confrontation. Brower played the troublemaker and the board was reasonable. This was a method Brower would later speak of with pride when he quoted Russell Train of the Conservation Foundation, who had said, "Thank God for Dave Brower, he makes it so easy for the rest of us to look reasonable."[194] Brower allowed the board to use the kind of argument Martin Luther King, Jr., would use in the next few years when he pointed out that he was a moderate, and if nobody would conciliate with him, then they would have to deal with the radicals, like Malcolm X. As an increasing number of conservation organizations formed, one saw a range of positions, yet to the Forest Service Brower had made the Sierra Club the most radical organization in the spectrum. Did the Club want to be on that end of the spectrum, so the National Audubon Society could say, "Thank God for the Sierra Club, they make us look reasonable?" Probably not. The board was not composed of Grant McConnells or David Simonses, but of more conservative men. Yet it was increasingly clear that Brower, more than any of them, had continued to change with the times. People like Leonard, Robinson, or Nate Clark, not as attuned to the new ecological view of wilderness, were more likely to abide by traditional stances. Even Wayburn, who sided with Brower more often than the others, and who was attentive to ecological thought, preferred convincing to confronting.

Intended or not, good or bad strategy, the 1960 controversy directed the evolution of the Club, shaped the future campaign for a wilderness bill, and determined the strategy the Club could use to preserve wilderness in the Northwest and elsewhere. Whether the controversy was a result of blundering or intuition, the time for reconciliation with the Forest Service was past. The controversy did solidify the Club's view and it brought influence with the new presidential administration, a new public image, and a leading role for the future. But there were undercurrents, lasting dissension and bitterness on the board, lasting bitterness in the Forest Service and perhaps even in the Park Service. Brower had made enemies and the Club had made enemies.

The sudden need to move swiftly masked a question which Club presidents, especially Nate Clark and Edgar Wayburn, would consider through the rest of the decade. What, they wondered, was the proper way to develop an ideal Sierra Club campaign? Should campaigns begin with public input, evolve through professional advice from wilderness conferences, then be administratively organized by the board of directors, and finally turn to strategic action by the executive director? If so, Brower had at times circumvented his role by entering into the first step, public input, by orchestrating wilderness conferences, and by anticipating board policy with strategic acts. Brower saw his role as executive director differently. He wanted first to act locally, by activating the grass roots and enlisting individuals; second, to influence the conservation community through councils and private contacts; third, to create nationwide publicity; and fourth, to confront federal agencies and lobby Congress in Washington, D.C.

He also wanted the Club to have a clear set of policies to follow, and by the end of 1960 the Club would publish a nearly complete statement of its policies and priorities. These were dull reading but necessary. A decade previously Brower had some copies of the 1951 *Annual* specially bound, he said, "as the club's first attempt to bring its periodical—and the articles and illustrations of permanent value within it—before the general public."[195] The volume was filled with wonderful tales of wilderness adventures. Very little of its contents could be construed as conservation. Now, the 1960 *Annual* still had the adventure: it reported a Club expedition to Masherbrum in the Himalaya and the second ascent of the South Buttress of El Capitan. (George Sessions—future advocate of Deep Ecology—climbed the Ahwahnee Buttress.) But primarily, in clear if somewhat stilted prose, the Club spelled out its policies on national parks, standards for national park and other scenic roads, and on national forests.[196] After nearly a decade of labor, the Club could point and say, This is what we want. Abstracted:

We want to "round out the national parks" (Albright's

phrase). We want master planning in the parks, with guide-lines for development. We want consideration for new na-tional parks to include places like the Cascades, Wheeler Peak in Nevada, the Sawtooths in Idaho, the Wind Rivers of Wyoming, the White Mountains and Minarets in the Sierra, and Point Reyes, north of San Francisco. We want roads built that put scenery first and speed second. We want national forests administered under a comprehensive land-use classi-fication system, with plans subject to public scrutiny. We want forest lands to be reviewed for potential uses. We want the Forest Service to list its general criteria when considering conflicting and compatible uses. We want these criteria ex-plained and interpreted in detail. We want all of these in the public interest. We will use these policies in the future as tools for critical analysis, and perhaps even turn critical analysis of government policy toward litigation.

For those members who knew the Club, there were articles in the 1960 *Annual* which added the depth of history to those policies. One, a personal recollection on "The Campaign for Kings Canyon National Park" by Frank A. Kittridge, re-minded members that the Club was formed to create and protect national parks.[197] The Club's official historian, Hol-way Jones, wrote in introduction to Kittridge that "conser-vationists are a stubborn and, by political necessity—if the truth be known—a patient breed of men; they are willing to wait for the right moment and the right circumstances." Jones commented that "there are lessons here for the cru-sades yet to be waged in the Pacific Northwest."[198]

The *Annual* concluded with Will Colby's memorial essay to Walter Huber, who had coordinated his successful role as a public figure with his interest in the growth of the Club dur-ing his life of 77 years. An older member of the Club burying his dead friend. But who would bury the young dead? David Brower had that difficult task. He noted the death of David Si-mons, "after a two day illness at Fort Bragg, North Carolina, where he was stationed. . . . Few will know," Brower thought, "how great a loss his death means to conservation." Few would know how much he did, "including the stirring of people at least twice his age into action, and well advised action."[199]

Speaking   *The West of which I speak is but another name for the*
for   *Wild, and what I have been preparing to say is, that in*
Wilderness *Wildness is the preservation of the World. Every tree sends*
           its fibers forth in search of the Wild. The cities import it at
           any price. Men plow and sail for it. From the forest and
           wilderness come the tonics and barks which brace
           mankind.   Henry David Thoreau

Brower first assumed his duties as executive director "speaking for the club within the context of club policy."[200] By 1956 Ansel Adams wished to see the voice of the Club reach a larger and more diverse audience; so he wrote to Brower, arguing that the Club's publications should reach beyond the conventional rational conservation literature toward a more dynamic artistic and literary expression of sentiment.[201] Soon Brower was submitting a revised job description which included coordinating book publishing and public relations programs based on "development of photographic and literary material."[202] It was important to have the very best Sierra Club artists and writers speak well for the Club.

Although the *Bulletin* had evolved since 1951, and the new format introduced in 1959 made it more of a piece for public consumption, Brower knew that a more professional program of publications would be even more effective, particularly in attracting new young members like Dave Simons. The problem was not simply to impress confirmed conservationists—though some argue that the real audience for mythmaking is those who do the same work, those who professionally make the myths about land use that the nation uses to make up its mind. No, the idea was more ambitious. The campaign against the Forest Service underscored the need for professional use of media. For its campaign against the Bureau of Reclamation the Club had put together *This Is Dinosaur*, but that book was hastily produced, not printed by the Club, and as Stegner put it, was not a "fighting book."[203] Further, it was linked to one campaign. If the Club was ready to sell its story to the public at large, if it needed something to move Congress to control the huge bureaus like Interior and Agriculture, it needed a more durable, more aggressive, more moving, and in a sense, more general kind of literature.

The first new book, which Brower began to plan as early as 1958, was an expanded version of the photograph exhibit "This Is the American Earth," hung in 1955 in the Club's LeConte Memorial Lodge in Yosemite. This collaboration between Ansel Adams and Nancy Newhall had been "put together to tell the world a conservation story it needed to know, and tell it beautifully."[204] The Club had called upon Adams' art some twenty years earlier with his folio *Sierra Nevada, The John Muir Trail*, which prepared for the campaign for Kings Canyon National Park. As Adams argued often, he was not willing to produce propaganda. He said about his Kings Canyon folio, "I feel secure in adhering to a certain austerity throughout, in accentuating the acuteness of edge and texture, and in stylizing the severity, grandeur, and poignant minutae of the mountains."[205] Yet *Sierra Nevada* drew praise from the heads of both the Park Service and Forest Service; it constituted "a silent but most effective weapon" which would justify the park, even if to many—especially during the depression—such a fancy book was "a bowing to the rich" simply because it looked so good. Adams' work was even criticized as being inhuman. "Doesn't anybody go there?" asked art critic Lincoln Kirstein.

Adams was beginning to come into his own as an artist. And for the exhibit "This Is The American Earth" he had enlisted Nancy Newhall, the wife of Beaumont Newhall, photography curator of the New York Museum of Modern Art. She had credentials as a designer of photographic exhibits, and had also distinguished herself as a writer about photography and conservation. In the next few years she would write a biography of Adams and call Brower's attention to the work of Eliot Porter.

When Brower, Newhall, and Adams began to think of turning the exhibit into a book, of making a series of books of this sort, the obvious name for the series would be Exhibit Format Book. Newhall was willing and able to enlarge the text, which was a part of the original exhibit.

By October of 1959 the *Annual* had advertised this beautiful book, "timely yet timeless" as Brower put it, a book which would consider what our ability to change the world portended for our standard of life, or our very survival.[206] This book would not be hastily produced, but would be a perfect work of art, the glory and the profits going entirely to the Club. Brower suffered over his preface, revising it again and again. Adams' standards for photographic reproduction were exacting. *This Is The American Earth* would not only set the standards in the field, it would present the Sierra Club vision as a philosophical standard for the nation to live up to. Most important, it would attempt to present the conservationist message in *positive* terms, as a celebration. It even celebrated its own intellectual progenitors, not simply the late Bernard DeVoto, but "the poets, historians, philosophers and scientists, from Isaiah and Plato down through Thoreau, Marsh, Muir, and Pinchot to Aldo Leopold, Robert Marshall, Harrison Brown, John Kenneth Galbraith." Indeed the text would become the major source for Brower's inspirational "sermon" for another twenty-five years.

Newhall introduced her subject by describing the modern age as frantic, constricted, choked, where "hopes darkened," an age of greed, power, terror, clouded mind, starved eye, and empty heart.[207] Meanwhile Adams' images provided a kind of overture to her rhetorical questions about "the price of exaltation," "the value of solitude," and "the cost of freedom."

Then Brower's foreword, a continuing feature of the series, indicated exactly what the book was after.[208] It was no less than a transformation of the American myth of the frontier. As anyone who has studied American history knows, the so-called myth of the American frontier—that set of ideas and images which allowed the expansion of capitalism into this seemingly infinite resource, in the name of virtues like freedom—allowed men to speak of conquering the West when they were extracting wealth and killing Indians. Indeed Brower's foreword was set in the Tetons, the "real" West, "a place that is just about as much the way it was when trappers first saw it as a place could be and still be a part of a national park a million people see each year." Set in the "magic" of the West, in wildness, it was also set in the value of the real American "freedom of wilderness," which Brower argued was *not* materialistic, "just to be spent for the comfort, pleasure, or convenience of the generation or two who first learn how to spend them . . . wilderness is worth saving for what it can mean to itself as part of the conservation ethic; that . . . saving is imperative to civilization and all mankind, whether or not all men know it." Wilderness was the only hope for "a wide spacious freedom that can remain in the midst of the American earth." And, as Brower argued, freedom was directly connected to the national parks, which were both ecological islands and barometers for the health of the American environment—an idea which would be taken up by other conservationists soon.

Newhall's text was panoramic, a kind of free verse, apparently derived from the poet Robinson Jeffers, not entirely divorced from the optimistic Whitman, but having the kind of optimism more characteristic of Carl Sandburg, another who used Whitman's poetic form. Her purpose too was panoramic. She attempted no less than a history of conservation in America, including the causes and cures of our present condition.

Her history moved through geological ages, into the entire cultural and environmental history of man, to the decay all over the earth—fallen Rome, despoiled Greece—lamenting "an exhausted, exasperated Europe . . . where even the memory of wilderness had vanished."[209] But in the new world, "here still was Eden," as writers as disparate as Roger Williams, Jonathan Edwards, and Ralph Waldo Emerson recognized. Here "a new esthetic, that wilderness is beautiful, was being born."[210] Here the idea of national parks "began a new relation between Man and the earth."[211] Then the coming of the machine: would the end of the frontier mean "the end of Eden?" "Reckless we tore at the last great virgin resources." We might have learned conservation from Marsh, Pinchot, Muir, Theodore Roosevelt. We began to see it clearer after 1929. But "now, by machines, we are torn loose from the earth."[212] Here then was the "Mathematics of Survival": earth would be exhausted within a century. Was this worthy of man? Not if he was willing to learn the dynamics of nature. "The wilderness holds answers to more questions than we yet know how to ask."[213] "What do air, water, life require of man?" The answer had to do with the simplicity of man's basic needs. "How lightly might the earth bear Man forever." In the end, the crucial resource was man's spirit. Next to the final photograph, a print called "Aspens, New Mexico," Newhall wrote these words:

> Tenderly now
> let all men
> turn to the earth.[214]

It is easy to satirize the text, but it did exactly what it was designed to do. Adams and Newhall did more than engage the emotions, they worked on the mythical level, the words and images braided in powerful ways. Brower used the final photographic image by Adams for the rest of his years as executive director, at the top of Sierra Club stationery, representing all the Club stood for.

Reviews were impressive. Justice William O. Douglas called it "one of the greatest statements in the history of conservation." In Adams' "magnificent photographs" and Newhall's "eloquent blank verse," John B. Oakes of the *New York Times* found "the philosophy of conservation and the necessity for it." Hal Borland wrote in the *Saturday Review*: "Essentially it is a song of praise to the earth, a prayer and supplication for its endurance. We can use such songs and prayers." Even the *Deseret News* in Salt Lake City, the newspaper owned by the Mormon Church, admitted, "Let's face it. The Sierra Club has been in the forefront of virtually every effort to lock up the West's scenic resources, and this book is a most skillful, persuasive part of that campaign."[215] If, as Brower hoped, *This Is The American Earth* epitomized what the Sierra Club had been seeking on behalf of the nation's scenic resources, then the Club also finally had a vehicle for its message. Here was the sermon. The Club would come to be known in some circles not as an organization, but as the producer of Sierra Club books.

After Cedric Wright's *Words of the Earth* (1960), *These We Inherit: The Parklands of America* followed—a republication of Adams' *My Camera in the National Parks* (1950), which defined "The Park Concept" and "National Park Ideals." Adams depended on Whitman's faith in nature:

> The earth never tires,
> The earth is rude, silent, incomprehensible at first;
>   nature is rude and incomprehensible at first. . . .

Joined to Whitman's faith in democracy, "the concept of the National Parks was America's unique contribution to the democratic idea." For Adams, the national parks represented "those intangible values which should not be turned directly to profit or material advantage." The national parks should represent "an enlightened relationship of nature and man."[216]

It was not an easy job revising the myth of the West. People like Brower and McCloskey remembered what they had learned about conservation and Gifford Pinchot in elementary school. How could this utilitarian and materialistic influence—this political ideology of the Forest Service—be countered? The answer was with as many voices as possible. Adams and Newhall were the beginning; Brower would soon enlist Wallace Stegner, Eliot Porter, and Joseph Wood Krutch.

The mantle of Bernard DeVoto had fallen on Stegner—with Brower's help. More than half of the May 1959 *Bulletin* was devoted to Stegner's "The War Between the Rough Riders and the Bird Watchers."[217] Using DeVoto's terms, Stegner made a powerful statement on wilderness and the western consciousness. It was not, however, an optimistic piece in the end, concluding, "It has never been man's gift to make wildernesses. But he can make deserts, and has." Stegner's most powerful statement was to come the next December, just when it would do the most good.

Dave Pesonen, a research assistant working for James Gilligan on the wilderness portion of the Outdoor Recreation Resources Review Commission (ORRRC) report, was concerned that the report on the "Place of Wilderness in National Outdoor Recreation" might be loaded against wilderness preservation, recreation meaning only play. He thought someone might write something on wilderness as idea: "When a young man looks across a wilderness he can enjoy not only looking at it, but indulging the hope of tramping in it. But what is there in it for a sedentary old man?" What about recreation in the mind, targets for the imagination? This might be used to refute the very potent argument of wil-

derness opponents that wilderness was undemocratic because of the limited number of man days of use, as opposed to
its size. So Pesonen told Stegner, "You are the only person I
know of who is qualified to articulate these two points: the
value of knowing and the unity sprung from a cultural image
between frontier-like activities and residual frontier."[218] Stegner would write a six-page letter, to be incorporated into the
report.

Stegner remembers that Brower pushed a little. In any
case, the Wilderness Letter—as it came to be called—effectively defined wilderness "as opportunity and idea," as "a
means of reassuring ourselves of our sanity as creatures, a
part of the geography of hope."[219] That phrase, "the geography of hope," was just the thing, as it turned out. Not only
would it be an often repeated refrain in Club rhetoric, but also
it would catch the imagination of Stewart Udall, who recognized its congruence, as idea and slogan, with Kennedy's
New Frontier.

Brower saw the need to advance the Club's publishing program in a way that would make conservation—and the
Club—ever more visible in the spectrum of national issues.
Wallace Stegner alone could not illuminate the wilderness
philosophy of the Sierra Club. Neither could Ansel Adams
supply all the images the Club would require. *In Wildness Is
the Preservation of the World* represented a major advance in
the publishing program. Here, with color photographs by
Eliot Porter, was the text of Thoreau, selected by Porter and
introduced by Joseph Wood Krutch. Again, Nancy Newhall
was involved. As an active member in the Atlantic Chapter
and a resident of New York, she had seen Porter's exhibit
named "The Seasons" in Rochester and had called it to the attention of Brower after six publishing houses had passed it by.
For Brower, the material was so moving that he would "vow
openly to see it published even if I had to take up a life of
crime to get the funds for it."[220] Ten years out of Harvard med-

ical school, Porter gave up medicine and took up photography in 1939. He was most noted for his work with birds. Adams tended to capture the sublime, the power in landscape, and was best known for his images of grand geological, almost cosmic shapes and forms, perfect for interpreting the "crown jewels." Porter's work in *In Wildness* used documentary close-up detail; he was a recorder, his moment was not special, but typical. As a critic said, "One feels that the earth usurped Porter's vision and that Porter was willing to let it."[221] Brower saw immediately that Porter and Thoreau together constituted "symbiotic art." And Krutch in his introduction to the book pointed out that Thoreau too took for his theme "the daily and hourly of the usually unnoticed beauty that is close at hand."[222] The Adams vision was close kin to Muir's; Porter's was close kin to Thoreau's.

But the message in Adams and Muir was also expressed by Thoreau. As Krutch indicated, the conviction in Thoreau which underlies all others is that "this curious world which we inhabit is more wonderful than it is convenient, more beautiful than it is useful; it is more to be admired and enjoyed than used."[223] Krutch was the perfect man to interpret this message which Brower thought so timely, a century after Thoreau's death. For Krutch had been the voice, more than thirty years earlier, of *The Modern Temper*, which, as one historian puts it, "summarized his generation's disillusionment with the cheery prewar faith in inevitable progress,"[224] with science, and with the ideals of the progressives. But he had not remained the voice of disillusion. Like Porter, he had experienced a revelation and renewal by reading Thoreau; he had left his urban environment for the desert near Tucson; he had changed his profession, from studying literature and writing drama criticism to studying botany and writing about natural history. It was the very transformation of Joseph Wood Krutch that the Sierra Club wanted to make more widespread. Consequently, to acquire his voice for the Club was a turning point.

With color, *Exhibit Format* books glowed. Their audience would be widespread, urban, and perhaps upper middle class. These were not inexpensive books. Just as the function of the parks was to regenerate the minds of urban citizens in an industrial age, these books would have a similar aim.[225] Their audience was the potential wilderness user, but was also the consumer of art. This was, of course, as traditional as could be, the aesthetic tradition par excellence. Yet in the late twentieth century the link between art and nature was tenuous. Even a century earlier Thoreau had written, and the Club had later reprinted:

> October 9, 1857
> It has come to this,—that the lover of art is one, and the lover of nature is another, though true art is but the expression of our love of nature. It is monstrous when one cares but little about trees and much about Corinthian columns, and yet this is exceedingly common.[226]

Krutch himself puzzled over this. "The more the painter invents," he thought, "the further he takes us from the world which actually exists and to that extent he may even encourage us in an alienation from the real." But the photographer, Krutch decided, "discovers rather than invents," and so teaches Thoreau's most insistent biblical injunction, namely, "Be not among those who have eyes that do not see, and ears that do not hear."[227]

It was expensive to produce this kind of a publishing program. Though Brower did not take up a life of crime, he did go begging. Development of *This Is The American Earth* received help from Walter Starr, who had served for years on the Club board but was by 1957 chairman of the board of Yosemite's concessionaire, Yosemite Park and Curry Company. The book required more philanthropy, from Max McGraw and the McGraw Foundation, as well as from the late Marion Randall Parsons. With *In Wildness* Brower surely did not have to make any promises, but he received a $20,000 grant and a $30,000 interest-free loan from Kenneth and Nancy Bechtel through the Belvedere Scientific Fund. The Bechtel Corporation was not unknown in conservation circles. Created by Stephen Bechtel, Kenneth's brother, it was building Glen Canyon Dam. At various times it would employ as executives Caspar Weinberger, future secretary of defense, and George Shultz, future secretary of state. It was one of the Six Companies, as they were called.[228] It did not matter that the money came from such sources at the time, when the Club was worried about government agencies; but at the end of the decade national land-use planning would be directed not simply toward government agencies, but also toward private developers.

A View from the Northwest 1960

The Club was prepared to face the new challenges of the Kennedy administration with strong chapters, geographical diversity, a publishing program and voice even in New York, Brower's charisma, a brain trust, Phil Berry and the Foundation, Wayburn as president, McCloskey in the Northwest. It would soon have a Washington, D.C., office. Coming out of the turmoil of the 1950s, it seemed to be a healthy, growing organization.

This is how the conservation scene appeared to Michael McCloskey who had earned his degree from Harvard in 1956, served two years in the military, and had come back to Oregon, entering law school in 1958. There he met Karl Onthank, a former dean of men at the University of Oregon who was active in the Sierra Club and the local conservation group, the Obsidians. Even while a law student McCloskey "fell under Onthank's influence," and was soon working as a volunteer as chair of the Obsidians' Conservation Committee.[229] Onthank was a special sort of person to McCloskey, an old timer who had learned conservation in the Teddy Roosevelt school but had continued to develop, a kind of human bridge between the old and new kinds of conservation. Onthank was his tutor in practical conservation. In 1959 McCloskey went to a convention of the Federation of Western Outdoor Clubs and was exposed to the exciting realm of national issues. He met Brower. Meanwhile, as a student he began to do serious research on the history of conservation, and by 1961 had published his analysis of the Multiple Use–Sustained Yield Act. By that time he knew that "unless you had a wilderness line drawn it was just standard logging terrain."[230]

As he said:

> I had learned in Oregon in my early years how bitterly
> the Oregon Dunes National Seashore proposal had
> been resisted, with advocates being denounced as
> Communists, and I learned in my own community of
> Eugene, Oregon, how much a pariah one could become
> in trying to save virgin forests from the lumbermen in
> the lumber capital of the world. I had seen fistfights
> break out on the courthouse steps at wilderness
> hearings.[231]

For that reason he was prepared to admire Brower, "his fighting spirit in resisting a situation that seemed to us all at the time to be outrageous." Brower expressed the outrage, and young people like McCloskey felt less like pariahs in a time when "it was conventional wisdom that we were just overreacting."[232]

Soon he found himself working for a whole collection of conservation organizations, including the Sierra Club. He read Simons' "magnificent proposal for an Oregon Cascades National Park," which became a precursor for his own work. Though he came into the issues too late to influence initial Club policy decisions about the disposition of wilderness in Oregon or the North Cascades, he helped (in consultation with Brower) to make the strategic decision that they would push for the North Cascades as a priority over Oregon Cascades, because in the aggregate it had a higher value. "We all realized that once [the North Cascades] became a national park we would have to protect it from the Park Service."[233] During the summer of 1960 he worked with Philip Hyde to protect a valley in the Wallowa Mountains from lumbering— for Brower, at Justice William O. Douglas' request.

As a young Democrat, McCloskey looked forward to the Kennedy administration: "We felt we were on the threshold of a wholly new period and it proved to be, with what Udall later called a third wave in conservation which was environmentally oriented and qualitatively oriented rather than quantitatively."[234] As he entered this period he found it was not the fiery and impatient Brower who was most congenial, but Wayburn. Wayburn reminded him of Karl Onthank. He was not as old, but was a similar kind of person, with a sense of history; "his outstanding quality was a kind of persistence and a long sense of vision. . . . I learned from him . . . to set your sights high, not to underestimate what you could accomplish over the course of time."[235] So it was that Mc-Closkey was recruited to the Club, first as a volunteer, but within a few years as a professional. This was more than fortuitous, since he came on at exactly the time when Wayburn became president of the Club, a position he would hold for much of the 1960s.

CHAPTER SIX

The Third Wave

Wilderness Conference, 1961

The 1961 Wilderness Conference, like all great ceremonial occasions, marked the passing of the old, the coming of the new, yet celebrated the past worth preserving. In the last month of his presidency, Nathan C. Clark presented the first annual John Muir Award to William E. Colby. Clark reminded the audience that the Sierra was one of the best-protected mountain ranges in the new world, and the Sequoia the best-protected species of tree, both the result of Muir's devotion. Clark presented a framed Ansel Adams photograph of redwoods to Colby, "whose devotion has been equal to Muir's." Colby too had been a friend of the redwoods: "His achievement carries forward the historic work of John Muir in rescuing for our time the primeval places epitomized in the great national parks."[1]

Edgar Wayburn presided, reminding the participants that for ten years, since the 1951 Wilderness Conference, since the Club entered the national realm, "there was an awareness of the basic fact that threats to the wilderness of the Sierra Nevada were essentially the same as the threats to unaltered lands in any part of the world."[2] The usual group of distinguished speakers appeared: chair of the conference, John B. deC. M. Saunders, provost of the University of California's

San Francisco Medical Center; Ansel Adams, Grant Mc-
Connell, Paul Sears, Howard Zahniser, Sigurd Olson, Joseph
Wood Krutch; and Gerard Piel, publisher of *Scientific American*. In addition, the speakers' list included Edmund G.
Brown, governor of California, Stewart Udall, secretary of
the interior, William O. Douglas, U.S. Supreme Court justice,
and John P. Saylor, powerful member of the House Committee on Interior and Insular Affairs.

William O. Douglas, who had just written *My Wilderness:
The Pacific West* (1960), was well known as a naturalist, hiker,
and interpreter of the Constitution. He announced that
healthy men must take inspiration from life in all its forms.
"Preservation of values which technology will destroy. . . is
indeed the *new frontier*." Man was more than a cog, a statistic,
or a consumer; he was a spiritual being. Wilderness was a
human right. By the end of the conference Douglas had taken
up an idea expressed by Gerard Piel, that western wilderness
is identified with our Bill of Rights, that wilderness is in particular related to an understanding of the First Amendment.
Douglas drafted what he called the Wilderness Bill of Rights,
the core of a later book, which included prohibitions of pollution, a need for roadless, picnic, and camping areas, but
most important, a set of ethical standards for government officials and government decision-making. Because bureaucrats needed protection to make wise decisions, he felt that
state and federal officials should not, on retirement, work for
groups they had regulated, and that "the judicial function" of
administration should be freed by law from pressure politics.[3]

Stewart Udall would offer a surprise. Addressing many of
his remarks directly to David Brower, he suggested making a
film of *This Is The American Earth*, financed—he joked—by oil
philanthropy money. He spoke of the close and friendly relations between himself and Orville Freeman, secretary of agriculture, a situation that boded well for the creation of new
national parks, and then he read aloud Stegner's Wilderness

Letter. Never had a secretary of the interior taken his text from the Sierra Club's own canon.[4]

Although Congressman Saylor spoke enthusiastically about the progress of the wilderness bill, the real encouragement for the Club to enter the political process came from Grant McConnell, who said that conservationists would have to fight more aggressively the stereotypes they had acquired as a "selfish interest" and as "starry-eyed idealists"; otherwise, the attitudes that politics are "dirty" and that conservationists must be "realistic" became a "self fulfilling prophesy." To avoid politics was to repudiate democracy, McConnell insisted; consequently to take up a cynical or dangerous passivity was "morally wrong and contrary to the American Ethos." Passivity resulted in the Tioga Road, or in multiple use as practiced in the North Cascades.[5]

During the long dry spell of the Eisenhower administration, the Club had been waiting for this day. Douglas had been introduced to many in the Club during the summer of 1959 when Brower, the Wayburns, Berry, and future Club president Raymond Sherwin traveled through the Sierra on a pack trip with him.[6] Later, Brower and McConnell discussed with him the problems associated with the Forest Service, since Douglas was particularly concerned with wilderness. What would become known as the rights of nature would begin to bear fruit nearly ten years hence.[7] In 1960, Douglas was elected to the Club's board. He left after a short term, probably because he foresaw environmental suits coming to the Supreme Court and did not want to disqualify himself, although he told Brower that "he thought the board sometimes was a cross between a mourner's bench and an old ladies' sewing circle."[8] Douglas was a staunch and outspoken supporter of a North Cascades national park and of the Wind River wilderness.

Udall's presence at the conference was in part a result of his good relationship with Brower. Also, Stegner had sent Udall a copy of *Beyond the Hundredth Meridian*, hoping that a dose of Powell would be good for him. Results came soon; when Kennedy addressed Congress on natural resources early in 1961 (his message was acclaimed in the *Bulletin*) he called for passage of the wilderness bill, surveys for new national parks, and establishment of national seashores, including Point Reyes. He insisted on cooperation between Forest Service and Park Service.[9] Udall could cite Kennedy's conservation objectives as his own.[10]

In practice, it appeared that Udall's actions would be even more favorable than his words. Until Udall arrived in Washington, Wayburn had never been able to speak to anyone above the director of the Park Service, but Udall knew who Wayburn was, and was interested. More important, Udall had a graph on his wall showing the dramatic amount of acreage he planned to add to national parks. As Wayburn remembers, "I was duly impressed, and we became very good friends."[11]

The June 1961 issue of the *Bulletin* showed pictures of Udall rappelling from Rainbow Bridge, coached by Brower. In July the *Bulletin* reported that Udall and Freeman had made a historic tour of the Colorado Plateau during which they conducted a joint press conference.[12] Over the objections of Utah's governor George D. Clyde, who feared that the new administration was about to "bottle up enormous quantities of Utah's natural resources" and "wreck the development" of the state, Udall proposed turning over a million acres of Bureau of Land Management land into a huge new national park; Udall appeared to have the support of Freeman. This canyonlands national park seemed a bold step, or perhaps, to those who knew some history, a resurrection of the ideas of Harold Ickes. Conservationists hoped Udall would not lose Freeman's support when it came to turning Forest Service land into national parks in the Cascades.

It was a relatively easy thing to propose parks in the

"worthless lands" of Utah, Mike McCloskey thought. When he was appointed Northwest conservation representative for the Club in October, in anticipation of the new administration's policy, he discovered something less encouraging. By December he was reporting the same old "stacked deck" forestry hearings.[13] In 1962, McCloskey remembers, "Orville Freeman got hornswaggled by the timber industry into making a number of commitments . . . to step up the allowable cut in the National Forests." Many held great hope, but when Kennedy toured the West in 1962, speaking on conservation, they perceived "an effort to reinvoke the natural resource policies of FDR in the thirties, which were make-work projects."[14]

The Club believed the administration would need to be reeducated and had placed just the men within the administration's ranks. Stegner had been "vastly enthusiastic" when Udall became secretary of the interior.[15] And soon he was invited to work on Interior's program. Although Stegner stayed in Washington for only two months, as "special assistant to the secretary," his influence was immense. Udall had obviously been seduced by the Wilderness Letter, and now Stegner was enlisted to help write Udall's book, *The Quiet Crisis*.[16] Stegner helped work out the outline before he returned to other commitments, and left behind two former students, Don Moser and Harold Gilliam, to work for Udall. Stegner said, in his modest way, "It was a good book, I think. It had some impact. A lot of people accused me of writing it, which was not true at all."[17] In the meantime Stegner talked to Udall about the wilderness bill. The thesis of Udall's book—that the root of America's environmental problems was an "uncritical acceptance of conventional traditional notions of progress"— was exactly the Stegner theory and was closely associated with the thesis of *This Is The American Earth*.[18] *The Quiet Crisis* could not be criticized as rehashed FDR. Considering that Stegner, like Udall, was enthusiastic about preserving the Colorado Plateau, the proposed canyonlands park, the enlargement of Arches and Capitol Reef monuments, it is no wonder that Stegner believed Udall "was completely on the side of the environment, a good steward."[19] As Brower has observed, Udall "came out strongly against mindless growth[,] population growth and development. . . . He was the first public official in any high place who ever did that that I know of, and no one has done it since."[20] So began the honeymoon. But issues on the Colorado River closer to Udall's home state would create problems; issues closer to the Forest Service would be out of his hands and would loom large in the future, and issues having to do with commercial interests, like the redwood timber industry, would trouble his entire administration.

Udall was not a monarch. Conrad Wirth was still director of the Park Service, and his Mission 66 was still a top priority. According to Brower, Wirth did not even include the North Cascades on his list of possible new national parks. According to Stegner, the Park Service was more conservative in its programs than Udall had hoped, and it seemed that Udall might be hampered by the power of the Bureau of Reclamation.[21]

As the 1961 Wilderness Conference suggested, there were new problems on the horizon. Joseph Wood Krutch had presented a double thesis: "I personally believe that if we do not permit the earth to produce beauty and joy it will not, in the end, produce food either. . . . I sometimes fear that, if we continue to act as though men were machines, they may actually, in the end, become something very much like machines."[22] What Krutch had to say about man's mechanistic treatment of nature and of himself applied to conditions in the cities as much as to conditions in the wild, and by linking his statements he argued that the two were themselves inextricable.

Gerard Piel pointed out that the physical sciences had become the death sciences with the coming of the atomic age. If conservationists spoke in Malthusian terms, they would be suggesting, particularly to urban Americans, that the life sciences too were death sciences, and that there was no hope to be found in wildness. Catherine Wurster, a distinguished city planner from the University of California–Berkeley, told her audience, "Both the mounting need to save wild areas, and the rising demands that destroy them, stem from the same universal forces: population growth and urbanization, with rising incomes, leisure, and education."[23] She thought that the great and destructive suburban push was motivated by a desire for a piece of nature; the more successful the nature movement was, the more problems it would create for itself. Dan Luten, the retired oil company biochemist now lecturing in geography at the University of California, argued that the next wilderness conference could either prepare to examine the twin issues of urban growth and population growth or admit that "concern for wilderness is sentimentality."[24]

Environmental problems like population, pollution, and energy development along the coast of California would loom large in the coming years, even while the Club grew in stature. It was not yet clear what the Club's role ought to be in these matters. At the same time, the Club's internal problems would become formidable, and the board would have to deal with them.

Edgar Wayburn became Club president in 1961 and his rise through the ranks constituted a significant change in Club politics. His arrival as a board member in 1957 was overdue, for he had lost twice to outings leaders. But his hands had been tied, since overt electioneering was scrupulously avoided. That was always how it had been, as Wayburn remembered; "the people who were the outing leaders in their twenties and thirties became the conservationists who led the club in their forties to sixties."[25] There was a group which

The Wayburn Administration 1961–1964

included Brower, Leonard, and Farquhar that Wayburn called a "mutual admiration society." Wayburn was something new, being neither a Californian nor a climber.

Within four years of being elected to the board, Wayburn had become president. What had happened? There were few of the traditional people left to preside. Lewis Clark (1949–1951), Harold Crowe (1951–1953), Dick Leonard (1953–1955), Alex Hildebrand (1955–1957), Harold Bradley (1957–1959), and Nate Clark (1959–1961) had served. Though Edgar Wayburn believed Ansel Adams had wanted to preside, Leonard does not believe this was true. In 1961 most directors did not find Adams an appropriate president, perhaps because of his emotionalism with regard to the Tioga Road. In 1961 the decision was made informally; the board did not then vote for a president, it chose one by consensus.[26]

After the term of Nate Clark it was clear that the president had an increasingly onerous role. Not only did the greatly increased visibility of the Club require more time, but there were increasing internal problems. If Clark was willing simply to preside, and by necessity from his home distant in Los Angeles, Wayburn announced his intention to be a strong president who would remain in close touch with the professional staff. Though Brower had "enormous potential," as Wayburn put it, and they could work closely together, the president was still the chief executive officer of the Club.[27] The president would have to be available to make decisions in a crisis.

There were problems with Brower. Wayburn remembers that there was "a paranoid streak in him, a strong paranoid streak."[28] Brower threatened to quit a number of times in the late 1950s and early 1960s, and was often in open conflict with certain members of the board, particularly with Bestor Robinson. Wayburn thought, and was seconded by Brower, that the Club had to present a strong front, and so he often went out of his way to attain Robinson's support after Robinson saw that the balance of power had shifted away from his own view. But Brower was not getting along well with the board. Nor was Brower likely to get along well with such men in Washington as Congressman Wayne Aspinall, who constituted the single biggest block to a wilderness bill.

An increased work load would make it necessary for other staff members to do some of what Brower had done in the past. In several ways the Club had outgrown itself. It had fostered a public image that far outstripped its actual strength. When Wayburn assumed the presidency, it had grown to 16,500 members from fewer than 7,000 when it began its Dinosaur campaign in 1952. By the time Wayburn ended his first term in 1964, membership would be at 25,000. When he reassumed presidency in 1967, on the Club's diamond anniversary, membership would have leaped to 55,000. Though its staff was small and its resources limited, the Club could not turn back.

It could not evade modern challenges either. Wayburn was aware of the changes in the ideology of conservation. He knew too that Brower commenced to do what his critics would call packing the board, making suggestions to the Club's Nominating Committee for a new group of prominent directors like William O. Douglas, editor-in-chief Paul Brooks of Houghton Mifflin, hydrologist Luna Leopold, Wallace Stegner, John Oakes of the *New York Times*, George Marshall, and Eliot Porter. Later would come Dave Sive, Fred Eissler, Patrick Goldsworthy, Larry Moss, Phil Berry, and Martin Litton, all perceived as "Brower men."[29] Whether this was ethical or not, and whether these individuals really were Brower men, Brower's views gained more credence with the board, and Wayburn no longer presided over a mutal admiration society. In retrospect, Wayburn tended to agree that before these new members arrived "there were members of the board who were not ready for the conservation challenges of the sixties."[30] The new board members were more congenial to his own views. But he also worried that the grass-roots structure of the Club was being threatened. These people who had not moved up through the ranks would be resented, if not by the Club membership in general, then by the older, more conservative regional leaders. This was apparent in the Sierra Club council, which represented the chapters in an advisory capacity to the board, and was often in open conflict with Brower.

Wayburn decided that Brower could devote an increasing amount of time to publications, while the president could handle conservation.[31] As Brower grew more occupied with his publishing program, he also became increasingly restive under what he called the board's interference. The publication program itself, highly successful with *This Is the American Earth* and then with *In Wildness Is the Preservation of the World*, would not in the long run make money if its profits were calculated by book sales alone, though it would accelerate both the Club's growth and income from membership dues.[32] Many felt that the publication program took Brower too much away from conservation and that he was too involved in his books to make objective decisions about them. Wayburn created a more powerful Publications Committee. The Club would have to choose between the great financial risk and the enormous philosophical or political value of the books.[33]

Yet these problems grew slowly, as the Club grew more powerful, more diversified in its aims; and the problems were not entirely due to Brower. Wayburn believed he could deal with some internal conflict with diplomacy, some organizational problems through a clear separation of powers and by expanding the organizational capacity of the Club.

By September of 1963, on the advice of George Marshall, the board had chosen a very few issues and given them campaign status. The list read: the Colorado River, the redwoods, the North Cascades, the wilderness bill, and "rounding out" the national park system.[34] These campaigns would be closely associated with the publishing program and would be regulated through a five-year plan which Wayburn had been pushing. Each campaign would require professional help. Wayburn was the first Club president to require an executive assistant. These major campaigns would also require regional and national help.

The Club had gradually been obtaining a network of regional representatives, but it had great difficulty funding their work.[35] McCloskey was retained as Northwest conservation representative soon after Wayburn took office; his performance there and elsewhere would prove outstanding, but the board met increasing problems funding his position. At various times, the board attempted to hire other regional representatives, including one in the Southwest and one in Sacramento. These could not be volunteer posts if the Club was to be assured of continuing effective work. The most important opportunity would be in Washington, D.C. In 1962 Brower advocated that the Club retain as its lobbyist William Zimmerman, Jr., arguing, "We are national in the influence we can bring to bear, and we are looked to for what we are *not* producing—for lack of a nail, I would say."[36] Nevertheless, the Club treasurer objected on budgetary grounds, and even Wayburn, while granting Brower's point, doubted that the Club could continue to fund field workers and also maintain an office in Washington, D.C.[37] A Washington office implied that the Club would support lobbying, yet as late as 1963, at the Wilderness Conference, Wayburn could continue to say, "We are not a lobbying outfit."[38]

Throughout the 1960s the Club continued to work on its agreed-upon priorities—the North Cascades, the Colorado River, redwoods, Point Reyes, as a part of the California coast worth preserving, a wilderness bill, and the disposition of de facto wilderness. Brower and Wayburn wanted to act aggressively on these campaigns.[39] Yet the Club was continually distracted by problems of energy development and environmental pollution, which resulted in crises of conscience that divided the

Energy and the Coast 1958–1963

board of directors. Each of the Club's priorities proved to have a dimension associated with broader environmental problems, and environmental issues were to eventually shape the decade.

In Washington, D.C., the Club wanted Congress to pass a decent wilderness bill.[40] It wanted to see an Outdoor Recreation Resources Review Commission report that recommended wilderness.[41] It wanted to see the national parks protected in their natural condition. But most immediately the Club wanted to see a national seashore at Point Reyes, in California. This seemed a simple task, but was to have broad implications. As early as 1958 the Club had devoted an entire issue of the *Bulletin* to proposing establishment of a seashore recreation area along the coast of Point Reyes peninsula, in Marin County. Hal Gilliam pointed out in the *Bulletin* that the peninsula was an "island in time," unchanged, undeveloped.[42] California congressman Clair Engle introduced a resolution urging Interior to acquire the land. The acquisition was likely to cost about $12,000,000, according to Newton Drury. But this undeveloped coast drew increasing interest from lumbering concerns and real estate developers. Dairymen were not interested in selling out and they were supported by the Marin County Chamber of Commerce. Point Reyes was itself not a sunny southern beach, but a rugged, wild piece of coast. In other words, it did not seem to be a popular sort of recreation area, but a wonderful place. "Drive along the San Andreas Valley between Bolinas and Tomales Bay," wrote Gilliam, "and peer into the deep woods where trails could be built through dozens of miles of magnificent fir forests alongside streams and lakes." Explore the beaches, wander among the sand dunes, he continued. And consider whether a California with a projected fourfold increase in population will need such a place.

Land acquisition at Point Reyes funded by the federal government would constitute a precedent.[43] But popular support

in San Francisco was great, and local citizens created a Point
Reyes Foundation. Wayburn belonged, and Doris Leonard,
married to Richard, was vice president.[44] In fact, Doris Leonard had formed with Dorothy Varian and George Collins an
organization called Conservation Associates, an independent
foundation designed to mediate between conservationists
and industry. As Wayburn said, Varian's money allowed
George and Doris to work. They apparently had an interest in
Point Reyes, particularly in buying up land before its value
went up.[45] This may actually have confused the issue, since,
as Wayburn said, "they considered themselves as the conservationists who could make the decisions for other conservationists."[46] Another thing was confusing. Suddenly, Brower
believes, there seemed to be a lot of support for Point Reyes
from people who were close to Pacific Gas and Electric
(PG&E).[47]

The issue became complicated when the *Bulletin*, in the
course of a year, reported three separate events. First, Pacific
Gas and Electric had announced plans to build an electric
power plant at Bodega Head on Bodega Bay, fifty miles north
of San Francisco and just north of Point Reyes.[48] Then in January 1962 the Outdoor Recreation Resources Review Commission completed its report, which was followed by Kennedy's 1962 conservation message. The *Bulletin* noted that on
Point Reyes progress was being made, though "predicting the
fate of Point Reyes National Seashore has been like spotting
the pea in a shell game."[49] Six subdivisions had been approved for Point Reyes since the seashore bill had been
drafted.

David Pesonen saw a pattern in these events. The son of an
administrator for the Bureau of Reclamation whose father
had appeared at an early wilderness conference, Dave Pesonen had studied forestry, had worked for Gilligan in producing the wilderness and recreation report for the ORRRC, and
had solicited Stegner's Wilderness Letter. Now, according to

the *Bulletin*, he was conservation editor for the Sierra Club while going to law school. As Wayburn remembers, PG&E had first proposed its power plant as early as 1957. At that time the Club had supported a move to make the area part of a state park.[50] Pesonen reported now that PG&E wanted a nuclear power plant right on Bodega Head, "a seismic stepchild of the San Andreas Fault." At this point, Pesonen reported, all the Club seemed willing to do was complain at the public hearings that it was shameful if the demands for energy would "result in the systematic picking off of irreplaceable scenic and recreational sites," particularly if the only virtue of PG&E's plan was its cheapness.[51]

In "An Analysis of the ORRRC Report," appearing in the *Bulletin* one month earlier, Pesonen had aggressively denounced the report itself as "really a compromise . . . the whole document will look at home on a shelf crowded with dusty plans for The Orderly Development . . . and The Wise Management of . . . and Planning for America's [future] . . . sound without fury. The report is confusing, it contradicts itself; but saddest of all, it leans wearily on the obvious, the indisputable, the conventionally wise, the irrelevant."[52]

As far as Brower remembers, the report went astray because the Izaak Walton League assumed control of the conservationist influence.[53] Pesonen himself was disappointed not only with the report but with the committee that produced it, which included such stalwarts as Laurance Rockefeller, Fred Smith, Joseph Penfold, and others from industry, government, and conservation groups. In particular, Pesonen wondered what the report's recommendations would mean to the Bodega Head and to Point Reyes. His *Bulletin* article "The Battle of Bodega Bay" was illustrated with reprinted advertisements for subdivisions at Point Reyes (Drake's Bay Estates) and a cartoon from the *Examiner* showing a small subdivided Point Reyes park with text from the report: "'It is not growth itself that is the problem, but the pattern of growth.

Even with the great expansion to come, there will still be a certain amount of open space within urban areas.'"⁵⁴ Pesonen feared growth. Even as Kennedy announced formation of the Bureau of Outdoor Recreation to coordinate recreational planning, with Edward C. Crafts as its head, even as Kennedy seemed to support Point Reyes and other desirable parks, people like Pesonen thought the administration was not taking a sufficiently forceful stand in protecting natural resources.

Pesonen was rising in the Club ranks; so were people who would oppose him. William (Will) Siri (b. 1919) had joined the board in the traditional manner. He was a famous climber and had led a Club-sponsored expedition to Makalu in the Himalaya in 1955. He was also a biophysicist and worked at the Lawrence Livermore Laboratory. As Siri saw himself, he was not a conservative on the board. Unlike Alex Hildebrand, a chemical engineer and the head of research at Standard Oil, Siri was a scientist. Of Hildebrand, he thought, "If an engineer presented an analysis, you had to accept that as a factual assessment and therefore adjust your plans accordingly." But Siri understood the difference between engineering and science and "couldn't buy that." "For Bestor and Alex," he remembers, "long experience in their professions may have convinced them that the most effective practice was the kind of relations they would have with other lawyers and businessmen, i.e., negotiate the best deal you could."⁵⁵ Unlike Leonard, who was a lawyer but "had a fair command of technical matters" as a result of his corporate role at Varian Associates, Siri believed he was a more disinterested party.⁵⁶ Siri compared himself to Leonard: "Dick was not a man who compromised; he wanted to fight through battles." On the other hand, Siri recalls, "the board didn't think it appropriate for us to be involved in these technical issues. The Sierra Club had not yet emerged from its preoccupation with wilderness preservation. Most of the members felt that was where the club's emphasis should continue to be placed."[57] Siri did not approve of Pesonen; as he later said, "Dave Pesonen appeared to discover at Bodega Head a major goal in life—to head off nuclear energy and maybe the Pacific Gas and Electric Company."[58] In fact, Siri thought that the two goals were indistinguishable in Pesonen's position. That was irrational, Siri believed, since there was no escaping the growth of California and the required planning, especially for energy. As Leonard would later say, after the Club changed its position in the 1970s, "What [the Club is] after is zero growth in the economy and in power, which is not politically realistic."[59]

Like Leonard, Siri thought Pesonen was too radical and an amateur.[60] Even Brower believed at first that Pesonen tended to overdramatize, but in retrospect said that "I don't think he was more radical . . . I think that he was simply right, and I wavered." When Brower had responded to the gag rule in 1960, he had argued that conservationists like Pesonen were by nature amateurs; they were watchdogs.[61] Though Siri was no compromiser, according to his own lights, he wanted the Club to be more sophisticated. When he commented on another opponent of nuclear power, Fred Eissler, he noted that the man was an English teacher, quite intelligent, but only familiar with the lay literature; as a result, Eissler "was quite enterprising in selecting what was consistent with his own feelings about the subject." Siri's influence on the matter of nuclear power and other environmental issues would grow, and he would become president of the Club in 1964. In the meantime, much of his time was devoted to planning for the American Everest Expedition. As he remembers, "Perhaps the observation of men under stress on Everest was good training for the years that followed in the Sierra Club."[62]

This matter of trust or distrust of technology—in this case nuclear technology—was dramatized in September of 1963 when Dave Pesonen and Phil Berry came to the board with an argument against the Bodega plant, based on safety factors. The result was, as Wayburn said, a "stormy session" of the board. By this time Point Reyes had been declared a national seashore, though with an insufficient land acquisition budget of $14,000,000—not enough to buy out ranchers who were increasingly enthusiastic about selling out.[63] Meanwhile, Pesonen had put together a booklet on the planned power plant at Bodega, and Brower helped finance its distribution, sending out a note to "Conservation Cooperators" indicating that the "details of the presentation and the analysis are the author's and not necessarily the opinion of the club," but also admitting that the Club started Pesonen on the project and that many members helped.[64] Harold Bradley, for one, wondered how the Club could fight nuclear power when it had used the argument at Echo Park that dams were outdated because nuclear technology was "right around the corner." "I suspect we shall be fighting the Echo Park dam again one of these days," Bradley concluded. "How strong will the old argument sound if we oppose nuclear reactors today on the ground of danger?"[65]

At the same time, PG&E had long-range plans for another nuclear power plant at Nipomo in the vicinity of Santa Maria–Oceano Dunes, part of the California coast that some wanted preserved as a state park.[66] The Club had reaffirmed its interest in "scenic and community values" at Bodega.[67] Wayburn and others met with PG&E the next month and discussed plans for power plants along the coast and in High Sierra primitive areas. The Club asked that the state Public Utilities Commission plan a new hearing for the Bodega Bay plant. This was refused. Then Phil Berry presented his proposal that the Club file a brief before the California Supreme Court, "limited to conservation issues only."[68] Berry's proposal was hotly debated, then rejected, only to be accepted a month later.[69] Yet its acceptance constituted a compromise. The board would take no stand on nuclear power plants per

se. Indeed, it passed a resolution, sponsored by Alex Hildebrand, declaring that since "plants using fossil fuel would be
equally disfiguring," it was opposed to any power plants on
shorelines of high scenic or recreational potential.

The issue of methods and tactics came up again. This time
Alex Hildebrand wanted to extend the gag rule of December
1959 as a result of Pesonen's report. Hildebrand believed that
arguments presented in the name of the Club "should not
normally include professional opinions of the type that are
controversial within the profession itself. . . . Safety arguments frequently fall into this category."[70] Another heated
discussion ensued, the motion was tabled, and a committee
appointed to review the issue. Hildebrand wished not only to
disassociate the board's position from Pesonen's, but to condemn Brower for distributing Pesonen's analysis. Though the
Club's policy was to prevent the scenic California coast from
being sacrificed, as far as Brower remembers, certain members
of the board meant, "That's our policy, but we're not going to
do anything about it."[71]

The board chose to see Pesonen's antagonism to PG&E as a
kind of paranoia. The Forest Service had already been alienated; why start making enemies of private industry? Brower
on the other hand wanted to know why PG&E had been secretive from the beginning about the power plant, hiding the
fact that it would be nuclear.[72] Martin Litton, in retrospect,
wonders. After all, he thinks, few were much dismayed by
the prospect of nuclear power in 1963.[73] Brower believes that
PG&E support helped push through the Point Reyes National
Seashore because, as one of his advisers suggested, it wanted
space down wind from its nuclear reactors. And he believes
that Conservation Associates knew what was going on.
Many years later he would joke, "If you have to choose between being naive or paranoid—I don't think there are any
other choices—I guess I would rather be paranoid. Naive
people look so simple minded."[74] The board was not willing

to be naive, but neither was it going to be paranoid. Dave Pesonen would have to carry on his campaign alone.

In 1962 Rachel Carson's book about pesticides, *Silent Spring*, was published.[75] In stark and shocking terms she described the heritage of death as it traveled right up the chain of life. Carson popularized the idea of ecology and criticized man's conquest and management of nature. To a greater extent than the Club may

Wilderness and Pesticides 1962–1963

have considered, she was writing about wilderness in a way that would change Club policies, not only about wilderness management, but about the Club's very involvement in environmental issues and questions of safety. Wilderness and environment could no longer be separated.

Man's desire to overprotect himself from pests, predators, or weeds, Carson thought, had to be tempered by a recognition that man shared the earth. "As crude a weapon as a cave man's club," she said, "the chemical barrage has been hurled against the fabric of life."[76] By turning his own knowledge against the earth, man erred philosophically: "The 'control of nature' is a phrase conceived in arrogance . . . when it was supposed that nature exists for the convenience of man." When men broadcast in a nonselective way such suffering as Carson documented, the question became "not only scientific, but moral. . . . The question is whether any civilization can wage relentless war on life without destroying itself, and without losing the right to be called civilized."[77]

Carson laid this problem on three doorsteps. First, modern man did not understand ecology or the effects of chemicals on ecosystems. Second, "This is an era of specialists, each of whom sees his own problem and is unaware of or intolerant of the larger frame in which it fits." And third, "It is also an era dominated by industry, in which the right to make a dollar at whatever cost is seldom challenged."[78] *Silent Spring* was the most influential critique of technological progress to appear in the 1960s, and primed the pump for Udall's *The Quiet Crisis*, as the similarity of the titles suggests.

The Club had created a general policy on pesticides in the late 1950s, even though many on the board had felt that the subject was beyond the realm of Sierra Club concerns.[79] Pesticides became a local issue in 1959 when the Park Service announced plans to spray for needle-miner moths in part of the lodgepole pine forest in Yosemite National Park. The Club concurred in the proposal, approving spraying in campgrounds only, urging "that the need for intensive study of the ecological effects be recognized as a specific part of the spraying project."[80] But this concurrence came home when the Club allowed the service to spray its own property at Soda Springs in Tuolumne Meadows, since it was used as a campground.

Carson's book sharply divided the Club ranks precisely along the lines of amateurs and professionals. *This Is The American Earth* had included a brief criticism of pesticides, which called out a vigorous response from professional chemist and Club member Tom Jukes, who worked for American Cyanamid. His attitude toward *Silent Spring* was predictably sharp, negative, and unswerving. But his argument was not entirely to be ignored. He defended DDT, which protected people against malaria and perhaps saved millions from disease:

> I saw a basic conflict between my philosophy and that of the new movement within the Sierra Club. I believe that I should help people to be protected against diseases and starvation. Which means using science to improve food supply and improve methods of treating diseases. This is really what I have been spending my professional life in doing.[81]

Alex Hildebrand—an engineer by training—was not impressed by Carson. In 1981 he remembered, "I can't think of her name now, but some woman who is not a scientist, wrote a story about terrible pesticides."[82] As Hildebrand remembered, she made "a tremendous impression on Dave [Brower] and others," and there was "something to what she said." The problem was that members of the Club "started getting into things like this where they weren't technically qualified to understand what we were talking about, and then they became too broad, and not selective enough in their criticism." Alex's father, Joel, was also bothered by an amateurish interest not only in pesticides, but in chemical fertilizer. What he perceived as Brower's neglect of scientific accuracy finally led to his own resignation from the Club.[83]

Brower, on the other hand, invited Carson to attend the Wilderness Conference of 1963. As Will Siri knew, the academic community itself was divided in its view of Carson's book, and most biologists found her writing, as Siri phrased it, "somewhat hysterical and not well founded." Nevertheless, there was general agreement among biologists that her basic thesis was correct. As a biophysicist, Siri realized that the academic debate was not as important as the effectiveness of Carson's book in making a vital issue visible.[84] It was too visible for the Club to ignore.

Brower wanted the Club to begin considering environmental issues close at hand. He thought the education of children in their own home towns was where conservation should begin. For that reason he promoted and narrated the Robert C. Stebbins film *Nature Next Door*. He began to see that the popularity of environmental issues would strengthen, rather than dilute, the wilderness movement. The *Bulletin* soon printed a long and reasonable review of the reaction among scientists and others to *Silent Spring*.[85] But Club discussion of pesticides would take place at first in a limited context. Were they appropriate in national parks? This issue was discussed in the Leopold Report on wildlife management in national parks, written by A. Starker Leopold and other biologists in March of 1963 and reprinted in its entirety in the *Bulletin* shortly after it was made public.[86] Bruce Kilgore, editor of the *Bulletin*, said the report advocated "a new era of ecologically-oriented management," relating it to Carson; the parks, like the environment generally, had become victims of overprotection and insufficient ecological knowledge.[87] The thesis of the report itself reflected the composition of the group that produced it, all professional wildlife biologists: "The major policy change we would recommend to the National Park Service is that it recognize the enormous complexity of ecologic communities and the diversity of management procedures, required to preserve them."[88]

The report criticized some methods at that time used by the Park Service as "potentially dangerous," and raised serious questions about mass applications of insecticides. It advocated control of wildlife populations, but said that "insofar as possible, animal populations should be regulated by predation and other natural means." Further, the Leopold Report argued that the Park Service was in the dark about ecological issues and had to recognize in its research that national park boundaries were not ecological boundaries. The same issue of the *Bulletin* noted that despite the Leopold Report, an intensive program of spraying for needle-miners would be undertaken in Yosemite that July, using technical assistance supplied by the Forest Service.

Though the 1963 Wilderness Conference did not after all include Rachel Carson, who was already ill from the cancer which would take her life, it did include a speech by her editor, Paul Brooks, and her presence was felt throughout.[89] Robert L. Rudd, a zoologist from the University of California–Berkeley, talked about DDT concentrations in fish taken from the San Francisco Bay. Speakers like Wallace Stegner could say only, "I certainly cannot speak from scientific knowledge. Nor can I speak from wisdom. But I *can* speak from fear. I am running scared. I can speak also, I suppose, from the mourn-er's bench, because this unbright cinder unfortunately is one world. The seas and the land and the air do interpenetrate, and we live in air as fishes live in water, though we live on land."[90] Even in such a mood, the Club presented John Muir Awards to Ansel Adams "in gratitude for his insistence that the great gestures of the earth not be transformed into some-thing less," and to Olaus Murie "in appreciation of his wis-dom, simplicity and integrity, which shine through his paint-ings and drawings, his spoken and written words, and infuse his philosophy for wilderness."[91]

Stewart Udall assured the audience that his views re-mained unchanged after two years. He further listed what he called obsolete assumptions, including "the assumption that man must destroy nature in order to 'conquer' it . . . . The as-sumption that science alone can solve all our problems . . . . The assumption that the population explosion is inevita-ble."[92] James Gilligan's summary of the ORRRC report on wilderness cited among the environmentally related values of wilderness "scientific research potentials," "essential habi-tat for many species of scarce plants and animals," and "pure air and water," as well as wilderness values for watersheds, culture and history, beauty, recreation through sports, and "refinement of sensory impressions."[93]

But the most controversial talk was given by Stephen Spurr, dean of the School of Natural Resources at the Univer-sity of Michigan. A forester, ecologist, and pioneer in the field of aerial mapping as applied to natural resource inventory, he challenged the wilderness advocates in his discussion of "The Value of Wilderness to Science."[94] He believed "in the intelli-gent use of our technical skills to create desirable wilderness ecosystems in the future," since "we are already managing wilderness in a very real sense. We should continue to do so. We should openly bring the immense skill of modern science and technology to bear to create more and better wildernesses." His was the dark side of Carson's thesis. If, as she argued, man's influence on his environment was more pervasive than anyone had supposed, man was inescapably changing his environment, and there was no turning back. He could only learn how to tinker or manipulate better. Spurr confronted many assumptions, including those of the Leopold Report. A truly biocentric approach to wilderness, he argued, would show no balance or permanence in an ecosystem, would show that "stability is only relative, and only superficial," that the term "exotic" is meaningless, since from the standpoint of wilderness there is no difference between native and introduced species, that there is no such thing as climax, that "natural succession will never recreate an old pattern, but will constantly create new patterns." So, he argued, "it is impossible to reestablish the wilderness that we in our nostalgia desire . . . we may create a wilderness in the twentieth century . . . but it will not be the wilderness of our youth." Interest in such a thing as "forest primeval" or "virgin forest" was anthropocentric and finally unrealistic. Meanwhile, since "we cannot turn back the clock," the managers were ready to create new ecosystems.

In publishing the proceedings of the conference, Brower could not resist rebutting Spurr's proposal. Therefore he devoted two pages to commentary by his assistant, Robert Golden, who recognized what a threat Spurr's "synthetic ecosystems" represented to the wilderness movement. Brower finally commented in a note that management might be applied to Golden Gate Park or Central Park, or in multiple-use projects, but that we should save "as much unspoiled and unmanaged wilderness as possible, just in case Professor Spurr happens to be wrong."[95] He also used his publisher's preface to argue with Spurr. Though Wayburn tried to prevent these comments from being published in the "objective" proceedings, writing, "It is repugnant . . . to have to write to you like this, Dave," Brower's views were so strong that he disregarded Wayburn's command.[96]

The Leopold Report recommended creation of a policy to preserve wilderness in the parks and "where necessary to re-create . . . the ecologic scenes viewed by the first European visitors," and the wilderness bill would recognize wilderness "as an area where the earth and its community of life are untrammelled by man"; but the full horror of *Silent Spring* suggested that it might be too late. So it was problematic whether the coming of environmentalism supported the wilderness movement or detracted from it. As Michael Mc-Closkey was later to write, "In the context of the new environmental movement, wilderness preservation appears to many as parochial and old fashioned. It looks suspiciously like retreat to fantasy or withdrawal from the problems of the 'real world.'"[97]

McCloskey's rebuttal to the argument that a desire for wilderness is a retreat into fantasy was written in 1972 and focused on another issue which Spurr had passed over rather quickly. Wilderness constituted both a biological standard and a reservoir for genetic material, as ecologists like Frank Fraser Darling had argued. And, as McCloskey remembered A. J. Rush saying, "When man obliterates wilderness, he repudiates the evolutionary force that put him on this planet. In a deeply terrifying sense, man is on his own."[98]

The coming of environmentalism required the Club to take a stand on pesticides and other environmental issues, Will Siri believed; but it would not do so until Siri became president of the Club. Wilderness, and parks as well, would have to be perceived not as islands, but as part of the larger environment. A wilderness bill would have to be pushed through.

Entering into its new and problematic publishing program under the Wayburn administration, the Club continued to publish its enlarged *Bulletin*, printed the proceedings of the wilderness conferences, and engaged a historian; furthermore it capitalized on the success of *This Is The American Earth* with a series of *Exhibit Format*

Publications 1960–1964

books, including five theme books, educational and directed toward public attitudes on wilderness and conservation: *This Is The American Earth* (1960), *Words of the Earth* (1960), *In Wildness Is the Preservation of the World* (1962), *These We Inherit* (1962), and *Not Man Apart* (1964). On the other hand, *The Last Redwoods* (1963), *The Place No One Knew* (1963), *Time and the River Flowing* (1964), *Gentle Wilderness* (1964), and *The Wild Cascades* (1964) were published to enhance and perhaps spearhead Club conservation priorities.[99]

This ambitious program was Brower's. As Will Siri recognized, Brower was almost always ahead of the board. And Brower may have wanted to use the publishing program to "bring the board along."[100] He never saw the publishing program as anything less than a natural extension of the Club's educational and conservation priorities, and he saw it as a chance to act unencumbered. "In his own mind, and on the outside, Dave *was* the Sierra Club," said Wayburn.[101] Brower has always indicated that this was not so at all.[102] Soon after being appointed executive director, when he drafted a publications policy which included an editorial board to be chaired by the editor of the *Bulletin*, Brower mentioned that someone might want to control the content of publications through guidelines. By 1957 he was chafing against the restraints of guidelines set down by the board. At first he thought the publications "should be presented interestingly, with suitable dignity . . . in an attractive format (but not necessarily an expensive or elegant one)."[103] A decade later he was producing expensive books in great quantity. The contention of ideas in the 1960s required a more elaborate editorial policy, including checks on the discretion of the *Bulletin*'s editor. But Brower was after bigger game. In a whimsical way he wrote in 1963 that the population of California doubled every fifteen years, but the Club was doubling every seven. "You can project those two curves and find that before long we will have everyone in the state belonging to the

Sierra Club."[104] Yet his ambitions generated problems for the board because of what Wayburn called his "freewheeling personality," or in more practical terms, because the Club had not established a sufficient set of economic and administrative procedures.

Nate Clark tried to address the administrative procedures of a growing organization late in 1960. Under his leadership, the Club divided its operations into publishing, conservation, lodges and lands, outings, and administration (including member services), each area controlled by a committee. That meant the Club would appoint a Publications Committee to review, evaluate, and authorize publication of manuscripts, to control expenditure of funds and review the budget, to "determine the standards of appearance and tone" so that publications were consistent with Club policy, and to assure cooperation with other areas of the Club.[105] Clark had in mind a rather traditional group for the committee. He asked August Frugé, director of the University of California Press, to chair the Publications Committee, George Marshall to be vice chair, Francis Farquhar to be the financial authority, and Martin Litton of *Sunset Magazine* and Robert C. Miller, director of the California Academy of Sciences, to serve as members. Yet the board continued to oversee personally the practical details of the publishing program, deciding in each case whether a book was to pay its own way or come within the category previously judged by the board as justifiable for appropriate conservation causes. By the end of 1962 it was clear that Brower resented coming before the board for approval so frequently, and that the task detracted from the board's attention to conservation matters.[106]

Meanwhile, as Wayburn remembered, the success of *This Is The American Earth* "changed Dave's whole way of looking at the conservation movement. He saw what a book could do— I think he recognized it before any of the rest of us did—and he was the creator."[107] Sometime in 1961 Brower arrived at

Wayburn's house with photographs by Eliot Porter which would become *In Wildness*. Wayburn was impressed: "These were a revelation in color photography." And the time seemed right, with improved technology and the coming popularity of the 35-millimeter camera. Wayburn "helped pave the way in the board of directors," which was necessary because color books were innovative and could be very expensive.[108] Wayburn also willingly accepted a larger portion of the conservation duties while Brower devoted himself to the books. Though the costs of the publishing program began to appear menacing in the next few years, Wayburn believes that "the books made the Sierra Club a nationwide organization before the membership did."[109] Conversely, the books made the membership figures for the Club leap ahead. Between 1958 and 1965 membership grew from 12,346 to 29,153 and assets of the Club from $372,598 to $1,179,953.[110] But its liabilities grew also, at an astronomical rate.

With great growth things did not go smoothly. Brower was pushing himself very hard and had a tendency to alternate between self-confidence and depression. He had reason to feel stress. Despite the high quality of the books he was producing, he continued to operate on what he believed was a shoestring budget. He tried to fund the books from gifts and grants, but raising money was itself an onerous task. As everyone knew and feared, if he ever published a money-losing book the Club would be in deep trouble.[111] He chafed at the Publications Committee's restraint. In retrospect, placing Brower's program in the control of a committee which included Farquhar, a former editor of the *Bulletin*, and Frugé, Brower's former employer at the University of California, was a dangerous tactic.

Nevertheless, Brower had the strong support of Adams, who had not only published two books with the Club and was scheduled for his third, but had become a member of the

Publications Committee. By the end of 1962, Adams believed that the publications of the Club constituted its strongest foundation and most important activity.[112] Consequently, he advocated expanding the program and including a showcase *Annual* for the *Bulletin*. Adams—the photographer best represented in the Club's publications—was coming to be identified with the very image of the Sierra Club. Nevertheless, he praised the program as Brower's, and feared for Brower's personal health. Adams believed that Brower had been overextending himself, and in a friendly way Adams warned Brower that for the public, the executive director of the Club had become "Mr. Sierra Club." This name, with its import, would be in common use over the next few years and would add to Brower's taxing duties. Adams' enthusiastic, almost frantic mode of expression in writing in support placed a heavy and highly personal burden on Brower to make his publications successful. However, Adams' high estimate of publications was not universal; in August of 1963 the publications program was challenged by the chair of the Club's own Publications Committee.

August Frugé requested a meeting of the Publications Committee with President Wayburn to clarify the proper place of publishing in the Club, since nobody knew where this program, which "takes up a major share of our energies and resources," was leading.[113] Frugé's memorandum requesting the meeting spoke for more conservative members of the Club, like Francis Farquhar, who desired to limit growth. It also called out strong responses from Brower and Adams. The Frugé memo and its responses became a focus for dissenting views about Club direction; it asked some basic questions about the direction of Club growth, and because it attacked Brower's pet program, even five years later it was still being circulated by people like Richard Leonard in an attempt to curb Brower's discretion and perhaps have him deposed.[114]

"The basic issue, in practical terms, is whether 1) publishing shall be the servant of the conservation and the other activities of the Club . . . not a goal in itself; or whether 2) we want to embark on a long range general publishing program," Frugé wrote.[115] Frugé went beyond priorities to ask that the executive director "be ready to predict the effect this [publishing] will have on the Club, financially and in every other way, during the next several years," a task to daunt any administrator. Further, Frugé announced on the second page of his five-page document that the Club was heading toward becoming "primarily a publishing organization," and "it is not impossible for the Club to become something like a smaller and less commercial version of *American Heritage*." He criticized such books as Porter's *In Wildness* as "general nature propaganda," and deprecated the second Porter book, *The Place No One Knew*, "since the battle was already lost and the book was designed more as art than as propaganda."

For Frugé, the Club was "not committed to *book* publication and especially not to expensive books; when a pamphlet or a magazine article promises to be more effective, even if it provides no income, it will be preferred." "We intend to husband our resources, human as well as financial," he wrote; the Club should publish "useful books," and those "with a close and direct relationship to the Sierra Club," and "books that take a direct and immediate part in the battle to preserve parks, wilderness areas, and other outdoor regions."

Insensitive to the sophisticated relationship between Brower's publishing and conservation aims, Frugé dismissed *The Place No One Knew*, saying, "A book on the part of the canyon that is not yet lost would strike closer to the mark." He disagreed with Adams' central tenet that Club publicity begin to reach emotions, and with Brower's judgment that a book which played upon emotion might have more effect than a straightforward crusade.

Adams responded vigorously.[116] Not only did he defend the

artistic merit of *The Place No One Knew*, but he argued that the book was meant to initiate a vigorous campaign centered on the lands of the Colorado Plateau. If it did not, that was the fault of the conservation department. Adams could not believe that Frugé misunderstood the purposes and intended audience of the *Exhibit Format* books. They were meant to expand conservation influence beyond the readers of pamphlets and magazine articles. As an artist, he recoiled from Frugé's desire for plain methods. He believed art played an important role in the conservation movement. Frugé doubted the ability of the books to bring in new Club members, but Adams knew from personal experience that the books did bring in new members. And on the question of membership, Adams had an acute sense that Frugé did not appreciate the evolution of the Sierra Club. The Sierra Club was no longer only a club. It was not likely to become only a publisher any more than it had ever been only a recreational organization. Changing times would require new emphasis in Club activities, and some risks. Adams emboldened his most important assertions by typing in capitals. Without boldness, the Club, like a man, would grow old. As Adams understood clearly and expressed decisively, limitations on the Club's publications would in the end limit the Club's sphere of influence.

When Wallace Stegner weighed the Adams and Frugé perspectives, he decided that the Club had many advantages as a publisher, in timeliness and in "dedicated and concentrated effectiveness." Though he could see the cause for Frugé's perturbation, he decided to side with Adams and encourage a vigorous publication program: "So in spite of my enthusiastic agreement with August's plea for a clear policy, I'm personally all in favor of our going ahead, involving the club in a publication program that will be right up to the edge of the club's financial possibilities."[117]

Brower was particularly upset, saw conspiracies, believed

Frugé and Farquhar were resisting the Club's natural evolution. Earlier that year, for instance, Farquhar had responded to a reader's criticism of the *Bulletin* by asking that "something is done to keep the Sierra Club on the main track and not go whirling all over the country. . . . I'm all for our doing our share in the national Conservation field, but not for trying to take on the whole job at the expense of the distinctive character of the Sierra Club."[118] Brower admitted that he owed Farquhar his stint as editor on the *Bulletin*, but not agreement about limiting Club growth. Farquhar, Brower wrote, "wishes we would recede to a club of about 3,000, with all emphasis on the Sierra."[119] As Wayburn and Litton remember, Brower attributed Frugé's criticism to professional jealousy and to Frugé's fear that Sierra Club Books would compete with the University of California Press.[120] If that was so, Brower did not try to air the issue in public; Frugé, in turn, put his argument in terms of finances and long-range goals of the Club.

When he defended his goals and finances, Brower complained about what he called "sand in the gears," "red tape," and the "High Cost of Consensus," and pointed out Farquhar's strong opposition to *In Wildness* and *The Place No One Knew*, books "widely held to be some of the most beautiful and effective conservation publishing yet to have happened." He also pointed out that disagreements among members of the Publications Committee had resulted in costly delays in publishing books. "I know, because I have been in the thick of it for ten years, that nothing the Sierra Club ever did in print or in film has been so effective. I have been close to the situation for 25 years in all, so this is not just a flash judgment." If there was any sense in beginning the program, and if this important part of conservation was to continue past "our publishing honeymoon," then the Club would have to look ahead. "Let me get on with the books and spare me— and yourselves—the constant exhange of memos," he pled;

"I request that you rely upon my judgment." He would take responsibility, "but for the good of the cause, *let us not worry our publishing program out of existence!*"[121]

Brower was persuasive, as everyone agreed who witnessed his orations from the quarterdeck and before the board. Though the board would delegate more power to the Publications Committee for overseeing Brower's work, it also continued to give him his head.[122] Because Frugé's original questions did not get answered, they would be raised over and over for the next five years; because they were not resolved decisively, they would fester and the situation would worsen. In retrospect, Brower was so completely committed to the *Exhibit Format* books—even now he thinks of them almost as children—that he could not judge the cost of their birth in a larger context. But if Brower pursued the glory of publishing, he also labored for the Club, and produced *Exhibit Format* books to support the three major Club campaigns of the 1960s: for the Grand Canyon, a Redwoods national park, and a North Cascades national park.

Thousands of people contributed, and in 1931, with the   **Redwoods**
help of the Save-the-Redwoods League and the Rockefeller   **1960–1965**
family, the State of California acquired some 9,400 acres,
including Bull Creek flats, for Humboldt State Park. . . . The
grove of giants was christened the Rockefeller Forest and California
took great pride in owning this, perhaps the very finest of all
stands of sempervirens.
Peggy Wayburn, "The Tragedy of Bull Creek"

Sempervirens: green forever. A state park, everyone supposed, guaranteed that the trees were saved forever. But in the winter of 1955–1956 great storms came to the California coast, and the redwoods in Rockefeller Forest were devastated. How could this happen? Peggy Wayburn pointed out in the

Bulletin that logging in the watershed above the forest had been going on unnoticed sinced 1947. Perhaps, as she supposed, because the logging was not done by one of the "old-line companies," it was irresponsible. When the rains came, they swept down sediment and debris and devastated everything; 420 giant redwoods fell in the winters of 1955–1957, 22 redwoods fell in 1959. The moral, she wrote, was plain: "Scenic resources cannot be considered out of context with the land that supports them. Protection of a whole ecological unit of land is essential if there is to be valid protection of any part at all."[123] The old school of noblesse oblige conservationists, like John D. Rockefeller, Jr., had not considered ecological issues seriously enough.

Martin Litton had sent a few dollars for the Save-the-Redwoods League, and had collected money for redwoods while he was a second lieutenant during World War II. As he guessed later, "the Club had never bothered with the coastal redwoods because that was the province of the Save-the-Redwoods League, which supposedly had done enough. We found out it hadn't done enough, not because it hadn't wanted to, but because everything Save-the-Redwoods League had done had been pretty much under the control of the logging companies."[124]

The state parks were where the League had acquired land, and that was where the logging companies wanted them to be; the very location of the parks in turn often made them vulnerable to the practices of the logging companies themselves, who owned all the redwood forests the League might want to buy. Even if enough money could be raised—and that would be increasingly difficult as the value of redwood soared—it was neither possible to force the logging companies to sell land nor make them act responsibly toward land they could affect with their upstream practices. Phil Berry put this in legal terms when he described the "legal loopholes" in the California Forestry Act which "encourage damage to forest and soil productivity and loss of important redwood parks."[125]

What was to be done? The Club was careful not to criticize the League, which had provided the many redwood parks the state owned. Such Club notables as Will Colby, Duncan McDuffie, Newton Drury, Francis Farquhar, and Richard Leonard had served on the board of the League. It was a mark of great social distinction to be a part of this elite group. Newton Drury reminded members "how much poorer the natural scene in the United States would be but for [John D., Jr.] Rockefeller's realization of its importance and his determination to aid in its preservation."[126] When John D. Rockefeller, Jr. died in 1952, his son Laurance became a force in the League. Brower believed the financial resources of men like the Rockefellers and McGraws and Mallinckrodts would be needed to reserve irreplaceable redwood forests.[127]

By 1960 the situation seemed critical. With the exception of the 75,000 acres in the redwood belt that the League had managed to acquire and donate as state parks, all of the virgin redwood forests in the State of California were in private hands and being cut at an alarming rate. As a result of the article Peggy Wayburn wrote for the *Bulletin* and the explorations she and her husband made, Edgar Wayburn had a growing "sense of almost personal guilt—I had been too busy with other things to do anything about the redwoods."[128] Meanwhile, Litton had been just "exploring around," as he remembers, seeking material for a *Sunset* article. He came across the forest in Redwood Creek, near the town of Orick, half way between Eureka and Crescent City: "There was Redwood Creek, and there was this ridge-to-ridge forest. . . . You could still see virgin tributaries where there had been no logging at all from the top on down."[129] There were other places too, like the King Range in Humboldt County where Litton flew the Leonards and other Sierra Club people. Fine forests grew along the Klamath, but they were going fast.

A lot of conservationists were converging on the coast, as Wayburn recalls:

> There was influence going back and forth. We were
> looking for the optimum redwood forest to preserve.
> We wanted not just to find groves, as Save-the-
> Redwoods League and the state of California wanted;
> we were looking for a redwood forest which could be
> preserved in perpetuity. We were looking for a forest to
> preserve from ridge to ridge, from the coast to the
> inland limits of the redwoods.[130]

All of this exploration turned up some wonderful country, but the sticking point was, in Litton's words, that "the redwoods would have to come back into our hands by money."[131] As Muir had written in the 1890s, "God has saved [the *Sequoia gigantea*] from drought, disease, . . . leveling tempests and floods; but he cannot save them from fools—only Uncle Sam can do that."[132] In this case it was not the strong arm only, but the bankbook of Uncle Sam that was needed.

Peggy Wayburn, as general secretary for the 1961 Wilderness Conference, arranged to sit at the conference next to Stewart Udall, to propose that there be a redwood national park. He was interested and sent John Carver, an assistant, to take a look. The Club suggested the possibility of forests on the Klamath, but Wayburn remembers Udall thinking "that there was too much of a fight involved."[133] There was increasing resistance from the redwood industry, and Litton remembers Udall mouthing the logger's line:

> "Do you realize that if you gentlemen get this park
> that you want with all the state parks and all that, that
> more than half of the standing redwoods remaining will
> be in parks?"
> We said, "Mr. Secretary, if we get *no* national park at
> all, it's only a matter of a very few years until one hun-

dred percent of all the standing redwoods are in
parks."[134]

But Udall remained interested and sent two planners from
the Park Service, Chet Brown and Paul Fritz. Everyone converged on the house of the Hagood family in Orick, California, right on Redwood Creek. Litton recalls, "It got to be a
regular party place . . . always a very festive situation." The
Park Service planners, the Hagoods, local supporters young
and old were there. "The Wayburns became part of the Hagood family, practically. They came and went with their
daughters."[135]

In April of 1963 Udall announced plans for a redwood national park, and a month later the Park Service brought *National Geographic* into the picture, for public exposure and because the Geographic Society would provide research money
for the extensive surveys necessary.[136] Brown and Fritz agreed
that Redwood Creek was the most suitable area and began to
put together a report. But the politics, within the Club and
without, had only begun. Brower and Litton believed that
Newton Drury of the Save-the-Redwoods League did not
know of the existence of Redwood Creek's superb forest, and
believed that was why the League advocated a plan by Drury
to "round out the state parks and then somehow accommodate these into a redwood national park."[137] Rather than suggesting a whole new watershed at Redwood Creek as a national park, the League proposed increasing the areas of
already extant state redwood parks by acquiring lands surrounding them. The League was proposing, in essence, three
smaller parks, while the Club wanted one much more extensive park encompassing a separate and entire watershed.[138]

Then came what Litton calls the tree-slapping, described in
the pages of *National Geographic* as "World's Tallest Tree Discovered." One day Litton, standing with Chet Brown at the
edge of the redwood forest, slapped a tree, saying "As far as

you know, this could be the tallest tree in the world right
here."[139] Brown took him seriously, came back later with a
Geographic crew, and measured the tree. As Litton has observed, trees near the edge of a forest have always been the
world's tallest trees, since they are the only ones that can be
measured by triangulation. The Wayburns and Litton had begun to call the forest at Redwood Creek "the lawn," because
it was so thick and uniformly tall. If this was the tallest tree
left, Litton and Wayburn were thinking in terms of forests,
not trees. But here was a way to get *National Geographic* into
the campaign to save the redwoods, and Litton, laughing, remembers people saying "You had to save the world's tallest
tree! . . . Everyone said the *Geographic* found this great tree—
great! Anybody could find it, but just let's save it."[140]

Showmanship might counter the publicity of the lumber
companies who would say that there was plenty of redwood
for ten thousand years but if you take any for parks there
won't be any left. Showmanship might counter the signs that
said Tree Farm, and the exhibits which showed new breeds of
redwoods, and the billboards which claimed that an area had
been reseeded but did not say it was reseeded with Douglas fir
or Sitka spruce. Litton thought it was high comedy when *National Geographic* announced that it had found the world's
tallest tree, "the Mount Everest of All Living Things," but
such hyperbole had the smell of success.[141]

Meanwhile, Brower began to produce Philip Hyde and François Leydet's *The Last Redwoods*, a book which would come
out at about the same time as Brown and Fritz's Park Service
report. The Sierra Club's publication would not be *National
Geographic* hyperbole. Brower met immediate resistance in
the Publications Committee. "Francis Farquhar," he remembers, "didn't want . . . to do anything that Newton Drury
wouldn't approve of."[142]

The book would have to skirt several issues. The Club did

not want to alienate state government, though Brower felt
that the state had been responsible for the tragedy at Rockefeller Forest, and Litton wanted to include strong criticism of
Governor Brown's road-building through the redwood forests. The Club did not want to alienate the Save-the-
Redwoods League, though Wayburn and others wished to
make a strong statement about the necessary ecological planning for a national redwoods park. Further, as Brower remembers, if the planners wanted to "indicate where a park
ought to be and what the key elements were," they were in a
bind, "because we didn't want to identify too clearly what
was needed at a time when [redwoods] lacked protection, for
fear that it would lead to a rapid logging, as punitive or vin-
dictive logging."[143] Udall would write a foreword to the book,
as he had for the one on Point Reyes, only if the specific park
the book proposed agreed with the report of Udall's own
planners. The result, Wayburn noticed in his publisher's note,
could not help but juxtapose "a requiem for what we could
have saved and didn't" and "a salute to the men of vision and
generosity who did save some small part."[144]

Nevertheless the Club had a first-rate writer in François
Leydet, who had extensive schooling in the humanities, history, and business at Harvard and Johns Hopkins, as well as
journalistic experience on the *San Francisco Chronicle* from
1954 to 1962. It had the services of Phillip Hyde. Martin Litton "provided not only information but advice, stimulation,
and a feeling of urgency." Litton drove, flew, and toured with
the authors, "all the while keeping up a steady monologue of
information and observation."[145] Adams assisted with some
photographs, Beaumont Newhall obtained old photographs
of early logging. Even the exacting Adams would later say of
the book that despite some inferior pictures and very poor
color, despite the fact that it showed too much haste in design, sequence, and balance, it was "undoubtedly a very important document."[146]

Udall set the tone of the Club's argument when he wrote in his foreword that "We have learned, in managing the isolated enclaves of Redwoods now under state or federal protection, that no guardianship is sure unless a unit—a whole watershed—is placed under a single management plan that is ecologically sound."[147] A good part of the Hyde–Leydet argument was about the failure of protection in the past. This did not make for an attractive book. As Brower commented later, *The Last Redwoods* had quite an effect, but did not sell very well, partly because "people didn't want that much carnage on their coffee tables."[148]

The Last Redwoods was the hardest-hitting of the *Exhibit Format* series. In the early chapters Leydet wrote the biography of a tree as it grew for thousands of years, spanning the history of western culture; he distinguished the redwood from the sequoia, discussed the history of the species, and its ecosystem. Then began the attacks, on tree farming ("tree mining"), on "the Freeway Threat," on the California Forest Practices Act, and on the myths of the "heroic days," which made Paul Bunyan, as Udall had said in his foreword, a national hero. Leydet's version of the history of "saving" the redwoods lauded the Save-the-Redwoods League, but criticized it too, criticized implicitly the "illusory" protection the Save-the-Redwoods League had attained for redwoods, pointing out that "the need to preserve a region's ecological integrity applies just as well to the Grand Canyon or the Everglades." Leydet went on, "The well-deserved publicity that the Save-the-Redwoods League's work has enjoyed, the glowing descriptions in print and by word of mouth of the beauty of the California Redwood state parks, the photographs that are frequently published of Redwood groves illuminated by slanting rays of sun—all tend to obscure an important fact: Of the estimated original redwoods stand before logging began, only five percent has been saved."[149] And those, left for publicity purposes by lumbering companies, had "primarily a soporific

effect on the public," which did not realize that they constituted "little more than a Hollywood facade," often extending
only a few hundred feet from the road.

Hyde juxtaposed images of the forest with images of devastation, images showing "the road that let people see trees"
with "the route that speeds the logging trucks." Leydet attacked the ideas of Governor Brown, who said, "We are following definite principles in our freeway program in these
matchless areas. A basic premise is to open up new vistas to
Californians."¹⁵⁰ Hyde's images and Leydet's text demonstrated that vistas were entirely inappropriate in a redwood
forest. The text charged a breach of trust by the state; it
quoted a number of letters of protest and resignation written
by citizens who asked the League, "Why contribute money to
buy land that will be despoiled?"¹⁵¹

Even the Park Service plan for a Redwood Creek national
park—really three plans—would not contain what Wayburn
considered the "optimum plan." The optimum plan was, in
the minds of Wayburn, Litton, and others, the "ninety-
thousand-acre plan" which had been in the original Brown
and Fritz report, but which Brown and Fritz were told "they
could not offer . . . publicly."¹⁵² Such a park would contain
more redwoods than the League had managed to save in its
long and illustrious history. Wayburn would stand fast, pursuing doggedly the kind of vision people like Litton admired.
But contacts with Udall and Rockefeller were disillusioning.

Wayburn worked closely with Udall during the period
1961 to 1965, spreading maps on the floor and going over
them in some detail. He had consulted with Drury in the
early stages of his own planning, but "Drury was discouraging and, as I remember it now, he felt that the Redwood
League had done everything necessary for redwood protection."¹⁵³ The Club would have to go it alone if it wanted a
large redwood national park. And for a while, in 1964, it
looked like Laurance Rockefeller supported the optimum

plan, or something like it. Finally, as Wayburn remembered, Rockefeller said, "'I have taken no public position. When I do, I will be guided by my longstanding advisors, Newton Drury and Horace Albright.' At that point something dropped on the floor. It was my heart." By 1964 Wayburn "was quite convinced that Laurance was not our man, and I knew that Newton was not our man. As I learned in the summer [1965]—although I'd suspected it very strongly before—Stewart Udall was no longer our man."[154]

Meanwhile, the Club's board could not decide whether it was wise for a comparatively small citizen conservation organization to advance its own proposal or support the professional work of the Park Service, which it assumed would automatically get administration support.[155] The problem was that the board itself contained strong League influence. Though Farquhar was no longer on the board, Leonard was, and he remained perhaps the most influential member. Litton believes now that Leonard was "not in the club," in the sense that "if there was another organization for which Dick had respect that was going the other way, he would rather have the club brought around to their way." Further, Litton and Wayburn believed that "the League didn't want a real redwood national park. The League wanted the federal government to take over the state parks" and buy Mill Creek, which the League could not afford.[156] Leonard, on the other hand, remembered that "Litton was a dangerous person," and claims that Litton once said in public that "Newton Drury has destroyed more redwoods than any of the lumber companies ever had."[157] Feelings ran high.

Norman (Ike) Livermore complained about the title of the Club's book, and believed that it did more harm than good.[158] But even Leonard thought it was "a very fair book."[159] As Wayburn turned over the presidency to Will Siri in the spring of 1964, he said that "this past year might well be called the 'redwood year' for the Sierra Club," not only because the book acted as a catalyst, but because the Club had protested freeways being routed through state redwood parks and had invested more than $150,000 to buy virgin trees for Big Basin Redwoods State Park.[160] Though such an expenditure was a large financial risk for the Club, it was small by comparison with Rockefeller money, which might run into many millions, or federal money. When Wayburn retired from the presidency, he took up the cause of a redwood national park with even greater urgency.

By the end of the year, the Executive Committee had approved Wayburn's response to the Park Service's report, *The Redwoods*. Wayburn advocated that "a major redwood park be established as soon as possible," that it be in the Redwood Creek area, that its boundaries be an enlarged version of the Park Service plan. He advocated as "equally imperative" that the watershed of Mill Creek, which the League favored, "be preserved as a redwood park." He thought that the report's idea that "reasonable and acceptable safeguards can be worked out by a coordinated management plan with commercial forest interest" was "wishful thinking." Only if the entire watersheds became public could these forests be preserved. He knew that this was an expensive proposition, but, as he put it, "our scenic heritage is worth a fraction—indeed a minute fraction—of the cost of putting man on the moon."[161] Litton put this in more strident terms: "Let's have a moratorium for one day on the Vietnam War. If we take one day's expenditures in Vietnam, we'll have all the redwoods we could ever want."[162] In any case, Leonard "admired Wayburn for the watershed approach," and later submitted the same kind of proposal to The Wilderness Society.[163]

But the watershed approach would constitute a sticking point between the League and the Club, indicating differences which ran deeper. By this time the Club was very different from the League as a conservation organization: the Club would use the public as a force, would not look for wealthy connections.[164] Further, the Club had a more modern approach to the nature of national parks, seeing them as complete ecological systems with faunal variety and geographical wholeness.

North Cascades   Retained by the Club as Northwest conservation
1960–1965   representative in the spring of 1961, Michael
                     McCloskey remained for several years employed
also by a number of other conservation organizations, including the Federation of Western Outdoor Clubs and the North Cascades Conservation Council. It was, as he recalled, "an interesting yeasty period, and attitudes were changing rather quickly."[165] As a local resident, he was interested in specific places like the Oregon Cascades and the North Cascades. He had been politicized by Wayne Morse and Richard Neuberger and would run for the Oregon House of Representatives in 1962.

When McCloskey arrived on the scene, he remembers, local conservationists were still arguing about whether to give up on the Forest Service and propose a North Cascades national park. But given the regional forester, J. Herbert Stone, "a totally unreconstructed devotee of logging," and the lack of wilderness legislation, even an overdeveloped national park was a more attractive idea than a pure but vulnerable "limited area."[166] Like Brock Evans, who would become the Club's Northwest representative a few years later, McCloskey was surprised that the Sierra Club did not have a battle plan: "people had just made this decision to go for a park, but I found that they didn't have a strategy; they didn't have a plan. I said, "Look, we can't sell an idea until it becomes concrete, until we have something specific to promote!"[167]

In October of 1960 Grant McConnell reported in the *Bulletin* that the North Cascades wilderness was "almost half safe," since nearly a half-million acres of the Glacier Peak wilderness had been given temporary protection. McConnell thought one of the world's scenic climaxes deserved a better fate, and that the next step beyond the Forest Service's lack of policy was "an objective study of the park potential in the total area."[168] Pat Goldsworthy, president of the North Cascades Conservation Council, a chemist now at the University of Washington, who was elected to the Club's board in 1967, did not know whether to applaud the Forest Service or criticize it for excluding so much.[169] But the Club policy remained, as McCloskey had observed, vague at best. Indeed, official board policy consisted only of the map drawn several years earlier by Dave Simons. Though Brower had made the film *The Wilderness Alps of Stehekin* and had published photographs of the Cascades area in the *Bulletin* over the years, there was no official written statement. As Wayburn told the board in the fall of 1961, "If the directors did not comment . . . the Club would lose its initiative in the court of public opinion."[170]

Though McCloskey admired the "grand vision" Simons had for an Oregon Cascade national park, the two had never met. When the Club decided to push for the North Cascades, which were more important in the aggregate, McCloskey would put his legal training to work and try to put together a prospectus for a North Cascades national park. Based on a 1937 National Park Service study, a 1938 wilderness study by Robert Marshall, and Simons' 1958 survey, McCloskey's 120-page Prospectus included a sample draft of a specific legislative bill for a national park. The Prospectus coordinated a variety of local viewpoints. It described the desirable natural features of the park, extending boundaries to areas of significant scenic value that might otherwise be subject to future impairment. It minimized conflicts with alternative commodity use. In particular it would make concessions to hunting, while attempting to limit future road building. So the Prospectus offered a national park and a "Chelan National Mountain Recreation Area," where hunting would be permitted. McCloskey's Prospectus constituted a significant advance for the Club. It indicated the means by which the secretary of the interior might acquire land, provided for the administration of the area, dealt with the possibility of future mining, and planned for the already underway North Crossstate Highway. It proposed methods of dealing with compensatory payments to counties for reduced timber sales, and payments in lieu of taxes on acquired private land. It spelled out appropriations needed to finance establishment of the park.[171]

By January of 1963 McCloskey had presented his legislative program to the board. It was endorsed immediately, with the provision that there also be wilderness at the heart of the proposed park, as suggested by the Seattle Mountaineers.[172] The board also endorsed McCloskey himself. Because the Prospectus drew admiration from the Northwest Chapter of the Club and from board member Lewis Clark, who praised McCloskey's ability to coordinate efforts of several organizations while understanding the problems of various land-use agencies, it insured the Club's continued support of a Northwest representative and the later addition of other regional representatives.[173] Wayburn recognized the precedent McCloskey was setting: "We realized we would have to go to Congress, and in the early sixties we made the jump."[174]

The Prospectus, in turn, was used as the key document to persuade the Kennedy administration to study the park idea. Stewart Udall formed a study commission, which began to develop a proposal. The study team's plans would be much less ambitious than McCloskey's or Simons', and McCloskey remembers being surprised when Brower pragmatically accepted the "highly restrictive proposal that came out of the federal study"; McCloskey played the idealist, resisting the federal plan.[175] The study team commenced hearings in October of 1963. Though Pat Goldsworthy doubted that a nineday tour would make a "sufficient visual impact on the Study

Team," he was more troubled by the small number of preservationists who showed up to counter testimony in support of "policy stressing multiple commodity-use management." No matter that the testimony of park and wilderness opponents was "highly repetitious and stereotyped, supporting the status quo," Goldsworthy complained in the November *Bulletin*, "the missing conservationists must make themselves heard, frequently and with conviction."[176]

Meanwhile, in an interesting turn of affairs, the North Cascades Conservation Council—with Goldsworthy as president and McCloskey as professional consultant—rather than the Club's Northwest Chapter, had carried the burden. As one commentator notes, it "became something of a pattern for single-issue organizations to form with members from the Club and other groups," with the single-issue group then taking the lead in a campaign.[177] By the end of 1964 the McCloskey Prospectus gained support from the Federation of Western Outdoor Clubs, the Mountaineers, the Mazamas, and the National Parks Association. The Wilderness Society was reluctant because, as Brower has said, "they were after the Wilderness Bill and didn't want to antagonize the Forest Service unnecessarily."[178] Nevertheless, a study team made up of members from both the interior and agriculture departments would constitute a major advance in land-use planning if the chair of the team, Ed Crafts—working for Udall as head of the Bureau of Outdoor Recreation, formerly of the Forest Service—could successfully coordinate the antagonistic agencies.

Brower had planned to produce an *Exhibit Format* book on the North Cascades. At various times he sounded out William Heald, Grant McConnell, and David Simons as authors. *The Wild Cascades: Forgotten Parkland* was written by Harvey Manning and published in the spring of 1965.[179] The study team would not make its recommendations until January of 1966. By that time McCloskey was working at the Club's San

Francisco office, and would soon be appointed conservation director.

Grand Canyon   In 1963 the Club had cause to celebrate Udall's
1960–1965   support of a Redwood national park, but also
                  had reason for pause. David Brower remembers
being less encouraged about matters closer to Stewart Udall's
home state, Arizona: "Udall had a major press conference for
the Southwest Water Plan at the time I was cooling my heels
in his outer chambers, waiting to get to him to try to stay the
closing of the gates at Glen Canyon. . . . but I was not allowed to see him. I was allowed to join the press conference,
however, and listen to the presentation. . . . That was early
January 1963, on the day they closed the gates at Glen Canyon and started its destruction."[180] All of this was disappointing, but not surprising. As a congressman, Udall had advocated the Echo Park Dam in Dinosaur. The Grand Canyon
would be Brower's next battle, another chapter in the Colorado River controversy. He remembers becoming active in the
battle by the late 1940s; "I suppose that I should say that I
went to the University of the Colorado River; I was a dropout
at Berkeley, but my education continued."[181] Over the years
he learned about agriculture, hydrology, sedimentation, city
development, alternate energy development. The loss of Glen
Canyon brought its own bitter lesson; as he said, "You don't
give away something you haven't seen; you don't suggest alternatives until you've been there."[182] And the bargain over
the protection of Rainbow Bridge turned into a bitter disap-
pointment. Udall could not guarantee protection of the monument. Perhaps the most important lesson was the one Richard Bradley expressed, that "conservationists can never really
win any fight, they can only prevent someone else from
doing so. The dam site is still there, neither out of sight nor
out of mind of certain people."[183]

For the rest of the year Udall discussed the Pacific Southwest Regional Water Plan, as it was actually called, which included comprehensive development of Colorado River water. The interior department's rhetoric, dominated by the Bureau of Reclamation, said its plan "aimed at relieving an increasing shortage of water" in Arizona, California, Utah, Nevada, and New Mexico, and would enable the region to "support its growing population."[184] After a long conflict over Colorado River water, particularly between California and Arizona, Arizona anticipated a favorable Supreme Court decision for Lower Basin water, received it on June 3, 1963, and hastened to build what it called the Central Arizona Project. Richard Leonard balked at the logic of the plan, saying, "They are going to pump that water uphill fifteen hundred feet into the Phoenix-Tucson area so that Arizona can have some water." But Leonard was also a pragmatist, knowing the plan "is an illogical waste of energy, but politically realistic. We haven't tried to fight that. You don't try to fight the states."[185]

To pay for all that pumping, two dams were proposed, one directly above Grand Canyon National Park, called Marble Canyon Dam, and one right below the park, called Bridge Canyon Dam—later called the Hualapai, as Brower and Litton thought, "to placate the Indians or try to enlist their support."[186] The Club had known these dams were in the plans of the Bureau of Reclamation even while it was fighting the Dinosaur battle. Now the dams would be justified as "cash register dams." There were other prospects on the drawing board. The problem was that neither dam was *in* Grand Canyon National Park, though water from Bridge Canyon Dam would back up into the park. For more traditional Club members the precedent was not clear.

Martin Litton did not care about precedents or about any limited idea of park boundaries. He cared about the Grand Canyon. He remembered that Bestor Robinson had advocated the Bridge Canyon dam, and Litton himself believed "the Sierra Club had endorsed and advocated the dams in the

Grand Canyon. The knowledge of the board members was so fuzzy and so thin, they didn't even know where the Grand Canyon was."[187] Litton knew that the park boundaries were inadequate protection for the Grand Canyon, that the two dams would seriously damage not only the inundated areas, but the canyon between. This time, Brower thought, the Club should get going before the Interior plans were even finished. So, in May of 1963, he planned for Litton to educate the board with charts and maps.

Even in 1963, there was Bestor Robinson. "I was on the staff, and he was board," Brower recalls, "and there was a peer group thing going on."[188] Robinson had made up his mind about the Bridge Canyon dam when he was president of the Club in 1948, and had decided that certain compromises were necessary. Even in 1974 he would stand by his previous decisions: "It's rather a second-rate canyon as you get down where the reservoir was proposed," he thought.[189] Acting as a political realist in 1948, he had recognized that "the economic loss would be staggering" if the Colorado were maintained as a wild river. Besides, he wrote as a member of the department of the interior's Advisory Committee on Conservation, the upstream dams on the Colorado would render the Grand Canyon free of silt, full of fish, and a pleasing picture. The reservoir from Bridge Canyon would hardly change the appearance of the Canyon from the rim, and boating in it would "afford a somewhat comparable experience" to running the rapids. Indeed, he wrote, a Marble Canyon dam would make certain features of the canyon like Vasey's Paradise and Red Wall Cavern more accessible to visitors. So Robinson objected neither to a dam upstream from the park at Marble Canyon nor a dam downstream.[190] This position, it might be said, was based on Club policies which held that the Club could protect dedicated parks and allow alternatives, and on the further assumption that parks were only scenic resources. Perhaps the Club was ready to advance beyond these policies, which Brower believed were in part responsible for the tragedy at Glen Canyon.

In May of 1963, in the same month that *The Place No One Knew: Glen Canyon on the Colorado* was brought out by the Club, Litton presented his river sermon to the board. A few months later he published it in the *Bulletin* under the pen name of Clyde Thomas.[191] "Leave [the Canyon] as it is," Theodore Roosevelt had said. "You cannot improve it. The ages have been at work on it, and man can only mar it." It was 279.4 miles of canyon, from Lee's Ferry, Arizona, to Grapevine Wash at the foot of Grand Wash Cliffs, most of it in Indian reservations, a national forest, a national monument, and a national recreation area. Litton pointed out that only 62.3 miles of river were within the national park:

> It is not an easy way out but rather a delusion to segment the Grand Canyon in our minds and try to comfort ourselves with the idea that we can give up chunks of the most magnificent wilderness of all and still keep our favorite roadside view from Bright Angel Point. The destruction of any part of the Grand Canyon is damage to the whole, and thus to every other part."[192]

Litton quoted the views of Dan Luten, who had argued that "it is folly to believe that the movement of large amounts of water anywhere will solve any problems." Litton went on to say that given the present situation—"complete agreement, on Capitol Hill as well as in Phoenix, that the Marble 'Canyon' and Bridge Canyon boondoggles are going to be built"— a massive campaign to prevent dams, and an eventual campaign to enlarge the park, were crucial. As Litton knew, "saving Grand Canyon will take as much effort as it took to save Dinosaur," and would stretch the resources of a Club now deeply involved in the redwoods and North Cascades. "It would be easier to fight only one battle, but we don't have that choice."[193] After an hour and a half of discussion by the board, according to Brower, Litton "so devastated Bestor Robinson's fifteen-year-old arguments that there was applause from the audience."[194] The board resolved to recommend that the park and monument be extended to include all 279.4 miles of canyon and to oppose any dams or diversions in the area.[195]

Four months later the board went on record as opposing Udall's Pacific Southwest Regional Water Plan because it contemplated Grand Canyon dams and because it also implied other dams which threatened scenic resources in California.[196] Though heavily engaged in his publishing responsibilities, perhaps because there was nobody else to do it or because of his feeling of personal responsibility in the tragic fate of Glen Canyon, Brower entered this campaign with great intensity. He brought members of his family into it. His son Kenneth assisted in preparing a book on the Grand Canyon. His daughter Barbara wrote Save Grand Canyon on the back of her hand, on the outside of her wallet, and on tables where food was served on Sierra Club outings. Brower sent out an avalanche of letters and dispatches.

In a sense, *The Place No One Knew* was the first step in Brower's campaign.[197] This was a subtle book with a strange combination of materials; perhaps it was misunderstood. Porter's images glowed and shimmered. They were dark, tortuous sometimes, and seemed to represent "caverns measureless to man." Scarcely a speck of sky in any of them, never a man, but the still, small voices. As Porter said, the place was big, but you learn to "focus on the smaller, more familiar, more comprehensible objects. . . . It is from them that the greatest rewards come." Always there was the light, reflected off water, off rock, glowing in the deeps. And these images had their own argument about "the place no one knew," the place before the birth of man, the womb of the world, the flow of blood, the flow of the Colorado. Maybe this was the greatest of the *Exhibit Format* books; certainly it was the saddest. As a requiem the book might say that "days flow through your consciousness," that "the current becomes the time on which you move," and Porter might end his introduction saying, "You glide into the day unpursued, living, as all good river travellers should, in the present." But it was not true.

"Glen Canyon died in 1963 and I was partly responsible for its death," wrote Brower in his foreword. "The least we can do is remember, with purpose, these things lost." The moral? "Progress need not deny to the people their inalienable right to be informed and to choose. In Glen Canyon the people never knew what the choices were." The text itself was, as Wallace Stegner suggested, a chorus of voices for the wilderness, excerpts from classical and modern writers: Clarence Dutton, John Wesley Powell, Frank Waters, Stegner himself, Joseph Wood Krutch, John C. Van Dyke, Loren Eiseley, William O. Douglas, Aldo Leopold, Mumford, Pope, Sears, Einstein, Thoreau. It was "the geography of hope." It was elegant propaganda.

As Brower began to send out copies of *The Place No One Knew*, he included a packet of material, including two letters to Steward Udall, written on June 22 and 24, 1963.[198] One spoke to Udall's conscience; the secretary had a continuing obligation to protect Rainbow Bridge, an obligation to "protection still required by law." This letter was also a statement about an emergency which Udall himself admitted in *The Quiet Crisis* and before audiences at two wilderness conferences, the crisis in conservation that demanded more than transitory technological fixes in the service of the market economy. The second letter spoke specifically to what Udall was now calling The Big Plan for the Colorado River. It asked that the Grand Canyon dams be taken out of the hands of the Federal Power Commission and placed before Congress. Citing the Club's "complete disinterest concerning the disposition of the waters of the Colorado," and concern "solely for the public interest in the public's great resources," Brower believed that the president "should exercise his authority under the Antiquities Act to proclaim an Enlarged Grand Canyon National Monument" for all 279.4 miles of the canyon, thus removing it from jurisdiction of the Federal Power Commission.

This was going to be a major campaign and an expensive one. By the beginning of 1964, even as the country was trying to recover from the shock of Kennedy's assassination, Brower threw all of his resources into the battle, organizing a Grand Canyon task force.[199] At first his list for the task force included technical experts like hydrologist Luna Leopold, physicist Richard Bradley, and chemist Phil Pennington, who with Brower would produce a slide show on Glen Canyon, later made into a film by Larry Dawson. There would also be a group of people involved in making a Grand Canyon book—François Leydet, Martin Litton, Wallace Stegner, Russell D. Butcher—and a group of river experts, including Otis Marston, Pat Reilly, Frank Masland, Jr. By this time Brower thought of a campaign in terms of a book, a film, and the technical arguments. Later he enlisted what he called the MIT trio: Jeff Ingram, a mathematician who would become Southwest regional representative, Alan Carlin, an economist with the Rand Corporation, and Laurence I. Moss, a nuclear engineer who would advance the increasingly untenable nuclear power alternative. As Brower hoped, "They went after the facts hard and brought their assorted expertise to bear."[200]

When Wayburn announced, as he left his presidency in 1964, that the Club was planning its campaign to protect the canyon, which "will be the area of a big push . . . in the coming months," Brower proposed a Grand Canyon book which was in fact well on its way.[201] In August he announced that the book would be ready by October. It was only a couple of months late. He also presented a budget, which included copies of Grand Canyon books for all members of Congress, distribution of the Pennington film on Glen Canyon, a Grand Canyon newsletter, costs for attending hearings in Washington, D.C., a new Grand Canyon movie, and extra coverage in the *Bulletin*.[202]

Was such a barrage of outreach necessary? Indeed it was. The Bureau of Reclamation was already busy countering the Glen Canyon book. It would make Lake Powell an example of its own good works and would use the rhetoric of the Old West. Stewart Udall praised the bureau as he introduced the book about its reservoir, *Lake Powell: Jewel of the Colorado*: "President and Mrs. Johnson have challenged us with an exciting new concept of conservation: Creation of new beauty to amplify the beauty which is our heritage as well as creation of more places for outdoor recreation. In this magnificent lake we have made such accomplishments."[203] Such a statement, suggesting that Lake Powell was a symbol of Johnson's Great Society, began the book that Floyd Dominy put together, a book which satirized the bureau's opponents with such poems as this:

> Dear God, did you cast down
> Two hundred miles of canyon
> And mark, "For poets only"?
> Multitudes hunger
> For a lake in the sun.

Dominy praised Glen Canyon Dam: "It has tamed a wild river—made it a servant to man's will." He praised the blue water in Glen Canyon as superior to the river, "brick-red, mud-laden; Big Red, the River Colorado; trickle or flood at Nature's whim since time began." In calling upon the old rhetoric of taming the West he said, "There is a natural order in our universe. God created both Man and Nature. And Man serves God. But Nature serves Man." And:

> To have a deep blue lake
> Where no lake was before

Seems to bring man
A little closer to God.[204]

All of this was directed not simply toward the reservoir which, to Litton's discomfiture, the bureau continued to call a lake. Just as the Club's book was directed downstream at the Grand Canyon, so was the bureau's propaganda, which defended the practicality of hydropower and advocated blue lakes behind "cash register dams" at Bridge Canyon and Marble Canyon.

Brower was concerned about Bestor Robinson because he found Robinson's ideas of 1948 echoed in Bureau of Reclamation brochures of the 1960s, which boosted the Pacific Southwest Water Plan. Just as it had a decade earlier, the bureau attempted to appropriate the domain of the Park Service, promising that a reservoir would provide "a water highway through the spectacular inner canyon gorge of the Monument to the lower reaches of the Park." At the same time it promised that "a minimum flow of 1,000 cubic feet per second will be maintained below Marble Canyon Dam through the Grand Canyon."[205] That low a flow would make running the river in the national park impossible. The barrage of Bureau of Reclamation promotion suggested that the Club would be involved in a big push to protect the canyon for much longer than a few months.

The Club answered the bureau's arguments with another book. Brower's preface to *Time and the River Flowing: Grand Canyon* reviewed past policy about the river, as well as controversies within the Club.[206] He also defended his publishing decisions, repeated many of the Glen Canyon arguments, and attacked the Bureau of Reclamation, while beginning to offer alternate power sources—which would prove to be hasty rather than wise. As Brower acknowledged, this book extended *The Place No One Knew* and suggested a new chapter for the Glen Canyon tragedy: "And wasn't the Colorado River

already dead, killed by Glen Canyon Dam? Would modest releases of water from that dam ever revive it?" But the book
accomplished what Litton had tried to show the board a year
and a half earlier. There still was a river in the canyon. There
still was a canyon, alive and changing, wild and beautiful.
Litton thought this was perhaps the best of the *Exhibit Format*
books because Leydet's text managed to guide the reader on
a river trip, to teach him geological history, and remind him
of the conservation history of the canyon. Many people contributed photographs for *Time and the River Flowing*, and the
results were mixed. But the overall effect suggested that the
world opened up into a broad sky in the canyon. Subscribers
of the Book of the Month Club would be surprised to find
color prints here by Ansel Adams.

The Bureau of Reclamation's propaganda for mecha- *Wilderness*
nized recreation on its reservoirs was a reaction to   1961–1964
wilderness as an idea. It suggested a backlash against
wilderness and especially wilderness recreation. Further, as
the wilderness idea seemed to gain strength in the Kennedy
administration, the wilderness bill brought many disappoint-
ments as it evolved. For instance, Hubert Humphrey, the bill's
first sponsor, later dropped it. By 1960 supporters of the bill
had only been able to have wilderness recognized as a
"proper use" of national forests in the Multiple-Use–
Sustained Yield Act. Yet supporters multiplied and wrote
hopeful letters. The Club was by no means the only organization supporting the bill, which remained largely the province of The Wilderness Society. Nevertheless, it was, in Wayburn's words, "one of our biggest general projects," though
the campaign was run by Trustees for Conservation since the
Club did not want to appear to be engaged in outright lobbying, even as late as 1963. Wayburn had appealed in 1958 for
letters through the Trustees, and Brower explained in publi-

cations by the Trustees why the Club itself could not advocate letter writing.[207]

Edgar Wayburn was led to say with historians of the Forest Service that "the Wilderness Act was a kind of culmination of a growing distrust of the Forest Service," though the act had been proposed before most leaders of the Club shared that distrust.[208] As Michael McCloskey has observed, "The fight for the Wilderness Act itself provided a clear focus for the efforts of the conservation movement . . . able for almost a decade to invest its hope and energy in moving a single vehicle of reform."[209] The wilderness bill also forced conservation groups to find new leaders, capable of undertaking essentially legislative tasks, expert in the framing, analysis, and use of legislation. Such a person was Michael McCloskey. McCloskey represented a new force in the Club, interested in campaigns but also in legislation as a tangible end. He followed carefully the progress of the various versions of the wilderness bill, whose original purpose, as he later defined it, was:

1. to provide clear statutory authority for the maintenance of wilderness areas;

2. to remove the administrative authority of Forest Service officials to decrease the size of or to declassify wilderness-type areas;

3. to protect National Forest wilderness areas against mining and the installation of water projects; and

4. to require designation of wilderness zones in units of the National Park system, federal wildlife refuge and range system, and within Indian reservations.[210]

The wilderness bill faced a formidable array of opponents. As Edgar Wayburn remembers, it was "bitterly resented" by the Forest Service when it "showed for the first time that conservationists had clout."[211] That clout was hardly apparent in the early years when, year after year, bills were introduced and failed. "These bills were initially opposed by both the Forest Service and the National Park Service," McCloskey wrote, "and were bitterly resisted to the end by lumber, mining, power, and irrigation interests."[212] Only when the Kennedy administration showed that the New Frontier was not simply the New Deal with a button-down collar, but constituted an attempt to put forth the "third wave" in American conservation, stressing ecological and aesthetic values; only when people like Stewart Udall recognized, as McCloskey has noted, that "wilderness has been the symbol of what the third wave was all about"; only then did passage of the bill seem possible.[213] Conservationists mobilized in the early 1960s.

Brower continued to speak around the country and to exploit his good relations with Stewart Udall, keeping in constant contact and continuing to advocate a strong bill.[214] Wayburn believed the very campaign for the bill had a salubrious result, since it forced the Forest Service, for instance, to show that it could protect wilderness better than Congress could. For that reason, Wayburn remembers saying at the time, "I don't care when the Wilderness Act is passed . . . as long as it's before Congress and it has as much support as it has."[215] But in early 1960 Wayne Aspinall, as the powerful chair of the House Interior Committee, developed a draft of the bill which omitted Indian reservations, eliminated an advisory council, allowed mining and reservoirs in wilderness, and allowed the secretary of agriculture to declassify nonqualifying primitive areas. by 1960, having obtained its own Multiple-Use–Sustained Yield Act, the Forest Service no longer objected in principle to the wilderness bill, and President Kennedy endorsed the legislation. The board of the Club in 1961 urged Kennedy to issue "Stop Orders on Land Development" for places like the North Cascades, Kern Plateau,

Oregon Cascades, Wind Rivers, Selway–Bitterroot Forests, and Idaho Sawtooths, "lands having apparent major wilderness or scenic values."[216]

Though in September 1961 and again in April 1963 the Senate passed a wilderness bill, Wayne Aspinall's House Interior Committee drew up a substitute bill which, McCloskey knew, "diluted the focus of wilderness legislation and erected unwarranted obstacles in the path of wilderness preservation."[217] This constituted a crisis much discussed by The Wilderness Society and by the Club. Ansel Adams decided that Aspinall's version was worse than nothing. A vote in favor of it, he wrote to one congressman, was a vote against wilderness. Brower noted that there was still time for a "good Wilderness Bill," but more letters to congressmen were necessary.[218]

Michael McCloskey encouraged people to come to public hearings in the Northwest. He also went to Colorado in 1962 and 1963 "to do some organizing work in Congressman Aspinall's district." Later, he went to a whole series of hearings in Denver, Idaho, and Washington. Sometimes he succeeded, as in Durango, Colorado, where everyone was supportive, and sometimes, as he remembers, he ran into trouble: "I made my pitch . . . [to] some local rancher who started scowling, and he looked at me in a ferocious way and said, 'There was a shooting here last week, and there is just about to be another one.' He was looking at me!" It was no breeze to testify in hostile places like McCall, Idaho, where miners and loggers turned out. Though Aspinall later complained bitterly about "outside agitators," McCloskey was willing to challenge the western opponents by taking the fight to their country, and felt that he "really got a lot of wires into Aspinall," applying pressure which eventually made the congressman let a version of the bill out of committee. McCloskey remembers, "In some ways the Wilderness Act fight was a very sophisticated campaign, but I think the tools or the lessons

out of that [campaign] really didn't get transferred very well."
McCloskey believes that only when the Club attempted to
draft and pass legislation for the redwoods in the late 1960s
was it introduced to "the full legislative process, the process
in congress of moving a bill along affirmatively."[219]

Spencer M. Smith, Jr. addressed exactly this problem at the
1963 Wilderness Conference. As a professional analyst, an
economist, and consultant, Smith had served for various
conservation organizations over the years. Why, he asked,
had conservationists taken such a licking in the House, having "the dubious distinction of ending, as Secretary Udall put
it, on second base?"[220] In comparison to business associations, labor unions, or farm organizations, conservationists
had no continuity, were unfamiliar with legislative process,
and were not interested in picking legislators to represent
their interest. "The so-called 'professional' conservationists
are certainly few," Smith noted, and "an awfully great number of people feel somehow that they have done their duty
when they have written their Congressman." He went on,

> Our opponents know us pretty well. They know we can
> mount an impressive campaign. But they also know if
> they can hold the status quo for a little while, that cam-
> paign will begin to taper off, and will hit a little bit of
> doldrums. And they can renew their pressure, knowing
> we lack finances, or rather our loose organization lacks
> the ability to again get the kind of ground swell we
> need.[221]

Conservationists could no longer apologize that "this won't
cost very much," nor could they help but confront what
Smith called the "pioneer developer," or "emotional fron-
tiersman," not with more emotion, but with "long term concerted efforts . . . with patience and a resistance to frustration." When, at the end of the conference, Wayburn

challenged Smith's disparagement of letter writing, Smith replied, "I meant you have to do that, plus other things."²²²

In the end, wilderness proponents agreed to compromise with Aspinall and supported his proposal for a Public Land Law Review Commission while accepting a wilderness bill which allowed mining in the wilderness system for twenty more years. The real responsibility for the bill's success belonged not only to amateurs, but to Zahniser, Brower, McCloskey, and to some congressmen, particularly John Saylor of the House Interior Committee, who was the leading advocate in the House. For McCloskey, the whole battle had implications about the Club's mission. How could a volunteer organization, centered on the west coast, keep up with Congress? What kind of Club would be needed for such campaigns in the future? What kind of Club would be needed to implement the act itself?

The board could scarcely keep up with the progress of the bill in Washington, and by spring of 1964 had given the Executive Committee authority to express the opinion of the Club. Even after the act passed, the board needed to have it explained by its Washington, D.C., representative, William Zimmerman.²²³ Yet Zimmerman served more as a conduit of occasional information than a constant contact, and was in no sense an actual lobbyist for the Club. The Club quite simply did not have the means—and perhaps not the desire—to conduct a positive legislative campaign.

In his President's Report of 1964 Wayburn discussed an issue closely related to lobbying.²²⁴ Though the staff had grown, and though many members of the staff doubled as employees and volunteers, office work alone was a problem for the growing Club. Wayburn hoped that the new computer system might solve some problems, but the Club was facing a communication crisis. Members wanted information, and often they wanted personalized answers to questions. The president could not answer all letters, nor could a mobile representative like McCloskey. Wayburn wanted the Club to remain a democratic organization, but he also wanted a single-minded organization. For the first time, a group of members had offered amendments to the bylaws which would politicize the board by requiring that directors not serve more than three consecutive terms, that all members and employees have greater freedom of speech, and that directors running for reelection be required to publish their complete voting record. These amendments were not passed, only because of what Wayburn categorized as voter apathy.

In 1964, it appeared that a Wilderness Act would be passed. It would be weaker in several respects than the bill originally written by Howard Zahniser. Congress allowed the extension of mining rights in declared wilderness for twenty years. An itemized list of 153 areas was originally proposed for the National Wilderness Preservation System; now every inclusion was dependent on a subsequent act of Congress. Zahniser originally hoped a National Wilderness Preservation Council could make recommendations to Congress and the president; it was now gone.[225] The Wilderness Act was signed by President Lyndon Johnson on September 3, 1964.

As most scholars agree, the Wilderness Act of 1964 did not provide comprehensive protection from development; instead it was a complex product of compromise.[226] In its most important sections, it set out a definition of wilderness, the extent of the National Wilderness Preservation System and the political process for creating it, the uses and prohibited uses of wilderness, and special provisions.[227] In definition, wilderness was "hereby recognized as an area where the earth and its community of life are untrammelled by man, where man himself is a visitor who does not remain." An area of wilderness was further defined as *apparently* unaffected by man's work, as having opportunities for solitude and primitive recreation, and as having at least 5,000 acres, or sufficient size to manage successfully as unimpaired. In extent,

the National Wilderness Preservation System would have as
its core 54 areas comprising 9.1 million acres. The act set out
a plan for reviewing 34 Forest Service primitive areas (5.4
million acres) over ten years. It further required a review of
roadless areas administered by the department of the interior, including national parks, monuments, wildlife and
game refuges. In the process of establishing wilderness, the
president could make recommendations to Congress, and local public hearings were to be held as a step leading to
congressional approval. In its sections on uses, new roads,
motorized vehicles and tools, structures and other improvements were prohibited, with certain exceptions for health,
safety, and administration. However, special provisions allowed certain current uses to continue in wilderness: mining
and mineral leasing extended until December 31, 1983; established use of aircraft and motorboats; management of fire,
insects, and disease; water resource development authorized
by the president; livestock grazing, where established before
the act.

Passage of the Wilderness Act intensified the Club's need to
engage in legislative activities. Arriving after the assassination of Kennedy, in the midst of the civil rights movement,
and at the beginning of the furor over the war in Vietnam,
wilderness legislation seemed a calm event in the midst of
turmoil. As McCloskey recollects, "the Johnson administration was so preoccupied with the war and its own troubles
that it really did not pay attention much to wilderness legislation." Indeed McCloskey observes, "the truth of the matter
is that no president has ever taken an interest in wilderness
policy on a sustained basis."[228] Brower also realized that the
Wilderness Act "would not be the end of a series of problems,
but the beginning."[229] If literature of the kind the Bureau of
Reclamation distributed reached a sympathetic audience, it
could cause a backlash to the Wilderness Act. Conservationists would once again be on the defensive. As Wayburn was

to learn, "Congress might be more amenable to the establishment of larger areas of wilderness than the Forest Service
was"; the Park Service and Forest Serivce would perfect the
art of foot-dragging.[230]

So passage of the act meant increased need to work within
the system for affirmative legislative action. McCloskey
thought in 1972 that "the price of its passage, however,
[threatened] to be the Achilles heel of the Wilderness effort."
With congressional action pending on more than a hundred
wilderness areas by the end of 1964, that effort was in danger
of losing momentum and focus. The campaign for passage
had been a propagandistic tour de force, but the subsequent
efforts to implement the legislation would be dissipated by
bureaucratic technicalities. The public would be "befuddled
by an endless procession of hearings, reviews, and legislative
proposals."[231] This was not the time for protests, boycotts,
marches, or other currently popular political activities. It was
a time for professionalism. McCloskey decided,

> Our business was not to just bear witness. Our business
> was to secure the political change that would protect
> the environment. Once you embark upon that process
> of analysis, you go in an entirely different direction in
> most instances than you do with direct action because
> for the most part, direct action is a confession of either
> failure with respect to being able to work through the
> political process or a reflection of the fact that the politi-
> cal process somehow is closed to you, or you are being
> locked out of it.[232]

The Wilderness Act locked the Club into the political process,
and this might mark the passing from the scene of the charismatic leaders like Howard Zahniser and David Brower.
These men, with their "highly personalized style of leadership," would soon be replaced by men who would not be remembered for eloquent speeches, but would lead the move-

ment with managerial expertise, political savvy, and a high
level of professionalism.[233]

Reminding conservationists of change in the movement
were the deaths of Olaus Murie, Howard Zahniser, Rachel
Carson, and Will Colby in 1963 and 1964. Like Aldo Leopold
and Robert Marshall, they would not be the ones to make
wilderness legislation work. Was the amateur tradition
gone? Perhaps not, but the powerful figures in the Club, men
like Martin Litton, who was reminiscent of Robert Sterling
Yard, or Richard Leonard, who was increasingly allied to
Newton Drury, or George Marshall, or Michael McCloskey,
who would see himself as "facilitating, among other things,
a great many leaders to find prominent roles in the club,"
or Wayburn, the diplomat, or even Brower—all seemed to
be more than amateurs, if not all strictly speaking professionals.[234]

Will Siri would discover, when he assumed the presidency,
that he would have to preside over a board made up of men
who considered themselves leaders, wanted to direct the
Club toward different goals, and consequently pursued a
style of leadership which McCloskey felt was "only possible
in organizations small enough to be dominated by one individual." Few of them aspired to be "facilitators" like Mc-
Closkey. Many of the newer directors would be more aggressive, demanding, intolerant, and perhaps refractory.[235] Board
meetings become more acrimonious, though this was the
price a democratic organization had to pay. And the Club
would leave the implementation of the Wilderness Act to its
professional staff and chapters, while members of the board
directed their energies toward expanding and protecting the
national park system.

CHAPTER SEVEN
Diamond Jubilee

Will Siri and the Environment, 1963–1965

When Will Siri came home from the victorious Everest expedition of 1963 he was ready for new conquests. As president-elect of the Club in 1964, he decided, as had Wayburn, to be "an effective president, spending the necessary time and effort and utilizing the authority of the office." Though he had sat on the board for a number of years and participated in discussions on environmental issues, Siri had not been a leading voice for the Club up to that point. As he remembered, he felt it was time for the Club to cease compromising and "to wage a determined battle even at the cost of losing at times." The Club was growing rapidly—from about 24,000 in 1964 when Siri became president to about 38,000 at the end of his term in 1966—and it was time for that strength to make itself felt. He would not take the job unless his "role was that of an active leader." Recognizing that he needed support from old hands like Leonard and Wayburn, acknowledging the growing alienation of Dave Brower from his old friends Bestor Robinson, Alex Hildebrand, and even Richard Leonard, Siri also knew that "Dave's intuition on environmental matters often approached omniscience."[1]

The demands on the president were growing all the time, and Siri asked Mike McCloskey to come down from Oregon and become his assistant. By this time McCloskey had established himself as overqualified for such a position, and Siri soon proposed that McCloskey establish a conservation department.[2]

Long discussions among friends at board meetings were over. Siri stressed the necessity for the board to be decisive. The Club could not stop and study everything to death. "For God's sake," he remembers saying often, "let's do *something*; anything's better than nothing even if it's faulty. . . . Let's set a position; we'll modify it later, but action is of paramount importance." Conservatives would resist taking stands on environmental matters like pesticides, population, pollution, land-use planning, energy, and urban amenities. As Siri remembers, "A few argued that the Sierra Club was a wilderness conservation organization, and [should] stay in the woods."[3] Nevertheless, the Club was under pressure to formulate policies that applied to the environment. Unfortunately, making such policy required nudging along a recalcitrant board and finding expert advice for making technical decisions. Nothing illustrates the problems associated with environmental policy more clearly than the discussions and conflicts which preceded the Club's stand on pesticides.

At first, the Club considered pesticides only as they related to the management of national parks. As early as 1953 Richard Leonard had asked the Club's Natural Science Committee to make recommendations about aerial spraying of DDT to control needle-miner moths in Yosemite. Milton Hildebrand, a biologist at the University of California, chaired the committee. At that time he had carefully responded that indirect effects on wildlife were difficult to determine, and given insufficient knowledge, any recommendations to the Park Service should be based "solely on the advisability and appropriateness of forest management in a national park."[4]

That was as far as things went for a decade, until the publication of *Silent Spring* in 1962. Because of the writings of

Carson and others, and because of the events of the 1960s, ecological consciousness was rising in conservation circles and in the general public; pesticides were soon viewed as a universal problem.

Wildlife, especially birds, used national parks as migratory paths. For that reason Park Service policy was doubly suspect, since DDT had been sprayed repeatedly in Yosemite and Kings Canyon. In 1963 Richard Leonard, acting unilaterally, sent a strong telegram to Stewart Udall noting that needle-miner moths had existed for a million years, controlled by predators and parasites, that "I have studied Yosemite needleminers 35 years," and that no spraying should be allowed in any national park. Brower followed this wire with one of his own to Udall, and letters too, some of which appeared to speak for the Club. The Park Service insisted that "although you do not agree with us, the action being taken is in the interest of the public."[5]

The Park Service sprayed for needle-miners in Tuolumne during the summer of 1963, as planned. Meanwhile, Leonard appealed to Milton Hildebrand of the Natural Science Committee to advise to the board. But advice was not forthcoming, and Wayburn presided over a hectic and inconclusive board meeting in September. Though everyone, staff and board alike, agreed that there was a general lack of scientific data, attitudes broke down into traditional patterns. Robinson thought that dead lodgepoles were unsightly, while Robert Golden, a staff member, and Fred Eissler, a new young board member, stressed the natural place of the moth in the Yosemite ecosystem. Brower pointed out that the Park Service was not taking advice from its own biologists. Though everyone was "appalled to see the spraying going on," as Alex Hildebrand said, people like Alex Hildebrand and George Marshall did not want to be adamant until they had conclusive data. Knowing the improbability of obtaining definitive data, Siri thought the Club might simply take a stand on "deliberate alteration of ecology on the basis of direct introduction of perturbing factors." Finally, three separate policies on pesticides were offered, while the board decided to await recommendations from the Natural Science and Conservation committees.[6]

In the meantime, Leonard participated in a meeting of the International Union for Conservation of Nature and Natural Resources, in Nairobi, Kenya. When that organization came out with a strong statement against spraying pesticides in national parks, Leonard brought a copy back to the board.

While Leonard was away, Brower wrote impatiently to Milton Hildebrand. Using an argument familiar to a professor at the University of California–Berkeley in the mid 1960s, Brower pointed out that "too many scientists have too little social conscience or too little humility. If not that, too many of them are on someone's payroll and their opinions cannot be attributed to them. Others are prone to chase facts all over the lot, but decline any responsibility for what is done with the facts they captured. The exception, I thought, would be the biologists." Brower believed that "conservation needs good sound advice" to counteract reports from companies like American Cyanamid and people like Tom Jukes. He reminded Hildebrand that "most of the decisions in this country are made by attorneys" who will "not come to scientifically sound conservation decisions if the scientists play hard to get and won't inform themselves."[7]

Hildebrand's reply was what it had been over the past decade; he argued still that the Club could at best build a case on the principle of habitat manipulation in a national park, and should not address the larger environmental issue. Further, he argued that the Club could not conduct research, and that the problem was "far too technical for laymen to advance." Even at his own university it was difficult to hire a competent man to direct such research. If, as was apparent, the Club had as yet no policy, what was one to make of all

Brower's public pronouncements? he asked. Hildebrand noted that a lawyer might properly say that he had studied needle-miners for thirty-five years, but for a true scientist to make such a statment was irresponsible: "You must not equate the scientist's reluctance to throw wild pitches with lack of guts or social conscience."[8]

Nearly a year later, in September 1964, Milton Hildebrand resigned as chair of the Club's Natural Sciences Committee, not in anger, but because his committee had failed: "At no time in the history of the committee has the club asked for a policy recommendation of importance before one or more officers of the club had, in effect, announced the club's stand to the agency concerned," he said. Though recognizing the problems of meeting crises, he also observed that reports were asked for too late to be forthcoming in time to meet a crisis, and were "forgotten when the crisis passed." Why, for instance, had the board taken no action after he submitted his second report on aerial spraying the previous October? The board should create "a climate of understanding and receptiveness."[9]

Milton Hildebrand was persuaded to withdraw his resignation, and by the next spring, as Siri recalls, "provided us with a well formulated, comprehensive policy, which we enthusiastically embraced. It dispelled any lingering doubt which some may have had about the Club's position on pesticides."[10] Eventually Milton Hildebrand, who presided over a group of eminent biologists in the Club's committee, provided a thorough, clear statement for the Club to embrace on policy with regard to public lands.[11] He also came back two months later with a specific policy with regard to chlorinated hydrocarbon pesticides: "Be it resolved that the Sierra Club opposes aerial and other general application of chlorinated hydrocarbons as pesticides, on all lands and waters, both public and private."[12] Several people could be credited with this resolution. Litton believed it passed because Brower had packed the board with people like Eliot Porter, Fred Eissler, and Wallace Stegner, while Siri believed it passed because he managed to control conflict on the board and keep Milton Hildebrand on the project.[13]

This resolution marked the first clear and thoroughly articulated environmental policy stand made by the Club. The board demanded "cognizance by public agencies of all potential uses of the land," required public disclosure of long-range effects of tax-supported control programs, and insisted that such proposals be "made with considerations for the total environment." Further, the resolution insisted that "no species should be considered inherently and always as a pest or 'bad' species," and noted that "the use of pesticides tends to reduce the diversity of natural environments, and simplified environments are relatively unstable and subject to depletion by pests. The use of pesticides tends, therefore, to perpetrate a need for such use."[14]

The response from Tom Jukes was not surprising. Jukes had been a vigorous supporter of the use of pesticides and had bitterly condemned any criticism of their use, as early as the brief mention in *This Is The American Earth*.[15]

Now also Joel Hildebrand, the father of Alex and Milton, resigned from his honorary position as vice president of the Club, not over the issue of pesticides, but what he considered a careless statement by Brower in the December 1964 *Bulletin* on the use of fertilizers.[16] When Joel tried to answer in the pages of the *Bulletin*, his letter, entitled "Means and Ends," was finally refused by Hugh Nash, the editor. Joel Hildebrand had in his letter criticized Brower's lack of technical expertise in discussing a matter involving chemistry. Hildebrand was never taken with Carson's book, which he had not read, since in his view it was not scientific. But he was worried about the trend in Brower's thinking. "Now to warn against pesticides is one thing. But to warn against chemical fertilizers is another."[17] And he was apprehensive about Brower's power, especially because of his own powerlessness to reply in the *Bul-*

letin. As far as he was concerned, Siri was not holding Brower in check, and Brower in turn was trying to control the media of the Club. In a larger sense, Hildebrand was dissatisfied with the direction of the Club, not only in regard to technical matters, but in regard to power politics, where voting strength counted. "Our strength earlier was moral strength rather than numbers, but when you do not have a majority you had better try to achieve what you want to do through moral strength and cogent argument rather than threats and confrontation."[18] Matters of technical expertise, Club media, Brower's authority, and changes in Club strategies all brought on Joel Hildebrand's dissatisfaction.

Every Club president would now have to contend with Brower. Siri knew that, and when he took office had tried to make such accommodations clear. He sat down with Brower to discuss their respective roles. And in a sense, Siri did retain good relations with Brower, telling Dave *New Policies and Policymaking 1964–1965* that there would be much latitude as long as Brower's actions did not jeopardize the structure or finances of the Club.

Nevertheless, Brower became more openly defiant of board policy, Siri remembers. Brower was under increasing fire from a variety of directions since, as Siri put it later, the Club was an elitist organization where there weren't many followers and everyone wanted to lead. "They weren't eager to see one man dominating the whole scene and doing things often that they didn't agree to or approve of, or that appeared to usurp the volunteer's role in the club."[19] McCloskey recognized almost immediately, when he became assistant to Siri in 1965, that he "in some ways was assisting the president to compete with the executive director." Though many board members might have been "mired in the past," McCloskey also began to see that Brower "wanted to provoke a showdown," if not with Siri, then with the board.[20]

But the board itself was a divided entity. By May of 1965

traditional members like Nathan and Lewis Clark, Richard Leonard, Alex Hildebrand, George Marshall, Ansel Adams, and Charlotte Mauk were answered by new voices. Fred Eissler (elected to the board in 1963), Martin Litton (1964), Wallace Stegner (1964), Pauline Dyer (1960), and Eliot Porter (1965) would generally be less troubled by consistency with past policy than with the urgency of making appropriate decisions for the future. The next two years would see even greater diversity in Paul Brooks (1966), John B. Oakes (1966), Patrick Goldsworthy (1967) and Richard Sill (1967). They too seemed eager to guide the Club on new campaigns and to shape policy on new issues. Will Siri and Edgar Wayburn were hard pressed to bridge the gap between old and new ideas. They began to experience further troubles when, in the mid 1960s, members from local chapters came into open conflict with board decisions.

The changes on the board were clearest not when the Club's major national priorities were at issue, but when local California issues like Mineral King and Diablo Canyon arose. These were exacerbated by debates over the relationship between the members and the board in 1963 and 1964, when the Club was asked by petitions to reconsider parts of its by-laws.[21] The petitioners demanded that the directors serve no more than three consecutive terms, that board elections include publication of the voting records of incumbent directors, and that all members, including directors, have freedom of speech, including the right to publicly criticize board policies.[22] In a sense, over the next few years there would be no separating matters of conservation policy, the publishing program, the content of the *Bulletin*, Club finances, questions of the autonomy of the professional staff versus the board, the board's power over chapters in conservation issues, and even procedural matters within the board.

When, in 1965, the board reconsidered the policy it had established in 1947 and 1949 not to oppose development of

Mineral King as a ski resort, it ran head on into changes in the Club—changes not simply in philosophy and power, but in organizational structure. These are seen most clearly not from the point of view of Ansel Adams, David Brower, Lewis Clark, or Richard Leonard, who had been members of the 1947–1949 board, but from the perspective of John L. Harper, who had become chair of Southern California's Kern–Kaweah Chapter in 1965. Harper, a geographer, had joined the Club in 1961 and had involved himself increasingly in chapter affairs. In the fall of 1962 he became alarmed by rumors of possible development in his favorite region. By the beginning of 1963 he had put together a preliminary report, advocating that the watershed of the upper east fork of the Kaweah River be protected by the Forest Service, or, preferably, that it be annexed to Sequoia National Park, where he thought it rightfully belonged.[23] The report began to go through channels, but got laid aside, since the Southern Section of the Sierra Club Conservation Committee was once again engaged by proposals to develop San Gorgonio for skiing. Harper's report sat eight months on the table of the Southern Section Conservation Committee, until he made personal contact with Will Siri and George Marshall when the board met in Los Angeles in October 1964. As Harper remembers, not only were Marshall and Siri "unaware of the plight of the area, worsening every week," but both were "aghast at the suppression of the report for eight months."[24]

Even while the report was circulating in San Francisco, the Forest Service indicated its own commitment to development. Worse, Harper thought, was "a kind of metamorphosis [in the Club] that can only be described as peculiarly self-defeating." Bob Marshall, the chair of the Southern Section Conservation Committee—no relation to the brothers Robert and George—seemed willing to compromise with the Forest Service. Harper thought Wayburn seemed "soft on mounting a resistance movement." Yet, as Harper remembers, in awe of "the brass" of the Club and intimidated by the local conservation committee, he reworded his report so that it would allow for limited development.²⁵ Meanwhile, the Forest Service had put together a prospectus which called for a substantial resort at Mineral King, including tramways with a capacity for 2,000 skiers per hour, parking for 1,200 autos, overnight accommodations, and a 5-million-dollar access road through Sequoia National Park.

Siri called an emergency meeting of the Executive Committee, and Harper witnessed for the first time how things were done by the "names" of the Club. Lewis Clark advised that the Club not stray too far from its 1949 policy decision. Leonard, "with his attorney's mind keeping events and names in order, wasn't sure of our best tack. . . . Ed Wayburn seemed to be best informed, with friends in high places in the regional office of the Forest Service." While Siri "kept us oriented on the immediate problem of a decision on interim policy," McCloskey "counseled sparingly, from the background." In the end, Harper remembers, Bob Marshall and Wayburn convinced Leonard and Clark to go along in seeking avenues of accommodation with what appeared to be inevitable development. Harper "went away in a daze," afraid that Mineral King was about to be surrendered.²⁶

A few months later, Harper noted that Bob Marshall was apprehensive; even while the Forest Service had apparently approved of the Southern Section Conservation Committee's "articles of capitulation," as Harper called them, Brower was likely to stir up trouble on the board, probably arguing against any kind of permissiveness on the part of the Club. Still, nobody was prepared for what Harper called the "verbal melee," four hours of debate which disrupted the May 2, 1965 meeting of the board of directors.

When Wayburn and Alex Hildebrand moved that the Club uphold its 1949 decision and "urge that every effort be taken" to provide reasonable development, the debate began. Those in favor argued that the Club was bound by its 1949 resolution, that officers of the Club as well as the Forest Service had been relying on this policy. Besides, Mineral King was the best available ski area site outside classified wilderness and national parks. Those opposed, led by Martin Litton with his usual folio of maps, argued that conditions had changed since 1949, requiring a "new appraisal of conflicting values." They noted that the Forest Service needed to hold hearings in light of the long period between 1949 and 1964, that an improved road would damage Sequoia National Park, and that perhaps the whole region would be affected. The area itself was valuable. They thought that the old proposal of adding Mineral King to Sequoia might be reactivated.

Litton was shocked when Brower at first seemed willing to agree with Wayburn, and was appalled that Adams did not realize that the road to Mineral King would go through Sequoia National Park.[27] He "stood up in righteous outrage" and "raised hell." After that, the balance began to shift. Brower changed his mind. The board entertained four substitute resolutions, finally deciding by a split vote that it would oppose any recreational development and ask that no action be taken until after public hearings. "In short," recalls Harper, "a bold new Sierra Club policy had emerged that weekend."[28] The split vote was significant in itself; Ansel Adams, Pauline Dyer, Jules Eichorn, Nate Clark, Fred Eissler, Martin Litton, George Marshall, Charlotte Mauk, and Eliot Porter voted for the new resolution, while Lewis Clark, Alex Hildebrand, Richard Leonard, and Edgar Wayburn voted against it.[29]

To Alex Hildebrand, going back on the 1949 commitment was a poor precedent: "I think it was a case of rather bad faith, and they did so on a split vote."[30] In retrospect he blamed the new members, but the record reveals that Adams and others were significant exceptions. The road argument won Adams over. Siri, who abstained, witnessed with mixed feelings what he saw as the soul-searching of a board. Wayburn and Leonard would change their point of view a few months later, when the magnitude of the Forest Service's plans began to escalate and the cost of the project leapt by several orders of magnitude.[31] Like Leonard and Wayburn, Siri initially felt a strong moral obligation to preserve the Club's policy. Yet he saw the Mineral King debate as "part of the transition in the club's character," and believed further that while the conservatives argued that the Club be bound by its word, "the principle was not abandoned by others; it was differently interpreted. . . . The club's position on an issue could be changed at will as new information or attitudes required."[32]

In reaction, the Angeles, Kern–Kaweah, and Riverside chapters, which had endorsed development, protested the board's action, and San Diego was considering such a protest. Yet Harper was encouraged by letters from Adams and Brower, who counseled idealism and the avoidance of foolish consistency. Fred Eissler allied himself with Harper too, helping to distribute information on the issue. Harper was finally pleased to see McCloskey issuing precise statements of Club policy. By September the board had entertained objections from the chapters and then overruled them, supplementing its policy by recommending that Mineral King be made a part of Sequoia National Park. As Harper remembers, "I was coordinator, with Mike McCloskey's good help during the next two years of dedicated but quite ineffective resistance."[33] McCloskey points out that the Club was buying time and exhausting administrative remedies before bringing suit and going to Congress.[34]

Mike McCloskey was in a position to provide good help by the end of 1965, for by then he had become the Club's first conservation director and was organizing a conservation department. He realized that Harper's work on Mineral King provided an impetus to mend the gap in the borders of Sequoia National Park—a gap truly constituting a historical anomaly—a chance to complete Muir's boundaries and to repair previous policy mistakes.³⁵ Indeed, Siri's proposal for a conservation department, necessary to meet the size and complexity of the Club and its obligations, might well have been prompted by Harper's work and the resulting confusion of the board.³⁶ So McCloskey would be responsible for "coordination of effort, dissemination of information, adequate research"—not to replace volunteer work or local conservation committees, but to help them—and would perform other duties, including supervising the conservation budget.³⁷ He would be assisted by the Northwest, Southwest, and Washington, D.C., representatives. McCloskey recruited W. Lloyd Tupling as Washington, D.C., representative when William Zimmerman died.³⁸ Mineral King would set new precedents in Club strategies, but the first impact of the Mineral King decision may have been internal. The board had accepted the need for more staff support, and further, the need to reevaluate its policies and sometimes change them.

By the spring of 1964 the Club was experiencing heavy operating losses and concerned directors, led by Richard Leonard, considered cutting the ambitious publishing program. Brower, however, was sure his book program would begin to pay for itself. The previous fall, the Club had announced in the "Sierra Club Explorer," a pamphlet advertising books to members, that 1963 was "the year Christmas came too soon." The books would be shipped late. The Club had missed the season when Americans buy the most books. A business error had been made, and this was not the first error of this kind, though in early 1964 the major newspapers of the country were soon coming out with large and enthusiastic reviews.³⁹

Books

1964–1967

Business matters were not the only issue. Brower believed that resistance in the Publications Committee was financial and ideological. Color meant a significant increase in cost, and Farquhar, Brower claims, simply did not want any books which were not about the West.[40] Farquhar later claimed he was troubled because Brower began to pursue projects without approval of the Club and would often commit a considerable sum to a project before he received approval.[41] And Brower was shocked when he discovered that Adams had begun to criticize the program.

Adams said in a memorandum of February of 1964 that some publications which had been put out as *Exhibit Format* books were not of sufficient quality to merit that title and might better be produced in less expensive editions.[42] As a professional, he criticized the reproductions in some of the books, particularly the one planned for the North Cascades, and while he retained his enthusiasm for the program, he also insisted that it should not sacrifice quality. He was surprised when Brower responded three days later that the memorandum was "about the most discouraging thing I have come up against in all my efforts with Sierra Club Publishing."[43] Brower could not believe that Adams would be such a perfectionist, considering the number of awards Club books had already received.

Adams, in turn, saw that Brower was receiving objective professional criticism as if it were personal. He told Brower that he did not want to see the Club produce unworthy books, and that the Club could only maintain its high standards by constantly, even ruthlessly, judging itself.[44] In the midst of this rapid exchange between Adams and Brower, Adams also wrote to Wayburn, expressing privately his belief that Brower's reactions were "not rational" and might well indicate an emotional collapse.[45] Though Wayburn and Litton generally believed that Adams was unhappy with the new emphasis on color, and Brower remembers Adams saying "Eliot Porter is color blind," Adams' critique of Club publications was accurate.[46] The issue at first was quality. In fact, Adams contributed color prints to *Time and the River Flowing*.

Adams was also worried that a book planned for the

Carmel–Big Sur coast would turn into a "Jeffers book." The
purpose of publishing *Not Man Apart* was to propose that the
Big Sur coast be preserved in its wild state, not to publicize
Jeffers' poetry or espouse his philosophy. Adams considered
Jeffers one of the great poets in the English language, because
of the grand images in the poems, not the philosophy espoused; and he did not wish to see a book of poetry.

George Marshall had a different view of Jeffers. When he
received one of the Club's new "Eloquent Light Notes," which
indicated that the sender would like to say, with Jeffers,

> A little too abstract, a little too wise,
>   It is time for us to kiss the earth again . . . ,

Marshall wrote to Stegner that the note nauseated him a
bit by reminding him "of the over-sentimentalized anti-
intellectualism which I encountered in Germany . . . in 1933
in the midst of disintegrating minds which led more and
more people to commit or accept vicious acts. . . . Much of
Jeffers' writing strikes me as being anti-human or a-human
and I should not like us to publish a book of this kind."[47]
What Marshall meant was important, subtle, and revealing.
As a Jewish humanist and civil libertarian, he was concerned
that the Club's public voice might become vicious, perhaps
authoritarian, and certainly noxious. He wrote that he would
not "like to say with Robinson Jeffers." He praised *Time and
the River Flowing* and *Gentle Wilderness*, but restated to Adams
what he had told Stegner, who was reading the manuscript
for *Not Man Apart*. Adams thought this problem could be
solved by judicious excerpting of Jeffers, yet expressed concern about the use of color.[48] Stegner recognized a danger
that "it won't be a Sierra Club book but a Nietzsche–Jeffers
book with Sierra Clubbish photography." He feared that
Brower was operating in haste, and hoped to slow the book.
As Stegner revealed to Marshall, Brower's son Kenneth had
selected the poems and their tenor indicated perhaps the

young man's immaturity: "Some of them have the difficulty that you quite rightly note: if we followed them we wouldn't be trying to conserve a coast, we'd simply wade out and breathe deeply."[49]

Later Stegner would be joined by Joseph Wood Krutch and Loren Eiseley in disapproving of Kenneth Brower as editor.[50] Part of their complaint had to do with nepotism, part with Kenneth Brower's undiplomatic way of writing editorial comments, and part with a seeming immaturity slipping into Club publications. Stegner said that Jeffers had read too much Nietzsche too early. In a sense the comments of Marshall and Stegner constituted professional criticism by conservative humanists, which was analogous to the professional criticism by conservative scientists. Kenneth Brower, beyond the fray, went on to a distinguished literary career.

There was a certain paradox implicit in the Club's publishing program. As it began to publish its high-quality *Exhibit Format* books and began to exploit the aesthetic taste for scenery, the Club also began to think in terms which went beyond the aesthetic. Such thinking was particularly exhibited in the work of Jeffers. Marshall was right: Jeffers was no humanist. The Club feared to make its argument for wilderness in terms which went beyond humanism. The humanistic argument was the heritage of Robert Marshall and Howard Zahniser. At the same time, Loren Eiseley, who wrote the introduction to *Not Man Apart*, and whom Brower hoped would become a new and important voice for the Club, represented a newer, colder view of nature, one increasingly present at the wilderness conferences, in which wilderness was not pretty, but a world of mindless evolution. Eiseley's view accepted, as the poetry of Jeffers did, the violence, death, chaos, and change of environmental history, where man himself was frighteningly alone and acted often as an animal.[51]

Artists like Adams were increasingly incensed by the vulgar aesthetic treatment of national parks in such magazines as *National Geographic* or *Arizona Highways*.[52] Martin Litton, who had worked so many years for the glossy and noncommittal *Sunset*, was also afraid that the Club's redwoods book would be "too pretty." At the same time, then, that the *Exhibit Format* books were representing nature idealized and picturesque, the avant-garde of the Club was moving beyond that kind of thinking. Yet the Club did not change its use of slick commercial photographic images.

The Club reinforced through its publications the aesthetic of the monumental West, a view its forward-looking thinkers were already transcending. And the enemy, the Bureau of Reclamation, used the aesthetic in imitation; indeed it had acquired the services of full-time photographers and a full-time publicity agent. The Club's publications program was pressured to meet certain public expectations. As late as 1967 Secretary of Agriculture Orville Freeman charged the Club with the following responsibility: people must be convinced "that a new national park, or an additional wilderness, or the buying of another national seashore area is as important to them personally as is a second car or a larger motorboat."[53]

Brower exploited the extraordinary beauty of Glen Canyon because he felt the public could only understand such things in aesthetic terms. There was also the Place No One Knew strategy: wild places could only be saved if people knew what they were. "If enough people want" is a typical beginning of the forewords Brower wrote in the 1960s. If this phrase meant anything, it meant that Brower believed the preservation of wild lands in America could only be accomplished by democratic means. And his appeal to the general public was in part an effort to refute the idea that the Club was elitist. The aesthetic perception of wilderness created the Club's constituency.

Brower's genius was his ability to evoke certain parts of the myth of the American frontier—the notion, for example, that man is a visitor on a continent not his own, a notion shared by much of the American public. The relation of this myth to the rapid social changes of the 1960s is complex. Nineteen sixty-three, the year the gates of Glen Canyon Dam were closed and the Club published *The Last Redwoods*, was also the year of the Birmingham demonstrations, of Martin Luther King, Jr.'s "Letter from the Birmingham Jail," and of John Kennedy's assassination. Civil rights would be followed by Indian rights. These events were held together in a common cultural context that included bitter contention over the Vietnam war and, in the rhetoric of the war, over the "defoliation of the earth." The common perception of many young people was that American society had somehow become a mindless juggernaut.[54] The introduction of Jeffers into the Club canon made it difficult to avoid a more complex and comprehensive critique of American civilization.

The more conservative members of the Club were not ready for the philosophy of Robinson Jeffers, and they were likely to be unprepared for another manuscript Brower received early in 1965. *On the Loose* was a book that celebrated frankly the immaturity of youth, following the epigraphs by Shaw, "What is life but a series of inspired follies," and by Aldo Leopold, "I am glad I shall never be young without wild country to be young in. Of what avail are forty freedoms without a blank spot on the map?" Here was a hand-lettered manuscript which promised, "The photographs in this book are of the lowest fidelity obtainable. They are as far from the photographer's vision as cheap cameras, mediocre film, and drugstore processing could make them." If Jeffers read too much Nietzsche too young, as Stegner claimed, the self-proclaimed "crazy kid" authors quoted Mark Twain and Steve McQueen. Terry and Renny Russell reminded the reader that the year of Kennedy's assassination was also the year a river was throttled at Glen Canyon, their Eden drowned. Their critique of American civilization was naive and honest. They made a self-glorifying book, one that did not fulfill its ambitious philosophical aspirations; yet they pointed in the direction the Club had taken long before, "Not to escape from but to escape to: not to forget but to remember. We've been learning to take care of ourselves in places where it really matters. The next step is to take care of the *places* that really matter."[55]

Brower took the manuscript of *On the Loose* to Ian Ballantine of Ballantine Books, who remembers recognizing that "the book articulated ideas of a strong appeal to young people, and it was obvious that the retail price of the hardcover edition had to be low."[56] This would be a best-seller. If the Publications Committee was worried about cash flow, here was one answer.

The board was now ambivalent about publications; while it commended Brower's accomplishments and looked forward to new paperbacks and color calendars, it worried about quality and content. As Brower continued to press for the program, he seemed to be hasty in assembling high-quality photographs and he met increasing board scrutiny of his manuscripts.[57] Thus a proposed book on Kauai was criticized by Frugé as confused and because it contained unnecessary attacks on the sugar companies. McCloskey agreed.[58] Perhaps the publishing program was creating financial strains because it was growing too rapidly; and quality was not helped, in Siri's view, because "Brower began to make some shortcuts in his arrangements for books." The optimism Siri had expressed in the spring of 1966 changed to pessimism by the next year. "By that time," Siri remembers, "the Club was in desperate straits."[59] The concerns Frugé had expressed in 1963 seemed more urgent when everyone realized that by 1967 the Club was spending about 40 percent of its budget on publications.[60] As McCloskey saw the situation, a modest publishing program stimulated financial growth of the Club, and certain Brower ideas about diversifying the program, particularly with calendars, would bring in considerable financial gains, but the Club simply did not have the financial base to support an expanding book program.[61]

Though the board continued to hope that the books would pay off, it feared that publishing was becoming, in Frugé's words, the "tail that wags the dog." When production was moved to New York in 1966, Brower found himself needed in two places at once. Publications suffered, Marshall thought, because Brower involved himself so deeply in the Grand Canyon campaign,[62] while Wayburn and McCloskey thought publications interfered with Brower's conservation work. Though Marshall had hope, and Siri enthusiasm, for paperback books produced in conjunction with Ballantine, Siri recommended reorganizing publications into a separate corporation.[63] Brower knew that this was a plan to exile him to New York, where he would be removed from Club politics.[64] Before that could be accomplished, Wayburn would once again inherit the Club presidency.

The Advertisements: Redwoods and the Grand Canyon 1965–1967

By the end of 1965 the Club had responded to the Park Service report on a redwood park, put out a book to elicit public response, and with Wayburn free of the presidency and McCloskey as conservation director, put a full-time team on the redwoods project. News appeared in the *Bulletin* almost every month. McCloskey went to Congress to lobby that spring, enlisted legislators to introduce in Congress the Club's bill for a 90,000-acre Redwood Creek national park. Nobody thought the bill would pass on the first try. As Stewart Udall had told Wallace Stegner, the fight for a redwood park would make Canyonlands look like a picnic.

By this time, Wayburn, McCloskey, Litton, and Brower had agreed that Redwood Creek represented the kind of park the

Club should advocate. Though the Save-the-Redwoods League preferred Mill Creek, Redwood Creek seemed to offer "the greater total opportunity for doing something substantial," not only because of its size, but because of its wilderness quality. It was not, as McCloskey has said, "a little thin fringe along the road," so the League and the Club broke ranks, not simply because Wayburn and Drury had some kind of personality conflict, but for philosophical reasons: "We were seeking something evocative of the wilderness experience in the redwoods, where I think Newton's notion was more oriented to specimen groves, campgrounds, and roads."[65] Brower always thought that Drury himself was "a superb example of a preservationist," and had great admiration for his policies—except his policy for a redwood park.[66] Just as Olaus Murie had resisted the specimen orientation in the Tetons twenty years earlier when it was advocated by conservationists like Laurance Rockefeller, so the Club would do battle with what it considered an archaic notion of parks. But Leonard disagreed. He believed that the League had an "ecological plan" and argued later that the Club need not break faith with the League.[67]

Meanwhile Udall, as McCloskey remembers, "seemed to be bogged down with indecision." The Club people felt they were "having to do the work of the administration" in supporting the Park Service's own plans for Redwood Creek. They felt that "Udall was constantly caught in an inconsistent position between urging us on to greater heights in a rhetorical way, but in the clinch buckling and sitting on his hands."[68]

The Club felt it was ready to test its own strength. After the campaign for the Wilderness Act, McCloskey remembers, the wilderness "movement was emerging from being a bunch of outcasts into gathering strength" and had "reached a whole new level of support."[69] Was it able to challenge the "great mythology attached to Laurance Rockefeller's 'invincibility' in those days"? Rockefeller over the years had an aura of authority which was essentially bought by investing money in conservation groups like the League.[70] The Club would utilize a popular constituency to counter old money and the old policies old money supported.

But there was a clear split within Club ranks and a tacit division of labor, with Brower leading the Grand Canyon campaign while Wayburn and McCloskey directed the redwoods battle. Some people came and went. Litton's style, as McCloskey remembers, "was to suddenly appear out of nowhere with intense interest in a subject . . . and then suddenly disappear for months on end."[71] Meanwhile, "Ed Wayburn and Dick Leonard were to some extent, while of the same generation, competitors as moral leaders among our volunteers." But Leonard found no place in the division of labor, and "drifted off into identifying with the league."[72] So did Adams and Farquhar.[73] These positions hardened so that Brower could later speak of Rockefeller, Drury, and Albright of the League as the "redwood power group."[74]

The situation came to a crisis in December 1965. It was not clear that Udall could get the Bureau of the Budget to fund a Redwood Creek park, and he was facing increasing opposition from Governor Brown of California, who was worried about his own reelection among voters in the Northern California counties.[75] Udall, who was later to say that he "wanted to pick a park, not a fight," leaned toward the more pragmatic course of going with the League.[76] As Leonard remembered, Udall called "all the leading foundations—the Ford Foundation, the Kellogg Foundation, and many others—to a meeting in his office with Newton Drury and me. His purpose was to get the foundations of the United States to support a redwood national park and agree to put up part of the cost."[77] Though Leonard called this a "generous idea" on Udall's part, Brower thought the meeting co-opted the Club's position; it signaled a turn-about in Udall's position, as far as Wayburn, McCloskey, and Brower could see. Maybe, they thought,

Udall wanted to back a winning team. Laurance Rockefeller seemed to have great power in the Johnson administration, without being an ostensible lobbyist, as Brower has pointed out.[78] Maybe Udall was yielding to the influence of Rockefeller, or worse, to the pressure of the lumber companies who did not want to give up Redwood Creek.[79]

Under the circumstances, it appeared that the Club was being locked out of the process of choosing a redwood park. It was time for a dramatic act, performed before the court of public opinion. Brower remembered the effectiveness of the full-page newspaper advertisement run by the Council of Conservationists to counter the Denver meeting of boosters of the Upper Colorado dams twenty years earlier. Just as the council could go on record, even while it was excluded from the meeting, could promise in 1955 that it would "exercise every honest, democratic prerogative" to fight the vested, moneyed, political interests, so too the Club was prepared ten years later in 1965 to use the same strategy. As Leonard knew, the Club was now in a position to lobby in its own name, since it could fall back on the Foundation, created in 1960 when the board began to worry about tax status.[80] By this point, Siri remembers, "we were pressing congress constantly and realized the hazard."[81] Further, the Club's position on a redwood park was being undermined by Udall and the League.

So Wayburn, McCloskey, and Brower began to work on the first Sierra Club advertisement.[82] Later the Club used a prominent San Francisco advertising agency, Freeman, Mander, and Gossage. Brower liked this agency because "Howard Gossage disapproved of conservation through guilt" and because Gossage also believed that an ad ought to be talked about, ought to be an event.[83] The Wayburns drafted the ad and delivered it to Brower for his edit. It appeared on December 17, 1965; the headlines read,

An Open Letter to President Johnson
on the last chance *really* to save the redwoods.

There were maps and pictures, and the letter itself. The letter, signed by Siri as president, Wayburn as vice president, Brower as executive director, and Michael McCloskey as conservation director, claimed to speak for "most of our 35,000 members all over the country." It pointed out that Udall himself had written the foreword to *The Last Redwoods* and that the Club supported the Park Service Plan (Plan I). "Redwood Creek is the place, the last real chance." What, then, was the problem?

> Others do not like it. Particularly those who would be intimidated by a powerful industry and its extensive public-relations program. Some leaders in the industry have been public-spirited. Others, and those they could influence, would let the best be destroyed. They would settle for a false-front redwood national park. . . . Or an existing state park, relabeled as a national park. Some voices, too, are calling for an easy, bargain-basement national park. . . .

Though the letter in the ad noted that "industries, like people, would rather die than change their habits" and "the price will be high," it also pointed out that in two years "there will be nothing worthy of the name [Redwood National Park] left to save." The ad concluded that "you can help establish a real Redwood National Park. Write the President and Governor Brown yourself; support the organizations that support the real park."[84]

It *was* an event, appearing in major newspapers all across the country. As Leonard remembers, "Secretary Udall had a copy of the *Washington Post*, which he held up before [a] group of fifteen or twenty foundation executives. Udall was so angry he was red in the face."[85] Leonard thought the ad was "vicious," a slap in the face of the League. Perhaps it was, but it was also a clear, open statement about integrity in park planning. That, at least, was how Wayburn described the Club's strategy to the board the next month.

The ad dramatized publicly the Club's break with the League. One historian says that such Club advertisements had a tone of "the shrillness of the betrayed," and she notes that Udall responded to the first ad by asking the Club to maintain a flexible position.[86] The ad was effective, thought McCloskey, because the message hit a clear target and was meant to get the administration off dead center. The Club's effectiveness, in turn, was dramatized for Siri in the combination of Wayburn and Brower. Wayburn was a leader of dogged determination and thoroughness, "the kind of thing that really pays off" in a long campaign. On the other hand, the campaign's "brilliant moments were generated by Dave."[87] Most important, Wayburn and Brower considered the League's Mill Creek proposal a "confession of failure," not only because the place was unsatisfactory, but because the means of obtaining a park should be open, honest, public, democratic.

A newspaper ad was exactly the medium for cultivating public consciousness, particularly because a private meeting of foundation executives could have the effect of subverting public interest. Though the ad itself claimed to be "made possible by the buyers of Sierra Club Books," some future ads would be paid for by special appropriations by the board. Many of the ads would pay for themselves in the new memberships and contributions they generated. This time the board was willing to provide increased funding for the Redwood National Park Fund.[88] By the end of the year, the board would fund such ads on a case-by-case basis.[89] By that time, the board was faced with a whole new set of developments.

By spring of 1966 the issue of dams in the Grand Canyon was heating up. The Club had been successful in its campaign to publicize the issue; an article by Richard C. Bradley on the proposed dams had been condensed for *Reader's Digest*, and led to a conference at the canyon for which Brower and the Club's Southwest representative, Jeff Ingram, helped plan the program. It was a fiery time, with proponents and opponents discussing what in fact constituted the Grand Canyon. Even the senator from Arizona, Barry Goldwater, surprised some people by not entirely favoring the dam-builders. But the congressman from Arizona, Morris Udall, did. Meanwhile, Brower had seen an internal Park Service memorandum which indicated in explicit terms that the director of the Park Service felt called upon to stifle internal dissent and perhaps limit the dispersal of information on dams.[90] But copies of interior department memoranda also indicate that the Park Service had made the strongest possible case against dams in the canyon, and that its arguments did not prevail. Secretary Stewart Udall had made his decision for dams and refused to budge.

Brower always believed that Stewart Udall was pressured by the Bureau of Reclamation, which was too strong to control, so he tried to work on Udall's conscience. Late in April 1966 he wrote to Udall "as a conservationist who has supported you strongly and wants to improve that support"; using the strongest language he could, he indicated that a secretary of the interior who let the dams go into the canyon "could hardly win a blacker mark. . . . so far as I can see it, your conservation career is at stake, and our parks and wilderness too."[91] Nevertheless, Udall was adamant. As far as dissent within the Park Service went, the secretary of the interior wrote to Brower, "the orderly working of government requires that all officers and career employees in the performance of their official duties adhere to government policies that are finally evolved."[92] There was no doubt in Udall's mind: policy had been set.

Brower reported in the May 1966 *Bulletin* that "the Grand Canyon chips are down in the House Committee. Action ur-

gent!!"[93] That issue of the *Bulletin*, devoted entirely to the
Grand Canyon, was sent out not only to Club members but to
the mailing lists of the Audubon, Natural History, and Wilderness societies.

The Club also announced a last-ditch effort to draft a bill, to
be introduced to Congress by John Saylor, John Dingell, and
Henry Reuss, which would protect the entire region from
Glen Canyon Dam to the Grand Wash Cliffs. Meanwhile, the
Bureau of the Budget had recommended that a Bridge Can-
yon dam be deferred. In May 1966, the House Interior Subcommittee on Irrigation and Reclamation held hearings in
Washington on the bills to authorize the Marble Canyon and
Bridge Canyon dams. Brower testified, as did Hugh Nash and
the group Brower called his MIT trio: Alan Carlin, Laurence
Moss, and Jeff Ingram. As a result of Ingram's testimony,
Floyd Dominy, commissioner of reclamation, was forced
grudgingly to admit that the Central Arizona Project was the-
oretically feasible without the dams.[94] The Club continued to
distribute the Pennington film on Glen Canyon, and discovered in June that the Park Service prohibited the film from
being shown by the concessionaire in Yosemite Park because
it "presents a point of view contrary to Department of Interior
Policy."[95]

Once again, as McCloskey notes, there was a clear target.
This time it was the adamance of Stewart Udall and Wayne
Aspinall in supporting the bill (H.R. 4671) for Lower Colorado River development. The bill itself, Brower knew, would
soon be brought by the all-powerful Aspinall to the House
floor for a vote. This time there would be a series of four full-
page ads run in the *New York Times*, called by Brower the
"Grand Canyon Battle Ads." The first, which appeared on
June 9, 1966, was extraordinary in the way it was produced.[96]

There were two different advertisements printed in a split
run of the *New York Times* as a test of amateur writing against
professional expertise, one version written by Brower, which

he felt was a "relatively quiet letter to Secretary Udall, asking him to save Grand Canyon and asking the public to speak up too." The second version, written mostly by Jerry Mander of the advertising agency, was more aggressive and contained not just one coupon to be sent to the Club (with a contribution, it was hoped) but a number of coupons addressed to the president, Udall, Aspinall, and the readers' own unnamed senators and congressmen. Brower's version—"Who Can Save Grand Canyon? *You* Can . . . and *Secretary Udall can too, if he will*"—claimed that the Bureau of Reclamation's "blind planning" would "flood out 130 miles of the living Colorado" if the bill passed. It quoted Theodore Roosevelt, as *Time and the River Flowing* had done: " 'Leave it as it is. You cannot improve on it. The ages have been at work on it and man can only mar it.' " Brower's letter to Udall finally asked, "Won't you please find them [the bureau] something better to do?" Mander's ad—"Now Only You Can Save Grand Canyon From Being Flooded . . . For Profit"—was more effective, as the number of coupons returned to the Club indicated. It spoke more directly to the House bill, and spoke more directly to the issue: "Remember, with all the complexities of Washington politics and Arizona politics, and the ins and outs of committees and procedures, there is only one simple, incredible issue here: This time it's the Grand Canyon they want to flood. *The Grand Canyon*."[97] The advantage of professional expertise was clear. These advertisements produced an event of multidimensional proportions.

On June 10, 1966, the day after the first Grand Canyon advertisement, as Wayburn and Leonard remember, a "small faceless man in a dark blue suit" from the Internal Revenue Service hand-delivered a letter which indicated that the IRS could no longer guarantee the tax deductibility of contributions to the Sierra Club. This swift response suggested to Leonard, Siri, and others that someone very high up had given the order. Leonard felt at the time that the very success of the Club in the Grand Canyon campaign had angered the water power interests.[98] Wayburn quipped that the government had never been known to act so swiftly except in national emergencies. He also reported in the *Bulletin* that this was one of the Club's most historic events.[99] McCloskey's theory was that Morris Udall had read the ads and immediately asked the undersecretary of the treasury, Joseph Barr, "How the hell can the Sierra Club get away with this?"[100] It may not have been judicious to make an enemy of Stewart's brother Morris, the man who eventually ascended to head of the House Interior Committee, but Morris Udall became one of the strongest conservationists in Congress and later friendly to the Club.[101]

In any case, Morris Udall rose before Congress on June 9 and denounced the "inflammatory attacks" on the Colorado River Basin Project Act which he had just introduced. "While I have high regard for many of the people who comprise the Sierra Club," he said, "I must say that I have seldom, if ever seen a more distorted or flagrant hatchet job than this."[102] The board of the Club had included, since May, John Oakes, senior editor for the editorial page of the *New York Times*; the *Times* responded on June 17, blaming the IRS for "gratuitous intervention in this controversy," calling the Bureau of Reclamation a "powerful bureaucracy which lobbies Congress and the public tirelessly and shamelessly with the public's own money," and criticizing Stewart Udall as an Arizonan who "has silenced several other agencies in his department." Other major newspapers, like the *Wall Street Journal*, followed in a similar vein. The attack on the Sierra Club was a serious error; as Brower has observed, "the threat to the Sierra Club was headline news all over the country. People who didn't know whether or not they loved the Grand Canyon knew whether or not they loved the IRS."[103] The ads paid remarkable dividends in the outpouring of public sentiment, and the IRS action was a backfire of colossal proportions.[104] It turned a conservation issue into a civil rights issue and, at a time when the young American public was particularly receptive, took the ferment of Berkeley to the national stage.

Nobody in the Club was surprised by a loss of tax status. As far as Brower was concerned, whether success in the Grand Canyon led to the loss or whether the loss led to success in the Grand Canyon, the time had come. But many were surprised by the positive benefits.

Will Siri, who had become treasurer of the Club when he stepped down from the presidency in May 1966, recognized that the financial consequences perhaps revolutionized the nature of the Club.[105] If the action of the IRS cut off large gifts and bequests, in compensation there was a flood of smaller contributions to the Club. Though the Foundation might now receive large bequests, the Club was going to be dependent in the future on grass-roots financial support. And it began to get such support. Membership jumped between June of 1966 and June of 1969 from 39,000 to 78,000, and small nondeductible contributions multiplied.[106] As one sociologist observed in the late 1960s, the kind of member did not change, but the number of members increased, and the nature of their involvement in the Club changed.[107] This would further separate the Club from the tradition of paternalistic philanthropy, as represented by the League. Maybe the Grand Canyon ads were farfetched, as Richard Leonard thought, or gauche, as some historians have thought, but they inspired the large public support the Club would need in the future.[108] Yet the ads also seemed to take authority in matters of strategy from the board and reflected a troubling trend in Club policy making.

The Grand Canyon ads of June 1966 were only the beginning of the Battle Ads. Indeed Sierra Club ads became more aggressive as time went by, and more effective. In 1967 one read, "Mr. President: there is one great forest of redwoods left on earth; but the one you are trying to save isn't it. . . . *Meanwhile they are cutting down both of them.*[109] The most famous ad, and the one most fondly remembered by connoisseurs, appeared late in the summer of 1966: "SHOULD WE ALSO FLOOD THE SISTINE CHAPEL SO TOURISTS CAN GET NEARER THE CEILING?"[110] Brower attributes this one to a Club member living in Princeton, New Jersey, and believes its emotional appeal stimulated people to write letters, attend hearings, do what they could.[111] In fact, Ansel Adams, a chief advocate of the use of emotion in publications, wrote to Brower and Marshall on July 2, 1966, that he was disgusted by the way exploitation seemed to be the controlling factor in national park management; any project which allowed people to *easily* see scenery previously difficult of access seemed to get approval. Adams suggested filling the Sistine Chapel with water so that visitors could float around and see Michelangelo's frescoes more clearly.[112]

But McCloskey saw problems with the ads. As with any publicity campaign, this one would eventually produce diminishing returns and would not work if there was not a clear target. The ads also might inhibit the Club's ability to lobby effectively or engage fully in the legislative process.[113] Brower, for instance, was making many powerful enemies in Washington, D.C., enemies like Wayne Aspinall. Though Wayburn kept reasonably good relations with the congressman and the congressman had been known to cry over *The Place No One Knew*, Aspinall was not a friend of the Club.[114] As Wayburn puts it, "Aspinall was an honest man in his terms, but he was a friend of the mining interests and the timber interests."[115] He would listen, Wayburn thought, but not to Brower. The Club would come to rely more and more on its Washington, D.C., representative. In addition, by August of 1966 relations between the Club and Morris Udall were very poor. Not only was Morris Udall bitter about "allegations made by the leadership of the Sierra Club that either I or Secretary Udall caused the Internal Revenue Service to take this action," but he indicated that as a result of certain United Press International stories and Brower's "false and unprincipled attacks on members of Congress" he could only say: "I want to continue to work with the Sierra Club, but I frankly think that Mr. Brower's effectiveness in the cause of conservation is nearing an end."[116] This was a serious charge by a man who was an avowed conservationist, who had introduced the Club's own redwood bill to Congress.

Though Brower wrote in a conciliatory way to Morris Udall, blaming the misconceptions of personal attacks on "bad reporting" by the newspapers and television, though he stated categorically that "I have not attacked you personally" and that their only disagreement was over the Grand Canyon dams, he would feel the repercussions of his own publicity.[117] At the same time he felt pressure from certain factions within the Club telling him not to concede other Colorado River development, or the Central Arizona Project, and, categorically, that no dams be built in the Grand Canyon.[118]

Leonard, for one, considered some of the ads insulting to the president and to Stewart Udall.[119] He thought they were indicative of Brower's inappropriate conservation tactics. In April of 1967, he could point to a letter from seven past presidents of the Club, and others, which stated that the Club must choose between responsible elected leadership and "irresponsible, uncompromising leadership by the executive director and his sympathizers." The letter accused Brower of using "biased, emotional, and irresponsible statements in Club correspondence and publications" and claimed that he "impugned the motives and good faith of public officials."[120] There were other accusations too: that Brower had misused Club media, had established Club policy before it had been considered by the board, and had made unauthorized expenditures. The result, said the letter's signatories, was that Brower had "lost the trust of many key persons both in and out of the Club."[121] The first step, the cosigners thought, was that the board take firm control of Club policy and publications.

No doubt these men responded not simply to Brower and his aggressive use of media; yet the executive director was so much in the public eye that any problem which arose as a result of the Club's campaigns was likely to find Brower as target. Traditional members expressed a fear that the Club no longer had the kind of solidarity that it had in the past, given the ever-increasing complexity of issues and a new board of directors whose members frequently disagreed about Club policy.[122] Brower feels that the April 1967 letter was occasioned by vigorous discussions of policy on Diablo Canyon.[123] There was a divided board now, as the debates over Mineral King had suggested and the contention over Diablo Canyon would soon dramatize in public. What was the essential nature of these divisions? Was it a generation gap? Will Siri did not think so.[124] Was Club growth in itself—the source of the Club's new-found power—also responsible for the turmoil that older members regretted? Or was the problem Brower, after all? Brower being able to exceed his authority for too many years, as Phil Berry has said?[125]

When George Collins retired from the Park Service *Diablo* and became a member of Conservation Associates, 1963–1967 along with Doris Leonard and Dorothy Varian, he made it a top priority to save Nipomo Dunes. Situated south of San Luis Obispo along the California coast near the town of Oceano, the dunes were of recognized scenic value and geological interest, but also an excellent site for a nuclear power plant, or so Pacific Gas and Electric thought when the company took an option to buy the property from Union Oil in 1962. Since Collins had studied the coast as a professional park planner, his priority, thought the Leonards, was based on an objective assessment of the California coast. According to Richard Leonard, PG&E had no idea that the area had been recommended for park status several times in the late 1950s and early 1960s. Meanwhile, Kathy Jackson, who was the first chair of the Sierra Club Council, took an increasing interest in the area and began her own campaign to preserve the dunes. At first, it seems, she could not get the board interested in her problem.[126] But in March 1963 she introduced PG&E to Conservation Associates, as a line of communication with the conservation movement. Though PG&E discussed plans with Doris Leonard, it still believed that Nipomo Dunes constituted the best site for its plant. This was where the Club stepped in.

In June of 1963, the Executive Committee of the board recommended preservation of the Nipomo Dunes. Wayburn and others met with PG&E to discuss alternatives, and negotiations continued over the next two years between Conservation Associates, PG&E, Kathy Jackson, the Los Padres Chapter, and various members of the board. One option, to move the plant back inland, was generally thought to be too expensive. Siri, President Robert H. Gerdes of PG&E, Jackson, and Doris Leonard visited the dunes and discussed the environmental problems. In May 1965 the board reaffirmed the Executive Committee's decision; by then Siri had appointed Kathy Jackson the Club's coordinator for the Nipomo Dunes campaign.

After reconsidering its options, PG&E offered to build its plant up the coast in Diablo Canyon, at the mouth of an isolated, undeveloped canyon just south of Montana de Oro State Park. As Siri remembers, he conferred with Kathy Jackson and others, including Fred Eissler. Eissler thought the Club had a clear policy opposing power plants along scenic coasts.[127] As McCloskey remembers, Siri and Jackson negotiated an understanding with PG&E to move its site to Diablo Canyon, but he "never felt comfortable with the way that that was done behind closed doors. In fact, I cannot think of any other instance in the twenty years I have been employed by the club where there was a unilateral negotiation of such a conclusive nature. The fact that there was no collective judgment employed on the club's side bothered me considerably."[128]

On the strength of his negotiations, Siri recommended to the board that the Club not oppose construction of the power plant in Diablo Canyon, provided that Nipomo Dunes were made available for acquisition by the state and PG&E not develop its property there.[129] Indeed Conservation Associates had approved the alternate site of Diablo Canyon late in April. Siri anticipated board approval in May of 1966.

At the May 1966 board meeting, Siri explained to the directors that PG&E had sought the alternate site because of Club opposition to development at Nipomo Dunes. He told the board that while the Club would take no stand on nuclear energy per se, a decision on siting "would be in accord with the club's long tradition, and its most effective practice, of urging the selection of alternative sites." In addition, such a resolution would mean that PG&E would consult the Club in the future. Diablo Canyon was not, he insisted, of park quality.[130] As Brower remembers, Jackson characterized it as a "treeless slot" where the power plant would be hidden from view.[131] The board accepted her description as accurate at that time. Nevertheless, Brower responded that he was disturbed by the speed with which the matter was brought before the board; such a decision should require more on-the-ground study. Eissler agreed that the Club should oppose development at the dunes, but thought it was not the Club's business to choose alternate sites. He felt further that recommending the Diablo site would be tantamount to approving nuclear power generation. He pointed to a precedent, when the Club had disapproved "construction of powerplants along the ocean and natural shorelines of high recreational or scenic value."[132] Nor could the Club be certain that PG&E would relinquish its dunes property. Yet the board resolved that Nipomo Dunes should be preserved and Diablo Canyon accepted as a satisfactory alternate, provided that marine resources would not be adversely affected, that the power transmission lines be out of sight, and that air pollution and radiation would not exceed licensed limits. Adams, the Clarks, Eichorn, Leonard, Marshall, Mauk, Siri, and Wayburn approved. Brooks and Dyer abstained. Only Eissler opposed the motion. Martin Litton, who had been to the site, was traveling in the Middle East.

By July PG&E was prepared to uphold its side of the agreement, by either leasing or selling the dunes to the California Department of Beaches and Parks. Richard Leonard wrote to Shermer Sibley, the new president of PG&E, thanking the company for allowing Conservation Associates and himself to see Diablo Canyon. Though he admitted that he found charm in the canyon and its oak groves, he also believed that the alternate site was necessary, given financial and political realities. "The barren seaside beaches at the mouth of Diablo Canyon are common on the California Coast," he wrote, "and far more attractive in other areas. The fine oaks of Diablo Canyon are much more plentiful in many other canyons close to Avila State Park." On the other hand, Nipomo Dunes were internationally known, and so, he wrote, "I strongly support your selection of Diablo Canyon as being less harmful to public values than . . . Nipomo dunes."[133]

While PG&E arranged to lease the land in Diablo Canyon, Martin Litton wrote an entirely different kind of letter to Sibley, asserting that the board's resolution of May 7–8 was a "fraudulently obtained vote." What he meant, as he later explained, was that the board had been taken in—not told the truth about Diablo Canyon—and that this was particularly unfortunate "on the eve of likely victory in the Nipomo dunes matter."[134] Though Siri and others complained that Litton had written in haste, as near as Litton could make out from the minutes the reasoning of the board on this matter seemed "either false, irrelevant, or contrary to Sierra Club ideals."[135] Why, he wanted to know, should the Club believe PG&E? Diablo, as he suspected and Leonard himself later affirmed, would split the Club ranks as seriously as Hetch Hetchy had over fifty years earlier, and for many of the same reasons.[136]

At bottom, there was the strategy of offering alternatives. In the past, the Club had suggested nuclear and coal power alternatives to dams on the Colorado River. At Hetch Hetchy, Glacier National Park, and perhaps even in the choice between a higher Glen Canyon Dam instead of Split Mountain and Echo Park dams, the Club had recommended alternate sites for dams. Who approved of such decisons? Brower, because any strategy that saved wilderness was worth trying; Leonard, because it was right to offer alternatives; and Siri, because it was necessary to face reality. In the past, offering alternatives seemed to work, made the Club appear reasonable, and provided the only possible strategy when growth was inevitable. But Litton wanted a new strategy, best stated, he thought, in Raymond Dasmann's *The Destruction of California* (1965) where "Dasmann says the way to stop 'growth' is not to prepare for it."[137] Litton said of self-fulfilling prophesies, as Brower would later, that "if a doubling of the state's population in the next twenty years is encouraged by providing the power resources for this growth, the state's scenic character will be destroyed."[138]

Siri and Leonard, on the contrary, believed that it was not the role of the Club to fight progress. Siri argued, "Consumption of energy has for decades accurately followed projections of need."[139] The best the Club could hope was that the power plants be clustered in only a few areas along the coast. Leonard considered Litton's comment about population control "a different problem," and wrote, "We *must* have comprehensive long-range land-use *planning. That* is what the Board of Directors of the Sierra Club has acted on."[140]

A second issue was the matter of trust. What if Conservation Associates, as Siri has indicated, may have been used as a conduit by others to arrive at compromises on environmental issues?[141] As far as Litton was concerned, "PG&E did not start backing away from the dunes because of public-spiritedness";[142] it did so because it knew the Sierra Club was uncompromising.

Phil Berry, who attended these meetings but did not become a member of the board until 1968, thought the Club had gotten off on the wrong procedural foot and the board had acted prematurely.[143] But it *had* acted, through Siri. McCloskey felt that Siri had made a commitment in good faith, and whether the decision was right or wrong, the board members of the Club felt they were "honor bound to support Siri."[144] Wallace Stegner too felt that a deal was a deal, and that the Club's public integrity required consistent policy.[145] The Nipomo Dunes–Diablo Canyon choice, once made, became a policy which demanded strict adherence. Loyalty now was essential to the well-being of the Club; Leonard felt any public dissent was treasonous.

Now there would be increasing personal conflicts, especially between Litton, who had little patience with "procedures," and Leonard, who patiently pursued organizational matters. "There was the Litton view, which required that the land come absolutely first and Sierra Club procedures a distant second," Berry thought. Such a mind, though well intentioned, presented a challenge to the incomplete organizational structure of the growing Club. In retrospect, Berry thinks, "the orderliness of the Leonard mind [ultimately] prevailed for procedures within the Sierra Club, but the philosophy of the Litton mind succeeded within the Sierra Club mind."[146] The battle between the two would engage the board for several years, and its paroxysms would change the structure of the Club.

In the meantime, perhaps as a result of procedural error,

acting on uncertain information supplied by an incomplete
Club infrastructure, using a behind-closed-door negotiation
with the help of an independent agent (Conservation Associates), basing its decision on the assumption that the Club
must accede to growth, and using an alternate-sites strategy,
the board had made a bargain with PG&E, a bargain which
gave the Club increased political power. But at a cost.

George Marshall was more than sixty years old when he assumed the Club presidency in 1966. He had served on the
board since 1959 and as secretary during Siri's presidency.
Three years younger than his better-known brother Robert,
George had been a mountain climber in his youth, though
not in California. He was a charter member of The Wilderness Society, and had edited its journal, *Living Wilderness.* He
had devoted a good portion of his time to conservation for
nearly thirty years, though not in the Club. Though he lived
in Los Angeles, he considered himself the first non-
Californian president of the Club. Attracted to the Club by
Brower's aggressive style of conservation, he nevertheless
was sponsored for membership by his other close companions in the Club, Ansel Adams and Richard Leonard. An enthusiastic supporter of the wilderness conferences, he kept
abreast of modern thinking on wilderness, but he also had a
good sense of organizational realities. He had advocated that
the Club begin to think in terms of priorities, and yet the year
he would preside was marked precisely by a breakdown of
the Club's Conservation Committee, by general dissatisfaction among the chapters, who wanted a greater voice in conservation policy, and by the Club's devoting immense effort to
Diablo, a low-priority issue. It started with the very first
meeting he chaired in September 1966.

In that meeting, Fred Eissler kept up his campaign for preventing development at Diablo Canyon. Though he had no
more success in changing Club policy than he had the pre-

vious spring—indeed, many thought that his aggressive presentation solidified the positions of Leonard and Adams—his effort did bring a change in Club politics. By the end of the year Brower was challenging the board, first of all by running for election, then by offering to withdraw his name from the ballot if the board would make him an ex-officio member with a right to vote, but without right to hold office.[147] He had a voice, now he wanted a vote. He remembers explaining that his vote would not change things, but that the right to present or second a motion was, in the Club at that time, critical.[148] The board approved this idea, with the provision that Brower not serve on the Executive Committee.[149] At the same meeting, Fred Eissler presented a petition asking that the Diablo Canyon–Nipomo Dunes question be put to the membership. What followed was a complex and desperate organizational battle taking up nearly two full board meetings.

The exact wording of Eissler's petition gave the Club membership a choice between favoring construction of a power plant at Diablo or urging that the Diablo region remain unaltered. Siri considered such wording unfortunate and appealed to a panel of lawyers, comprised of Berry, Leonard, and Leonard's law partner, Stewart Dole. The panel reported that the board had the right to determine the form in which a ballot question could be submitted to the membership. So Siri and Adams recommended giving Club members a choice between reaffirming or rejecting the policy passed by the board, using the wording of that policy. Though Berry argued that this was not to present the question raised in the petition, which was whether the preservation of Diablo Canyon was worthy of Club efforts, and though Litton and Eissler were now joined by Jules Eichorn, who admitted that he had voted wrongly the previous May as a result of inadequate information, the board chose to reword the petition to favor its own position. It also appointed two committees to investigate the economic and ecological aspects of the Diablo proj-

ect, and promised that the controversy would be aired in the
Bulletin, with equal treatment for both sides. In a last-ditch
effort, Dyer, Eichorn, Eissler, Litton, and Porter asked that the
board resolve for a one-year moratorium on all power developments along coastal sites, including Diablo Canyon and
undeveloped shores of the Great Lakes.[150] This resolution
lost, 7 to 5. Brower planned, on that very day, a strategy for
reintroducing the moratorium.[151]

Brower requested a special meeting of the board, citing not
only Diablo Canyon but a variety of serious organizational
problems which beset the staff. He felt that he was being
hampered by the Publications Committee, by an ineffectual
Conservation Committee, and by a president who usurped
staff decisions.[152] Marshall replied vigorously to a strong and
provocative letter from Eliot Porter which supported Brower's complaints.[153] Litton wrote Porter that "bringing in the
unbalanced influence of the Siri/PG&E/Leonard combine
. . . the conflict of interest had become all too apparent, and I
am surprised and disappointed that George [Marshall] did
not openly recognize it a long time ago."[154] He meant that the
Club could not afford to think for corporations like PG&E or
it would begin to think like corporation.

A month later, in a special meeting, the select committees
reported that inland sites for power generation were possible,
though more expensive, and that "the Diablo Region was remarkably worthy of preservation" on ecological grounds.
Board member Brooks believed that the directors did not
want a plant at Diablo. By this point they probably did not,
but felt they were not at liberty to discuss the issue in these
terms. Siri stood fast, Marshall deplored the dissension
within the Club, and Adams declared, "The Club's stand . . .
is based on a degree of adulthood that accepts the utility's
mandate to supply power and recognizes the public's need for
power."[155]

Adulthood required the supporters of the May 1966 decision to ignore what Litton characterized as overwhelming committee evidence. After a respresentative from the Club's Legal Committee indicated that the board did not have the right to change the meaning intended by the petitioners, a split vote once again reaffirmed that the referendum would be presented to the membership in the form approved by the board. Brower, as the minutes quoted him, "deplored the growing tendency within the club to give procedure priority over achievement, to interfere and stifle in the attempt to control, and to consider the Board to be the club and not the members."[156] Brower also cited attempts to keep information out of the *Bulletin*. There was open warfare now, not only between two factions on the board, but also between the board and the staff, which supported the Eissler–Litton faction on Diablo and supported Brower in his bid for more executive discretion.

When Will Siri required that each argument on the Diablo issue be given two pages in the February *Bulletin*, Hugh Nash, Martin Litton, and David Brower planned their Diablo strategy; they would present their argument in the format of an advertisement or campaign pamphlet.[157] Meanwhile, Brower had been releasing details of the controversy to the press.[158] Siri asked Marshall to stop Brower on the grounds that such action was divisive and would weaken the Club.[159] Soon Richard Sill, as chair of the Sierra Club Council, circulated an open letter accusing Litton and Eissler of undermining the board so that the staff could step into total control of the Club.[160] Brower responded publicly; he copied for Sill and the board a discussion of the Hetch Hetchy controversy out of Holway Jones' recently published Club history, *John Muir and the Sierra Club: The Battle for Yosemite* (1965), changing the words so that the discussion of Hetch Hetchy could be read as a discussion of Diablo.[161] Need history repeat itself so soon? he asked. He attempted to conciliate Marshall, writing, "It seems to me that we have all made some mistakes, and I have certainly made my share. But isn't the biggest mistake of all the mistake of letting the face of the coast be despoiled to save our own [face]—or in the illusion that we thereby save our own?"[162] Litton spoke in even stronger terms, saying the issue was "whether the comfort of entrenched Directors shall override the highest principles of the Club, and the obligation of the Board to look before it leaps."[163]

In this contentious atmosphere, the Club election of 1967 approached. Along with the ballots, the Club sent out an informative sheet on the amendment to the bylaws which would give Brower a vote and on the board's version of the referendum concerning Diablo Canyon.[164] On the information sheet, Eissler justified voting privileges for Brower, and was opposed by such Club stalwarts as ex-presidents Phil Bernays, Harold Bradley, and Harold Crowe, who were joined by representatives of local chapters now in open rebellion against Brower, perhaps because of their recent disagreement over the Mineral King ski area. George Marshall introduced the Diablo referendum, claiming that this was the first time in the Club's seventy-five-year history that the membership had been asked to review an action of its board of directors. *"The use of a petition to reverse Board action should not be initiated lightly; it could set a precedent to hamstring the Board and the club,"* he wrote in his explanation of the wording of the ballot proposition. Statements by Will Siri and Ansel Adams supported board action on Diablo, and opposition was signed by David Brower, Pauline Dyer, Fred Eissler, Martin Litton, Daniel Luten, David Pesonen, Eliot Porter, and George Treichel, chair of the Select Committee on Ecological Issues. The enclosure stated that more information on the Diablo issue would appear in the long-delayed February *Bulletin.* "If you can do so without risking your ballot's delivery at club headquarters later than the April 8 deadline, you should await your *Bulletin's* arrival before voting."

The *Bulletin* was not forthcoming because Siri and Adams

were three weeks delinquent in delivering their arguments. Finally Hugh Nash attempted to replace their copy with a letter from Brower. And Nash issued the notorious "Half Bulletin," an issue of 700 copies which included only the Nash, Brower, and Litton text, leaving blank pages where the Siri and Adams argument was meant to appear.[165] Though Brower later apologized for this act of rebellion, he pointed out that chapters were meanwhile putting out their own one-sided arguments.[166]

Martin Litton distributed to directors and chapter chairmen his own analysis of "the distortions, significant omissions, and heavily emphasized irrelevancies in George Marshall's supposedly neutral 'background' information on the Diablo Canyon issue."[167] Consequently, Marshall joined what was coming to be called the "Xerox circuit." Reading these communications, chapter chairmen must have felt like the chorus of a classical drama. They could recognize the validity of both positions, but also witnessed the tragic intractability of both sides. Without question, not only had the Diablo issue split the board, it had politicized the process of Sierra Club elections. For a number of years Club elections grew more windy and the board swayed in many directions. If Diablo was, as Wayburn claimed, "an unfortunate aberrancy, but not the most important issue in the Club's schism," nevertheless the board made it the most important symbol of schism.[168]

The State of the Club in 1967   The Diablo Canyon controversy was not only a cause but also an effect of changes in the Club too numerous and diverse to organize into a simple thesis. Organizational growth alone created its problems. As George Marshall left office in May of 1967, he reported that membership grew in one year by 28 percent, to 50,000 members.[169] There were twenty-one chapters now, and these were active groups, each desiring to bring its own conservation agenda to the board. Meanwhile the Club had reached a new constituency through publications and advertisements. This meant a large number of what Marshall called "de facto members-at-large" who were valuable but neither interested in outings nor committee work. To a greater extent than ever, the Club had a grass-roots constituency, yet that constituency was diverse in its assessment of priorities and policies. "How can volunteer member activity and leadership—much of which is on a professional level— be encouraged, developed and coordinated?" Marshall asked. The growing staff of the Club, even if it was insufficient to keep up with its tasks, was now large enough to require that the relationship of staff members to the board be regularized, perhaps bureaucratized.

The board itself was beset by a diverse constituency and an increasing number of important national issues, many of which went far beyond matters of parks and wilderness. Soon board members like Ansel Adams would begin to doubt their own ability to deal with technically complex environmental issues; how then was it possible for a regular member of the Club to make informed decisions? The Club struggled with financial problems and pressure from the IRS. With increased external and financial pressures, increased work load, and a greater diversity of viewpoints represented, the rapidly changing board would find it difficult to remain consistent in its policy decisions.

To aid in orderly administration, the board turned to the Sierra Club Council. Though the council had no clearly defined scope when it was established in 1956, it evolved rapidly. Composed of representatives from all chapters and all major Club committees, its instigation was an attempt by the board to channel advice coming from the grass roots and to create an instrument which could in turn provide advice and assistance, particularly on organizational problems. It had authority only to govern itself and make recommendations to the board. From its inception the council organized biennial information and education conferences. By 1963 it had been made responsible for chapter boundaries. In 1963 and in 1967 it recommended a set of policies limiting electioneering in board elections.[170]

Marshall believed that the Sierra Club Council was becoming a substantial help with internal organizational issues. The Sierra Club Council, chaired by Richard C. Sill, had sponsored in late March 1966 its sixth Information and Education Conference, in San Diego, entitled "The Individual in a Growing Club." Such a conference was necessary precisely because chapter and group leaders felt increasingly alienated from the board, and felt also that the board was isolated from the individual members by a staff which limited communication rather than fostering it. When Michael McCloskey spoke, he described the Club bureaucracy and indicated that "increasingly, the membership must look to its own resources for creativity on behalf of the Club's purposes." Edgar Wayburn tried to explain how conservation policy was established. "Conservation policy always begins with a person and his idea," he began, but "only the Board can establish policy and say how it is to be carried out." Richard Sill showed how the individual could work through groups, chapters, and the council to reach the board. But his most urgent point was, "Don't let the board or the staff forget you or run over you."[171] In particular, "You can understand Dave [Brower], and most of us almost have reverence for him, but *don't let him run over you.*"[171]

Was the purpose of the council to stimulate member activity and strengthen members' rights? It had been created to deal with internal matters, "housekeeping" as Wayburn put it,[172] and with representatives from all the principal committees and all the chapters was itself becoming unwieldy by 1967. In fact it had no clearly discernible role until Sill was encouraged by Siri to make a role for it when Sill assumed chairmanship in 1964 and began to deal with some local conservation disputes.[173] Perhaps its most important role, as Siri saw it, was as "a source of experienced people for election to the board."[174]

Richard Sill thought of himself as a representative of the grass roots of the Club. A professor of physics at the University of Nevada, Reno, he was a mountaineer and felt strongly that the root of Club involvement was a love and understanding of the outdoors. Nevertheless, he foresaw a future when the board would be composed of full-time, big-name conservationists, estranged from individual members. For that reason he hoped that the council would have more say in the affairs of the Club. So when he ran for the board in 1967 he tried to represent the volunteer sector. He insisted that the *Bulletin* be a more useful instrument of communication to the membership. Young, in his thirties, and as Wayburn remembers, brash and brilliant, he had a propensity for long memos.[175]

The board was pressed by grass-roots representatives like Sill, Bob Marshall, and Richard Searle of Los Angeles, and was pressed by the traditional elite. In April 1967 the board and the council received the critical letter from eminent older members and seven ex-presidents demanding that the board take full control of Club affairs and wrest leadership from "the Executive Director and his sympathizers." Like Sill, these men argued that the *Bulletin* had been usurped by the staff. Though they did not refer specifically to the "Half Bulletin," they did ask for dismissal of Hugh Nash.[176]

And with the 1967 election results, the new board seemed to have a mandate. The bylaw amendment which would give the executive director ex-officio membership on the board failed to get the required two-thirds vote, 9,059 voting for and 6,994 against. On Diablo, 11,341 voted to uphold the board policy to approve the power project, and 5,255 opposed it.[177] The total vote represented less than a third of the membership. Nevertheless George Marshall, in his final presidential report, was gratified that the membership had upheld the board, although he complained that the referendum was unwise and the bylaws faulty, since the referendum was occasioned by a petition including only about one hundred signatures.

At its first meeting in May 1967, the new board established a *Bulletin* Policy Committee and made the editor directly responsible to the Club president. At the instigation of Siri, it also suggested reorganizing publishing, proposing to make the program a separate corporation. At the same time, under President-elect Wayburn's guidance, it tried to conciliate Brower, reaffirming its confidence in the executive director and further reaffirming its determination to pursue vigorously its conservation programs. Returning President Wayburn took part of his mandate to include better communication with grass-roots leaders and tried to remedy this problem not only by direct supervision of the *Bulletin*, but by occasional letters "To Sierra Club Leaders." [178] By October he could point to a new edition of the long-awaited *Handbook* and to continually effective advertising—"Legislation by Chainsaw," published in the *Wall Street Journal*—which brought in 500 new members. During his first six months as president, membership increased by more than 7,000, to 57,620. To meet the challenges ahead, he appointed separate blue-ribbon committees to handle the growing membership, publications, conservation activities, the *Bulletin*, bylaws, and finances. He modified the Conservation Committee to include the regional conservation committees (RCCs), of which there were now five. Meetings, as he said, continued to multiply. Yet he could also report some good news by November, on the eve of the Club's celebration of its Diamond Jubilee. Publishing continued to flourish, with new books on Baja California and the Navajo country, posters, and the new line of calendars. Three major legislative breakthroughs suggested that there would be a Redwood national park at Redwood Creek, that the department of the interior had finally decided not to recommend dams in the Grand Canyon, and that there would be a North Cascades national park.

Perhaps the biggest external problem facing the Club was its tax status, but that too had its good side. The Torre brief, written to defend the Club against the IRS, contained the first inclusive and thorough description of the Club ever written.[179] It was highly regarded by Siri, Marshall, and Wayburn, and articulated their idea of the structure and function of the Club.[180] Gary Torre was one of three senior members of one of the largest tax firms in California. He had been a clerk to William O. Douglas but was not a member of the Club. As Wayburn remembers, "he learned the history of the Sierra Club at that time better than anyone else because we were his client." Berry thought the Torre brief was a beautiful statement. Brower thought it was backward looking and did not allow for future legislative effort.[181]

The Club, Torre explained, was organized into four separate operations—outings, publications, conservation, and general membership services—none involved in partisan campaigns. Any legislative involvement was collateral to its educational programs. All activities, when properly understood, furthered the educational program of the Club, as clearly stated in the bylaws.

The outings program continued to be *the* major enterprise, "the base on which the club rests." Measured in man-days, the amount of time involved was prodigious. "As the outings program provides the laboratories and classrooms, the publications program provides the library for use in the educational process."[182] The published proceedings of the wilderness conferences, for instance, were of high scholarly quality. As the awards and acclaim won by *Exhibit Format* books indicated, these books achieved major artistic and educational goals. In any case, the brief said, none of these books was simply propaganda. In 1965 and 1966, publications accounted for more than 40 percent of total Club expenditures and by far the greatest amount of staff time.

The *Bulletin* constituted the largest single membership service. The brief measured space in the *Bulletins* published in 1965 and 1966; one-third of the pages was devoted to individual experience and appreciation of the outdoors, many pages were devoted to general conservation issues, and less than 20 percent of the pages dealt with major legislative goals in the Grand Canyon and redwoods. "Assuming that all these pages seek to influence pending legislation, what is surprising is the restraint that has been exercised. . . . The Sierra Club Bulletin is no lobbyist's pamphlet; instead it is a responsible publication which attempts to inform its readers on the variety of issues and influences which are constantly developing in the field of conservation."[183]

Conservation, continued Torre, could by no means be equated with legislative activities. Not only was the Club a diverse political group, it was rooted in the mainstream nineteenth-century ethos of progressivism, of private citizens who could determine the country's future through "the reasonableness and good will of an informed citizenry." When it sought to intervene in the private sector, as it had with PG&E with regard to Nipomo Dunes, "the Club, by keeping its views before the public and avoiding economic domination and partisan controversy, . . . won for its policies widespread support that assures an audience will be granted."[184] Given the tremendous expansion of public law during the last fifty years, the Club served the government's need for public input. Indeed, it was doubtful that the Wilderness Act could work without the volunteer activity of such organizations as the Sierra Club. So too, the Club acted as a legislative consultant. Yet of the Club's total expenditures in 1965 and 1966, Grand Canyon and Redwood Park consumed only 2.6 percent of the total, and general conservation less than 10 percent. Though the Club did support one court case in 1966, to the tune of $50,000, this was an unusual circumstance. Even the advertisements could be seen as within the educational purposes of the Club, the brief concluded.

The Torre brief depicted in rosy terms the Club of the past; Grant McConnell described the new world in which the Club needed to function. Brower's chief adviser about Forest Service politics, McConnell had lectured the 1961 Wilderness Conference on wilderness and politics. Club members also might have read his article "P.R. in The Forest" in the April 1966 *Bulletin*, an article reprinted from *The Nation*.[185] There McConnell argued that "it is one of the tragedies of political life that a one-time crusading agency of government should become a major threat to the public interest it was created to defend." In the same year McConnell published *Private Power and American Democracy*, an exposition of his thesis about the collaboration between business and government.[186] He argued that the Forest Service constituted a microcosm of "the basic ambiguities and perplexities of Progressivism itself."[187] Progressivism, the ethos that Torre described as the ideological root of the Sierra Club, had failed to develop criteria for public virtue and was impotent in the face of private power in a democracy. The Club was involved in what McConnell termed "the Quest for the Public Interest" and could no longer cherish the illusion that power need not exist. It must accept the facts that McConnell established: "Power is at the heart of all politics," and "Power is inescapably a reality."[188] And power, he thought, resided in the collaboration between government and business. "The modern age corporation," McConnell argued, as others in the Club also would argue by the beginning of the 1970s, "is in some respects no more than a special case in the pattern of business politics. It seeks autonomy and defends its political boundaries with determination . . . an autonomous body politic in a legal order of decentralized power."[189] No wonder, then, that multiple use had meant only "an assertion of unlimited discretion in the disposal of public resources according to the personal tastes and power needs of the administrators." In the late twentieth century, a federal agency like the Forest Service "was a trackless wilderness in which men in office unlearned in reading the signs upon the land itself and ungifted with the sense of moral direction wandered before the pressures of all the winds that blew."[190] From the McConnell perspective, the Club's tax problem was a consequence of its successful intervention between government and business.

The Club's effectiveness in the future, McConnell's conclusion suggested, would "require rejection of the illusions that informality of government produces justice, that political power can be abolished, and that the surrender of public authority to private hands results in democracy."[191] McConnell preached a lesson that applied to the internal workings of the Club as a private association as well. First of all, he noted that "strong distaste for anything less than unanimity seems to be one of the principal characteristics of private associations." Pressure for what he called "orthodoxy," based on the illusion of group homogeneity, led to oligarchy, which was inescapable and not remarkable, but also meant that a private organization (like the Sierra Club) "generally lacks the limitations that guard against tyranny and injustice to minorities and individuals." It was a "wishful view that the private association [be it a corporation *or* the Club] is the natural home of democracy."[192] These warnings would be a useful gloss on the turmoil that followed the Club in the next two years.

When the Club prepared to celebrate its Diamond Jubilee in the fall of 1967, it could look upon the Torre brief as a clear exposition of its recent past; yet the Club was still rooted in the ideas of Muir. It had celebrated its first quarter century only a year after the formation of the National Park Service, and its second quarter century in 1942 with the completion of Muir's project, the preservation of Kings Canyon National

Park, through the efforts of its officers and of Francis Farquhar and Will Colby in particular. Now, entering its fourth
quarter century, its president could still say, "Muir epitomized
the Sierra Club of his day—and even the club of our day."
Even as the Club honored Muir in 1967, it would look forward, as Wayburn exhorted, to its national role, "to the continuing battles for the Grand Canyon, and the redwoods, and
the North Cascades . . . to new efforts for Muir's own territory, Alaska . . . and to the quickening battle for the quality of
man's own environment."[193] Speakers at the Diamond Jubilee, like Farquhar, warned, "Let us not forget the beginnings." Leonard told "How Will Colby Started Outings,"
Brower expounded on "Rock Climbing: How Cragmont Won
the War." There was much talk of outings. Yet the Club Farquhar remembered ("No need in those days to publish descriptions of candidates for election to the Board of Directors—everyone knew who Colby, LeConte, Tappaan, Huber,
McDuffie, and Aurelia Harwood were, and had confidence in
them")[194] was not the Club of the 1960s.

The same issue of the *Bulletin* which reprinted the speeches
from the Diamond Jubilee contained an "Important Notice to
Sierra Club Members" warning that pursuant to board recommendation on the day following the Diamond Jubilee,
"No Sierra Club lists, files, facilities or personnel in any location shall be made available to be used by anyone for purposes of electioneering," and that "organized campaigning in
any form for any nominee is contrary to club policy."[195] A
contentious board had made its break from an earlier, easier
time.

At the May 1968 board meeting it was clear that *Conservation*
a majority of the new board wished to recon-   *1968–1969*
sider the Diablo issue. Wayburn promised action
in September. Meanwhile, there was increasing evidence
that thermal effects from a nuclear power plant would adversely affect marine life. So a majority of directors asked Phil

Berry and Dave Brower to draft a letter to PG&E making the company aware of the imminent policy review. Directors Berry, Eissler, Goldsworthy, Leopold, Litton, Moss, Oakes, and Porter authorized having their names appended.[196] Wayburn asked that Brower not send the letter. But Litton "acted in behalf of the Majority's wish to speak out" and sent the letter to Shermer Sibley.[197]

The results distressed Wayburn as he read editorials in the *San Francisco Examiner*, which not only spoke of a "new anti-atom majority" on the board, but criticized the "Inconsistent Club," which had damaged its prestige and cast serious doubt on the wisdom of consulting with the conservation group.[198] When Brower attempted to write to the newspapers to clarify the situation, Siri, Leonard, and Adams were unhappy. Because the letter to PG&E did not contain actual signatures, Shermer Sibley wrote to Wayburn asking for confirmation of the document's accuracy.[199] Wayburn wrote to the directors, saying that sending such a letter, without personal signatures and independent of official Club action, put him in an awkward position: "In other words, this is a hell of a way to run a railroad."[200]

There was a furious debate in September. Phil Berry cannot remember any board meeting before or since as highly charged.[201] The terms of the discussion had not significantly changed. The new majority believed that the original Diablo policy contravened Club principles, that the Club should not bargain away a unique scenic area. Eliot Porter argued in a way convincing to Phil Berry and even Will Siri that "the Sierra Club should never be a party to a convention that lessens wilderness."[202] Further, a change in circumstances had occurred as a result of the belated recognition and growing awareness of what would be termed "thermal pollution" from coastal power plants. Adams, Leonard, Siri, Wayburn, and Sill, supported by several individuals and chapter representatives, argued that any change in Club policy, at this late

date, would only weaken Club prestige. Berry said he could vote in clear conscience for a resolution overruling membership only because there had been a change in conditions. After several trial resolutions, the board said it "regretfully acknowledges its belief that it made a mistake of principle and policy in attempting to bargain away a place of unique scenic beauty in its prior resolutions in regard to Diablo Canyon and environs." This resolution also included a more comprehensive policy opposing the use of coastal lands for industrial purposes.[203] Unfortunately, the directors did not agree about the meaning of the resolution. Berry believed that the resolution did not overrule the membership referendum of 1967, and wrote to PG&E that "in my opinion the new resolution does *not* change the existing club stand with respect to the particular site."[204]

Although Berry may have hoped that his statement would allow the Club to affirm appropriate principles without damaging its prestige, the membership was confused. Litton thought Berry wrong about the import of the resolution, and wrote to Club leaders that such a change of mind not only permitted "but requires active opposition to development at Diablo Canyon."[205] Wayburn was more concerned about Club solidarity and sent a telegram to Club leaders, pleading:

KEEP FOREMOST IN YOUR MIND ALL THE GREAT
GOALS AND PURPOSES FOR WHICH WE HAVE
WORKED SO LONG. OUR ACHIEVEMENTS HAVE
NEVER BEEN GREATER. OUR DISSOLUTION OVER
DIABLO CANYON OR ANY OTHER SINGLE ISSUE OR
DECISION CAN MAKE A DIFFERENCE . . . 100
YEARS FROM NOW.[206]

Wayburn was right—about making a difference and about achievement. In 1968, the *Bulletin* followed carefully the major Club campaigns. On February 1, 1967 Secretary Udall had announced that the Johnson administration would oppose dams in the Grand Canyon. Udall had determined that Arizona could get its Central Arizona Project without these dams, saying "I can confess now that I approached this problem with a less-than-open mind in early 1963, when we began our planning in Interior."[207] In October 1967 the Senate Interior Committee reported a compromise redwoods bill which authorized a 64,000-acre park, including some but by no means all of the Redwood Creek acreage that the Club proposed for the park. Edgar Wayburn detailed seven additions the Club wished to add to the bill before the Senate.[208] In April 1968 Brock Evans, the Club's Northwest representative, detailed the current status of proposals for a North Cascades park, indicating that there were three possibilities: one bill passed by the Senate, one being discussed by the House, and the "Conservationists' Preferred Plan," which included a larger national park and more Forest Service wilderness than either house of Congress had proposed. As he said, "conservationists view the legislation passed by the Senate as compromise legislation, designed to appease the timber and hunting interests, but still support it because it represents a substantial step forward in the drive for full protection of the area."[209]

At the September 1968 board meeting, McCloskey reported major successes either achieved or close to achievement in Congress: a Redwood national park of 58,000 acres, a North Cascades national park of 671,000 acres, a Biscayne Bay national monument, a Flaming Gorge national recreation area in Utah, as well as legislative protection for scenic rivers, national trails, and estuaries. Many dams had been delayed; both dams in the Grand Canyon had been defeated. McCloskey expected President Johnson to sign a bill in a few days which would give statutory protection to the entire Grand Canyon from Glen Canyon Dam to Lake Mead. There was encouraging legislation for protection of endangered species, for pesticide research, and for protection of national wildlife refuges.[210]

As McCloskey reported to the board, "the record of this congress will make it one of the great conservation congresses in history." The Club could take particular pride in three major victories. On the redwoods, it overrode the recommendations of the presidential administration, overcame a powerful combine of lumber companies, persuaded Congress to appropriate $92,000,000 for a national park, more than had ever been spent for a park. The North Cascades Park legislation, McCloskey noted, turned what had seemed ten years earlier a political impossibility into a reality. The Forest Service would cede more than 500,000 acres to the Park Service. McCloskey described how, in the case of Grand Canyon, "the Club under the leadership of Dave Brower has done the impossible." The Bureau of Reclamation would be locked out of the Grand Canyon. The Club had prevailed over its strongest opponents.[211]

But as McCloskey later wrote for the *Bulletin*, the victories sometimes fell short of what conservationists hoped to save. The redwood park was "the best that political conditions allowed." There were still concerns about inappropriate recreational development projects in the North Cascades. But on balance, the Club could be pleased. Giving credit to The Wilderness Society and North Cascades Conservation Council, he said also that "Senator Henry Jackson deserves recognition as the conservationist in Congress who deserves our profound thanks."[212] McCloskey's report should have boosted morale. At any other time this news would have been a cause for rest and recreation. But the times were demanding. When he spelled out the conclusion of these epochal efforts for the November *Bulletin*, McCloskey warned that now "begins a period of painstaking follow-through to fill the systems out, and . . . a continuing challenge to make the parks realize the high purpose which inspired them."

By the end of the year McCloskey found he had to combat apathy in the Club. It was not true that conservationists would soon have nothing to do. Compromises had left the boundaries of a number of parks "far short of what we know they should be," and it was time for a second effort on the Grand Canyon, Redwoods, and North Cascades parks.[213] In the next two years the Club would bring out a new edition of *The Last Redwoods* and another book on the Grand Canyon, *Grand Canyon of the Living Colorado*, in an effort to increase the sizes of Redwood National Park and Grand Canyon National Park.[214]

The Redwood National Park was shaped by politics, and its historian has argued that its political shape defied the contours of the land, was untenable, and was the result of conflict between the League and Club. The Club would continue to campaign for a complete national park at Redwood Creek. So too the North Cascades National Park was political in shape, its boundaries the result of a complex of compromises among lumbering and mining interests, hunters, highway boosters, the Forest Service, the Park Service, and conservationists. Wayne Aspinall worried that the park would be "the private preserve of a few hardy mountaineers," while those of a more purist persuasion worried it would be developed too much. The Glacier Peak Wilderness Area would be administered by the Forest Service and vulnerable to mining. The Grand Canyon was without dams, but the status of the lands and the river itself was in no sense secure. As conservationists would soon realize, the Colorado River in the Grand Canyon had been seriously compromised by the Glen Canyon Dam, and the health of the bottom of the canyon could and would be determined by those who controlled that dam. The forests on the canyon's rim could be partly controlled by Forest Service policies on cutting timber. The politics surrounding these priceless regions had not ceased, and the flaws in these parks could only be remedied by new legislation.[215]

As for the wilderness system, politics would shape its fate too. Grass-roots politics. At the midpoint of the ten-year survey authorized by the Wilderness Act of 1964, only five of the fifty-four proposed units studied had been added to the national wilderness protection system. The Sierra Club's conservation department had prepared materials for members on the meaning of the Wilderness Act, had distributed a policy guide for action under the Wilderness Act, and an outline explaining "How to Make a Wilderness Study."[216] Chapters were participating with considerable autonomy in local wilderness proposals, and even if there was a risk that the national organization could not entirely control these proposals, it was generally agreed that the magnitude of the job at hand required delegation of authority.[217] All wilderness would have to be established by congressional action, but if every wilderness proposal produced a battle royal like that for the redwoods, McCloskey "feared Congress simply was going to lie down on the job and give up in disgust."[218] More than four dozen additions to the wilderness system would be up for consideration in the ninety-first Congress. Implementation would require constant encouragement of the grass roots, as well as of Congress, and efficiency required coordination by the Club's conservation department. By now it was clear that the task of preserving wilderness in Alaska would constitute a major club effort, and most of the 1969 Wilderness Conference would be devoted to Alaskan wilderness, in particular to preserving wildlife.

The Club's legislative program for 1969 would include eight points: (1) tax reform for nonprofit membership organizations, (2) implementation of the Wilderness Act, (3) new units in the national parks, (4) additions for the Redwood, North Cascades, and Grand Canyon parks, and some national seashores, (5) appropriations for national parks, (6) active participation in the hearings of Wayne Aspinall's Public Land Law Review Commission, (7) testifying on various major pieces of environmental legislation, including proposals on water pollution, endangered species, a presidential council of environmental advisers, and problems of nuclear plant location and thermal pollution, and (8) warding off various dams.[219]

Litigation would follow legislation as environmental law grew up rapidly in the late 1960s. Dave Sive, a New York attorney and chairman of the Atlantic Chapter, replaced John Oakes on the board in October 1968, Oakes having resigned because he was unable to attend board meetings. The next month Sive contributed an article to the *Bulletin* on the Storm King Mountain case.[220] The importance of the case was found in the ruling by the Court of Appeals that scenic beauty must be considered along with economic costs by the Federal Power Commission, so attorneys for the Club were able to submit testimony by experts on scenic beauty, including professors of art and art history as well as leading administrators of conservation organizations. Men like Charles Callison of the National Audubon Society and David Brower of the Club joined professors from Harvard and Yale, testifying before the Federal Power Commission on the beauty of the Hudson River at Storm King. Their testimony could be used in appeals, right up to the Supreme Court. As Sive pointed out, the depth and breadth of this precedent would have far-reaching effects on the fundamental issues of the use of national resources.

Encouraged by this kind of success and urged on by McCloskey, the board authorized "appropriate legal proceedings to protect the Mineral King area and Sequoia National Park."[221] This would be the first substantial litigation the Club undertook by itself, and would be financially demanding.[222] It would depend on funding from the Foundation, whose president, Leonard, believed that it was inappropriate to engage in litigation only as a delaying tactic.[223] On the other hand, McCloskey knew that "the lawsuit was absolutely critical in gaining us four or five years of time to build up our campaign."[224] Phil Berry, as he remembers, welcomed this bold move toward aggressive conservation litigation.[225] Perhaps nobody recognized the extent to which the Mineral King case would change the direction of Club strategy in the 1970s, when the Club's influence and power would be felt in the field of conservation litigation. Nineteen sixty-nine would mark an "environmental awakening," and the Mineral King case would be cited as a major event in this "Big Bang of the Environmental Revolution."[226]

In the last days of the Johnson administration, Brower lobbied Udall to reserve something like seventeen million acres for national monuments and wildlife refuges in Alaska and the lower forty-nine states.[227] But the last-ditch effort achieved only limited success. Prospects for the next four years were grim. Nixon's new administration nominated Alaska's Walter J. Hickel to succeed Stewart Udall as secretary of the interior. In December 1968 the Club's Washington, D.C. representative, Lloyd Tupling, did what he termed a little detective work and warned the board that Hickel appeared to favor exploitation of resources.[228] McCloskey consulted with Wayburn and put out a memorandum regarding strategy on the Hickel nomination, suggesting that the Club gain facts before it spoke too sharply. Since it was likely that the Club would be working with this man, McCloskey advised expressing concern, calling for facts, generating pressure, but withholding final judgment.[229] In other words, the Club should not burn its bridges. Nevertheless, a barrage of letters from Club members to Congress in January protested Hickel's nomination, and the Club would officially oppose Hickel soon.[230] Brower's statement to the Senate Committee on Interior and Insular Affairs would ask that Governor Hickel remove his name from consideration for the post.[231]

At the beginning of 1968 Litton and Eissler had asked the board to act on oil drilling in the Santa Barbara channel. Nothing was done. But on January 28, a blowout at the Union Oil Company platform spewed crude oil over thirteen miles of oceanfront beach and a marine sanctuary, killing many birds. There was a fine irony that such a disaster should point out the need to protect wildlife just when the Club was becoming increasingly sensitive to issues of wildlife management. Beyond that, the oil spill was perhaps the single most galvanizing national event, the final straw, leading to the environmental revolution, coming as it did in the midst of the controversy over the Hickel nomination. The Club passed a resolution in February asking that the state and federal tidelands leasing program be thoroughly reviewed.[232]

Challenged by many ongoing campaigns whose successful resolution would consolidate an already impressive set of advances in environmental legislation, faced with a significant political shift in the national political scene, confronted by new and widening environmental issues, the Club found that its most serious crisis was internal. By 1969 it was impossible to ignore unambiguous signs that the Club's organizational structure and solidarity were breaking down at exactly that time when there should have been a great deal to celebrate.

CHAPTER EIGHT
The Brawl

The Historical Mission

The debates over Mineral King and Diablo Canyon were also debates over the Club's historical mission. They were debates that Richard Leonard took up with gusto. Leonard and many of the board were in their professional lives members of corporations, universities, and other large organizations; they knew that consistent policy and organizational stability were absolutely essential in any large entity. This was a characteristic too of the Club's opponents. Compare the institutional structure of the Sierra Club with that of the Park Service. The Park Service had a historical mission, though it was variously interpreted, sometimes with considerable contention. So did the Club. A mission indicated limits, yet during the 1960s both organizations had been expanding the size and scope of their activities. In other ways these entities were different. In staffing, the Park Service, a steep hierarchic bureaucracy, valued consistency, specialization, professionalism, and career motivation. The Club considered itself democratic, with power flowing up from the membership; it valued vitality, a generalist perspective, volunteerism—even in its professional staff—and selflessness. Further, there was the question of ideological authority. The Park Service took advice from political sources, often in private, sometimes in a closed board room. It had close ties to American business and listened to corporations. The Club had once had similar ties but by the 1960s prided itself on its openness, on listening to disinterested, objective, nonpolitical parties, ecologists, social analysts. It was proud of its non-economic perspective. Indeed one could accurately predict future Club policy by listening to the idealistic discussions at wilderness conferences.

The ideal Club was an open forum. But the membership was arguing that the board usurped regional authority during the Mineral King dispute, and Will Siri's negotiations with PG&E or Richard Leonard's with Shermer Sibley were not open. Even the Diablo referendum which put policy to the general membership was manipulated by the board in a way that created contention. Factions on the board were not simply discussing policy in an open forum. They were also seeking political power and organizational influence. All of this suggested that the ideal Club was in danger.

By the mid 1960s the Club was polarized into two camps. Leonard, Siri, and Adams wanted to move a little closer to the Park Service and the Forest Service and PG&E to negotiate; they thought that was the mature course. Brower, Litton, Eissler, and others wanted to keep their distance; they thought that distance was essential to protect the Club's integrity. Brower would argue that the Club needed to distance itself from the Forest Service at Mineral King and while implementing the Wilderness Act, and from the Park Service and the department of the interior in the North Cascades and Grand Canyon controversies, and from lumber companies during the redwoods campaign. Meanwhile, the Club's size and power grew; other organizations expected the Club to act consistently and in traditional ways.

Growth and the complexity of pushing through legislation in Washington, D.C., required a larger, more professional and perhaps more bureaucratic staff, and required making hard economic choices. In fact, the Club's grass-roots organizational structure created pressure for authoritarian and rigid Club policies—a contradiction expressed by warring factions on the board. (These same pressures would be applied to the Park Service as it tried to expand its own historical mission from the Mather–Albright ideals; many would argue in the sixties that it should return to the progressive ideology and mission of its origin.)

The Club's sense of its historical mission was changing. By the early 1950s the Club had distinguished its views of recreation from the progressive concept of mass recreation, as espoused by the National Park Service. The Club found it harder to admit that what it meant by conservation—a term it did not wish to give up—was different from the Pinchot–Roosevelt ideal. That difference was part of its confrontation with the United States Forest Service in the late 1950s. In the late 1960s it might have to separate itself further from the progressive-conservationist idea of progress, from growth itself.

The Club came of age in a pioneer western town, San Francisco, and prided itself on its region's aspirations toward art, philosophy, literature—aspirations, it thought, sustained by the spirit of the land, not by the material wealth of resources. But the Club had never gone so far as Bernard DeVoto in equating material exploitation of western land with the enslavement of its citizens, because, as Gary Torre suggested, the Club was rooted in a Jeffersonian ideal which included, even emphasized, "man's need to master the earth." Horace Albright and William Colby were trained in mining law. Alex Hildebrand was an executive in a major oil corporation, and at one time directed its offshore oil operations. The board had included subdividers, developers, and men involved in resource-based industries over its entire history. In that context, what did purism mean in the late 1960s?

To young members of the Club staff, Martin Litton represented the new purism of the Club. One would describe Martin Litton as "one of the great guys. . . . He was a travel editor

and then senior editor at *Sunset*, but he kept writing things
that were too strong for *Sunset*'s stomach . . . very strong on
the redwoods and Grand Canyon primarily . . . . He is a purist. He even talked Brower out of some compromises that
Brower considered at the time. He won't budge."[1] Stegner too
admired Litton, who knew the terrain of California and the
West by the square inch. "When he takes a position, he takes
it from knowledge," Stegner said. The Litton style was "tough
and unswerving," "abrasive and unyielding," "never soft,"
and "generally very effective."[2] Yet Ansel Adams, the purist of
the late 1950s who had tendered his resignation to the Club
over the Tioga Road, expressed in very strong terms a complete disapproval of the personal and professional traits of
Martin Litton.[3] Alexander Hildebrand thought Litton dishon-
orable because he would not respect the precedent of Club
policy on Diablo Canyon.[4] How could Martin Litton call out
such disparate responses? This was a conflict not simply
about style or character, but about the Club's sense of itself.

Late in 1966, for instance, McCloskey had recommended
that the Club adopt an "urban amenities" policy supporting
"programs in settled areas to maintain scenic views of natural
landscapes and a suitable amount of open space, to obtain
pure air and water, and to establish and maintain a suitable
number of regional, county, and city parks and greenbelts."[5]
Though it would call out limited Club action, here was a step
toward a policy on environmental quality, and perhaps social
activism. Hildebrand insisted that such a program would require changing the Club's bylaws, which limited Club interest to "scenic resources, natural ecology, and wilderness." It
might be appropriate for the Club to study such matters, but
"to press for *action* on a purist basis could, at times be technically or socially either wrong or doubtful."[6] Litton agreed, in
a qualified way. Though he thought that "*everybody* deserves
a better environment," he thought in the 1960s and still believes that the Club might pervert and dilute its own purposes
if it took on many social issues.[7]

And Brower's publishing effort was drawing the Club into a broader sphere. In 1967 he published a book on the wilderness of Mexico, *Baja California and the Geography of Hope*. Brower reported that the Club had "territorial ambitions"; it was time for Sierra Club books to "travel afield."[8] The Club published *Central Park Country* in 1968, celebrating the park planned a century earlier for New York City by F. L. Olmsted, "the living core around which the city organizes and by which it is nourished."[9] Was the Club making policy with regard to urban planning, as *Central Park Country* suggested? Another book suggested in 1967 that the Club had recommendations for the Navajo Tribal Council on the protection of Navajo land. Brower argued in *Navajo Wildlands* that "the problem that New Yorkers and Navajos share stems from the very understandable urge to grow . . . from a recent conclusion that progress and growth are good and interchangeable and that both consist of an ever-increasing quantity of the works and numbers of man."[10] *Almost Ancestors* (1968) included a collection of portraits of California Indians from tribes exterminated by white men. Brower's foreword acknowledged that there was not a single photograph of a Navajo in *Navajo Wildlands*, but that "perhaps these faces can be symbols for us, can make more poignant the tragedy we are inflicting on living things less like ourselves."[11] These were fine books, but they suggested a breadth of interest which the Club might be incapable of sustaining.

So the Club was divided about its mission, the breadth of its programs, and the strategies it would use to attain its aims, while some of its organizational mechanisms for resolving conflict seemed powerless in the face of rising dissension.

When Wayburn had become president for a second term in 1967—only the second time this had happened since Muir's era—the Club was *Organization 1967* faced with deteriorating relations between board and staff, conflicts between chapters and board, and serious concerns about Brower. Pressed by a financial crisis, the Club had to repair its organizational structure. Since publications constituted such a massive expenditure of staff time and money, the board began there.

The board meeting of May 6, 1967 marked the beginning of major reorganization that had been anticipated for months by extensive correspondence among board members. Most important had been a shift by Adams with regard to Brower and with regard to the Club's publishing operation. As he wrote to Eliot Porter, he believed that the Club would have to enter a new phase, advocate a new program called the "Conservation of Man," and implement a more advanced strategy that was more cooperative, more civilized, and more sophisticated.[12] In this letter Adams was frankly disdainful of Brower's newest production, *On the Loose*. In a way that would trouble many, Adams seemed to focus all his concerns about problems in the Club on Brower, as if the executive director was the objective correlative of all the difficulties the growing Club faced. He found what he perceived as Brower's antagonism toward members of the board hard to accept. He found a parallel to Brower's style in Richard Hofstadter's *The Paranoid Style in American Politics* because Hofstadter revealed many situations similar to those faced by the Club.[13] Adams did not mean that Brower was paranoid in a medical sense, but that Brower's policy of treating people who did not understand the significance of wilderness as if they were enemies had often turned them into enemies. Further, Adams feared that board procedures were breaking down and that policy decisions were not being treated as "law." Adams was careful to avoid impugning Brower's motives, and more careful to credit Brower with dedication and genius; but because Brower frequently disregarded the board of directors, and because the board had duties to the members, Adams felt that the situation had to be rectified, either by limiting Brower's discretion or by dismissing him. Policy was, Adams claimed, his primary concern. The Club, as an institution, would have to survive. Secondly, he noted that financial management was an increasing problem, and that the quality of the publications program was in decline.

When Porter attempted to defend Brower, Adams hardened his position and said he thought that Eliot had perhaps been "brain-washed" by Brower, as he suspected Litton and Eissler had been. Brower's singlemindedness, as Adams saw it, could destroy the Club.[14] Adams also felt that Brower had perhaps brainwashed the staff, and it was not an especially fine staff, he thought, with the exception of Cliff Rudden and Michael McCloskey.

George Marshall tried to intervene, suggesting that "the Sierra Club is always at its best when members of the staff and the Board work together with mutual understanding on major issues, and I hope that once more we may be in this happy state most of the time."[15] But by the middle of the month Adams had written to the directors that he had withdrawn his support of David Brower as executive director.[16] Sorry that it had become necessary, he asked: (1) that Brower be relieved of his duties immediately, with a clear statement of reasons; (2) that Mike McCloskey be appointed acting executive director and given full power to reorganize the staff; (3) that the comptroller, Clifford Rudden, be given full power to operate the business aspects of the Club; (4) that publishing enter a period of moratorium; (5) that the Club analyze its finances, estimating future needs for conservation; (6) that the Club establish a position of coordinator; (7) that the board establish a procedure for controlling debate and policies which would circumscribe the personal discretion of directors; and (8) that the board separate national conservation issues from local issues. Adams proposed these steps because he believed the crisis was so serious that the Club as an institution was in danger of collapse.

Adams explained to August Frugé in December 1968 that

he had begun to rethink the publishing program after Frugé's 1963 report, and began to suspect that in his idealism he had not assessed seriously enough the economic realities of the Club's operations.[17] His letters to Porter suggest that he had begun to compare the organizational problems of the Club with those of major corporations with which he had been associated—Kodak, PG&E, and others. Early in 1967 he told Frugé there was no mistaking Brower's intention to dominate the Sierra Club. If Brower was successful, he thought, this would subvert the ideals and aims of the organization.

A week before the May 6, 1967 board meeting, Will Siri proposed to the directors a "reorganization of Club publishing activities," a plan which might solve financial, organizational, and perhaps Brower problems. "While the publishing program is a creative, vital force in conservation, it is also a business," he wrote. As a major part of the Club's budget, it was, as Frugé had predicted four years earlier, "the tail that wags the dog." Underlining the seriousness of the problem, Siri pointed out that a 10 percent deficit in publishing could wipe out the operating resources of the Club. The directors did not have "the moral and legal right" to take this risk. Though he indicated no person was at fault, he also suggested a way in which "David Brower can devote his full attention and considerable talents" where his "most enduring and effective contribution to the Club and to conservation will rest," that is to say in the publications, to be based in New York, in a separate nonprofit corporation.[18]

As Wayburn remembered, when the board met in executive session before its official meeting in May 1967, Adams spoke vehemently against Brower but then moderated his position.[19] In official action, Siri's recommendation was passed; a committee was established to plan for reorganization. Wayburn authorized it to investigate "all questions related to reorganization, consistent with guidelines." Wayburn would finally charge the committee with much broader responsibilities, including the reorganization of the Club to

meet growth for the next seventy-five years.[20] To dispel any
rumors that Brower was about to be fired, the board reaffirmed the vigorous conservation campaigns and expressed
confidence in the executive director. That resolution was
moved by Siri and seconded by Adams.[21]

McCloskey, who was conservation director, sent out a
press release on publication reorganization, which included
comment by Wayburn that "no organization which grows at
a rate of 24% a year can be free of stress," and which protested, perhaps a little too obviously, that "we have every desire to retain the full services of our talented Executive Director," and "there is no liberal-conservative split on the Board
over conservation," and "there was no concerted move to dis-
pense with the Executive Director's services, as some press
reports have suggested."[22]

Brower did not see reorganization in a rosy light. As he
wrote to Wayburn, he thought rumors of his dismissal, reported in the Angeles Chapter newsletter, were meant to test
reaction to a proposal to dismiss him. He believed that Siri's
plan was designed to get Brower "to pull up stakes in Berkeley, and go on detached service in New York, or else." At least
Siri had promised that Brower could continue to work on the
Grand Canyon campaign. Brower saw other hidden things.
He thought that Tom Jukes had drafted the letter by Club ex-
presidents—the letter critical of himself and the *Bulletin*—
and Jukes was close to Siri. Brower was not reconciled to his
fate, but wrote to Wayburn: "Books, however, must go to
New York, and me too." He worried about the composition of
the Reorganization Committee. Siri should not be chair and
others should be screened to avoid any conflict of interest.[23]
When the committee was formed, it included, among others,
Paul Brooks, Will Siri, and August Frugé.

It would be an oversimplification to blame the Diablo controversy, or growth, or financial problems in publications, or
Brower himself for the Club's organizational turmoil. For one

thing, there was the serious conflict between staff and board. When the board made the editor of the *Bulletin*, Hugh Nash, directly responsible to the president, Wayburn began actively to involve himself in editing, which angered Nash and made mounting problems worse.[24] As far as Brower could see, Wayburn tended to treat the staff as "lackeys" and created personnel problems.[25]

Writing to Paul Brooks—one friend on the Reorganization Committee, Brower suspected—Brower could only guess at what had made himself so unpopular.[26] Brower claimed that the chair of the Reorganization Committee, Chuck Huestis, was brought into Sierra Club circles by Siri. Brower suspected that Siri and Leonard wanted him removed most of all because he interfered with their plans for compromising with PG&E over Diablo Canyon, but he could not guess the motivation behind Adams' hostility.

Nevertheless, he thought his primary administrative weakness was in not getting the board to hire a big enough staff. The board did not want to hire enough staff because "of individuals who do not want the club quite to grow up." So Brower applied the following principle in hiring:

> . . . if you aren't big enough or rich enough to describe
> jobs precisely and then find people who will accept the
> Procrustean bed, then you find people who are bright
> and have religion and build a job around them that fits
> closely enough to be part of them, letting them be
> people in working hours as well as on their own
> time. . . . The further point is that when we do get
> someone who demonstrates great competence in addi-
> tion to brightness and religion, we delegate to him.[27]

This was not a policy appreciated by certain members of the board. It was also resented by many members in chapters. Their chief spokesman would be Richard Sill.

By the end of 1967 Richard Sill had served on the board for

half a year. He thought the Club's essential problem was a breakdown in the determination, expression, and implementation of Sierra Club policy. Ideally, he believed, the members determined policy. He suspected most members believed that the board determined policy but the staff expressed and implemented it. Yet his experience on the board during his first few months suggested, as he announced in a widely disseminated speech, that the staff rather than the board set Club policy.[28] A struggle between staff and board harmed the Club and its programs. As far as he was concerned, the problem was apparent in such fiscal matters as Brower's pursuing the idea of Sierra Club posters and negotiating a contractual arrangement with Ballantine Books, both without advising the Club president. Far more serious was his charge that Brower and his Southwest representative, Jeff Ingram, decided not to oppose a Hooker dam on the Gila River, which would inundate part of the Gila Wilderness. Sill believed Brower and Ingram made this compromise to strengthen efforts to obtain legislative protection for the Grand Canyon, despite the Rocky Mountain Chapter's complaint that such a compromise would undermine its own effort to protect the Gila Wilderness and the board's clear policy of opposing a Hooker dam.[29] Sill's charge must be read against Brower's October 1967 *Bulletin* editorial arguing against the construction of the dam.

Careful to say that the staff was not being rebellious but was simply guided insufficiently by the board, Sill projected an organizational problem which he said would cripple the Club's future. The future might take one of two paths. One was toward a figurehead board made up of prestigious people but directed by the staff. Under such circumstances even the *Bulletin* would cease to be published for members, but would instead be used to communicate positions to those outside the Club and would be filled with articles by the Loren Eiseleys and Justice Douglases for political impact. Another path to the future would follow the grass-roots tradition; directors would retain authority and use the *Bulletin* to communicate with members. Indeed, Sill pointed out that the Club must take the second path for legal reasons. If the corporate structure of the Club was not altered, he argued, should the staff "bankrupt the Club, it is the Directors who must make good the deficiencies." For that reason, he personally had obtained legal counsel.

If the staff resented being treated as hired hands, Sill could only answer that they were. It was "*far* more important that the Club be a social and political movement, in reality, than that it merely appear to be one." He knew only one avenue out of this crisis, and it was political. Members would have to vote carefully in the 1968 Club election, and needed information on the actual positions of board candidates. Only members, he thought, could protect a board captured by the staff. The Sierra Club Council was, in Sill's view, "the bulwark against excessive professional dominance of the Club." In the next election the membership would deny a bylaw amendment designed to weaken if not eliminate the council.

The 1968 Election   As the Club muddled through its organizational problems while approaching its 1968 election, controversy continued over Diablo Canyon and Sill made his charges in the speech he called "The Mad Hatter's Tea Party, or What Every Sierra Club Member Should Know" at the annual banquet of the Los Padres Chapter on December 5, 1967. On the bright side, as 1967 ended it appeared that the Club might be easing out of its financial problems. Siri reported to the board that publications were beginning to pay off. Nevertheless, the board debated the continuing growth of the publications program. The discussion turned on the number of *Exhibit Format* books that should be published each year, three or four. George Marshall and Richard Leonard argued that publications needed for members were being sacrificed for the *Exhibit Format* books. Leonard pointed out that a new *Handbook* had been delayed for six years and the *Annual* number of the *Bulletin* had not been published for two years. Marshall said that publications were adding stress to an overburdened staff and weakening the conservation program. Siri, on the other hand, argued as treasurer that four *Exhibit* books were necessary if the program was to continue to be successful. The board decided, finally, not to curtail the four-book publishing program.[30]

Almost immediately, vigorous opposition to this policy from some chapters indicated that the board's actions were under close scrutiny. Bob Marshall of the Angeles Chapter used Sill's arguments to protest the board's action.[31] He argued that publications and its budget were interfering directly with the operations of the chapters, not simply by diminishing communication within the Club, but by producing an unnecessarily large professional staff and thwarting the grass roots. He complained that the funds available to chapters and to their best instrument of communication, the Sierra Club Council, were diminishing. Like Sill, Bob Marshall was running for the board on a platform of returning the Club to its members. That a board candidate had a political platform at all set a precedent.

Though the board had debated the advisability of political electioneering in the early fall, it had decided in December to accept a proposal by the Sierra Club Council permitting a 300-word "statement of qualifications" for each candidate, which would allow voters to determine the candidate's fitness for directorship.[32] At the same time, the board determined that "organized campaigning in any form for any nominee is contrary to Club Policy."[33] Such a determination was impossible to enforce, since factions had already formed. There was a strong Brower, Litton, Eissler contingent that based its campaign on aggressive conservation policies. There was the Sill, Bob Marshall contingent that wanted to bring increased regional representation to the board, and perhaps more power to the council. There was another group made up of Wayburn, Leonard, Siri, George Marshall, and the Clarks that wanted to minimize public campaigning altogether.

Sill and Bob Marshall's vigorous campaign elicited from their opponents a petition to change the composition of the Sierra Club Council. This was presented by Brower supporters as a change in bylaws, substituting regional councils for the Sierra Club Council and redistributing representation in accordance with the size of the chapters which participated.[34] In theory, the Sierra Club Council did not engage in policy decisions at all. As Edgar Wayburn described the paths in which recommendations on policy flowed to the board, chapter groups or chapter executive committees would submit ideas on chapter, regional, and national policy issues to regional conservation committees (RCCs), where such committees existed. The regional conservation committees would set priorities or instigate further study before passing on recommendations through the conservation director or the executive director to the board.[35] But few RCCs existed, and their experience was limited.[36] Only after 1971 would the RCCs be a truly effective part of Club policy making. Meanwhile, Brower felt that the Sierra Club Council was aspiring beyond its intermediary role and that the Club was in danger of having two heads.[37] Nevertheless, George Marshall reported in the minutes that the bylaw change was a proposal for "abolishing of the Sierra Club Council." Brower wrote to Marshall in an attempt to add his own comments to the minutes, which he felt unfairly stated the case against the change in bylaws.[38] George Marshall responded vigorously, not only pointing out that most of the board regarded the council as valuable, but also asserting that the petition for the change in bylaws contained an improprietously large number of staff member signatures. Marshall concluded bitterly that "the Executive Director has neither the right nor the privilege to rewrite the minutes."[39]

These letters, rather than the minutes themselves, were widely circulated on the "Xerox circuit." Sill enthusiastically joined the fray, not only complaining about the wide distribution of Brower's response to the minutes, but also charging that Brower had suppressed communications from the council chairman to council members and chapter chairmen.[40] As Siri noticed, the council was a thorn in Brower's side, a threat to publications and other programs.[41] And Brower's engagement in a campaign to weaken the council was viewed by the chapters as an attempt to resist the growing desire among grass-roots members for a stronger voice.

Meanwhile, Sill began to anticipate the report of the Reorganization Committee by outlining to a committee of the Sierra Club Council the principles he believed most important for reorganization. His ideas were not different from those which would be suggested by Wayburn's appointed committee, but his action, and the council's, was taken as an attempt to manage what the board had appropriated to itself. Richard Leonard warned Sill that reorganization would take a long time, need not be made a major public issue, and was best discussed by the board and its committee first.[42]

Increasingly, Brower's financial management came under scrutiny by various grass-roots members, particularly by Richard Sill. This was not simply a question of money spent, but of Brower's discretion, his independence in spending.[43] In February 1968 the board renamed Brower's contingency fund, changing it to discretionary fund but limiting Brower's discretion in using it.[44] Brower argued that he had always used these funds in ways consistent with Club policy and that he could show good results. Nevertheless, the board, with the dissent of Eissler, Litton, Goldsworthy, and Porter, required Brower to receive presidential approval for any monies committed under the fund. And replacement of expended funds was not guaranteed.

Never very good at keeping accounts, too rushed to submit

such things as travel requisitions, Brower found his freedom as an executive being eroded; the simplest thing for him to do, as Siri knew, was to ignore or evade the increasingly complex procedures.[45] At the same time, the board was growing increasingly concerned with an issue Sill had publicized late in 1967: the board was responsible for the finances of the Club, but did not control them. It now attempted to establish consistent procedures for making contracts.[46] Sill found this insufficient and asked for special meetings. When denied, he distributed a formidable sheaf of legal materials on the fiscal responsibility of board members.[47]

In a carefully drafted summary of the financial crisis, Leonard assessed the Club's situation.[48] The audited yearly losses from publications had gone from $14,665 in 1963 to a peak of $119,144 in 1966, and could be estimated at another $63,475 in 1967. This meant a total of $230,083 lost in five years. As of the end of 1967, the Club had $945,896 of its cash assets tied up in inventory and accounts receivable. A simplified financial statement showed, at the end of 1967, $1,623,704 in assets and $1,176,417 in liabilities; though its net worth was $447,287, and the Club was not technically bankrupt, it had invaded permanent and restricted funds by $118,109. Such a situation was contrary to the provisions of the bylaws and was morally improper, Leonard believed; these matters, he said, "drastically affect the personal moral and financial responsibility of each Director." And he concluded, "There is no other business as serious as the continuing life of the organization, and its ability to carry on its good work of the past 75 years." By April 1968, Rudden, as comptroller, would report that the net assets of the Club had decreased by $115,000 in the past year, and he reluctantly recommended that the board cut back on both conservation and publications programs so that it could operate on a sound financial basis.[49]

Such disturbing material alarmed Adams in particular,

who feared that a financial collapse might also spell the financial ruin of individual directors, who were legally responsible for the Club's debts.[50] Worse, the board believed it had discovered that Brower had apparently been publishing books without contracts.[51] All the while, the Club continued to deal with its IRS problem.[52] All of these financial and organizational problems became campaign issues in 1968.

It appeared that the board had little time to make room for its old agenda—its conservation campaigns. There was a troublesome proposal for a Minaret Summit trans-Sierra road, the problems of preserving the ecological integrity of Everglades National Park, the coming need for a major campaign for wilderness in Alaska, the continuing need to protect de facto wilderness until it could be considered under the terms of the Wilderness Act, and the matter of oil drilling in the Santa Barbara Channel.[53] In early 1968 the redwoods campaign reached a crisis; Georgia Pacific Corporation was cutting in regions which the Club believed belonged to the proposed Redwood national park.[54] There was the danger of strip mining near Glacier Peak, in the midst of the North Cascades wilderness, and there was the continuing controversy over Diablo. There were new issues that the board could not begin to deal with, like a proposed environmental protection act.[55]

But Wayburn's executive attempt to regularize procedures and maintain clear priorities began to show results. By spring of 1968 the conservation staff had prepared a new *Conservation Policy Guide*, a compendious and complete abstract of all the policy decided by the board between 1946 and 1968. On the other hand, there would be a need for policy in areas little known to Club members. The board added a new priority late in 1967, "the preservation of the wilderness and scenic values of Alaska."[56] The wording of such a priority owed its vagueness to the magnitude of Alaska's land mass and the variety of its resources. But as Siri noted, there was no point in making Alaska a priority unless the Club could move actively on specific issues. If only the Club could solve its internal problems, with Alaska perhaps there was a chance to propose a unified and well-researched program, before wilderness disappeared. But organizational issues continued to preoccupy the board.

In Nomine Diaboli Brower

Richard Sill placed grass-roots dissatisfaction with the Club's organization on Brower's doorstep. Adams argued that the Sierra Club was making enemies as a result of Brower's strategies. Leonard blamed Brower for the Club's financial problems. Yet the results of the 1968 Sierra Club elections seemed to support Brower; successful candidates included, in addition to Siri, four presumably pro-Brower men: Phil Berry, Luna Leopold, Laurence Moss, and Eliot Porter. However, the amendments to the bylaws, including substitution of regional councils for the Sierra Club Council, failed to pass. Though only about 25 percent of the membership voted, one way to read the results was that the membership liked a strong council but tended to support policy advocated by Brower, Litton, Porter, and Berry.

Wayburn expressed hopes for unity in his comments to the board.[57] It was not to be. The board would debate almost every issue which came before it and continue to review many past decisions. McCloskey viewed this dissension as rivalry for control. In the coming months, finances would loom large in these battles. McCloskey believes "finances were the most convenient thing to fight over."[58] But the problems went deeper than money.

What was at stake? Many believed that the future of conservation was endangered. On the board, there was the Eissler view that the Club had been infiltrated by industry and its purposes subverted.[59] Martin Litton believed that "PG&E is out of control."[60] This sense of urgency was pervasive in the conservation movement in the late 1960s, and Brower played a role in making it pervasive. In January 1960 he had responded to the board's Gag Rule with an article in the *Bulletin*, "A New Decade and a Last Chance: How Bold Shall We Be?" Brower had introduced his subject with the chilling statement by Allen Morgan, "What we save in the next few years is all that will ever be saved." Brower had enlarged on that apocalyptic statement with his own judgment from the 1950s: "Never have so few taken so much from so many—and so fast."[61]

Stewart Udall believes that Brower "helped start the train of thought that culminated in the bumper sticker 'Question Authority.'"[62] There was no question that Brower listened to young people and they in turn listened to him. Brower's intention had always been to keep the Sierra Club on the cutting edge of the conservation movement, to anticipate. In Berkeley in the 1960s it was impossible to ignore young people. For many youths of the 1960s there was reason to advocate government by conscience, since government by law had not abolished racial injustice, had led the United States into war in Southeast Asia, and had allowed the resources of the land to be consumed by corporate license.

Brower was certainly not the chief or most extreme exponent of distrust in government or advocate of government by conscience. The conservation movement was filled with such thinking, and in the late 1960s, as the war in Vietnam reached its peak, young Americans suffered unusually strong feelings of distrust. The radical left would soon argue that the National Environmental Teach-In in 1970 was a scheme devised by the stewards of the nation's wealth—such organizations as the Ford Foundation, Resources for the Future, and Laurance Rockefeller's Conservation Foundation—to contain the students' spring offensive against the ecological disaster in Southeast Asia. The more conservative members of the Sierra Club had perhaps found *Silent Spring* to be too apocalyptic, and would disapprove of Paul Ehrlich's *The Population Bomb* and Brower's apocalyptic foreword to it, which compared population growth to cancer and insisted on immediate action. Another young writer would argue in 1970, "a year is about one-fifth of the time we have left if we are going to preserve any kind of quality in our world."[63]

Not Brower alone, but the nature of the Club's style was at issue. How distrustful should it be? As Richard Hofstadter has argued, political style has to do with the way ideas are believed and advocated, rather than with the truth or falsity of their content. Hofstadter thought that in mid-century America many believed a vast or gigantic conspiracy was the motive force of history, saw the fate of this conspiracy in apocalyptic terms, regarding the age as a turning point in history. Militant leaders often acted as if a conflict between absolute good and absolute evil was at stake, and consequently as if nothing but complete victory would do, and militant leaders often committed themselves in a distinctly personal way, since decisive events were not part of a stream of history but the consequences of someone's will. Militant leaders often appealed to the mass of people over the heads of elected leaders, through disdain of established institutions.[64]

In fact, an organization like the Club, when it grew in size, staff, and complexity, would be less able to accommodate its own governance by individual conscience, and since, as McCloskey notes, "Brower's whole impetus was to follow his own intuitions," the Club became "less and less able to accommodate Brower's particular style."[65] Leonard believed that governance of the Club by law and policy was endangered.

Leonard, Sill, and Adams asked for Brower's dismissal at board meetings in September 1968 and again in October 1968. They had an arsenal of financial arguments concerning losses in the publications program, Brower's use of royalties from *Exhibit Format* books for conservation expenses, and

other financial irregularities: Though they would never publicly accuse Brower of financial wrongdoing for personal
benefit, others in the Club would.[66] Beneath all this discussion of finances, they distrusted Brower's assumption that he
was operating against conspiracies, against external threats
to the Club, and they resented his reluctance to compromise
on management matters. They may have felt that his aim in
the publishing program was to go over the heads of the board
to the court of public opinion. They began to slow, if not stop,
the growth of the Club's publishing program, ostensibly for
financial reasons. Even Berry began to be concerned about
Brower's use of the discretionary fund.[67]

Brower did think there were external threats to governance of the Club. Brower, Berry, and others were sure that
their phones at the Sierra Club were tapped, perhaps by
PG&E. Many times those forces which hoped to damage the
Club focused directly on Brower and sought to discredit him,
as Richard McArdle had done. Morris Udall had attempted in
the halls of Congress to discredit Brower as a conservationist.

And Brower had to fight the rear guard. In the early 1960s
he had not considered nuclear technology dangerous, and
had willingly accepted a grant from the Belvedere Scientific
Fund, supported by the Bechtel Corporation, to print an *Exhibit Format* book. It is unreasonable to suggest that he or
anyone else thought he had compromised the Club at the
time. In the late 1960s an increasing number of young activists would reconsider such sponsorship. Now Brower had to
answer militant activists like Fred Eissler and Dave Pesonen,
who opposed nuclear technology with an energy that most of
the older members of the board could not fathom.

Eissler and Pesonen had a great distaste for corporate
power in any form. Eliot Porter was able to speak for their
views in a way that was convincing, even to Will Siri. The
context of the Club's mission had changed since it was
founded, Porter argued, and the Club had chosen to meet the

growing forces of the late twentieth century. When it found private interests, developers, exploiters, and agencies of government arrayed against Club principles, it "set no boundaries to the field of its engagement, no limits to its responsibility." Porter acknowledged that some within the Club viewed with trepidation a conservation policy which would lead the Club into conflict with the most powerful private organizations in California and in the nation:

> Many among us believe that only by compromise and accommodation can the club retain its influential position with the government and the people. They believe that only through stubborn consistency can the Club maintain respect for its actions and a fair image in the land. I say that compromise and accommodation with industry and private interests and as well with bureaucratic agencies will destroy the influence and standing of the club.[68]

Brower sympathized with this view. He had referred to the Forest Service and to the Bureau of Reclamation as enemies. Porter too spoke unashamedly of "corporations whose deeds belie their words, and whose interests are diametrically opposed to ours." For a corporation "concerned first, last, and always with material gain," conservation was only useful for the "public relations image." Such a corporation, Porter thought, was PG&E.

But Brower's problem as executive director was vastly more complicated than having to face opponents in government agencies and corporations. He also expressed fear of the "enemy within." He argued that Bestor Robinson served on the board in the 1960s as an *agent provocateur* for the Forest Service. And he knew that Tom Jukes, founder of the Club's Atlantic Chapter, was a leading behind-the-scenes participant in the campaign to oust him. Jukes was a tough case for the Club at large, according to the Sierra Club eastern representative, Gary Soucie. Jukes advised Wayne Aspinall that Brower's militant position on the Grand Canyon did not reflect Sierra Club opinion, and Jukes attempted to undercut the Club's case for preserving its tax status in 1966.[69]

Brower had been accused of conflict of interest in his management of the publications program. He in turn believed this problem clung to his colleagues. For example, as early as September 1963 Phil Berry had demonstrated incontestably that the Club had a clear policy on coastal power plants; yet the board was rendered powerless to act by directors who argued that the cost of $500 for an *amicus curiae* brief was too great, that the Club was not a party to the proceedings, that the appeal would be unsuccessful, and that a bargain could be struck with PG&E. Berry found these arguments, by Robinson, Leonard, and Randall Dickey, Jr., untenable. "Impliedly, the face PG&E's managers must save before its stockholders is more precious than the Sierra Club's public image," he commented.[70] Berry simply did not believe that the board had the right to act on such conflicting allegiances. Unlike Dave Pesonen, who was disillusioned, Berry hung on in the face of such behavior by the board. Four years later, in 1967, Brower thought this ethical problem was still with the Club. And there were other conflicts.

Martin Litton obtained a copy of a letter from Richard Leonard, writing as president of the Sierra Club Foundation, addressed to Shermer Sibley, president of PG&E. The letter thanked PG&E for contributing $500 to the 10th Biennial Wilderness Conference, and extended "personal appreciation for all the courtesy and cooperation" PG&E had extended to Wayburn, Siri, and himself. Leonard expressed admiration for Sibley's help to Conservation Associates and the Resource Agency of the State of California: "Such cooperative long-range land use planning is an exceptionally valuable contribution to the people of California, *and* the 2,000,000 customers of the company."[71] Litton felt that such a combination of issues constituted potential, if not actual, conflict of interest for the Club and for Leonard as president of the Foundation. Litton distrusted "courtesy and cooperation."

One member of the Club's Reorganization Committee was Robert Cutter, of Cutter Laboratories. In 1967 Brower had written to Wayburn, "You will remember, I am sure, that Bob Cutter told the Wilderness Conference Planning Committee that he could get chemical-industry contributions if we agreed not to invite Rachel Carson to speak at that conference."[72]

Wayburn himself had spoken of Laurance Rockefeller and Newton Drury as "not our kind of people." Wasn't this a polite statement of a deeper distrust? As it grew in the Club, distrust focused on economic growth produced by a technical or corporate elite. There were special interests who lobbied Congress or controlled public utility commissions, whose wealth allowed them to create undue influence or traffic in conflict of interest. They could not be allowed to influence Club policy.

In this atmosphere of distrust, the board reviewed in September 1968 the Reorganization Committee's report. The committee listed as its major areas of concern:

(a) Rapid expansion of publishing

(b) The consequent risk to other programs

(c) The financial vulnerability inherent in publishing

(d) The need to redistribute workload and responsibilities among staff and volunteers

(e) The need for the staff to follow consistently policies set forth by the board

(f) The need to avoid major financial commitments without proper approval

(g) The need to remedy the organizational and procedural weaknesses of the Club

(h) The need to increase involvement and better define
the responsibilities of volunteers

(i) The need to reapportion funds to support an
increased role in conservation activities on a local level

(j) The need to develop additional sources of funds

(k) The need to improve communication[73]

The Reorganization Committee's report recommended
higher membership dues, but not a separate publications
program. It advocated a full-time professional president for
the Club, to be above the executive director. It argued that ra-
tionalization of the Club organization, rather than additional
staff, was a remedy for the problems of growth. It suggested a
stronger Publications Committee, a change in the Sierra Club
Council so that it would include only elected delegates from
the chapters. It recommended that staff operations be organized in six divisions—publications, conservation, information and education, member services, finances, and outings—to be coordinated by an executive vice president.[74] It
offered a corporate structure one could expect from a committee made up primarily of professional institutional and
corporate executives.

The reorganization report did not address any of the problems that Brower considered important, since it did not offer
a means of meeting urgent conservation crises as they came
up. Nor did it guarantee that the kind of decision made about
Diablo Canyon would be avoided in the future. Surely the
chief problem faced by the Club and the whole conservation
movement was the continual fighting of rear-guard actions.
Speed was of the essence. The Club was not an institution
needing protection, but was a means of protecting the land.

Brower's very personal sense of urgency was, he felt, entirely justified; "you see too many things about to be lost too soon because too few care, and you can't walk away," he wrote to Paul Brooks.[75] And he believed that reorganization would only slow down the Club's—and his—ability to act swiftly. He had opposed splitting authority between staff and board from the early 1960s, and he expected that split-level authority would become a greater detriment to swift action if the board accepted the Reorganization Committee's report. He felt the council was a poor means of governing conservation policy because local groups could be captured by local economic interests. He believed that the Club required a chief of staff, but he expected that the Club was on the verge of the kind of disaster often brought on by use of professional consultants; a management consulting firm would study the problem and recommend that a high-priced man be hired to solve it. This was a horrifying specter to Brower: a professional executive hired not for his devotion to conservation, but for his organizational skill. Brower could see the coming of the MBA and a sterile if efficient and expedient future for conservation. He pled:

> Let there be a contract for 1969 that will let me have the
> authority to do what you hold me responsible for, dis-
> courage the sniping, clarify the organizational lines,
> and require me to live up to the budget I present . . .
> that the Board approves, and that I have control over. If
> I don't live within it, do not renew the contract.[76]

Later, Brower would see his intervention in the Diablo controversy as the issue that destroyed his relationship to the board. But others in the Club, certainly members of the Reorganization Committee, were concerned not only about style but about institutional structure. Compared to Brower, they had a far more sophisticated, if also a more mechanical and specialized, view of the way an organization worked. Organizational experts might argue about the Club as they argued about government: the structure of an organization may be more important in understanding its problems than are its aims or functions.[77] As analysts like Sill had argued, Brower's very creative skill in advertising and publishing had shaped the Club for more than fifteen years, but perhaps at the expense of the needs of the members.

Michael McCloskey recognized that the grass roots would be more and more necessary if the Wilderness Act was to fulfill its promise and if the Club was to continue to expand its interest in land use at a greater distance from San Francisco. There was no chance for Brower's proposal for personal autonomy, because to avoid having the Club represented by any one person the board considered serious reorganization imperative, and because the board no longer trusted Brower as a financial administrator.

On October 19, 1968, Sill, Leonard, and Adams were able to bring charges against Brower at a special, and to Wayburn's dismay, very public board meeting. *The 1969 Election* They orchestrated three separate allegations. Sill argued that Brower had unlawfully attempted to divert Sierra Club funds from publishing royalties to his own discretionary fund, where he could use them for conservation activities if he so chose. Adams argued that Brower would not accept a position subordinate to the Club and demonstrated his thesis by detailing what he called "the Galapagos Book venture," wherein Brower flagrantly disregarded decisions of the Publications and Executive committees. Leonard argued that Brower was fiscally irresponsible. As he said, "Dave will just not permit control."[78]

These charges were carefully documented, but not proven. Leonard, Sill, and Adams made it clear that they were not charging Brower with an attempt to benefit himself personally, and they did not explicitly ask for dismissal since they did not have the votes to accomplish such an aim. They had made their case public. Brower was given thirty days to respond to their charges. After the allegations, there was an attempt at a compromise measure, based on the work of the Reorganization Committee. The Club could establish the post of "administrative vice president," and when that position was filled Brower would become "organizational vice-president." Director Pat Goldsworthy reported that Brower had stated that he could live with such a situation, "though not entirely happy with it." Leonard remembers Brower arguing vigorously that such a division of authority would cause chaos.[79] The board resolved to investigate the possibility, but nothing came of it.

It is doubtful that Sill, Leonard, and Adams wanted a compromise. Behind their actions were a number of disgruntled members, particularly Tom Jukes, who Adams praised for his outspoken criticism of Brower. Adams had written to Tom Jukes nearly two weeks before the October 19 meeting, sending copies to Sill and Leonard, expressing distress that he had to oppose an old friend like Wayburn on the Brower matter.[80] But he, Sill, and Leonard would stick to their position, Adams said, first by having Brower discharged, and if that failed by resigning as a group. Adams knew that Brower's position had been strengthened by the conservation victories of 1968. Wayburn had pointed this out. But Adams knew too that the Club was not the only group to work for these victories. The Redwood National Park would have been larger and better, Adams thought, had the League's plan been supported by the Club, and had the Club not attempted to further an unreasonably ambitious plan. It was unethical for the Club to break ranks with other conservationists. Further, it was unethical for Brower and his allies to use Club resources against the board and against others outside the Club. This last was a surprising perception; the people Adams called Brower's associates held a majority on the board at the time. The allegations of October 19 were only the first step in a political campaign to unseat Brower and his associates on the board.

Adams was willing to impugn the redwoods campaign and include Wayburn by implication in his condemnation of Club conservation strategy. Brower wrote to members of the Grand Canyon Task Force in November that "the victory came in such a way that it did not receive the notice in our own publications that the victories in the Redwoods, North Cascades, etc. received."[81] Such proprietary interest in credit for conservation victories indicated the extent to which Club solidarity had broken down. The board polarized into pro- and anti-Brower factions and the two groups began to campaign on formal candidate slates—the A.B.C. and C.M.C.—in October 1968. A.B.C was the Brower faction, and C.M.C., the Leonard, Sill, Adams faction.

Richard Sill noted to himself that A.B.C., as an acronym, actually stood for Aggressive Brower-Style Conservationists in 1968 and Active Bold Constructive in 1969, according to its own group, but meant Aggressive Berserk Conservationists to Sill, and Ave Brower Caesar to Jukes. C.M.C. actually stood for Concerned Members for Conservation, but the Brower group, according to Sill, thought it meant Conservatives for Minimum Conservation, or even Conservatives for Midget Cerebration. In any case, this was a public campaign and would be covered heavily by the press. People walked around with buttons on their lapels which said "Great Hero Book Club," and Phil Berry would write satirical plays like *Prometheus Unboundaried.* As one Concerned Member for Conservation wrote to Sill, it was "High Noon for the Sierra Club."[82]

Brower took the offensive in his response to the allegations and to the campaign mounting against him in the 1969 election. In October 1968 he wrote to Adams—with copies to the board, the chapters, the council—that the allegations had greatly damaged the Club and conservation; he considered Adams' charges at the meeting and in subsequent letters "actionable, libel, and slander," and demanded that Adams undo his wrong.[83] By the end of the year Brower announced that he was willing to be a candidate for the board, since he was nominated by petition. In his statement to the secretary of the board he indicated he would resign as executive director at the organizational meeting of the new board, whether elected or not, and "if a substantial number of these candidates are elected who have been advocating that the club diminish its program, that resignation will be final."[84]

More important, Brower continued to act according to his own priorities, as if he were setting Club policy and direction. He had recommended publishing an "international series" of books, extending the idea begun in *Exhibit Format* books on Baja California, Kauai, Mount Everest, and Navajo wild lands.[85] In October 1968 he published another issue of the *Sierra Club Explorer*, an occasional newsletter he had used for advertising Club books during the 1960s. This edition, he pointed out, was supported by $0.50 of each member's $9.00 dues. Its purpose was to launch a campaign called "Toward an Earth International Park" by publishing the two-volume Galapagos set, which would also initiate the Sierra Club International Series.[86] It was not clear where the funding for this issue of the *Explorer* came from.[87] On January 14, 1969, two days before he testified at the Hickel hearings, Brower published on his own initiative in the *New York Times* a page-and-a-half advertisement announcing:

New Sierra Club Publications advance this urgent idea: an international program before it is too late, to preserve Earth as a "conservation district" within the Universe, a sort of . . ."EARTH NATIONAL PARK."[88]

The ad included three coupons, one for contributions to the Sierra Club Foundation, one urging President Nixon to commit his administration to world leadership in conservation, and one enabling the reader to apply for membership in the Sierra Club and purchase Club publications, including Ehrlich's *The Population Bomb* and the volume edited by Kenneth Brower, *Galapagos: The Flow of Wildness*.

It was hard for objective observers to understand where or how Brower's program had evolved. Why, at such a critical time, would Brower attempt to launch an international Club policy on his own authority? And where had Brower gotten the idea for the program? Perhaps through discussions with Stewart Ogilvy and Hugh Nash. Ogilvy had been an editor at *Fortune* magazine, and left that post in 1969 to pursue a conservation career focusing on two concerns, the need for democratic federal world government and the need for an international program of population control. Ogilvy had introduced Brower to Hugh Nash, and facilitated Nash's appointment as editor of the *Bulletin*. All three were involved in the Diablo campaign, all three shared Ogilvy's international interests, and all three would be instrumental in creating Friends of the Earth.[89] Without question, the program was intuitive, as Brower would describe it; it was also political, international, and meant to aggressively meet the challenges of the new Nixon administration. Brower was initiating a new visionary direction for the Club, trying to bring the Club along as he had for nearly twenty years. But the board did not follow.

To Wayburn, Brower's unauthorized "Earth National Park" advertisement was the final straw. For months Wayburn had been besieged by demands to suspend Brower. Even Phil Berry was increasingly disturbed by Brower's lack of discretion, and Siri was no longer willing to support Brower. On January 29, 1969 Wayburn suspended Brower's authority to make or fulfill financial commitments for the

Club. When he explained his action to the board, he cited the advertisement and its cost of $10,500, and he also denied Brower's right to commit the Club to a whole new program. In addition, Brower's intervention in the Club's final pleas in Washington to regain its tax status the previous May, and Brower's unauthorized mailing of the *Explorer*, were at issue.[90] Brower had issued the *Explorer* because, he claimed, Wayburn would not allow Hugh Nash to publish advertisements for the Galapagos books in the *Bulletin*.[91] Brower defended his acts with regard to the Publications Committee's approval of international publications, but the Club Legal Committee supported Wayburn's actions, judging that a new international program went beyond the purposes of the Club as granted by its Articles of Incorporation.[92]

The board decided at its February 1969 meeting that Brower should take a leave of absence as executive director until the Club elections were over, on April 14, 1969. Michael McCloskey was appointed acting executive director.[93] All of this was publicized in the local press; perhaps the strongest statement to ensue was by Wallace Stegner, who wrote to the *Palo Alto Times* a letter which was widely reprinted.[94] In his letter Stegner asserted that those who opposed Brower did so "because they fear that in his grab for absolute power he will wreck the Sierra Club." Though Stegner spoke of Brower as "a kind of genius," he thought the man had "been bitten by some worm of power," while it was imperative that Club policies "be decided by the full board, and not by one individual, however brilliant and however histrionic." Like Adams and Leonard, Stegner regretted having to make such a statement public, because he held such warm regard for Brower as a man, and because he respected Brower so highly as a conservationist.[95]

Perhaps any one of Brower's indiscretions might not have been critical, but in sum they made him the issue of the election of 1969. Leonard, Adams, and Sill had begun their campaign in October with support primarily from the more conservative old guard and a few eccentrics like Tom Jukes, and they found that Brower's precipitous actions gained them great support from Club chapters and from increasingly alarmed unimpeachable members like Stegner. The Brower faction had legitimate aspirations toward a vital and aggressive Club for the future, aspirations now sullied and confused by Brower's haste.

Wayburn had grudgingly reported to the membership in December of 1968 that the board had rescinded its ban on electioneering, that "the time-honored democratic practice of campaigning—with all its potential for good and not-so-good—is now with us in the club."[96] Electioneering could be constructive or destructive, depending on how it was used, he said. In February 1969 members discovered that they were being asked to vote, once again, on the Diablo Canyon controversy. The C.M.C. and A.B.C. published campaign brochures, including platforms and slates. Every Club member received these brochures through the mail.

The A.B.C. advocated Brower's international program, asking, "Shall the Sierra Club revert to its days as a society of 'companions on the trail'?" The five candidates—George Alderson, Polly Dyer, Fred Eissler, David Sive, and David Brower—promised an extensive program. "In the struggle to save the Earth's wild places and environment, it is now the 11th hour. Anything short of total commitment in this battle wherever it is joined, is reprehensible." The pamphlet said that "the land is not ours to compromise," and promised to win conservation struggles, using whatever means necessary: "When faced with Goliath, try to find something better than a slingshot." There would be a nationwide program for the Total Environment. Candidates supported the International Series of publications and believed the *Bulletin* should make ecology a household word; they promised to expand the conservation program, continue outings, and fight the

IRS. Brower responded in the campaign pamphlets to allegations which were becoming less than fair in many chapter publications. The A.B.C. slate represented geographical diversity, while the C.M.C. candidates were all from the Bay Area. Finally, the pamphlet announced that on March 7 Wayburn had suspended *Bulletin* editor Hugh Nash for refusing to publish what Nash called "political material that would have promoted Wayburn's own candidacy."[97]

The C.M.C. asked members to join all living past presidents of the Sierra Club in voting for its slate, and published a list of dedicated members who recommended voting for Ansel Adams, August Frugé, Maynard Munger, Raymond Sherwin, and as an addendum to the pamphlet, for Edgar Wayburn. This pamphlet spoke of "the Crisis," focused on finances and on Brower's role in embarrassing the Club when he publicized the Diablo controversy and produced the "Earth National Park" ad.[98] For the C.M.C., membership activism was the key to the future. In brochures illustrated by Ansel Adams photographs, its platform advocated a vigorous conservation program based on sound financial management, balanced publications, increased support of member activities in conservation and outings, and a balanced productive relationship among board, staff, and membershp.

The Results of the 1969 Election   The election of 1969 marked a decisive defeat of the Brower faction. All five C.M.C. candidates received more votes than Brower, the leading A.B.C. candidate. By a greater majority than it had in 1967, the membership refused to reconsider Diablo.[99] Because this election was so important, so carefully observed by journalists and students of the conservation movement, its significance has been studied carefully.

The political battle within the Club suggested the degree to which the Sierra Club was no longer a *club*, but a political entity. If the Sierra Club had once been an organization in San

Francisco, Brower's publishing program had made the Club a national force. As an article published in *The Nation* suggested, turmoil within the Club mirrored turmoil within national politics; it may have indicated a step backward in California state politics and the conservation movement.[100] Though the formation of factions might have begun a two-party system in the Club, it also seemed to mirror the political shift in the country which brought Nixon to the presidency and Reagan to governorship of California. The C.M.C. had called upon the "silent majority" in the Club, as Nixon had called upon the silent majority in the United States. (California, the most populous state in the union, would soon bring to the national stage the kind of figure Stegner had characterized at the beginning of the decade as "two gun Desmond." Ronald Reagan would be the first political figure that the Club would openly oppose for election. As one history put it, this California phenomenon was "not the real cowboy but Ronald Reagan, the man who plays cowboys."[101])

This universal significance of the 1969 Sierra Club election was generally denied by Brower, Siri, and others. The Club had always discussed specific issues; just as analysts of California politics suggest that voters respond to specific issues in critical elections precisely because of the state's political instability, so too Club voters in various parts of California showed no marked geographical trends.[102] The Club voters in the more politically conservative Southern Californian chapters did not oppose the A.B.C. more strongly than others. Club-wide, those who voted for the C.M.C. slate overwhelmingly believed that the issue was Brower, his one-man control of policy, and particularly his fiscal irresponsibility. Those who voted for the A.B.C. did so primarily because of conservation policy; they wanted the Club to enlarge its sights, become a more aggressive and more vital conservation force.[103] The A.B.C. received its strongest support in the Atlantic and Southeast chapters, the C.M.C. its strongest support in California. Generally, the longer a member had been in the Club, the more likely he would be to support the C.M.C.[104] Of voters who had been Club members for ten years or longer, 90 percent supported the C.M.C. Yet even 63 percent of the newest Club members supported C.M.C. candidates. Though discussion preceding the election turned on proposals for returning the Club to the membership, particularly through extensive reorganization, and though many who voted for the C.M.C. slate believed they were voting for a more democratic future, the nature of the Club's governance, one sociologist argued, would not change.[105] It did change, but not immediately.[106]

Richard Sill had attempted before the 1969 election to project election results; though he had underestimated the numerical extent of the C.M.C. victory, he had been accurate in his projection of the board's composition.[107] He felt that Adams, Leonard, and himself, as a result of their acts toward Brower, would be branded as fanatics. Given the risk of premature aggressive action, with a reaction in the following election, he wondered, "Should we assume a role of sweet cooperation on a neutral controlled Board and bide our time?" He supposed that the neutrals would like to see "semi-professional control" of the Club, including a paid president. But the C.M.C. had argued for "national membership control," or what Raymond Sherwin called "a symbiosis of volunteer and staff" which would allow a volunteer presidency of manageable proportions. Yet the C.M.C. did not act as if it wanted to open up power to the membership. Instead it began to make plans for its own control of the Club.

Though Brower was willing to return to his position as executive director, even in a highly compromised role, the C.M.C. had already decided that he would be dismissed if he did not resign. And Adams believed that outgoing Secretary of the Interior Stewart Udall might accept Brower's post, as paid Club president.[108]

The old Executive Committee met on April 18, 1969, and no minutes were recorded.[109] The next day the C.M.C. caucused with Berry, Siri, and Wayburn, and took 60 percent of the new Executive Committee, or voting control. Now Leonard could orchestrate what would happen at the first meeting of the new board, on May 3, 1969. As Leonard planned it—though not exactly as it happened—Brower would be fired, by a 9 to 5 vote, with the motion by Adams and the second by a C.M.C. freshman. The Executive Committee would fire most of the senior staff. According to Leonard's plan, A.B.C. members would not be permitted on the Executive Committee, which would include Wayburn, Berry, Sill (as secretary, because of his "keen analytical ability"), Frugé, and either Maynard Munger or Sherwin. Charles Huestis would be treasurer. Wayburn wanted to be vice president, and Leonard felt that he would do no harm in that position. More important, the president would find himself in an extremely difficult position. Not only would he be required to fire all the senior staff except for McCloskey, Rudden, Brock Evans, and Lloyd Tupling, but he would be beset by dissident A.B.C. people and by C.M.C. people who wished for quicker reorganization than was possible. Leonard wrote, "I recommend that C.M.C. stay out of this *as President*, but accomplish the same long-range results by *voting control* of the Executive Committee."[110]

As Sill recognized, the C.M.C. planned to reorganize the Club from the Executive Committee, and the Executive Committee would be in a position to make the board delegate real line authority to itself. Sill thought the board must make major policy decisions if possible and through the president "must be constantly informed what action is to be taken," and that several vice presidents would be needed to administer Club policy, at least on an interim basis.[111]

In anticipation of taking control of the board, Adams and Leonard consulted with Ike Livermore, who was now secretary of resources for California governor Ronald Reagan. Livermore offered organizational recommendations, including a one-term limit for the Club president and three- or four-term limits for directors. He also suggested a conservative financial and publications policy. Given a forum, Livermore used this chance to condemn "Past Criticizable Acts" of the Club, including "vituperative and frequently unfactual" publications and statements and misleading campaign statements with regard to redwoods, Dinosaur, and other areas.[112] In notes written on a copy of the letter from Livermore, and in Adams' response to Livermore, Adams and Leonard concurred that Livermore provided a clear and reasonable solution to the Club's problems.[113]

At the May 3–4, 1969 meeting of the board, Leonard's plan was largely followed. Though Litton and Goldsworthy tried to prevent the final act, Brower submitted his resignation and it was accepted on the motion of Will Siri, who stated, "I offer this motion with the realization of all that it will create for the future . . . two giants have come to the parting of the ways. The two giants are the body of the Sierra Club and the other embodied in the person of Dave Brower."[114] A "Eulogy," as the Club's minutes called it, was passed praising Brower. It said,

> David Brower has served the club with dedication and brilliance first as a director and then since 1952 as Executive Director. More than any other person he has involved the public in our fight to preserve a livable world. He has pioneered in the effective use of films, *Exhibit Format* Books, paperbacks, posters, full page newspaper ads and other of the mass media. He has sought to expand the concerns of the club to include all of the environment. David Brower has been a leader. He

has tried to bring along those who have lagged behind, not always with success. And now his role in club affairs must diminish. We are saddened by this prospect. We wish him well in his new efforts to save and restore the quality of our environment. We salute David Brower and wish him to know that his unique contribution to the Sierra Club is appreciated.[115]

Brower's resignation concluded, "I hope to make many more speeches praising the good Sierra Club achievement. I intend this to be my last speech as a Sierra Club employee and it has ended."

Phil Berry was elected president, and in more controversial action, Charles Huestis, not an elected board member, was made treasurer. Though the board discussed the composition of the Executive Committee and the extent of its power, the political machinations of the C.M.C. guaranteed that the Executive Committee would not represent any minority portions of the board, and would include one C.M.C.-approved member who had not been elected to the board at all. Against the objections of Will Siri, the new Executive Committee indicated that it would not refuse to make policy. (Even more than the board, the Executive Committee was in danger, George Marshall argued, of being all from the Bay Area, and as a result provincial.) Though not on the Executive Committee, Adams and Leonard would do their best to see dissent stifled until they believed that the Club's crisis had passed. After much discussion, McCloskey was made chief of staff, rather than executive director.

The results were mixed. Siri felt that "almost the moment Dave [Brower] left there was an almost audible sigh of relief throughout the club, and people began to work together again and have a strong feeling of unity once more."[116] But Brower's supporters felt no relief when events followed the C.M.C. plans. They attempted to include in Brower's eulogy a line indicating that Brower wished to save the environment "in ways which the Sierra Club is not yet willing and able to pursue."[117]

At the May 3 banquet, Club president Berry began to attempt reconciliation. "The A.B.C. and C.M.C. are one Club," he announced. He promised that there would be no retreat: "There must be dynamic movement ahead—without compromise of principle—as far and fast as possible toward our conservation goals."[118] At the Club banquet Brower announced the formation of a new organization, Friends of the Earth, which would include a League of Conservation Voters, and encouraged the Club: "There's lots of work to do—let's!" He would take a good portion of the Club's senior staff with him. Litton would conduct a celebratory Powell Centennial river trip down the navigable portions of the Colorado River later that month. The Club would have to deal with its long-standing financial woes, its organizational problems, and its future direction as quickly as possible, and do so minus much of its experienced staff.

AFTERWORD

Earth Day and Beyond

Relatively uninvolved in "the Brawl," as Wayburn called it, and only thirty-two years old, Phil Berry could appeal to younger members. He was not inexperienced as a mountaineer or a conservationist. First serving the Club in 1950 as a pot scrubber on the High Trip, he had become a climber of considerable accomplishment. He had been a member of the Bay Chapter Executive Committee and for four years chair of the Legal Committee. He was a graduate of Stanford and a member of the Section on Mineral and Natural Resources Law of the American Bar Association. Phil Berry might represent not only the new youth, but a new professionalism that the conservation movement needed.

As new president, Berry was paired with Michael Mc-Closkey, himself a lawyer and representative of a new professionalism. McCloskey recognized that Brower had been an intuitive and "hands on performer," but that the new staff would require a more impersonal style of management. McCloskey would set goals for people, monitor their progress, assess their performance, and make them a team. He knew that a large, complex organization required "a very elaborate trail of paperwork" and an amalgam of different contributions.[1] He would have to be a facilitator. For years,

435

Ansel Adams had been asking that the staff present the board with better-organized material. McCloskey's "Recommendations of the Conservation Department" brought new clarity to board decisions; now agenda items were uniformly organized and clearly formatted to include the recommended policy, the facts, history of Club policy, current status, arguments and counterarguments.

McCloskey watched the membership of the Club change. If, in the mid 1960s, three-quarters of the members joined for the outings program and only a quarter for the conservation program, by the early 1970s the ratio was reversed. Members were paying their dues to see an effective conservation program.[2] As a main-line, reformist conservation organization, the Sierra Club had always committed itself to what was called "working within the system." The system had become increasingly legislative and legal. "Our business was not to just bear witness," said Michael McCloskey. "Our business was to secure political change that would protect the environment."[3] Conservation, thought McCloskey, required political expertise. It called for lawyers and experts in the practice of public policy.

So while Michael McCloskey rebuilt the staff which had been decimated as a result of the Brower controversy, and while Berry mended wounds, speaking at chapter meetings all over the country, they both attempted to guide the Club through its financial crisis without losing too much ground or launching new enterprises, at the same time garnering conservation successes and opening a new front in the field of conservation law.[4]

As Maxine McCloskey noted, the 1969 Wilderness Conference was the largest to date, and came at a time when "a new ecology movement was just beginning to gather strength across America."[5] This conference, called "Wilderness: The Edge of Knowledge," focused on the role of wildlife in wilderness, particularly in Alaska; the ecological integrity of parks and wilderness was uppermost in the minds of organizers and participants. A critique of policy in national parks in 1969 insisted that the ecological well-being of parks and per-petuation of their natural biological communities must come before recreational needs, and that parks were not islands; the condition of wilderness in America was a sign or symp-tom of the larger forces at work on the American continent, and on the earth.[6]

In his keynote address at the conference Paul Ehrlich de-nounced "the continuing delusion . . . that environmental problems can be separated from the population explosion."[7] The Club was besieged with a set of metaphors which sug-gested the subtle relationship between economics and ecol-ogy on our small blue planet. Ecology and economics had the same etymological root, as Kenneth Boulding had noted in 1966. He had coined a phrase, "The coming spaceship earth." That phrase was used not only by Boulding in a frequently re-printed essay, "The Economics of the Coming Spaceship Earth," but also by Adlai Stevenson: "We travel together, pas-sengers on a little spaceship, dependent on its vulnerable re-sources of air and soil; all committed for our safety to its se-curity and peace; preserved from annihilation only by the care, the work, and I will say, the love we give our fragile craft."[8] The spaceship metaphor was appropriated too by Buckminster Fuller, the utopian futurist who discussed for the 1969 Wilderness Conference "Conserving the Assets of the Spaceship Earth."

A darker view of the earth was suggested by Garrett Hardin when he wrote "The Tragedy of the Commons" in 1968.[9] As-serting that man was faced with problems which had no technical solution—that space was no escape—Hardin pre-dicted that the freedom to use the earth as a commons would diminish as population increased; the future would be forced to recognize certain necessities, "mutual coercion, mutually agreed upon." Contrary to hopes of the past, conscience was an insufficient tool for avoiding the destruction of the earth. Later, Hardin spoke even more darkly of the earth as a lifeboat. "Lifeboat Ethics: The Case Against Helping the Poor," brought vigorous opposition from humanists.[10] He meant to say that the earth was already overpopulated, and trying to save all its passengers was futile. Then everyone would perish.

On a more optimistic note, Edgar Wayburn, at the 1969 conference, presented the John Muir Award to Henry M. Jackson, the first non-Sierra Club awardee.[11] Such an unprecedented award not only recognized Jackson's role as chair of the Senate's Interior and Insular Affairs Committee in passing the Wilderness Bill and supporting new parks (including North Cascades and Redwoods), as well as his role in the Grand Canyon controversy, but also indicated the extent to which the Club had acquired political debts. So a politician joined John Muir Award winners William Colby (1961), Olaus J. Murie (1962), Ansel Adams (1963), Walter A. Starr (1964), Francis Farquhar (1965), Harold Bradley (1966), and Sigurd Olson (1967). (No award was given in 1968.) Jackson would sponsor the National Environmental Policy Act (NEPA) in the next year. Later the Club's Washington representative would have to oppose Jackson over the Supersonic Transport (SST), which promised to boost the senator's home-state economy, and the Club would discover that Jackson was willing to sacrifice NEPA for the Alaska Pipeline.[12] The more radical members of the ecology movement would ask why the Club was promoting the political career of a man sometimes called "the Senator from Boeing," the man who served as a chief hawk in the Senate, advocating nuclear superiority and the advancement of the military-industrial establishment.[13] In the next year there would be increasing pressure for the Club to take a stand on the war in Vietnam.

Such issues suggest the difficulty the board encountered when it began to consider new priorities, pushed along by

McCloskey, who observed that the Club's official statement was somewhat out of date. The major phases of the North Cascades, Redwoods, and Grand Canyon campaigns had been completed; priorities such as Alaska, and the completion of the wilderness and national park systems, seemed to lack focus. McCloskey wanted to chart the course and define what was meant by the term "priority," in terms of budget, staff time, and work by volunteers.[14]

In his usual pragmatic way, he suggested six criteria for choosing priorities: (1) the future well-being of natural resources of great inherent importance and national significance should be at stake; (2) success in protecting the resource should offer hope of establishing precedents of transcending importance or promise a beneficial change in power relationships; (3) projects should be capable of popular portrayal, by presenting either a clear choice, an uncomplicated issue, or a specific focus; (4) adoption of the project should offer the Club a distinctive role that does not duplicate the work of others and that fits the Club purposes; (5) the project should be of sufficient duration to allow a major campaign to be mobilized, and yet be capable of achievement within a reasonable time; (6) the project should be part of a scheme of national priorities having geographical balance and attracting national support.

By September 1969 the board was beginning to debate, in a friendly way, the future direction of the Club. While McCloskey steered a pragmatic course, Phil Berry proposed a broad new program he called "environmental survival." Wishing the Club's agenda to incorporate modern ideas on environment, Berry created an informal committee which came up with resolutions concerning survival, population, and pollution.[15] Survival: the Club should urge that preserving a livable environment be as important to the United States as national security or the challenge of the space age. Population: the Club should urge that the United States and all individual states abandon all programs or policies promoting population growth, that they actively promote educational programs to reduce population growth to zero, that the United States not only condition all foreign economic aid on implementation of birth control policies but give foreign aid solely for that purpose, and that all states of the United States legalize abortion unqualifiedly. Pollution: the Club should urge that the United States and each individual state outlaw the internal combustion engine for vehicles manufactured after 1975, and that taxes be imposed on petroleum-powered vehicles in proportion to the vehicle's fuel consumption and/or pollution of the air.[16]

Such an agenda had the potential to change the entire direction of the Club. Wayburn and Litton feared that these new priorities could dissipate the Club's efforts. As Litton said, "there is no one but the Sierra Club to fight for bits and pieces of the remaining wilderness."[17] However, Porter, Sherwin, Siri, and others argued that such long-range issues would affect every regional or specific problem in wilderness and parks; if the big issues weren't faced, matters of wilderness or parks would be meaningless. The board passed the resolutions on a livable environment and population, but left the matter of automobile pollution for further study.

Over the next months and years the Club would refine these policies and find ways to implement them. By December 1969 the board could supplement its policy on a livable environment by an "Environmental Bill of Rights" (as it came to be called), which would extend individual personal rights to include a clean and healthy environment.[18] The board would support a more reasonable, detailed, and qualified policy on automobile air pollution. It would also oppose noise pollution, and mount resistance to the proposed Supersonic Transport.[19] It would endorse Ralph Nader's campaign against private polluters.[20] It would involve itself increasingly in population matters.[21]

The Club would link policies on population growth and economic growth when it created an energy policy, begin-

ning in 1970. Not only would the board urge immediate legislation prohibiting any public or private utility from advertising or promoting increased use of power, it would go on
record as opposing "the concept of the inevitability of continued escalation of power needs."[22] By 1971 the Club had ample reason to consider oil an "environmentally hazardous
substance."[23] Club members, Berry included, picketed the
Standard Oil offices across the street from Club offices after an
oil spill in San Francisco Bay in 1972.

By October of 1972 the Club had a national energy policy,
including tenets on energy conservation and pollution control, in the face of increasing resistance from business and industry.[24] By 1974 the board, on the grounds of safety, resolved
for a moratorium on the building of nuclear power plants—
against the urging of Leonard, Siri, its own president (Laurence Moss), and its own Energy Committee.[25] So it was that
the Club found itself involved in what Raymond Sherwin
called "Battling the Corporate Giants," to Leonard's dismay.[26]
Oil spills at Santa Barbara, coupled with the Club's policy of
protecting coasts, made collision with oil corporations unavoidable. The proposed trans-Alaska pipeline touted by the
oil industry would have such a potentially immense effect on
Alaskan wilderness that the Club could not avoid resisting
the whole project.

Because the Club could scarcely evade its role in a larger
social movement which would call into question assumptions about economic growth in light of increased scarcity, it
would inescapably be in conflict with the major corporate interests of modern America. As Berry and others were aware,
many reputable scholars began to speak of the limits to economic growth and the relationship between economic
growth and the ecological history of man; an increasing array
of studies argued that civilization ought to curtail economic
growth and accord material things only secondary importance.[27]

All of these new priorities reflected what was coming to be

called the "environmental revolution," characterized by a series of events and an upsurge of popular sentiment.[28] Earth
Day, inspired in Wisconsin, where John Muir spent his boyhood, was celebrated especially on college campuses on April
22, 1970, one day after the 132nd anniversary of Muir's
birth.[29] Earth Day constituted an attempt to bring all conservation organizations together, refuting the notion widely
held in the Nixon administration that conservation was just a
fad. But the very popularity of the movement brought its own
dangers. As Berry reported to the board in February 1970,
the conservation platform was increasingly crowded. "We
welcome real converts, but the growing popularity of our
cause has attracted some whose motives must be questioned.
Politicians paying lip service, industrialists laying down public relations smoke screens, and anarchists voicing legitimate
concerns about the environment for the ulterior purpose of
attacking democratic institutions are all suspect."[30]

For Earth Day, McCloskey introduced an inexpensive paperback book, *Ecotactics*, to be published by Pocket Books.
Subtitled *The Sierra Club Handbook for Environmental Activists*,
Ecotactics boasted that "of some 28 individual contributors,
only two are over 40. More than half are under 30."[31] In his
foreword, McCloskey wrote, "The Sierra Club believes in action . . . we concentrate specifically on political action to
change public policy because that is how lasting improvements can be secured in our society . . . it is not enough simply to protest."[32] Though Ansel Adams called this handbook
"two dimensional," still believing that the Club should try a
new exhibit like "This Is the American Earth," McCloskey's
idea led to a series of inexpensive paperbacks called "Battle
Books."[33]

In the *Bulletin*, Connie Flateboe, the Club's campus representative, announced that Earth Day would be the occasion
for the first national teach-in on the crisis of the environment. The chief goal, she wrote, was "bringing individual

lifestyles into some measure of ecological balance."[34] In the same issue of the *Bulletin* Wayburn editorialized that "survival is not enough: . . . In many places this [survival] is being hailed as the emergence of a 'new conservation' as opposed to the 'old.' The 'new' is supposed to be spear-heading the just-discovered 'gut' issues of survival; the 'old' more narrow (and called by some 'elitist') is supposed to be still saving trees and worrying about Wilderness areas and National Parks." Though 1969 would go down as the year that man first stepped on the moon, and as the year of ecological awakening, Wayburn warned it could also bring a serious polarization to conservation: "We can also end up living in a concrete world and subsisting on algae, if survival is our only aim. The earth was meant to be a livable, beautiful place: none of us must settle for less."[35]

Nevertheless, the Executive Committee supported Berry when he instructed the Bylaws Committee to propose amendments to restate the Club's purpose, "to eliminate [geographical] restrictions (i.e. confinement to the United States) to include [as purposes] survival and its incidents relative to environmental quality," and also to eliminate the requirement of sponsorship for membership, now unworkable in an organization that numbered more than 100,000 members.[36] Four hundred thousand copies of *Ecotactics* were published; staff, board, and volunteers participated in Earth Day activities.

McCloskey reported to the board, "Our very success . . . in fueling the environmental awakening is raising implications that it is well for us to understand."[37] Though the Club was highly visible, it could not be dominant in such a mass movement, which was by necessity an amalgam of the consumer movement (including corporate reformers), the movement for scientific responsibility, a revitalized public health movement, population control groups, pacifists, young people who stressed direct action, "and a diffuse movement in search of a new focus for politics." The Club could not speak for such a diverse array of interests. Skeptics from many special-interest groups questioned the Sierra Club's engagement in the political process, wanted to change America's lifestyle, distrusted any large institutions—believing them all beyond reform—or thought it was too late. While the Club was being asked to deal with literally all the environmental issues in the world, it would be wise to focus the limited Club means on what could be done.[38]

Many of the Club's priorities in the 1970s continued to be traditional environmental issues, relating to parks, wilderness, and preservation of the nation's coasts. Early in 1969 the board set a policy on the tidelands and outer continental shelf, urging legislation not only to assure that the Santa Barbara disaster would not recur and that pollution from spillage or cleanup would not destroy marine resources, but to protect areas of biological, scenic, and social value.[39] The Club was increasingly involved in a campaign to "Save the Bay," to protect San Francisco Bay from pollution and from a scheme to fill the bay to make room for population growth.[40] Across the continent, Everglades National Park faced ongoing threats from a massive but unfinished jetport only six miles north of the park.[41] While the board also continued to focus on expansion and completion of the North Cascades and Redwoods national parks, it extended its efforts for protecting the Grand Canyon, broadening its interest beyond the canyon to the entire Colorado Plateau. It continued to work toward completing the wilderness system. Completion of the national park system was closely tied to the fate of the public domain in Alaska, and Alaska would consume a major portion of Club resources for the next decade.[42]

To an extent greater than anyone might have imagined, the Wilderness Act of 1964 had led to a dizzying array of new federal legislation, much of it passed in 1969, the first year of

Nixon's administration, with more to come. Indeed, the new Wilderness Act was the first enacted of a new kind of legislation which would respond to the American public's desire for a higher quality of life. As some argue, the very nature of public land laws shifted: the late 1960s marked a transition from traditional land law, wherein private rights were in conflict with other private rights, to modern federal land and resource law, which sought the public interest.[43] Such a major reform had been the Club's goal from its inception. In line with its historic orientation, the Club was not only a major participant in enacting new legislation, but was a party to litigation which would test these laws.[44] The Endangered Species Act of 1966 would prove to be remarkable legislation, and as amended in 1973 would be a powerful tool for protecting species and their habitats.[45]

The National Environmental Policy Act (NEPA) of 1969, signed by Nixon on January 1, 1970, as his first official act of the new decade, would become by far the most important procedural public land management statute of the 1970s.[46] Michael McCloskey gave lead testimony for this law, and the Club did some lobbying. Nixon proclaimed the statute a herald of a new environmental era while believing privately that it was nothing more than an innocuous statement of policy; it became a good deal more.[47] In its three main parts, NEPA set forth goals of environmental quality for the nation; required that an environmental impact statement (EIS) accompany "every recommendation or report on proposals for legislation and other major federal actions significantly affecting the quality of the human environment"; and established a President's Council on Environmental Quality (CEQ). All federal agencies would have to give consideration, if not priority, to the environmental aspects of their programs; plans would be open to public scrutiny to a greater degree than ever before, and the documentation challengeable in court. Not only would NEPA affect the siting of power plants and oil pipelines, it would change the wilderness classification process for lands managed by the Bureau of Land Management and the Forest Service. With passage in 1976 of the Federal Land Policy and Management Act (FLPMA), also known as the Bureau of Land Management Organic Act, BLM lands would go through wilderness review in the 1980s and beyond.

No longer could the Club underestimate its needs in Washington, D.C. Not just its proposals, but all kinds of environmental legislation might affect the future of wilderness. The Club had begun to strengthen its Washington, D.C. office in 1967 when it acquired the services of Lloyd Tupling. Like so many others who had rejuvenated Club ranks in the 1960s, Lloyd Tupling came from the Northwest. Born in 1915, Tupling knew Washington, D.C. well, having served as the top staff person for Senator Richard Neuberger. He guided the environmental lobbyists who gathered at the Capital at the time of Earth Day. As McCloskey says, "Tup may have been the most important person in helping America's environmental movement get beyond rhetoric and get results."[48] Yet in the early 1970s Lloyd Tupling feared that his six-member staff was not going to be able to stop the special interests, once corporations realized that the environmental lobby was succeeding. He knew that corporate interests would try to dismember NEPA, and by 1973, as he put it, "the roof would fall in," with environmentalists once again on the defensive.[49]

Though McCloskey was more optimistic, he reported in a 1969 article for the *New Republic* that a strange paradox pervaded Washington: "While the vision is broadening, many sound programs are in trouble. Polluting and exploiting industries are on the counterattack." In 1968 the timber industry had successfully brought forward what McCloskey referred to as "an ingenious proposal," first known as the National Timber Supply Act, but renamed the National For-

est Timber Conservation and Management Act of 1969. Seiz-
ing on the need for timber generated by the Housing Act of
1968, the timber industry wished the Forest Service to abandon its policy of sustained yield.[50] Though a coalition of conservation organizations managed to defeat this "loggers' relief act" in the first key roll-call vote in the House in the
1970s, it was not an easy victory. McCloskey calls it a "heroic
save," a come-from-behind effort.[51]

Brock Evans, the Club's Northwest representative, knew
that the timber industry was only beginning its assault on
National Forests, and he too predicted a reaction to the conservation successes of the late 1960s.[52] As an active participant in the Washington, D.C., scene, he also recognized the
importance of the grass-roots campaigning which had
stopped the timber industry. Born in 1937 in Ohio, by the
1960s Evans had graduated in history from Princeton and
was in law school at the University of Michigan, reading
books like Eiseley's *The Immense Journey* for pleasure.[53] He began to visit the West, first Glacier National Park. He worked
there for two summers. When he graduated from law school
in 1963, he moved to Seattle, began climbing, thought about
the newly passed Wilderness Act, became active in the North
Cascades Conservation Council, read Sierra Club *Exhibit Format* books, worried about the clear-cut logging he saw, and
met Michael McCloskey. He also met Patrick Goldsworthy,
and acquired his political education during the hearings for
the North Cascades National Park. He met Brower in 1966
and was hired as the Club's Northwest representative in
1967. He began visiting Washington, D.C., and learned organizational skills when he ran his first major conservation
campaign, to save Hell's Canyon on the Snake River, in 1968.
He remembers his first official Club trip to the Capital, flying
in to help on the Grand Canyon campaign: "Back in the
teeming east again," and on a groggy morning, "there was
the terrible Wayne Aspinall, destroyer of the wilderness sys-

tem, putting the dams in."[54] He spent four to six weeks a year in Washington, D.C., working on Northwest issues. When the Club learned that Tupling was planning to retire in 1972, Ed Wayburn sounded out Evans to see if he would take over the job. And Evans thought, "Who would want to leave a place like *this*, like Seattle, to come back to a place like *that*?"[55] But when Brock Evans accepted the post in Washington, D.C., in 1973, the Club acquired an experienced and highly sophisticated lobbyist.

On June 23, 1970, Wayne Aspinall's Public Land Law Review Commission (PLLRC) released its final report.[56] The committee had been directed to review current practices within federal land management agencies, to predict future demands upon public lands, and to recommend changes in policy and law in order "to provide the maximum benefit for the general public." As McCloskey reported, "the Commission came into existence as a vehicle to express the views of its chairman, who embodies the traditional views of the rural West."[57] It was generally conceded that the Aspinall committee was serving the interests of rural resource exploiters who feared that the environmentalists might cut off their traditional paths of access to public lands.[58] Consequently the commission's report was, as Phil Berry said, "oriented toward maximum immediate commercial exploitation." Its twin premises of limitless population growth and an ever-expanding economy would only prolong what Berry called "the no deposit-no return, use-once-and-throw-away, Philistine culture that we have today."[59] Western commercial interests were regrouping.

Brock Evans had recognized the kind of economic, political, and grass-roots power it took to meet the timber industry, the fifth largest American industry in employees and gross production; but with the Arab oil embargo of 1973, "a shiver of panic went through the whole country," and "it was the most incredible thing to see the power, the unseen power, of all that oil money at work."[60] Evans knew he had dropped into what he called a very defensive situation. In retrospect, Michael McCloskey argues, the energy crisis of 1973 did not mark the death of environmentalism, but certainly announced a period of reaction and testing. This period was followed, in 1976, by a banner year for new environmental legislation.[61]

To use McCloskey's phrase of 1972, wilderness was "at the crossroads" in the early 1970s. Not only was the wilderness movement endangered as a result of a shift in national focus from wild lands to places where life was threatened, but the traditional concerns of the conservation movement—wilderness and parks—were in danger of being swallowed by the new environmental movement, which viewed matters of wilderness as "parochial and old fashioned."[62] At the end of 1969, the Club's Wilderness Classification Study Committee reported that the lack of congressional action on wilderness to date was largely a result of public apathy toward completion of the national wilderness preservation system.[63] As the board resolved, the Club would have to meet this apathy with "legal action, the initiation of legislative action, and massive public relations campaigns."[64]

On the other hand, after 1970 federal agencies had to draft an environmental impact statement for each wilderness classification proposal. Though the agencies thought of this procedure as added red tape, it allowed greater chance for public comment.[65] Sufficient public pressure and lawsuits also forced the Forest Service and later the BLM to conduct Roadless Area Review and Evaluation (RARE I and RARE II) procedures to identify wilderness for possible inclusion in the system, to assure that preserved wilderness would be dispersed throughout the United States and would represent a good sample of various ecological systems, and to locate wilderness areas close to population centers so they might be enjoyed.[66] But RARE I brought out the power of industry too. At local hearings all over the Northwest, as Evans remembers, conservationists were assaulted. Workers found slips in their pay envelopes saying, "Your job is threatened; you better turn out at these hearings." The oil industry was donating money to organizations of four-wheel-drive users; the timber industry enlisted motorbike people and other mechanical recreationists as its grass-roots frontline troops. "They would wear their leather jackets with tassels on them—thirty-two zippers and all that sort of thing on it," Evans recalls.[67] If reaction to wilderness began in Washington, it ended in the field. There was never going to come a time when grass-roots support could be forgotten.

Lay conservationists—the grass roots—discovered that it was no longer enough to pay their membership dues and write their congressmen. They would have to educate themselves to read environmental assessments (EAs), and environmental impact statements (EISs), analyze interim wilderness management plans, track wilderness inventories, and testify at public hearings. Meanwhile the national Club could test only some federal decisions in the courts.

Environmental law was confusing, dynamic, and technical. By 1967, however, a staff member could write, "Last year, the New York lawyers began joining the club at such a rate that I was afraid we were going to become the New York Bar Association."[68] "A few years ago," wrote Michael McCloskey in 1970, "our friends in law school laughed at us because we wanted to 'change the world.'"[69] By the early 1970s there were lots of young lawyers in the Club's ranks who wanted to change the world and use their profession to do it.

The Sierra Club went to court because it had the expertise, means, and opportunity to do so. It began to do so more frequently in the late 1960s because there was a prospect of success.[70]

When the Club brought suit over Mineral King in June of

1969, naming as defendants the secretaries of agriculture and interior, the superintendent of Sequoia National Park, the California regional forester, and the forest supervisor of Sequoia National Forest, it was attempting to establish its own right to protest, to speak for the rights of nature, and its right to protest on principle the misguided and irresponsible acts of discretion by federal agencies.[71] The Club argued that the Forest Service and the National Park Service were violating their trust and specific provisions of law in granting to Disney Productions a thirty-year permit for developing a ski area.[72] When the Club received a preliminary injunction in July 1969, this widely publicized action constituted one of the events that dramatized the environmental revolution.[73]

The idea of the rights of nature, as articulated by Aldo Leopold, had been translated into legal terms by William O. Douglas, and Douglas in turn had put that idea into the minds of many prominent Club members.[74] By the early 1970s the idea of the rights of nature was increasingly in the air. The Club would establish its standing in the Mineral King case, and Douglas's Supreme Court dissent—based on an essay by Christopher Stone—would be a source for much discussion and hope for the future, an opportunity to articulate the theory that "those people who have so frequented the place as to know its values and wonders will be able to speak for the entire ecological community."[75]

At the end of July 1969, after the Club had received its preliminary injunction in the Mineral King case, the Club Legal Committee summarized eight pieces of litigation it had been following. Since, "for all practical purposes we think we have achieved standing to sue in federal courts where any aggrieved party can contest government action," the committee recommended establishing such a precedent in the California state courts.[76] The courts were anxious to make environmental law, and over the years the Club would win three-fourths of its cases because the federal agencies had not complied with legal requirements or were asleep.[77] Court cases offered good chances for publicity. A lawsuit gave citizen groups parity with developers or federal agencies, as McCloskey noted:

> As much as I think corporations dislike litigation, government agencies dislike it even more. It completely pulls away the veil of pretense that they are the governors and we are the governed. Suddenly they are standing in court beneath the judge in the same way we are, with equal time.[78]

Richard Leonard at Brower's urging incorporated the Sierra Club Foundation in 1960 believing the Club would lose its tax status when the board authorized Brower to lobby "as effectively as he wanted to."[79] The Foundation was directed by previous presidents and officers of the Club, some of whom were no longer active in Club affairs. Berry himself created a new entity, the Sierra Club Legal Defense Fund. The fund raised its own money and acted as legal counsel for the Club. The directors of the fund could accept or reject cases proposed by the Club directors. On the other hand, the Club agreed to help finance the fund, through the Foundation.[80] All of this was necessary for the 1970s because so much legislation was already in place, more was coming, and the Club had to focus on testing and using legislation.

In June of 1969 Phil Berry called a special meeting of the board, including as well chapter representatives and members of the council, staff, and major committees. The meeting was to address "questions affecting internal organization and procedures," to provide a forum where any idea that would make the Club a more efficient organization would receive a hearing. Berry announced "his intention to charge the By-laws Committee to review the entire charter of the Sierra Club," and entertain the following question: What organizational framework should be used for making conservation decisions?[81]

Instead of establishing a national conservation committee, the Club would attempt through the 1970s to implement a decentralization that was necessary for membership trust. The board resolved not to overrule a regional conservation committee without consultation, assuring local and regional groups that the staff would be more responsive and available to grass-roots members for research and recommendations. In June 1971 Siri recommended an extended system of Regional conservation committees (RCCs) that would cover all regions of the United States, have considerable autonomy, and would develop broad conservation policy, suggesting the direction for the future.[82] In 1969 the grass roots wanted more variety in publications, more use of television, and fewer *Exhibit Format* books. McCloskey and Berry advocated that there be a "conservation newsletter" for "hard news," with the *Bulletin* to be used as a slick publication for recruitment. The board agreed to respect the time of members who came to make presentations, if the members would agree to respect the needs of the board.[83] The promises of the board would have to be institutionalized. That was a slow process which would include changing the bylaws.

By September of 1970 the board had submitted to the membership sweeping recommendations for revising the bylaws. First, the Club's purposes were changed to read:

> To protect and conserve the natural resources of the
> Sierra Nevada, the United States and the World; to
> undertake and publish scientific and educational stud-
> ies concerning all aspects of man's environment and the
> natural ecosystems of the World; and to educate the
> people of the United States and the World to the need to
> preserve and restore the quality of that environment
> and the integrity of those ecosystems.[84]

These new purposes not only absorbed environmental ideas and spoke the new language of ecology, but reflected international aspirations. They so clearly reflected the Brower ideas of 1969 that Richard Leonard would later say, "They were carried out simply because Brower was right. His ideas were sound ideologically."[85]

The bylaw amendment passed in 1971 by a majority of 78 percent.[86] The Club became increasingly active in international matters during the presidency of Raymond Sherwin (1971–1973), who established an International Conservation Committee.[87] This activity was reflected in the broadening focus of wilderness conferences. In 1971 the conference was held in Washington, D.C., and in 1975 it was called "Earthcare" and held in New York City. The Club sent representatives to the United Nations Conference on the Human Environment, held in Stockholm during June 1972.[88] Such international conferences generated ideas like "deep ecology," articulated in Bucharest in 1972 by the Norwegian philosopher Arne Naess.[89]

The Club's 1971 statement of purposes was more cosmopolitan, not as poetic as the earlier one had been. But a second amendment also passed: in the future, a two-thirds vote by the Sierra Club Council, followed by a vote of consent of the board, could change the Club's bylaws. Such an amendment not only institutionalized the role of the council in recommending policy on internal matters, but also facilitated the "continuing, changing, growing process" of the Club. It would allow the Club, in January 1973, to change in two days the phrase "protect" to "protect by all lawful means," when the Club's right to engage in lawsuits was challenged in the courts.[90]

The new phrase would also allow creation of the Sierra Club Committee on Political Education (SCCOPE).[91] As Brock Evans argued, the power of grass-roots voting was a still untapped resource for the Club. When Secretary of the

Interior James Watt said much later that he had the support of the West, he really only had the cowboy West; "two-thirds of the votes," Evans said, "are in Boise and Salt Lake City and Denver and San Francisco and Seattle and Portland and all those places. That's our vote; that's us."[92]

Over the years the style of the bylaws would be edited, so that they read, by the 1980s,

> To explore, enjoy, and protect the wild places of the
> earth; to practice and promote the responsible use of
> the earth's ecosystems and resources; to educate and
> enlist humanity to protect and restore the quality of the
> natural and human environment; and to use all lawful
> means to carry out these objectives."[93]

But in 1971, Richard Sill too was concerned about grass-roots control of the Club. In January he privately published a pamphlet called "The Future of the Sierra Club," which was widely distributed and affected the thinking of voting members.[94] Sill believed that the Club needed a way to avoid future campaigns as divisive as that of 1969. Even though he considered the C.M.C. a political necessity, he wished also to see the entrenched neutral members of the board, like Siri and Wayburn, phased out. As he argued, the board could not reform itself, so it would have to be reformed.[95] Adams and Leonard chose to support Sill.

Though Adams did not think that Sill's idea of limiting directors' terms could solve every problem, he believed that this was one step in the right direction, to make certain that never again would dominant personalities control the Club.[96] Sill wrote that a greater turnover would "provide the board with a flow of new ideas," would allow "accurate representation needed for a national rather than regional Sierra Club," would "result in a more responsive, better informed directorate," and would still allow popular directors to return after a "sabbatical."[97] Many of the more traditional members feared that the two-term policy might destroy continuity, result in what Wayburn called a "green board" which would have to learn the ropes over and over again.[98]

In April 1971, the Club membership amended article IV of the bylaws and limited directors to two consecutive terms, to be followed by a required sabbatical of one year. Later, the procedures for nominating directors were also changed so that nominations came from the chapters and provided a broader geographic representation among candidates.[99]

The composition of the board did begin to change and become more fluid. Ansel Adams resigned in 1971, feeling that it was time to make room for capable young people with new ideas. Eliot Porter ended his tenure in 1971. Richard Sill left the board in 1973, as did Richard Leonard and Martin Litton. These men never returned to the board, though Leonard was later appointed honorary president. Increasingly, the board of directors came to accurately reflect the geographic diversity of a Club which quadrupled in size over the decade of the 1970s. Women were elected in greater numbers and their voices became more prominent.

Edgar Wayburn took his sabbatical in 1972, and returned to serve through most of the 1970s and 1980s. Phil Berry too was reelected after sabbaticals in 1974 and 1981. In 1983, fourteen years after he stepped down as executive director, David Brower was elected once again to the Club's board of directors.

While the Sierra Club grew in size and influence in the post-World War II era, environmental issues became national issues. The Club itself became a major force in national politics as it worked for improving the quality of life in America. An organization which appeared at the dawn of a new age, a post-frontier age, it came to see its role as the protection of many of those American values the frontier had fostered.

The gains of the post-World War II era would be lasting because organizations like the Sierra Club had relentlessly pressed federal bureaus like the Forest Service to open their planning processes to public comment, and then insisted that this public comment be institutionalized; because organizations like the Sierra Club were able to encourage public interest in environmental issues and bring about a permanent change in public perceptions of the importance of these issues; and because environmental laws were enacted, tested, and enforced as a direct result of Club lobbying and litigation. In the 1970s the Club entered the electoral process as well.[100]

It has been argued that the environmental movement of the 1960s and 1970s had implications beyond itself, and constituted a resurgence of participatory democracy in late twentieth-century America.[101] This was as the Club hoped. As David Brower wrote when speaking of the Colorado River, "The rest will go the way Glen Canyon did unless enough people begin to feel uneasy about the current interpretations of what progress consists of—unless they are willing to ask if progress has really served good purpose if it wipes out so many of the things that make life worthwhile."[102] This was not a new message; one finds it in the journals of Muir, or Aldo Leopold, for instance. In the post-World War II era there was a difference; the Sierra Club and other organizations were able to make Americans ask the hard questions about progress. The environmental movement was at root a victory of the public at large, of amateurs, though environmental proposals required sophisticated planning by specialists. I believe this history bears that out.

Conversely, the rise of environmentalism was not merely a victory of amateurs. As Michael McCloskey argues with fervor, the 1970s did not mark a downturn in the environmental movement or in the strength or aggressiveness of the Sierra Club. The continuing advance of environmental reform during this decade, and its gains in improving the quality of life of all Americans—in urban, rural, and suburban situations—demonstrates the virtues of more sophistication, of political expertise, organizational continuity, and patience.

David Brower demonstrated in the 1960s that a conservation organization supported by many small contributors could work. Big-money conservation was not the only way to influence national environmental policy, because the American public wanted, needed, and was willing to pay for environmental reform. The Sierra Club applied this insight to its own organizational structure. When grass-roots members like Richard Sill demanded that the Club be run by more than a central board, and when members like Martin Litton demanded that the Club create policy on the basis of thorough on-the-ground experience, the Club's answer was a healthy decentralization of power, the result of improved channels of communication from local groups to the board, which evolved through the 1970s. None of these gains were accomplished without friction, none quickly. The Club did evolve. It continued to grow in size and strength in the 1970s, and balanced its policies on traditional land-use issues with policies on energy, pollution, and broader environmental issues.

Even while the Club enlarged the scope of its interests, the gains of these decades were true to the spirit of Muir, who understood well the two sides of environmental issues: the humanistic side and the biocentric side. As he wrote during the summer of 1890, "The mountains are fountains of men as well as of rivers, of glaciers, of fertile soil."[103] Muir was not only saddened by the destruction of wilderness, but also was appalled by the degradation of life in nineteenth-century American cities and farms. He never forgot the poor children he met in the 1870s, the "ragged, neglected, defrauded, dirty little wretches of the Tar Flat waterfront" of San Francisco. He would distribute flowers to them when he returned from his short excursions to Mount Tamalpais. And he would say, "No matter into what depths of degradation humanity may sink, I

will never despair while the lowest love the pure and beautiful, and know it when they see it."[104]

Muir understood that the role of the Sierra Club would
undergo a major shift in the twentieth century. As he told the
Club in 1895, "I have not lagged behind in the work of exploring our grand wildernesses, and in calling everybody to
come and enjoy the thousand blessings they have to offer."
But "with reference to their preservation and management, I
think I said truly that this part of the work of the Club dependent on the action of Congress was in great part lawyer's
work . . . ."[105] Muir could laugh at the new responsibilities of
a Club activist. "I must make speeches and lead in society affairs. This, as it appears to me, is not reasonable." He could
profess no aptitude for "formal, legal, unwild work."
Throughout the twentieth century, mountaineers, backpackers, river runners who loved most exploring the wilderness
would also learn an aptitude for unwild work. And they
would do it well.

Notes

Sources and Abbreviations

The minutes of the Sierra Club Board of Directors and Executive Committee used for the research on this history are housed at the Sierra Club offices, San Francisco, and are abbreviated in the book's notes as follows:

Minutes, BoD: (date)

Minutes, Ex Comm: (date)

The *Sierra Club Bulletin* is abbreviated as *SCB*. When *Bulletin* is used alone and italicized in the text, it always refers to this source.

The Sierra Club: A Handbook, frequently cited, was first published in 1947, and was subsequently reissued in revised editions in 1951, 1955, 1957, 1960, 1967, and 1971.

The main source for personal collections of Club materials, manuscripts, and correspondence is the *Sierra Club Archives*, located at the Bancroft Library, University of California–Berkeley. These archives are organized by the name of contributor, box or carton number, and file name. References are made in the following form:

Document description, *Sierra Club Archives*, personal contributor, box or carton number, file: name.

In addition, I have used extensively the following collections:

Richard Sill Papers, University of Nevada, Reno, which has no file names;

Nathan Clark personal papers, on loan to author.

Richard Cellarius personal papers, in possession of Richard Cellarius, pertaining to the Sierra Club By-laws.

This history also depends on two series of oral histories:

The Sierra Club History Committee interviews, housed at the Sierra Club Library, San Francisco;

The Bancroft Regional Oral History Office interviews, Sierra Club History series, housed at the Bancroft Library, Berkeley, and the Sierra Club Library, San Francisco.

Certain correspondence and records of conversations with the author, identified as such by notes, are in the author's possession.

All sources except Club minutes receive full notation on first citation for each chapter, and are abbreviated in subsequent citations for the chapter.

The three portraits—of John Muir, Walter Huber, and Norman Clyde—were conceived originally as interchapters, but were moved in a late editorial round into chapters one, two, and three. The footnote numbering for the portraits remains separate from that of the original chapter notes. I hope this does not cause the reader any inconvenience.

Chapter 1

John Muir in California, 1868–1890

1. *Sierra Club Handbook* (San Francisco: Sierra Club, 1967), text facing p. 8.

2. William Frederick Badè, *The Life and Letters of John Muir*, 2 vols. (Boston: Houghton Mifflin, 1923–24); Michael P. Cohen, *The Pathless Way: John Muir and American Wilderness*, (Madison: University of Wisconsin Press, 1984); Stephen Fox, *John Muir and His Legacy: The American Conservation Movement* (Boston: Little, Brown and Co., 1981); Frederick Turner, *Rediscovering America: John Muir in His Time and Ours* (New York: Viking, 1985); Linnie Marsh Wolfe, *Son of the Wilderness: The Life of John Muir* (1945; repr., Madison: University of Wisconsin Press, 1978).

3. Linnie Marsh Wolfe, ed., *John of the Mountains: The Unpublished Journals of John Muir* (1938; repr., Madison: University of Wisconsin Press, 1979), p. 84.

4. See Kevin Starr, *Americans and the California Dream 1850–1915* (New York: Oxford University Press, 1973), p. 101.

5. John Muir, "Yosemite Valley in Flood," *Overland Monthly* 8 (April 1872), p. 347. For a history of Yosemite as a state park, see Hans Huth, "Yosemite, the Story of an Idea," *SCB* 33 (1948), pp. 47–78; Hans Huth, *Nature and the American: Three Centuries of Changing Attitudes* (Berkeley: University of California Press, 1957); and Holway R. Jones, *John Muir and the Sierra Club: The Battle for Yosemite* (San Francisco: Sierra Club Books, 1965). For Muir's developing voice, see Cohen, *The Pathless Way*.

6. Starr, *Americans and the California Dream*, pp. 425–428.

7. Joseph LeConte, *A Journal of Ramblings Through the High Sierra of California by the University Excursion Party*, ed. Francis P. Farquhar (1874; repr., San Francisco: Sierra Club Books, 1960), pp. 73–74.

8. John Muir, *To Yosemite and Beyond: Writings from the Years 1863 to 1875*, ed. Robert Engberg and Donald Wesling (Madison: University of Wisconsin Press, 1980), p. 162.

9. Badè, *Life and Letters of John Muir*, vol. 2, pp. 28–29.

10. John Muir, *Steep Trails*, ed. William Frederick Badè (Boston: Houghton Mifflin, 1918), pp. 162, 202.

11. Fox, *John Muir and His Legacy*, pp. 87–99.

12. John Muir, *The Yosemite* (Boston: Houghton Mifflin, 1912), pp. 8, 9.

13. Alfred Runte, *National Parks: The American Experience* (Lincoln: University of Nebraska Press, 1979). See chap. 3, "Worthless Lands," pp. 48–64.

14. Quoted in Jones, *John Muir and the Sierra Club*, p. 44.

15. Badè, *Life and Letters of John Muir*, vol. 2, p. 237.

16. David Brower, executive director of the Club from 1952 to 1969, refers to this as "The Place No One Knew" argument: "Muir knew well that if Yosemite were a place no one knew, it would not be protected." Brower to the author, February 19, 1987.

Birth of the Sierra Club, 1892

1. Ethel Olney Easton, "Sierra Club Beginnings," *SCB* 54 (December 1969), pp. 13–15. See also William E. Colby, "The Story of

the Sierra Club," *The Sierra Club: A Handbook* (San Francisco: Sierra Club, 1947), p. 4.

2. Johnson to Muir, November 21, 1889, *John Muir Papers*, Holt Atherton Library, University of the Pacific, box 3.

3. Holway R. Jones, *John Muir and the Sierra Club: The Battle for Yosemite* (San Francisco: Sierra Club Books, 1965), pp. 7–11.

4. Holway R. Jones, "John Muir, the Sierra Club, and the Formulation of the Wilderness Concept," *The Pacific Historian* 25 (Summer 1981), pp. 64–78.

5. *Articles of Association, By-Laws, and List of Members* (San Francisco: Sierra Club, 1892).

6. Frederick Turner, *Rediscovering America: John Muir in His Time and Ours* (New York: Viking, 1985), p. 290.

7. Joseph LeConte, "The Sierra Club," *SCB* 10 (January 1917), p. 141.

8. Kevin Starr, *Americans and the California Dream 1850–1915* (New York: Oxford University Press, 1973), p. 189.

9. Walton Bean, *Boss Rueff's San Francisco* (Berkeley: University of California Press, 1968), p. 8.

10. Susan R. Schrepfer, *The Fight to Save the Redwoods: A History of Environmental Reform 1917–1978* (Madison: University of Wisconsin Press, 1983), pp. 11, 12.

11. George E. Mowry, *The California Progressives* (Berkeley: University of California Press, 1951), pp. 86–104.

12. Starr, *Americans and the California Dream*, p. 406.

13. Ibid., p. 285.

14. John Muir, *The Yosemite* (Boston: Houghton Mifflin, 1912), appendix A, p. 263.

15. David Brower has always argued that Yosemite is America's first national park. Brower to the author, February 19, 1987.

16. Robinson is quoted in Jones, *John Muir and the Sierra Club*, p. 57; see also pp. 59–61.

17. See Stephen Fox, *John Muir and His Legacy: The American Conservation Movement* (Boston: Little, Brown and Co., 1981), p. 127; Jones, *John Muir and the Sierra Club*, p. 113.

18. Robert Underwood Johnson, *Remembered Yesterdays*, (Boston: Little, Brown and Co., 1923), p. 293.

19. Muir, *The Yosemite*, appendix B, p. 297.

20. These issues are discussed in Jones, *John Muir and the Sierra Club*; John Ise, *Our National Park Policy: A Critical History* (Baltimore: The Johns Hopkins Press, 1961); Roderick Nash, "The American Invention of National Parks," *American Quarterly* 22 (Fall 1970), pp. 726–735; Ronald A. Foresta, *America's National Parks and Their Keepers* (Washington, D.C.: Resources for the Future, 1984); Alfred Runte, *National Parks: The American Experience* (Lincoln: University of Nebraska Press, 1979).

21. "The Sierra Forest Reservation," *SCB* 1 (January 1896), pp. 254–267.

22. "Proceedings of the Sierra Club," in *SCB* 1 (January 1896), p. 284.

23. Ibid., p. 270.

24. "Forestry Notes," *SCB* 3 (January 1900), p. 117.

25. "Proceedings of the Sierra Club," *SCB* 1 (January 1896), p. 271.

26. For Leopold's thinking, see Susan L. Flader, *Thinking Like a Mountain: Aldo Leopold and the Evolution of an Ecological Attitude toward Deer, Wolves, and Forests* (Columbia: University of Missouri Press, 1974). For Muir's thinking, see Michael P. Cohen, *The Pathless Way: John Muir and American Wilderness* (Madison: University of Wisconsin Press, 1984).

27. Linnie Marsh Wolfe, *Son of the Wilderness*, p. 275.

28. John Muir, *Our National Parks* (1901; repr., Madison: University of Wisconsin Press, 1981), p. 364.

29. Fox, *John Muir and His Legacy*, chap. 11, pp. 358–374.

30. *The Mountains of California* (1894; repr., Berkeley: Ten Speed Press, 1979), p. 4.

31. Samuel P. Hays, *Conservation and the Gospel of Efficiency: The Progressive Conservation Movement, 1890–1920* (Cambridge: Harvard University Press, 1959), p. 265.

32. "Are National Parks Worth While?" *SCB* 8 (January 1912), p. 237.

33. "Wild Parks and Forest Reservations of the West," *Atlantic Monthly* 81 (January 1898), pp. 15–28.

34. "Remembering Will Colby," *SCB* 50 (December 1965), pp. 69–78. This issue includes an extensive interview conducted by the Bancroft Library.

35. Jones, *John Muir and the Sierra Club*, pp. 21–23.

36. Ibid., p. 20.

37. See Cohen, *The Pathless Way*, pp. 311–321.

38. Jones, *John Muir and the Sierra Club*, p. 23.

39. Bean, *Boss Rueff's San Francisco*, p. 33.

40. Quoted in Turner, *Rediscovering America*, p. 340.

41. "Remembering Will Colby," p. 71.

42. Mowry, *The California Progressives*, p. 15.

43. "Remembering Will Colby," p. 72. For Muir's perspective, see Cohen, *The Pathless Way*, pp. 323–326.

44. For early background on the Hetch Hetchy issue, see Jones, *John Muir and the Sierra Club*, pp. 83–117.

45. Nash, *Wilderness and the American Mind*, p. 174; Fox, *John Muir and His Legacy*, p. 140.

46. Santayana is quoted in Starr, *Americans and the California Dream*, pp. 419–423, and in Cohen, *The Pathless Way*, p. 136.

47. Hays, *Conservation and the Gospel of Efficiency*, pp. 195, 196.

48. Harold K. Steen, *The U.S. Forest Service: A History* (Seattle: University of Washington, 1976), pp. 74, 75.

49. Grant McConnell, "The Conservation Movement—Past and Present," *Western Political Quarterly* 7 (March 1954), pp. 463–478.

50. Gifford Pinchot, *The Use of the National Forests* (Washington, D.C.: U.S. Department of Agriculture, 1907), p. 19. See also Steen, *The U.S. Forest Service*, pp. 78–81.

51. Jones, *John Muir and the Sierra Club*, p. 90. For the best short summary of the Hetch Hetchy controversy, and a bibliography, see Nash, *Wilderness and the American Mind*, chap. 10, pp. 160–181.

52. *San Francisco Examiner*, December 2, 1913.

53. David Brower remembers coining this slogan at a Democratic Party platform conference in Denver, circa 1956. Brower to the author, February 17, 1987.

54. *SCB* 6 (June 1908), pp. 318–319.

55. *SCB* 6 (June 1907), pp. 261–265.

56. "The Battle Within the Battle," in Jones, *John Muir and the Sierra Club*, p. 80.

57. *SCB* 6 (January 1908), pp. 265–268.

58. I am indebted to Susan Flader for this justification of Olney's position. Flader to the author, February 17, 1987.

59. Jones, *John Muir and the Sierra Club*, pp. 97, 112, 113.

60. Quoted in Jones, *John Muir and the Sierra Club*, p. 98.

61. Jones, *John Muir and the Sierra Club*, pp. 114–117.

62. Easton, "Sierra Club Beginnings," p. 15.

63. William Frederick Badè, *The Life and Letters of John Muir*, vol. 2 (Boston: Houghton Mifflin, 1923–24), p. 237.

64. Muir, *The Yosemite*, pp. 260, 261.

65. Edith Jane Hadley, *John Muir's Views of Nature and Their Consequences* (Ph.D. diss., University of Wisconsin, 1956), p. 740.

66. Kent is quoted in Nash, *Wilderness and the American Mind*, pp. 167–168; see also p. 174.

67. Jones, *John Muir and the Sierra Club*, pp. 105, 106, 127, 139.

68. Ibid., p. 122; Fox, *John Muir and His Legacy*, p. 141.

69. Quoted in Nash, *Wilderness and the American Mind*, p. 180.

70. *The Sierra Club: A Handbook* (1947), p. 8.

71. Jones, *John Muir and the Sierra Club*, p. 157.

72. Quoted in Fox, *John Muir and His Legacy*, p. 145.

73. Jones, *John Muir and the Sierra Club*, p. 95.

74. Quoted in Jones, *John Muir and the Sierra Club*, pp. 167, 168.

75. *The Sierra Club: A Handbook* (1947), p. iii.

76. Grant McConnell, "The Conservation Movement—Past and Present," pp. 477, 478. This issue is discussed in detail also by Stephen Fox in *John Muir and His Legacy*, chap. 11, "Lord Man, the Religion of Conservation," pp. 359–374.

77. "Remembering Will Colby," pp. 73, 74.

78. Jones, *John Muir and the Sierra Club*, p. 168; Linnie Marsh Wolfe, *Son of the Wilderness: The Life of John Muir* (1945; repr., Madison: University of Wisconsin Press, 1978), p. 341.

79. Nash, *Wilderness and the American Mind*, pp. 170, 181.

80. Richard M. Leonard, "Mountaineer, Lawyer, Environmentalist," interview conducted by Susan R. Schrepfer, Regional Oral History Office, the Bancroft Library, Berkeley, 1975, pp. 112, 114, 123, 283, 316.

81. Ibid., pp. 306, 130.

82. David Brower to Richard Sill, February 13, 1967, with enclosure, in *Sierra Club Archives*, Brower papers, carton 208, file: Diablo Canyon.

83. "Mountaineer," p. 121.

84. Martin Litton, quoted in Lee Green, "The Old Man and His River," *Outside* (May 1986), p. 44.

85. Colby, "John Muir—President of the Sierra Club," *SCB* 10 (January 1916), p. 2.

86. Quoted by Colby, "John Muir—President of the Sierra Club," *SCB* 10 (January 1916), p. 4.

87. *SCB* 10 (January 1912), p. 207, and map, p. 221.

88. Colby, "National Park Affairs," *SCB* 10 (January 1916), p. 81.

89. Osborn, "John Muir," *SCB* 10 (January 1916), pp. 29–30.

90. Wolfe, *Son of the Wilderness*, p. 345.

91. B. H. Lehman, "Marion Randall Parsons," *SCB* 38 (October 1953), pp. 35–39.

92. "To Higher Sierras," *SCB* 10 (January 1916), p. 40.

93. "The John Muir Trail," *SCB* 10 (January 1916), p. 87.

94. *The Yosemite*, p. 171.

95. "A Quarter of a Century of Service," *SCB* 10 (January 1916), p. 211.

96. Johnson, "John Muir as I Knew Him," *SCB* 10 (January 1916), p. 15; Charles Keeler, "Recollections of John Muir," *SCB* 10 (January 1916), p. 19.

97. See Joseph M. Petulla, *American Environmental History: The Exploitation and Conservation of Natural Resources* (San Francisco: Boyd and Frazer, 1977).

98. Foresta, *America's National Parks*, p. 17.

99. *SCB* 8 (January 1912), p. 205.

100. Horace Albright, *The Birth of the National Park Service* (Salt Lake City: Howe Brothers, 1985), pp. 1–14.

101. Robert Shankland, *Steve Mather of the National Parks* (New York: Alfred Knopf, 1970).

102. Foresta, *America's National Parks*, p. 9.

103. Shankland, *Steve Mather*, pp. 9, v.

104. Quoted in Albright, *Birth of the National Park Service*, pp. 16, 17.

105. Shankland, *Steve Mather*, p. 294.

106. Albright, *Birth of the National Park Service*, p. 21; Shankland, *Steve Mather*, pp. 58–63.

107. Stephen T. Mather, "National Parks—the Federal Policy, Past and Future," *SCB* 10 (January 1916), pp. 97–101.

108. Hal Rothman, "Second-Class Sites: National Monuments and the Growth of the National Park System," *Environmental Review* 10 (Spring 1986), pp. 45–56.

109. Badè, *Life and Letters of John Muir*, vol. 2, pp. 378–380; see also Holway R. Jones, "John Muir, the Sierra Club, and the Formulation of the Wilderness Concept," *Pacific Historian* 25 (Summer 1981), pp. 64–78.

110. Mather, "National Parks—the Federal Policy," pp. 97–101.

111. Shankland, *Steve Mather*, p. 104.

112. Foresta, *America's National Parks*, pp. 17, 18.

113. Albright, *Birth of the National Park Service*, p. 29.

114. Ibid., p. 24.

115. Albright, *Birth of the National Park Service*, p. 36; Public Law 235, 64th Congress (1916).

116. Albright, *Birth of the National Park Service*, p. 36.

117. Ibid., pp. 32–43.

118. Ibid., p. 59; William C. Everhart, *The National Park Service* (New York: Praeger, 1972), p. 196.

119. Albright, *Birth of the National Park Service*, pp. 68–73.

120. *SCB* 10 (January 1919), p. 478; the full letter is on pp. 478–482.

121. For analysis of the Lane letter, see F. Fraser Darling and Noel D. Eichhorn, *Man and Nature in the National Parks, Reflections on Policy*, 2d ed. (Washington, D.C.: Conservation Foundation, 1969), pp. 28–31.

122. For commentary, see Darling and Eichhorn, *Man and Nature*; Ise, *Our National Park Policy*, pp. 194–195; Foresta, *America's National Parks*, pp. 28–29.

123. Quoted in Shankland, *Steve Mather*, p. 8.

124. Albright, *Birth of the National Park Service*, p. 82.

125. Francis P. Farquhar, "Sierra Club Mountaineer and Editor," interview conducted by Ann Lage, Sierra Club History Committee, San Francisco, 1974, p. 25.

126. Shankland, *Steve Mather*, p. 267.

127. Ibid., pp. 207–208; Donald C. Swain, *Wilderness Defender: Horace M. Albright and Conservation* (Chicago: University of Chicago Press, 1970), pp. 107–109.

128. Foresta, *America's National Parks*, p. 28.

129. "Policy of the Sierra Club on Road Construction in the Sierra," Sierra Club Circular no. 25 (May–June 1927). See also Jones, "John Muir, the Sierra Club, and the Formulation of the Wilderness Concept," pp. 76, 77.

130. Francis P. Farquhar, "Legislative History of Sequoia and Kings Canyon National Parks," *SCB* 26 (February 1941), pp. 42–58.

131. Holway R. Jones, "First Kings," manuscript in the author's possession, p. 16.

132. On conflict between the Forest Service and the Park Service in 1920, see Foresta, *America's National Parks*, pp. 18–35, and Steen, *U.S. Forest Service*, pp. 18–21.

133. Henry S. Graves, "A Crisis in National Recreation," *American Forestry* 26 (July 1920), pp. 391–400.

134. Farquhar to Lovekin, April 6, 1922, quoted in Jones, "First Kings," p. 17.

135. Badè to William B. Greeley, February 17, 1921, quoted in Steen, *U.S. Forest Service*, p. 157.

136. Quoted in Jones, "First Kings," p. 17.

137. Jones, "First Kings," p. 36.

138. Francis P. Farquhar, editorial, *SCB* 12 (January 1926), p. 299.

139. The definition of purism I use is introduced by Donald C. Swain in *Wilderness Defender*, p. 137. For a different view, see Schrepfer, *Fight to Save the Redwoods*, p. 53.

140. Badè to Farquhar, November 26, 1921, quoted in Jones, "First Kings," p. 22.

141. Farquhar, "Sierra Club Mountaineer and Editor," p. 26.

142. For a good portrait of Yard, see Fox, *John Muir and His Legacy*, pp. 203–206.

143. Swain, *Wilderness Defender*, p. 67; Albright, *Birth of the National Park Service*, p. 54.

144. Albright, *Birth of the National Park Service*, p. 106.

145. Fox, *John Muir and His Legacy*, p. 203.

146. Parsons, review of *The Book of the National Parks* by M.R.P., *SCB* 11 (January 1920), pp. 108–110, quoted in Fox, *John Muir and His Legacy*, p. 206.

147. David R. Brower, "Environmental Activist, Publicist, and Prophet," interview conducted by Susan R. Schrepfer, Regional Oral History Office, the Bancroft Library, Berkeley, 1980, pp. 46, 47.

148. Leonard, "Mountaineer," pp. 50−52.

149. See comment by interviewer Susan Schrepfer in Brower, "Environmental Activist," p. 48.

150. See Enos Mills and Emerson Hough, quoted in Swain, *Wilderness Defender*, p. 139; on Yard, see Swain, *Wilderness Defender*, pp. 67, 247.

151. Martin Litton approved of Yard but never met him. Litton to the author, personal communication, May 1986.

152. "Remembering Will Colby," p. 75.

153. Editorial, *SCB* 12 (1927), p. 409.

154. Editorial, *SCB* 10 (January 1919), pp. 431−433.

155. See Robert A. Caro, *The Power Broker: Robert Moses and the Fall of New York* (New York: Knopf, 1974).

156. Robert W. Righter, *Crucible for Conservation: The Creation of Grand Teton National Park* (Colorado Associated University Press, 1982), pp. 131−134.

157. For the origin of the League, see Schrepfer, *Fight to Save the Redwoods*, pp. 3−37.

158. *SCB* 11 (January 1920), pp. 1−4.

159. Editorial, *SCB* 11 (January 1920), p. 87.

160. William E. Colby and David R. Brower, "Duncan Mc-Duffie—1877−1951," *SCB* 37 (December 1952), pp. 84−85; Schrepfer, *Fight to Save the Redwoods*, p. 51.

161. Farquhar, "Sierra Club Mountaineer and Editor," p. 32.

162. Schrepfer, *Fight to Save the Redwoods*, p. 30.

163. Ibid., p. 33.

164. "Remembering Will Colby," p. 76.

165. "Shall the Nation Continue to Own the National Forests?" and "Recognition of Public Service," *SCB* 12 (1926), pp. 298, 299.

Chapter 2

Walter Huber, 1883−1960

1. Will Colby, "Walter Leroy Huber," *SCB* 45 (December 1960), p. 81.

2. "Longs Peak," *SCB* 13 (February 1928), p. 64.

3. "The North Palisade Glacier," *SCB* 9 (January 1915), p. 263.

4. Conrad L. Wirth, *Parks, Politics, and the People* (Norman: University of Oklahoma Press, 1980), pp. 359–360.

5. Quoted in Colby, "Walter Leroy Huber," p. 83.

6. Minutes, BoD: January 19–20, 1957.

7. Minutes, BoD: December 6, 1947.

8. Minutes, BoD: January 7–8, 1956.

9. Joel Hildebrand, "Sierra Club Leader and Ski Mountaineer," interview conducted by Ann Lage, Sierra Club History Committee, San Francisco, 1974, pp. 28, 33.

10. Minutes, BoD: May 7, 1955. See also Farquhar's comments in Minutes, BoD: May 1, 1948.

11. *Sierra Club Archives*, Sierra Club History Committee, box 2.

Recreation, 1901–1950

1. William E. Colby, "Proposed Summer Outing of the Sierra Club—Report of Committee," *SCB* 3 (February 1901), pp. 251–253.

2. William E. Colby, "Twenty-Nine Years with the Sierra Club," *SCB* 16 (1931), p. 15.

3. *Our National Parks* (1901; repr., Madison: University of Wisconsin Press, 1981), p. 56.

4. *The Sierra Club: A Handbook* (San Francisco: Sierra Club, 1947), p. 16.

5. Ibid., p. 24.

6. Marion Randall Parsons, "The Twenty-Eighth Outing," *SCB* 15 (February 1930), pp. 9–20.

7. Robert Marshall, "The Problem of the Wilderness," *Scientific Monthly* 30 (February 1930), p. 146.

8. Francis P. Farquhar, *Place Names of the High Sierra* (San Francisco: Sierra Club, 1926); Walter A. Starr, Jr., *Guide to the John Muir Trail* (San Francisco: Sierra Club, 1934); Hervey Voge, *A Climber's Guide to the High Sierra* (San Francisco: Sierra Club, 1954). Early publications of the Sierra Club are listed in *The Sierra Club: A Handbook* (San Francisco: Sierra Club, 1960), pp. 104–106.

9. Francis P. Farquhar, *History of the Sierra Nevada* (Berkeley: University of California Press, 1965), p. 235.

10. Chris[topher] Jones, *Climbing in North America* (Berkeley: University of California Press, 1976), pp. 127–142.

11. Richard M. Leonard, "Mountaineer, Lawyer, Environmentalist," interview by Susan R. Schrepfer, Regional Oral History Office, the Bancroft Library, Berkeley, 1975, p. 8.

12. Bestor Robinson, "Thoughts on Conservation and the Sierra Club," interview conducted by Susan R. Schrepfer, Sierra Club History Committee, San Francisco, 1974, p. 51.

13. Ibid., p. 51.

14. Nancy Newhall, *Ansel Adams: A Biography. Volume I: The Eloquent Light* (San Francisco: Sierra Club Books, 1963), pp. 36–37.

15. "Ski Experience," *SCB* 16 (February 1931), pp. 44–46.

16. Brower to the author, February 19, 1987. Brower biographical material is from this source.

17. David Brower, "Far From the Madding Mules," *SCB* 20 (February 1935), p. 77.

18. Ansel Adams, with Mary Street Alinder, *Ansel Adams: An Autobiography* (New York: New York Graphics Society, 1985), p. 57.

19. Michael P. Sherrick, "The Northwest Face of Half Dome," *SCB* 43 (November 1958), p. 23.

20. John Mendenhall, "John and Ruth Mendenhall: Forty Years of Sierra Club Mountaineering Leadership, 1938–78," interview conducted by Richard Searle, Sierra Club History Committee, San Francisco, 1979, p. 25.

21. William E. Siri, "Reflections on the Sierra Club, the Environment, and Mountaineering, 1950s–1970s," interview conducted by Ann Lage, Regional Oral History Office, the Bancroft Library, Berkeley, 1979, p. 14.

22. "A Climber's Guide to the High Sierra," *SCB* 22 (February 1937), pp. 48–57. The climber's guide was completed in 1954; see Hervey Voge, ed., *A Climber's Guide to the High Sierra* (San Francisco: Sierra Club, 1954).

23. "Climbs by Norman Clyde in 1930," *SCB* 15 (February 1931) pp. 107–108.

24. Harriet Monroe's poem, composed in 1904, is printed in *The Sierra Club: A Handbook* (1947), p. 69.

25. Harold Crowe, in *The Sierra Club: A Handbook* (1947), p. 74.

26. Richard M. Leonard, Arnold Wexler, William E. Siri, Charles Wilts, David Brower, Morgan Harris, and May Pridham, *Belaying the Leader: An Omnibus on Climbing Safety* (San Francisco:

Sierra Club, 1956), pp. 80−84; printed earlier in *SCB* 26 (February 1941).

27. Leonard et al., *Belaying the Leader*, p. 55.

28. "Equipment and Technique for Camping on Snow," *SCB* 22 (February 1937), pp. 38−47.

29. Bestor Robinson, "The First Ascent of Shiprock," *SCB* 25 (February 1940), pp. 1−7.

30. Leonard, "Mountaineer," pp. 38−40.

31. David R. Brower, "Environmental Activist, Publicist, and Prophet," interview conducted by Susan R. Schrepfer, Regional Oral History Office, the Bancroft Library, Berkeley, 1980, pp. 35−37.

32. Nathan C. Clark, "Sierra Club Leader, Outdoorsman, and Engineer," interview conducted by Richard Searle, Sierra Club History Committee, San Francisco, 1977, p. 43.

33. David R. Brower, ed., *Manual of Ski Mountaineering*, 1st ed. (Berkeley: University of California Press, 1942).

34. Leonard et al., *Belaying the Leader*.

35. "Lake Tahoe in Winter," *SCB* 3 (May 1900), pp. 121−126, a reprinting of Muir's newspaper article.

36. Hazel King, "Ski Running: An Impression," *SCB* 9 (January 1915) pp. 271−273.

37. "An Introduction to Skiing," *SCB* 15 (February 1930), pp. 64−68.

38. "A Winter in the High Sierra," *SCB* 15 (February 1930), pp. 69−73.

39. For Farquhar's commentary, see *SCB* 15 (February 1930), pp. 97−98.

40. See "Winter Sports" in *The Sierra Club: A Handbook* (1947), pp. 39−47.

41. "Ski Heil!" *SCB* 20 (February 1935), pp. 1−7.

42. *The Sierra Club: A Handbook* (1947), pp. 88−92.

43. "Beyond the Skiways," *SCB* 23 (April 1938), pp. 40−45.

44. Ruth D. Mendenhall to the author, May 10, 1983.

45. "Retrospect: Nineteen-thirty-one" *SCB* 17 (February 1932), p. 7.

46. Minutes, BoD: May 4, 1935; December 7, 1935.

47. Joel Hildebrand, "Sierra Club Leader and Ski Mountaineer," interview conducted by Ann Lage, Sierra Club History Committee,

San Francisco, 1974, pp. 22–24. See also Stephen Fox, *John Muir and His Legacy*: *The American Conservation Movement* (Boston: Little, Brown and Co., 1981), pp. 214–217; David Brower to the author, February 20, 1987.

48. Richard Leonard to the author, August 18, 1987. Minutes, BoD: January 13, 1939. As another result of the Bohemian Club meeting, Ickes and Hildebrand formed a close relationship which allowed Hildebrand to recommend Newton Drury as future head of the National Park Service, an idea the secretary accepted. Hildebrand, "Sierra Club Leader," p. 19.

49. Arno B. Cammerer, quoted in Newhall, *The Eloquent Light*, p. 165. See also Adams, *Ansel Adams, An Autobiography*, p. 151.

50. On *Sky—Land Trails of the Kings*, see Brower, "Environmental Activist," p. 20.

51. "The John Muir-Kings Canyon National Park," *SCB* 14 (February 1939), pp. i–vii; "Further Support Needed for Muir Park Bill," *SCB* 14 (April 1939), pp. xiii–xiv.

52. Hildebrand and Farquhar, quoted in "The John Muir-Kings Canyon National Park."

53. "Further Support Needed for Muir Park Bill," p. xiii.

54. "How to Kill a Wilderness," *SCB* 30 (August 1945), pp. 2–4.

55. Brower, "Environmental Activist," p. 178.

56. Leonard, "Mountaineer," p. 95.

57. Robinson, "Thoughts on Conservation," p. 41.

58. Brower, "Environmental Activist," p. 22.

59. Leonard, "Mountaineer," p. 95.

60. Ibid., p. 96.

61. Minutes, BoD: September 1, 1946.

62. Minutes, BoD: December 7, 1946.

63. Brower, "Environmental Activist," p. 136.

64. "San Gorgonio Auction: *Going, Going, ———,*" *SCB* 32 (January 1947), pp. 3–10.

65. David Brower to the author, February 27, 1987.

66. "San Gorgonio: Another Viewpoint," *SCB* 32 (January 1947), pp. 12–15.

67. Brower, "Environmental Activist," p. 179.

68. David R. Brower and Richard H. Felter, "Surveying California's Ski Terrain," *SCB* 33 (March 1948), pp. 97–102.

69. Minutes, BoD: August 31, 1947.

70. Susan R. Schrepfer, "Perspectives on Conservation: Sierra Club Strategies in Mineral King," *Journal of Forest History* 20 (October 1976), pp. 176–190.

71. Leonard, "Mountaineer," pp. 96, 97.

72. "Brief in Support of San Gorgonio Primitive Area," *SCB* 32 (March 1947), pp. 18–27; italics in the original.

73. Public Law 235, 64th Congress (1916). See also Horace Albright, *The Birth of the National Park Service* (Salt Lake City: Howe Brothers, 1985) pp. 36, 39–44.

74. Brower, "Environmental Activist," p. 29.

75. Ibid., p. 28.

76. See Linda H. Graber, *Wilderness as Sacred Space* (Washington, D.C.: Association of American Geographers, 1976).

77. "Protecting Mountain Meadows," *SCB* 32 (May 1947), pp. 53–62.

78. Attributed to Colby by Leonard, "Mountaineer," pp. 19, 20.

79. Brower, "Environmental Activist," p. 20a.

80. Minutes, BoD: May 3, 1947. Brower remembers Barbara Norris (later Bedayn) using the phrase "render not too accessible." Brower to the author, February 20, 1987.

81. Minutes, BoD: September 5, 1948.

82. "Relocation of Tioga Road: Report of the Executive Committee of the Sierra Club on the Proposed Relocation of the Tioga Road, Yosemite National Park," *SCB* 19 (February 1934), pp. 85–88.

83. Ibid.

84. "Tuolumne Winter," *SCB* 32 (May 1947), pp. 89–95.

85. On Bradley's proposal and critique, see Minutes, BoD: August 31, 1947; "Tuolumne Meadows and Tomorrow," *Sierra Club Archives*, Bradley papers, carton 116, file: Roads. The proposal was printed as a pamphlet under the latter title, at Bradley's expense, when the board of directors would not allow it to appear in the *Bulletin*. Bradley distributed it on September 5, 1948, when the board met with officials of Yosemite National Park in Tuolumne Meadows.

86. Minutes, BoD: August 31, 1947.

87. Robinson in Minutes, BoD: December 6, 1947.

88. Harold C. Bradley and David R. Brower, "Roads in the National Parks," *SCB* 34 (June 1949), pp. 31–54.

89. Minutes, BoD: May 1, 1948.

90. Minutes, BoD: September 5, 1948.

91. "Park Roads," *Sierra Club Archives*, Bradley papers, carton 116, file: Park Roads.

92. Stewart Kimball to Richard Leonard, August 29, 1949, *Sierra Club Archives*, Bradley papers, carton 116, file: N.P.S. Roads. On Park Service Roads, see also Minutes, BoD: August 31, 1952.

93. Minutes, BoD: February 17, 1951. Results of general membership voting are reported in Minutes, BoD: May 5, 1951.

Chapter 3

Norman Clyde, 1885–1972

1. William B. Devall, "The Governing of a Voluntary Organization: Oligarchy and Democracy in the Sierra Club" (Ph.D. diss., University of Oregon, 1970).

2. Thomas Jukes to William Devall, September 17, 1969, in *Richard Sill Papers*, University of Nevada, Reno, box 48.

3. See "T. H. Jukes Interviewed by Mr. Nadzan Haron for Sierra Club History Project, February 1981," an oral history filed in the Sierra Club Library, San Francisco.

4. Richard M. Leonard, "Mountaineer, Lawyer, Environmentalist," interview conducted by Susan R. Schrepfer, Regional Oral History Office, the Bancroft Library, Berkeley, 1975, pp. 15–17.

5. Jack Kerouac, *Dharma Bums* (New York: New American Library, 1958), p. 68.

6. *The Sierra Club: A Handbook* (1947), p. 18.

7. Norman Clyde, *Close Ups of the High Sierra*, ed. Walt Wheelock (Glendale, Calif.: La Siesta Press, 1962); *Norman Clyde of the High Sierra: 29 Essays on Mountains by Norman Clyde* (San Francisco: Scrimshaw Press, 1971); Norman Clyde, *El Picacho del Diablo* (Los Angeles: Dawson's Book Shop, 1975); Harold Gilliam, "Old Man of the Mountains," *SCB* 46 (September 1961), p. 13.

8. Leonard, "Mountaineer," pp. 19, 20.

9. Ibid., p. 20.

10. *The Sierra Club: A Handbook* (1947), p. 16.

11. John Muir, *South of Yosemite: Selected Writing by John Muir*,

ed. Frederic R. Gunsky (Garden City, N.Y.: Natural History Press, 1968), pp. 70, 88.

12. John Muir, *Steep Trails*, ed. William Frederick Badè (Boston: Houghton Mifflin, 1918), p. 22.

13. Jules Eichorn, Prologue to *Norman Clyde of the High Sierra*, p. 12; David Brower to the author, February 20, 1987.

14. Leonard, "Mountaineer," p. 16.

15. Ibid., p. 8.

16. Ibid., p. 6.

17. Ibid., p. 17.

18. David Brower to the author, February 20, 1987.

19. "Snowbanners of the California Alps," in Muir, *The Mountains of California* (1894; repr., Berkeley: Ten Speed Press, 1979), pp. 41–47.

20. Leonard, "Mountaineer," p. 17.

21. Ibid.

22. Brower to the author, February 20, 1987.

The Wilderness Society, 1935

1. Stephen Fox, *John Muir and His Legacy: The American Conservation Movement* (Boston: Little, Brown and Co., 1981), pp. 203–212; Roderick Nash, *Wilderness and the American Mind*, 3d ed. (New Haven: Yale University Press, 1982), pp. 182–209.

2. Fox, *John Muir and His Legacy*, pp. 203, 204.

3. Robert S. Yard, "A Summons to Save the Wilderness" and "The Wilderness Society Platform," *The Living Wilderness* 1 (September 1935); Aldo Leopold, *A Sand County Almanac, and Sketches Here and There* (New York: Oxford University Press, 1949), p. 149.

4. C. J. Stahl, "Where Forestry and Recreation Meet," *Journal of Forestry* 19 (1921), pp. 526–529.

5. "The Wilderness Society Platform," p. 2.

6. Aldo Leopold, "Why the Wilderness Society?" *The Living Wilderness* 1 (September 1935), p. 6; italics in the original.

7. "The Types of Wilderness Recognized," *The Living Wilderness* 1 (September 1935), p. 2.

8. Leopold, "Why the Wilderness Society?" p. 6.

9. For background on Robert Marshall, see John Collier, "Wilderness and Modern Man," in David R. Brower, ed., *Wildlands in*

Our Civilization (San Francisco: Sierra Club, 1964), pp. 115–127; see also "Decisions for Permanence," chap. 12 of Nash, *Wilderness and the American Mind*, pp. 220–225.

10. Fox, *John Muir and His Legacy*, pp. 206–208.

11. Robert Marshall, "The Problem of the Wilderness," *Scientific Monthly* (February 1930), pp. 141–148; reprinted in *SCB* 31 (May 1947), pp. 43–52. Quotations from Marshall, and used by Marshall, in this and the next three paragraphs are from "The Problem of Wilderness."

12. Joseph Wood Krutch, *The Modern Temper: A Study and A Confession* (1929; repr., New York: Harcourt Brace, 1956).

13. Krutch, *The Modern Temper*, p. 56.

14. The definitive biography is now Curt Meine, *Aldo Leopold: His Life and Work* (Madison: University of Wisconsin Press, 1987).

15. Frederick Jackson Turner, "The Significance of the Frontier in American History," in Ray Allen Billington, ed., *Frontier and Section: Selected Essays of Frederick Jackson Turner* (Englewood Cliffs, N.J.: Prentice-Hall, 1961), pp. 38, 39.

16. Quoted in Richard Hofstadter, *The Progressive Historians: Turner, Beard, Parrington* (New York: Knopf, 1968), p. 74.

17. Hofstadter, *The Progressive Historians*, p. 74.

18. Susan L. Flader, *Thinking Like a Mountain: Aldo Leopold and the Evolution of an Ecological Attitude Toward Deer, Wolves, and Forests* (Columbia: University of Missouri Press, 1974), p. 29.

19. Quoted in Flader, *Thinking Like a Mountain*, p. 270.

20. Leopold, *A Sand County Almanac*, p. 188.

21. Aldo Leopold, "The Conservation Ethic," *Journal of Forestry* 31 (October 1933), pp. 634–643.

22. Harold C. Bradley, "Aldo Leopold—Champion of Wilderness," *SCB* 36 (May 1951), pp. 14–18.

23. David Brower to the author, February 20, 1987.

24. Robin Winks, "Conservation in America: National Character as Revealed by Preservation," in *The Future of the Past, Attitudes to Conservation 1174–1974*, ed. Jane Faucett (New York: Watson-Guptill, 1976), pp. 141–150.

25. Robin Winks, *The Myth of the American Frontier, Its Relevance to America, Canada, and Australia* (Leicester, U.K.: Leicester University Press, 1971), pp. 17, 18.

26. Minutes, BoD: February 17, 1951.

27. William Tucker, *Progress and Privilege: America in an Age of Environmentalism* (New York: Anchor Press, 1982).

28. John H. Hendee, George H. Stankey, and Robert C. Lucas, *Wilderness Management*, Miscellaneous Publication no. 1365, (Washington, D.C.: U.S. Forest Service, Department of Agriculture, October 1978), p. 9. This is the definitive text on wilderness management.

29. Glen O. Robinson, *The Forest Service, A Study in Public Land Management* (Baltimore: The Johns Hopkins University Press for Resources for the Future, 1975), pp. 257–261.

30. Marshall, "The Problem of the Wilderness," p. 148.

31. Hendee, Stankey, and Lucas, *Wilderness Management*, p. 62.

32. Louise E. Peffer, *The Closing of the Public Domain: Disposal and Reservation Policies, 1900–50* (New York: Arno Press, 1972), pp. 339, 342.

33. See the Preface to George Cameron Coggins and Charles F. Wilkinson, *Federal Public Land and Resources Law* (Mineola, N.Y.: Foundation Press, 1981), particularly p. xxiii.

34. Leopold, *A Sand County Almanac*, p. 224.

35. Roderick Nash, "American Environmental History: A New Teaching Frontier," *Pacific Historical Review* 41 (August 1972), pp. 363–372.

36. Norman B. Livermore, Jr., "Man in the Middle: High Sierra Packer, Timberman, Conservationist, and California Resources Secretary," interview conducted by Ann Lage and Gabrielle Morris, Regional Oral History Office, the Bancroft Library, Berkeley, 1983, p. 17.

37. Livermore, "Man in the Middle," p. 32.

38. Livermore's letter is included in Minutes, BoD: August 31, 1947.

39. Minutes, BoD: May 1, 1948.

40. Norman B. Livermore, Jr., "Sierra Packing and Wilderness Policy," *SCB* 32 (May 1947), pp. 96–98; Richard M. Leonard and Lowell Sumner, "Protecting Mountain Meadows," *SCB* 32 (May 1947), pp. 53–62.

41. Bernard DeVoto, "The West Against Itself," *SCB* 32 (May 1947), pp. 36–42.

42. Minutes, BoD: May 3, 1947.

43. Hendee, Stankey, and Lucas, *Wilderness Management*, p. 38.

44. Brower to the author, February 20, 1987.

45. Nash, *Wilderness and the American Mind*, p. 5.

46. Hendee, Stankey, and Lucas, *Wilderness Management*, p. 38.

47. Robinson, *The Forest Service*, p. 280.

48. "Wilderness: A Squandered Heritage: a Statement on Wilderness Policy Prepared by the Sierra Club," November 27, 1948, *Sierra Club Archives*, Bradley papers, carton 118, file: Wilderness.

49. Brower, ed., *Wildlands in Our Civilization*, contains selected speeches from wilderness conferences and the summaries of the first five biennial wilderness conferences, 1949–1957.

50. Livermore in Brower, ed., *Wildlands in Our Civilization*, p. 140.

51. Hendee, Stankey, and Lucas, *Wilderness Management*, pp. 15–21.

52. Robinson in Brower, ed., *Wildlands in Our Civilization*, pp. 146, 147.

53. Zahniser in Brower, ed., *Wildlands in Our Civilization*, p. 136; Sumner in ibid., p. 135.

54. Richard M. Leonard, "Mountaineer, Lawyer, Environmentalist," interview conducted by Susan R. Schrepfer, Regional Oral History Office, the Bancroft Library, Berkeley, 1975, pp. 409, 410.

55. A. T. Spencer in Brower, ed., *Wildlands in Our Civilization*, p. 140.

56. Livermore in Brower, ed., *Wildlands in Our Civilization*, pp. 140–141.

57. Brower in *Wildlands in Our Civilization*, p. 52.

58. Spencer in Brower, ed., *Wildlands in Our Civilization*, p. 141.

59. Zahniser in Brower, ed., *Wildlands in Our Civilization*, p. 155.

60. Pesonen in Brower, ed., *Wildlands in Our Civilization*, p. 140.

61. Russell in Brower, ed., *Wildlands in Our Civilization*, pp. 133, 145.

62. Scoyen in Brower, ed., *Wildlands in Our Civilization*, p. 151.

63. Gunsky in Brower, ed., *Wildlands in Our Civilization*, p. 150.

64. Losh in Brower, ed., *Wildlands in Our Civilization*, pp. 149, 150.

65. Brower in *Wildlands in Our Civilization*, p. 53.

66. Murie in Brower, ed., *Wildlands in Our Civilization*, p. 165.

67. Minutes, BoD: May 5, 1951; Brower, ed., *Wildlands in Our Civilization*, pp. 163, 164.

68. Zahniser in Brower, ed., *Wildlands in Our Civilization*, p. 47.

69. Michael McCloskey, "Sierra Club Executive Director: The Evolving Club and the Environmental Movement, 1961–1981," interview conducted by Susan R. Schrepfer, Regional Oral History Office, the Bancroft Library, Berkeley, 1983, p. 8.

70. Leonard in Brower, ed., *Wildlands in Our Civilization*, p. 175.

71. Russell in Brower, ed., *Wildlands in Our Civilization*, p. 133.

72. C. Nelson Hackett, "Lasting Impressions of the Early Sierra Club," interview conducted by Josephine Harding, Sierra Club History Committee, San Francisco, 1975, p. 21.

73. David R. Brower, "Environmental Activist, Publicist, and Prophet," interview conducted by Susan R. Schrepfer, Regional Oral History Office, the Bancroft Library, Berkeley, 1980, p. 55.

74. "Yosemite versus Mass Man," *SCB* 37 (October 1952), pp. 3–8.

75. Bernard DeVoto, "Let's Close the National Parks," *Harper's*, October 1953, pp. 49–52.

76. Conrad L. Wirth, *Parks, Politics, and the People* (Norman: University of Oklahoma Press, 1980), p. 237.

77. Minutes, BoD: January 7–8, 1956.

78. Wirth, *Parks, Politics, and the People*, pp. 262–267.

79. Minutes, BoD: January 7–8, 1956.

80. "Mission 66 . . . A Promise For The Parks," *SCB* 41 (April 1956), pp. 3–4.

81. Ansel Adams, "The Meaning of the National Parks," reprinted in *Celebrating the American Earth* (Washington, D.C.: The Wilderness Society, n.d.), p. 5.

82. Minutes, BoD: January 7–8, 1956.

83. Ansel Adams to David Brower, February 15, 1956, *Sierra Club Archives*, Bradley papers, carton 118, file: Wilderness.

84. "A Program for Yosemite Valley," *SCB* 42 (January 1957), pp. 14–16.

85. Adams in Minutes, BoD: May 4, 1957; Olaus Murie to Trustees of the National Parks Association, quoted in Minutes, BoD: May 4, 1957; Roland K. Griffith to Conrad Wirth, April 25, 1956.

86. Ansel Adams to Harold Bradley, August 30, 1957, *Sierra Club Archives*, Bradley papers, carton 116, file: Tioga Road.

87. Ansel Adams to Harold Bradley, July 12, 1958, *Sierra Club Archives*, Bradley papers, carton 116, file: Tioga Road.

88. Ansel Adams to Fred Seaton, Sinclair Weeks, and Conrad Wirth, July 7, 1958, *Sierra Club Archives*, Bradley papers, carton 116, file: Tioga Road.

89. Memorandum, Harold Bradley to BoD, July 18, 1958, *Sierra Club Archives*, Bradley papers, carton 116, file: Tioga Road.

90. Memorandum, Alexander Hildebrand to Ansel Adams, Lawrence Mirriam, John Preston, Harold Bradley, and David Brower, July 16, 1958, *Sierra Club Archives*, Bradley papers, carton 116, file: Tioga Road.

91. Ansel Adams to Alexander Hildebrand, July 19, 1958, *Sierra Club Archives*, Bradley papers, carton 116, file: Tioga Road.

92. Minutes, BoD: November 8, 1958.

93. Conversation reported in Wirth, *Parks, Politics, and the People*, p. 359.

Chapter 4

1. Elmo R. Richardson, *Dams, Parks, and Politics: Resource Development and Preservation in the Truman-Eisenhower Era* (Lexington: University Press of Kentucky, 1973), p. 58.

2. Quoted in Richard M. Leonard, "Mountaineer, Lawyer, Environmentalist," interview conducted by Susan R. Schrepfer, Regional Oral History Office, the Bancroft Library, Berkeley, 1975, p. 107.

3. On the history of American reclamation, see Donald Worster, *Rivers of Empire: Water, Aridity, and the Growth of the American West* (New York: Pantheon Books, 1985); and Marc Reisner, *Cadillac Desert: The American West and Its Disappearing Water* (New York: Viking, 1986).

4. Leonard, "Mountaineer," p. 134.

5. E. T. Scoyen, "Kilowatts in the Wilderness," address before the Annual Banquet of the Sierra Club, May 3, 1952, in *SCB* 37 (December 1952), pp. 75–83.

6. Richardson, *Dams, Parks, and Politics*, p. 52.

7. David R. Brower, "Environmental Activist, Publicist, and Prophet," interview conducted by Susan R. Schrepfer, Regional Oral History Office, the Bancroft Library, Berkeley, 1980, pp. 52, 53.

8. Margaret Murie, "A Matter of Choice," *Living Wilderness* 15 (Autumn 1950), pp. 11–14.

9. Leonard, "Mountaineer," p. 130.

10. Lewis Clark, "Down the Narrows of the Virgin River," *SCB* 36 (May 1951), pp. 6–13; Steven Bradley, "Folbots Through Dinosaur," *SCB* 37 (December 1952), pp. 1–8.

11. Gregory C. Crampton, *Standing Up Country: The Canyon Lands of Utah and Arizona* (New York: Knopf, 1964), p. 4.

12. Elmo R. Richardson, "Federal Park Policy in Utah: The Escalante National Monument Controversy of 1935–1940," *Utah Historical Quarterly* 33 (Spring 1965), pp. 110–133.

13. Memorandum to BoD, November 26, 1952, *Sierra Club Archives*, Brower papers, carton 225, file: S.C. Exec. Dir.

14. Brower, "Environmental Activist," p. 9.

15. Minutes, BoD: December 5, 1952 and May 2, 1953. See also *SCB* 38 (January 1953), p. i.

16. Memorandum to BoD, November 26, 1952, *Sierra Club Archives*, Brower papers, carton 225, file: S.C. Exec. Dir.

17. Ibid.

18. Minutes, BoD: December 15, 1951.

19. Minutes, BoD: June 3–7, 1953.

20. David R. Brower, "The Sierra Club: National, Regional, or State," in Minutes, BoD: October 17, 1953.

21. Minutes, BoD: December 2, 1950. This was the first chapter organized outside California.

22. Minutes, BoD: October 17, 1953.

23. Leonard, "Mountaineer," p. 156.

24. Minutes, BoD: August 16, 1953.

25. Minutes, BoD: December 12, 1953 and February 27, 1954.

26. Minutes, BoD: September 2, 1951.

27. Minutes, BoD: May 24, 1953.

28. Martin Litton, "Sierra Club Director and Uncompromising Preservationist, 1950s–1970s," interview conducted by Ann Lage, Regional Oral History Office, the Bancroft Library, Berkeley, 1982, p. 3.

29. Litton, "Sierra Club Director," p. 22.

30. Minutes, BoD: August 16, 1953.

31. Litton, quoted by Brower in letter to "Dinosaur Coopera-

tors," October 6, 1953, *Sierra Club Archives*, Bradley papers, carton 114, file: Dinosaur.

32. David R. Brower, Introduction to Litton, "Sierra Club Director," p. i.

33. Luna Leopold to David Brower, August 26, 1953, in *Sierra Club Archives*, Bradley papers, carton 114, file: Dinosaur. Brower remembers Luna Leopold telling him, "Stick to your birdwatching." Brower to the author, March 11, 1987.

34. "Confidential," n.d., report, enclosed with David Brower to "Dinosaur Cooperators," October 23, 1953, *Sierra Club Archives*, Bradley papers, carton 114, file: Dinosaur.

35. Minutes, BoD: December 23, 1953.

36. For the continuing developments in the Dinosaur campaign, see *SCB* 39 (January, February, and March 1954); Brower's testimony is reprinted in "Preserving Dinosaur Unimpaired," *SCB* 39 (June 1954), pp. 1–10.

37. *SCB* 39 (March 1954), p. 30.

38. Minutes, BoD: December 24, 1954.

39. Minutes, BoD: May 1, 1954.

40. Brower is quoted in Owen Stratton and Phillip Sirotkin, *The Echo Park Controversy*, Inter-University Case Program, Cases in Public Administration and Policy Formation, no. 46 (University, Ala.: University of Alabama Press, 1959), p. 70.

41. Minutes, BoD: October 16, 1954.

42. Leonard, "Mountaineer," p. 176.

43. Minutes, BoD: November 21, 1954.

44. Ibid.

45. Brower, "Environmental Activist," p. 137.

46. Leonard, "Mountaineer," p. 144.

47. Minutes, BoD: November 21, 1954.

48. *SCB* 40 (January 1955), pp. 3–5.

49. Minutes, BoD: December 27, 1955.

50. Minutes, BoD: October 15, 1955.

51. Minutes, BoD: December 27, 1955.

52. "Footnote to Hetch Hetchy," *SCB* 39 (June 1954), pp. 13, 14.

53. Brower, "Environmental Activist," pp. 128, 129.

54. Wallace Stegner, ed., *This Is Dinosaur: Echo Park Country and Its Magic Rivers* (New York: Knopf, 1955). Litton's role as ghost-

writer is from a conversation between Litton and the author, March 1986.

55. See Bernard DeVoto, "The West Against Itself," reprinted in *SCB* 32 (May 1947), pp. 36—42.

56. "The War Between the Rough Riders and the Bird Watchers," *SCB* 44 (May 1959), pp. 4—11; "Wilderness Letter," 1960, reprinted as "Coda: Wilderness Letter" in Wallace Stegner, *The Sound of Mountain Water* (New York: Dutton, 1980).

57. Wallace Stegner, "The Marks of Human Passage," in Stegner, ed., *This Is Dinosaur*, pp. 3—17.

58. Ibid., p. 15.

59. Ibid., pp. 14, 17.

60. *The Denver Post*, October 31, 1955; copy in the *Sierra Club Archives*, Bradley papers, carton 114, file: Dinosaur.

61. Roderick Nash, *Wilderness and the American Mind*, 3d ed. (New Haven: Yale University Press, 1982), p. 219.

62. Richardson, *Dams, Parks, and Politics*, p. 201.

63. Watkins' words and Stegner's reply are in Stegner, "The War Between the Rough Riders and the Bird Watchers," p. 41.

64. Wallace Stegner and Richard W. Etulain, *Conversations with Wallace Stegner on Western History and Literature* (Salt Lake City: University of Utah Press, 1983), p. 175.

65. David Brower, "*Confidential* to Dinosaur Coopters," October 23, 1953, with enclosures, *Sierra Club Archives*, Bradley Papers, carton 114, file: Dinosaur. See also Stratton and Sirotkin, *The Echo Park Controversy*, pp. 79—82.

66. Leonard, "Mountaineer," p. 125.

67. Raymond J. Sherwin, "Conservationist, Judge, and Sierra Club President," interview conducted by Ann Lage, Regional Oral History Office, the Bancroft Library, Berkeley, 1982, pp. 83, 84.

68. Stegner and Etulain, *Conversations with Wallace Stegner*, p. 175.

69. Peter Wiley and Robert Gottlieb, *Empires in the Sun: The Rise of the New West* (New York: G. P. Putnam's Sons, 1982), p. 37.

70. Brower, "Environmental Activist," p. 122.

71. Leonard, "Mountaineer," p. 113.

72. Ibid., pp. 123, 124.

73. Bestor Robinson, "Thoughts on Conservation and the Sierra

Club," interview conducted by Susan R. Schrepfer, Sierra Club History Committee, San Francisco, 1974, p. 23.

74. Leonard, "Mountaineer," pp. 120, 121.

75. Alexander Hildebrand, "Sierra Club Leader and Critic: Perspective on Club Growth, Scope, and Tactics, 1950s–1970s," interview conducted by Ann Lage, Regional Oral History Office, the Bancroft Library, Berkeley, 1982, p. 116.

76. Stegner and Etulain, *Conversations with Wallace Stegner*, p. 169.

77. Karl W. Luckert, *Rainbow Bridge and Navajo Mountain Religion*, vol. 1 of American Tribal Religions series (Flagstaff: Museum of Northern Arizona, 1977), p. 3.

78. Ibid., p. 24.

79. Brower, "Environmental Activist," p. 131.

80. Litton, "Sierra Club Director," p. 63.

81. Brower, "Environmental Activist," p. 142.

82. Ibid., p. 136.

83. Richardson, *Dams, Parks, and Politics*, p. 98.

84. John Muir, *The Yosemite* (Boston: Houghton Mifflin, 1912), p. 260; Brower, "Preserving Dinosaur Unimpaired," p. 5.

85. Muir, *The Yosemite*, p. 262.

86. Brower, "Preserving Dinosaur Unimpaired," p. 9.

87. Leonard, "Mountaineer," pp. 112, 115.

88. Brower, "Environmental Activist," p. 119.

89. Muir, *The Yosemite*, p. 262.

90. Leonard, "Mountaineer," pp. 337, 338.

91. Brower, "Environmental Activist," pp. 123, 130–133.

92. Leonard, "Mountaineer," p. 338.

93. Brower, "Environmental Activist," p. 133.

94. Ibid., p. 88.

95. David R. Brower, "Report to the Annual Organization Meeting," May 2, 1957, in Minutes, BoD: May 4, 1957.

Chapter 5

1. Grant McConnell, "The Conservation Movement—Past and Present," *Western Political Quarterly* 7 (March 1954), p. 464; Susan R. Schrepfer, "Perspectives on Conservation: Sierra Club Strategies

in Mineral King," *Journal of Forest History* 20 (October 1976), pp. 176–190.

2. Susan R. Schrepfer, *The Fight to Save the Redwoods: A History of Environmental Reform 1917–1978* (Madison: University of Wisconsin Press, 1983), p. 26.

3. Bestor Robinson, "Thoughts on Conservation and the Sierra Club," interview conducted by Susan R. Schrepfer, Sierra Club History Committee, San Francisco, 1974, p. 1.

4. John Ise, *Our National Park Policy: A Critical History* (Baltimore: The Johns Hopkins Press, 1961), p. 643.

5. Conrad L. Wirth, *Parks, Politics, and the People* (Norman: University of Oklahoma Press, 1980), p. 21; Harold K. Steen, *The U.S. Forest Service: A History* (Seattle: University of Washington, 1976), p. 278.

6. Ise, *Our National Park Policy*, p. 557.

7. Steen, *The U.S. Forest Service*, pp. 278–295.

8. Wirth, *Parks, Politics, and the People*, p. 358.

9. Steen, *The U.S. Forest Service*, p. 303.

10. Conversation with the author, October 24, 1985.

11. Michael McCloskey, "Sierra Club Executive Director: The Evolving Club and the Environmental Movement, 1961–1981," interview conducted by Susan R. Schrepfer, Regional Oral History Office, the Bancroft Library, Berkeley, 1983, p. 2; Harold K. Steen, *The U.S. Forest Service*, p. 156.

12. John H. Hendee, George H. Stankey, and Robert C. Lucas, *Wilderness Management*, Miscellaneous Publication no. 1365 (Washington, D.C.: U.S. Forest Service, Department of Agriculture, October 1978), p. 61.

13. Olaus Murie to William Parke, July 26, 1951, *Sierra Club Archives*, Wayburn papers, carton 187, file: Three Sisters.

14. Minutes, BoD: September 2, 1951.

15. McCloskey, "Sierra Club Executive Director," pp. 2, 3.

16. Ibid., p. 13.

17. David Brower remembers "wilderness on the rocks" as having been coined by Simons; correspondence with author, February 20, 1987.

18. Michael McCloskey, Foreword to Nancy Wood, *Clearcut: The Deforestation of America*, a "Battlebook" (San Francisco: Sierra Club Books, 1971), pp. 7, 8.

19. Ibid., pp. 8, 9.

20. McCloskey, "Sierra Club Executive Director," p. 14.

21. Edgar Wayburn, "Sierra Club Statesman, Leader of the Parks and Wilderness Movement: Gaining Protection for Alaska, the Redwoods, and Golden Gate Parklands," interview conducted by Ann Lage and Susan R. Schrepfer, Regional Oral History Office, the Bancroft Library, Berkeley, 1985, p. 49.

22. Ibid., p. 176.

23. Ibid., p. 22.

24. Ibid., p. 2.

25. Ibid., pp. 23, 24.

26. Ibid., p. 24.

27. Ibid., p. 25.

28. Minutes, BoD: May 3, 1952.

29. "Now If Ever," September 4, 1954, *Sierra Club Archives*, Charlotte Mauk papers, carton 145, file: Three Sisters.

30. Richard M. Leonard, "Mountaineer, Lawyer, Environmentalist," interview conducted by Susan R. Schrepfer, Regional Oral History Office, the Bancroft Library, Berkeley, 1975, p. 244.

31. Leonard, "Mountaineer," p. 245.

32. Richard Leonard to Pat Goldsworthy, January 14, 1955, *Sierra Club Archives*, Wayburn papers, carton 187, file: U.S.F.S.

33. Brower/McArdle correspondence, *Sierra Club Archives*, Art Blake papers, carton 112, file: Three Sisters Wilderness.

34. David R. Brower, "Environmental Activist, Publicist, and Prophet," interview conducted by Susan R. Schrepfer, Regional Oral History Office, the Bancroft Library, Berkeley, 1980, pp. 43, 149.

35. "Forest Service Conference on Wilderness: Excerpt from Notes by David R. Brower," March 13, 1953, *Sierra Club Archives*, Art Blake papers, carton 112, file: Three Sisters Wilderness.

36. Brower to McArdle, October 21, 1955, *Sierra Club Archives*, Art Blake papers, carton 112, file: Three Sisters Wilderness.

37. McArdle to Brower, November 8, 1955, *Sierra Club Archives*, Art Blake papers, carton 112, file: Three Sisters Wilderness.

38. Brower to McArdle, n.d., reply to McArdle's letter of November 8, 1955, *Sierra Club Archives*, Art Blake papers, carton 112, file: Three Sisters Wilderness; Brower's italics.

39. "Sierra Club—Confidential Draft Only," n.d., *Sierra Club Ar-*

chives, Wayburn papers, carton 187, file: Three Sisters. This document written by Hal Roth gives the history of the Deadman controversy. For another version of the history, see Hal Roth to Ezra Taft Benson, April 15, 1955, Martin Litton personal papers, on loan to author, file: U.S.F.S.

40. On Brower's disillusionment, see Brower, "Environmental Activist," pp. 83–85.

41. Minutes, Ex Comm: August 16, 1953.

42. Brower, "Environmental Activist," p. 84.

43. McArdle's official statement, issued December 20, 1954, is excerpted in "Sierra Club—Confidential Draft Only," n.d., *Sierra Club Archives*, Wayburn papers, carton 187, file: Three Sisters, and more completely in Hal Roth to Ezra Taft Benson, April 15, 1955, Martin Litton personal papers, on loan to author, file: U.S.F.S.

44. Brower, "Environmental Activist," p. 85.

45. "Sierra Club—Confidential Draft Only," n.d., pp. 14, 15, *Sierra Club Archives*, Wayburn papers, carton 187, file: Three Sisters; brackets in original.

46. Ibid., p. 1.

47. Brower, "Environmental Activist," p. 85.

48. Ibid., p. 84.

49. Steen, *The U.S. Forest Service*, pp. 302, 303.

50. Wayburn, "Sierra Club Statesman," pp. 25, 26.

51. Leonard, "Mountaineer," p. 340.

52. Quoted in "Sierra Club—Confidential Draft Only," n.d., p. 12, *Sierra Club Archives*, Wayburn papers, carton 187, file: Three Sisters.

53. Wayburn's notes in "Sierra Club—Confidential Draft Only," n.d., *Sierra Club Archives*, Wayburn papers, carton 187, file: Three Sisters.

54. Minutes, BoD: June 20, 1954.

55. Leonard, "Mountaineer," p. 340.

56. Ibid., pp. 339–342.

57. Ibid., p. 271.

58. Ibid., pp. 80, 271.

59. Ibid., pp. 242, 243.

60. Brower, Environmental Activist, pp. 181, 193.

61. Leonard to Arthur Carhart, January 7, 1948, *Sierra Club Archives*, Charlotte Mauk papers, carton 145, file: U.S. B.L.M.

62. Leonard, "Mountaineer," p. 340.

63. Steen, *The U.S. Forest Service*, p. 301.

64. Alexander Hildebrand, "Sierra Club Leader and Critic: Perspectives on Club Growth, Scope, and Tactics, 1950s–1970s," interview conducted by Ann Lage, Regional Oral History Office, the Bancroft Library, Berkeley, 1982, p. 18.

65. Hal Roth to Ezra Taft Benson, April 15, 1955, with Martin Litton's notes, Martin Litton personal papers, file: U.S.F.S.

66. McArdle to Albright, April 7, 1955, *Sierra Club Archives*, Wayburn papers, carton 174b, file: Deadman.

67. Albright to McArdle, April 15, 1955, *Sierra Club Archives*, Wayburn papers, carton 174b, file: Deadman.

68. McArdle to Albright, April 7, 1955, *Sierra Club Archives*, Wayburn papers, carton 174b, file: Deadman.

69. M. M. Barnum to Edgar Wayburn, May 26, 1955, with Wayburn's notes dated May 31, 1955, initialed by R. M. L., *Sierra Club Archives*, Wayburn papers, carton 174b, file: Deadman.

70. "REPORT DUE DECEMBER 31, 1955," with Wayburn's notes dated October 17, 1956, *Sierra Club Archives*, Wayburn papers, carton 174b, file: Deadman.

71. Minutes, BoD: November 20, 1955.

72. Memo from Brower to Hildebrand, Bradley, Wayburn, June 27, 1956, *Sierra Club Archives*, Wayburn papers, carton 174b, file: Deadman.

73. Minutes, Ex Comm: July 11, 1956.

74. "The Fate of Deadman Creek," *SCB* 41 (October 1956), pp. 5–9.

75. Peggy Wayburn, "Butano Story: An Object Lesson for the Future," *SCB* 41 (January 1956), pp. 10–12.

76. Minutes, BoD: September 22, 1956.

77. James P. Gilligan, "The Development of Policy and Administration of Forest Service Primitive and Wilderness Areas in the Western United States" (Ph.D. diss., University of Michigan, 1954).

78. Brower, "Environmental Activist," p. 64.

79. Minutes, BoD: January 7, 1956.

80. *SCB* 41 (December 1956), pp. 1–10, 73–84.

81. *SCB* 41 (December 1956), pp. 24–31.

82. *SCB* 42 (June 1957).

83. *SCB* 42 (June 1957), pp. 78, 79.

84. *SCB* 42 (June 1957), pp. 79—81.

85. A. Starker Leopold, "Wilderness and Culture," in David R. Brower, ed., *Wildlands in Our Civilization* (San Francisco: Sierra Club, 1964), pp. 81—85.

86. Stephen Fox, *John Muir and His Legacy: The American Conservation Movement* (Boston: Little, Brown and Co., 1981), pp. 307—313.

87. William L. Thomas, ed., *Man's Role in Changing the Face of the Earth* (Chicago: University of Chicago Press, 1956).

88. Lowell Sumner, "Are Beavers Too Busy?" in Brower, ed., *Wildlands in Our Civilization*, p. 86.

89. Thomas, ed., *Man's Role in Changing the Face of the Earth*, p. 1,152.

90. "Are Beavers Too Busy?" was first published in *SCB* 42 (June 1957), p. 19.

91. Ansel Adams and Nancy Newhall, *This Is the American Earth* (San Francisco: Sierra Club, 1960), p. 62; see also *SCB* 42 (June 1957), p. 80.

92. Brower remembers presenting this slogan to a Democratic Party platform committee in Denver in the mid 1950s. Correspondence with the author, February 20, 1987.

93. See Minutes, BoD: February 18, 1957 and March 19, 1957; "Fifth Wilderness Conference Backs Recreation, Wilderness Proposals," March 20, 1957, *Sierra Club Archives*, Brower papers, carton 229, file: Wilderness Bill, 1957.

94. Brower to Ervin L. Peterson, April 12, 1957, *Sierra Club Archives*, Brower papers, carton 226, file: Three Sisters.

95. "A Conservationist's Questions about National Forests," April 5, 1957, *Sierra Club Archives*, Brower papers, carton 229, file: Wilderness Bill, 1957.

96. "Sierra Club Official Urges New Look at National Forest Uses," April 5, 1957, *Sierra Club Archives*, Wayburn papers, carton 187, file: Three Sisters.

97. *Sierra Club Handbook* (San Francisco: Sierra Club, 1967), p. 44.

98. Leonard to Pat Goldsworthy, January 14, 1955, *Sierra Club Archives*, Wayburn papers, carton 187, file: Three Sisters.

99. Minutes, BoD: November 20, 1955.

100. Wayburn, "Sierra Club Statesman," pp. 34, 35.

101. "The Cascade Wilderness," *SCB* 41 (December 1956), pp. 24–31. See also Brower, "Scenic Resources for the Future" and "Reviewing Our Needs for Scenic Resources," *SCB* 41 (December 1956), pp. 1–10, 73–84.

102. Simons to Zahniser, ca. November 1956, *Sierra Club Archives*, Simons papers, carton 164, file: Correspondence, 1956–1957.

103. Simons to Murie, November 7, 1956, and Murie to Simons, November 16, 1956, *Sierra Club Archives*, Simons papers, carton 164, file: Correspondence, 1956–1957.

104. McConnell to Simons, November 1956, *Sierra Club Archives*, Simons papers, carton 164, file; Correspondence, 1956–1957.

105. *SCB* 42 (June 1957), p. 17.

106. "Arthur H. Blake," *SCB* 42 (June 1957), pp. 54, 55.

107. Minutes, BoD: January 1, 1957.

108. "Confidential," February 3, 1957, addressed to Pat Goldsworthy, Phil Zalesky, Polly Dyer, Karl Onthank, Howard Zahniser, Fred M. Packard, Irving Clark, Edgar Wayburn, and Grant McConnell, *Sierra Club Archives*, Wayburn papers, carton 179a, file: North Cascades.

109. "What Kind of Protection for the North Cascades?" February 27, 1957, *Sierra Club Archives*, Wayburn papers, carton 179a, file: North Cascades.

110. D. Simon to J. H. Stone, April 6, 1957, *Sierra Club Archives*, Simons papers, carton 164, file: Correspondence 1956–1957.

111. For Stone's reputation in Sierra Club circles, see McCloskey, "Sierra Club Executive Director," p. 17.

112. Minutes, BoD: May 24, 1957.

113. Brower to McConnell, March 13, 1958, *Sierra Club Archives*, Wayburn papers, carton 179a, file: North Cascades.

114. Simons to Brower, March 29, 1958, *Sierra Club Archives*, Wayburn papers, carton 179a, file: North Cascades.

115. Simons to Wayburn, April 9, 1958, *Sierra Club Archives*, Wayburn papers, carton 179a, file: North Cascades.

116. Ibid.

117. McConnell to Brower, May 15, 1958, *Sierra Club Archives*, Wayburn papers, carton 179a, file: North Cascades.

118. Simons to McConnell, May 6, 1958, *Sierra Club Archives*, Simons papers, carton 164, file: Correspondence April–May 1958.

119. Simons to McConnell, May 15, 1958, *Sierra Club Archives*, Simons papers, carton 164, file: Correspondence April–May 1958.

120. McConnell to Simons, May 15, 1958, *Sierra Club Archives*, Simons papers, carton 164, file: Correspondence April–May 1958.

121. Simons to McConnell, June 4, 1958, *Sierra Club Archives*, Simons papers, carton 164, file: Correspondence June 1958–December 1959.

122. "To North Cascade Cooperators . . . ," July 16, 1958, *Sierra Club Archives*, Wayburn papers, carton 179a, file: North Cascades.

123. See Minutes, Sierra Club Conservation Committee: June 19, 1958; Simons to McConnell, June 23, 1958, *Sierra Club Archives*, Simons papers, carton 164, file: Correspondence June 1958–December 1959. This letter is the source of quotes below.

124. Charles A. Gillett of the American Forest Institute, quoted by Steen, *The U.S. Forest Service*, p. 295.

125. See Brower, "A Conservationist's Questions about National Forests," April 5, 1957, *Sierra Club Archives*, Brower papers, carton 229, file: Wilderness Bill, 1957.

126. Steen, *The U.S. Forest Service*, p. 305.

127. Executive Director's Report, p. 12, Minutes, BoD: May 4, 1957.

128. Peggy and Edgar Wayburn, "Where Should Management Stop?" *SCB* 43 (January 1958), pp. 3–6; David R. Brower, "Straight Thinking," *SCB* 43 (January 1958), p. 2; Frederick Eissler, "Machines Violate Wilderness Philosophy," *SCB* 43 (January 1958), pp. 7, 8.

129. "Understanding and Management," *SCB* 43 (January 1958), p. 20.

130. "What Can We Do for Wilderness?" *SCB* 43 (April 1958), p. 6.

131. "Arthur H. Blake," *SCB* 42 (June 1957), p. 54.

132. Roderick Nash, *Wilderness and the American Mind*, 3d ed. (New Haven: Yale University Press, 1982), p. 222.

133. See *Sierra Club Archives*, Brower papers, cartons 228, 229, 230.

134. J. Michael McCloskey, "The Multiple Use–Sustained Yield Act of 1960," *Oregon Law Review* 41 (December 1961), pp. 53, 54.

135. Brower, "Environmental Activist," p. 91.

136. *SCB* 44 (February 1959), p. 10.

137. Nathan C. Clark, "Sierra Club Leader, Outdoorsman, and Engineer," interview conducted by Richard Searle, Sierra Club History Committee, San Francisco, 1977, p. 69.

138. "Wilderness Conference," *SCB* 44 (April 1959), pp. 10–14.

139. "Wilderness Conference," *SCB* 44 (April 1959), p. 12.

140. Daniel B. Beard, "Plants and Animals in Natural Communities," in *The Meaning of Wilderness to Science*, Proceedings of the 6th Wilderness Conference, 1959, ed. David R. Brower (San Francisco: Sierra Club, 1960), pp. 5, 6.

141. Caption to photograph of the Galapagos, *SCB* 52 (October 1967), p. 21.

142. Minutes, BoD: May 24, 1959.

143. "Confidential to Board of Directors," June 19, 1959, *Sierra Club Archives*, Brower papers, carton 226, file: U.S. Forest Service.

144. Minutes, BoD: July 4, 1959.

145. Brower to Nathan Clark, August 14, 1959, *Sierra Club Archives*, Mauk papers, carton 145, file: U.S.N.P.S.

146. Clark to Brower, August 20, 1959, *Sierra Club Archives*, Mauk papers, carton 145, file: U.S.N.P.S.; conversation of author with Nathan Clark, December 5, 1985.

147. Clark to Brower, August 20, 1959, *Sierra Club Archives*, Mauk papers, carton 145, file: U.S.N.P.S.

148. Grant McConnell, "The Multiple-Use Concept in Forest Service Policy," *SCB* 44 (October 1959), pp. 14–28; David R. Simons, "These Are the Shining Mountains," *SCB* 44 (October 1959), pp. 1–13.

149. "The Silent Procession," subtext for Phillip Hyde photographs, *SCB* 44 (October 1959), between pages 4 and 5.

150. Minutes, BoD: December 5, 1959.

151. For the so-called Gag Rule and the board discussion, see Minutes, BoD: December 5, 1959.

152. Wayburn, "Sierra Club Statesman," p. 290.

153. Brower, "Environmental Activist," p. 156.

154. Ibid., p. 154.

155. Phillip S. Berry, draft interview conducted by Ann Lage, Regional Oral History Office, the Bancroft Library, Berkeley, n.d., pp. 11, 13.

156. Berry, draft interview, pp. 15, 16.

157. Brower, "Environmental Activist," p. 154.

158. Clark, "Sierra Club Leader," pp. 69, 70; Minutes, Ex Comm: June 18, 1960.

159. Leonard, "Mountaineer," p. 144.

160. Minutes, BoD: July 22, 1962. See also Sierra Club, *Outdoor Newsletter* no. 2 (May 29, 1961).

161. Berry, draft interview, p. 73.

162. Steen, *The U.S. Forest Service*, p. 306.

163. *SCB* 45 (March 1960), back cover.

164. *SCB* 44 (April–May 1960), pp. 3–7.

165. Minutes, BoD: May 7, 1960.

166. "May Board Meetings," *SCB* 45 (June 1960), p. 2.

167. Clark to Murray, May 11, 1960, published in *SCB* 45 (June 1960), pp. 2, 3.

168. "Dear Friend of Conservation," May 13, 1960, *Sierra Club Archives*, Mauk papers, carton 144, file: Sierra Club: Dave Brower.

169. Steen, *The U.S. Forest Service*, p. 307.

170. Minutes, BoD: September 18, 1960, October 15, 1960.

171. Robinson to Clark, September 23, 1960, in Clark personal papers, on loan to author.

172. Minutes, Ex Comm: June 18, 1960; Minutes, BoD: September 18, 1960.

173. Minutes, BoD: September 18, 1960.

174. Minutes, BoD: May 24, 1959, December 5–6, 1959.

175. Minutes, BoD: July 21, 1959.

176. Brower, "Environmental Activist," p. 96.

177. Sierra Club, *Outdoor Newsletter* no. 6 (August 22, 1960); the cover letter is included in *Sierra Club Archives*, Wayburn papers, carton 188, file: U.S.F.S. See also Steen, *The U.S. Forest Service*, pp. 309, 310.

178. The outdoor newsletters are listed in "Rainbow Bridge and the Quicksands of Time," *Outdoor Newsletter* vol. 2, no. 1 (May 29, 1961), p. 2. A copy is in the author's possession.

179. Steen, *The U.S. Forest Service*, p. 309; Richard McArdle, in *Proceedings of the Fifth World Forestry Congress* vol. 1 (1962), pp. 143–145.

180. McArdle to Clark, October 28, 1960, in correspondence on *Outdoor Newsletter* no. 6, collected in "Controversial Forest Service

Action with Regard to Potential Parks," *Sierra Club Archives*, Wayburn papers, carton 188, file: U.S.F.S.

181. Brower to McArdle, November 1, 1960, in "Controversial Forest Service Action with Regard to Potential Parks," *Sierra Club Archives*, Wayburn papers, carton 188, file: U.S.F.S.

182. Henry Schmitz to Clark, September 12, 1960, in "Controversial Forest Service Action with Regard to Potential Parks," *Sierra Club Archives*, Wayburn papers, carton 188, file: U.S.F.S.

183. Robinson to Clark, November 2, 1960, in "Controversial Forest Service Action with Regard to Potential Parks," *Sierra Club Archives*, Wayburn papers, carton 188, file: U.S.F.S.

184. Clark to Robinson, November 11, 1960, *Sierra Club Archives*, Brower papers, carton 226, file: Forest Service.

185. "Notes on Forest Tactics," memo from Brower to BoD, October 12, 1960, *Sierra Club Archives*, Wayburn papers, carton 188, file: U.S.F.S.

186. McConnell to Brower, November 3, 1960, *Sierra Club Archives*, Brower papers, carton 226, file: U.S.F.S.

187. Ashley L. Schiff, "Innovative and Administrative Decision Making: The Conservation of Land Resources," *Administrative Science Quarterly* 11 (June 1966), p. 28; see also pp. 1–30.

188. McConnell to Clark, December 17, 1960, in "Controversial Forest Service Action with Regard to Potential Parks," *Sierra Club Archives*, Wayburn papers, carton 188, file: U.S.F.S.

189. Clark to McArdle, December 30, 1960, in "Controversial Forest Service Action with Regard to Potential Parks," *Sierra Club Archives*, Wayburn papers, carton 188, file: U.S.F.S.

190. Minutes, BoD: October 15, 1960.

191. Exhibit A, p. A-3, December 30, 1960, in "Controversial Forest Service Action with Regard to Potential Parks," *Sierra Club Archives*, Wayburn papers, carton 188, file: U.S.F.S.

192. Ibid., p. A-8.

193. Clark to McArdle, December 30, 1960, in "Controversial Forest Service Action with Regard to Potential Parks," *Sierra Club Archives*, Wayburn papers, carton 188, file: U.S.F.S.

194. Brower speech, University of Utah, December 5, 1985.

195. 1951 *Annual*, *SCB* 36 (May 1951), hardbound, dustcover copy.

196. 1960 *Annual*, *SCB* 45 (December 1960).

197. Frank A. Kittridge, "The Campaign for Kings Canyon National Park," *SCB* 45 (December 1960), pp. 32–46.

198. Holway R. Jones, introduction to Kittridge, "The Campaign for Kings Canyon National Park," *SCB* 45 (December 1960), pp. 32, 33.

199. "David Ralph Simons, 1936–1960," *SCB* 45 (December 1960), pp. 24, 25.

200. Enclosure in "To the Board of Directors," November 26, 1952, *Sierra Club Archives*, Brower papers, carton 225, file: Sierra Club Executive Director.

201. Adams memo to David Brower and others, November 19, 1956, *Sierra Club Archives*, Brower papers, carton 225, file: Sierra Club Committees, Pub. Com.

202. Memo, "Job Description," revised December 18, 1957, in Minutes, BoD: February 18, 1957.

203. Wallace Stegner, ed., *This Is Dinosaur: Echo Park Country and Its Magic Rivers* (1955; repr., Boulder: Roberts Rinehart, 1985), p. vi.

204. David R. Brower, "Francis P. Farquhar," *Not Man Apart* 4 (1974), p. 16.

205. Nancy Newhall, *Ansel Adams: A Biography. Volume 1: The Eloquent Light*, (San Francisco: Sierra Club Books, 1963), pp. 126, 164, 165.

206. Advertisement for Adams and Newhall, *This Is the American Earth*, in *SCB* 44 (November 1959), pp. 8, 9.

207. Adams and Newhall, *This Is The American Earth*, pp. i–ix.

208. David R. Brower, Foreword to *This Is The American Earth*, pp. xiii–xiv.

209. *This Is The American Earth*, p. 9.

210. Ibid., p. 18.

211. Ibid., p. 21.

212. Ibid., pp. 22, 23, 32.

213. Ibid., p. 62.

214. Ibid., p. 88.

215. Reviews; see *Sierra Club Archives*, Publications Scrapbooks, 7 vols.

216. Ansel Adams, *These We Inherit: The Parklands of America* (San Francisco: Sierra Club, 1962), pp. 13, 14.

217. "The War Between the Rough Riders and the Bird Watchers," *SCB* 44 (May 1959), pp. 4–11.

218. Pesonen to Stegner, June 15, 1960, *Sierra Club Archives*, Brower papers, carton 229, file: Wilderness. See also Wallace Stegner, "Saga of a Letter: The Geography of Hope," *Living Wilderness* (December 1980), pp. 12, 13.

219. First printed by the Club as "The Wilderness Idea [a letter]," in David R. Brower, ed., *Wilderness: America's Living Heritage* (San Francisco: Sierra Club, 1961), pp. 97–102; reprinted as "Coda: Wilderness Letter" in Wallace Stegner, *The Sound of Mountain Water* (New York: Dutton, 1980), pp. 245–253.

220. David Brower, Foreword to *In Wildness Is the Preservation of the World* (1962), p. 10.

221. Linda H. Graber, *Wilderness as Sacred Space* (Washington, D.C.: Association of American Geographers, 1976), pp. 60–74.

222. Joseph Wood Krutch, Introduction to *In Wildness Is the Preservation of the World*, p. 13.

223. Ibid., p. 15.

224. Fox, *John Muir and His Legacy*, pp. 229–233.

225. Paul Shepard, *Man in the Landscape: A Historic View of the Aesthetics of Nature* (New York: Knopf, 1967), pp. 265, 266.

226. Thoreau's words are reprinted in *In Wildness Is the Preservation of the World*. The body of the text in this book is not paginated.

227. Krutch, Introduction to *In Wildness Is the Preservation of the World*, p. 14.

228. Peter Wiley and Robert Gottlieb, *Empires in the Sun: The Rise of the New West* (New York: G. P. Putnam's Sons, 1982), pp. 35, 289, 290.

229. McCloskey, "Sierra Club Executive Director," pp. 14, 253.

230. Ibid., p. 11.

231. Ibid., p. 254.

232. Ibid., pp. 5, 6.

233. Ibid., p. 19.

234. Ibid., p. 7.

235. Ibid., p. 253.

Chapter 6

1. David R. Brower, ed., *Wilderness: America's Living Heritage*, Proceedings of the 7th Wilderness Conference, 1961 (San Francisco: Sierra Club, 1961), pp. 144, 145.

2. Wayburn in Brower, ed., *Wilderness: America's Living Heritage*, pp. 1, 2.

3. Douglas in Brower, ed., *Wilderness: America's Living Heritage*, pp. 13, 27, 166.

4. Udall in Brower, ed., *Wilderness: America's Living Heritage*, pp. 91–103.

5. McConnell in Brower, ed., *Wilderness: America's Living Heritage*, pp. 164, 165.

6. Raymond J. Sherwin, "Conservationist, Judge, and Sierra Club President," interview conducted by Ann Lage, Regional Oral History Office, the Bancroft Library, Berkeley, 1982, pp. 21–24; David R. Brower, "Environmental Activist, Publicist, and Prophet," interview conducted by Susan R. Schrepfer, Regional Oral History Office, Berkeley, 1980, p. 189.

7. See "Minority Opinion (Justice Douglas)," in Christopher D. Stone, *Should Trees Have Standing? Toward Legal Rights for Natural Objects* (Los Altos, Calif.: William Kaufman, 1964), pp. 73–82.

8. Brower, "Environmental Activist," p. 189.

9. John Fitzgerald Kennedy, "President's Message on Natural Resources," February 23, 1961, reprinted in *SCB* 46 (March 1961), p. 5. See also Brower, "Environmental Activist," pp. 97, 145.

10. Stewart L. Udall, "We Must Act NOW for More National Parks," reprinted from *Audubon Magazine* in *SCB* 46 (March 1961), pp. 4, 5.

11. Edgar Wayburn, "Sierra Club Statesman, Leader of the Parks and Wilderness Movement," interview conducted by Ann Lage and Susan R. Schrepfer, Regional Oral History Office, the Bancroft Library, Berkeley, 1985, p. 323.

12. "Udall and Freeman Make History at Four Corners," *SCB* 46 (September 1961), pp. 4–5.

13. "Forestry Hearings in Northwest," *SCB* 46 (December 1961), p. 3.

14. Michael McCloskey, "Sierra Club Executive Director: The Evolving Club and the Environmental Movement, 1961–1981," interview conducted by Susan R. Schrepfer, Regional Oral History Office, the Bancroft Library, Berkeley, 1983, p. 7.

15. Wallace Stegner, "The Artist as Environmental Advocate," interview conducted by Ann Lage, Regional Oral History Office, the Bancroft Library, Berkeley, 1982, p. 13.

16. Stewart L. Udall, *The Quiet Crisis* (New York: Holt, Rinehart, 1963).

17. Stegner, "The Artist," p. 14.

18. See Ronald A. Foresta, *America's National Parks and Their Keepers* (Washington, D.C.: Resources for the Future, 1984), p. 263.

19. Stegner, "The Artist," p. 121.

20. Brower, "Environmental Activist," p. 21.

21. Stegner, "The Artist," pp. 18, 21.

22. Krutch in Brower, ed., *Wilderness: America's Living Heritage*, pp. 72, 73.

23. Wurster in Brower, ed., *Wilderness: America's Living Heritage*, p. 117.

24. Luten in Brower, ed., *Wilderness: America's Living Heritage*, p. 179.

25. Wayburn, "Sierra Club Statesman," pp. 179–181.

26. Leonard to the author, September 22, 1987; Wayburn, "Sierra Club Statesman," pp. 181–183. During this period Leonard was a close friend of Adams and was Adams' attorney.

27. Michael McCloskey points out that the executive director was made chief executive officer of the Sierra Club in 1982. McCloskey to the author, January 1, 1987.

28. Wayburn, "Sierra Club Statesman," p. 186.

29. Ibid., p. 189. For a chronological list of Sierra Club officers until 1967, see *Sierra Club Handbook* (San Francisco: Sierra Club, 1967), pp. 57–60.

30. Wayburn, "Sierra Club Statesman," p. 202.

31. Ibid., p. 193.

32. Brower, "Environmental Activist," pp. 334, 335.

33. Wayburn, "Sierra Club Statesman," p. 206.

34. Minutes, BoD: September 7, 1963.

35. Minutes, Ex Comm: May 20, 1961; Minutes, BoD: October 13, 1962, July 20, 1963, September 7, 1963.

36. Minutes, BoD: October 14, 1962.

37. Minutes, BoD: October 14, 1962, November 25, 1962, July 27, 1963, November 23, 1963.

38. Edgar Wayburn in François Leydet, ed., *Tomorrow's Wilderness*, Proceedings of the 8th Wilderness Conference, 1963 (San Francisco: Sierra Club, 1963), p. 251.

39. "How Bold Shall We Be?" *SCB* 45 (January 1960), pp. 3, 4;

Edgar Wayburn, "The Sierra Club's Role in 1962," *SCB* 45 (January 1962), p. 3; and David R. Brower, "The Conservation Challenge for 1962," *SCB* 47 (January 1962), p. 2.

40. Ansel Adams to Charles M. Teague, with enclosure, September 25, 1962, *Sierra Club Archives*, Brower papers, carton 331, file: Wilderness, 1962.

41. David E. Pesonen, "Outdoor Recreation for America," *SCB* 47 (May 1962), pp. 6−9, 12, 13.

42. "Rediscovering a Peninsula," *SCB* 43 (September 1958), pp. 4−6. *An Island in Time: The Point Reyes Peninsula* is the name of a film by Laurel Reynolds and Mindy Willis, distributed by the Club.

43. Wayburn, "Sierra Club Statesman," pp. 93, 131.

44. Richard M. Leonard, "Mountaineer, Lawyer, Environmentalist," interview conducted by Susan R. Schrepfer, Regional Oral History Office, the Bancroft Library, Berkeley, 1975, p. 219; Wayburn, "Sierra Club Statesman," pp. 146−151.

45. Leonard, "Mountaineer," p. 219.

46. Wayburn, "Sierra Club Statesman," p. 57.

47. Brower, "Environmental Activist," pp. 192, 193.

48. "Struggle on the Seacoast," *SCB* 46 (April 1961), p. 9.

49. David E. Pesonen, "ORRRC Speaks," *SCB* 47 (January 1962), p. 15.

50. Minutes, BoD: July 5, 1958.

51. Wayburn, "Sierra Club Statesman," p. 58; David E. Pesonen, "The Battle of Bodega Bay," *SCB* 47 (June 1962), p. 9.

52. *SCB* 47 (May 1962), p. 6.

53. Author's interview with Brower, December 5, 1985.

54. Pesonen, "The Battle of Bodega Bay," *SCB* 47 (June 1962), p. 9.

55. William E. Siri, "Reflections on the Sierra Club, the Environment, and Mountaineering, 1950s−1970s," interview conducted by Ann Lage, Regional Oral History Office, the Bancroft Library, Berkeley, 1979, pp. 22, 23.

56. Ibid., p. 160.

57. Ibid., pp. 23, 157.

58. Ibid., p. 156.

59. Leonard, "Mountaineer," p. 141; see also pp. 311, 312, 402, 403.

60. Siri, "Reflections," p. 141.

61. Brower, "Environmental Activist," p. 199; "How Bold Shall We Be?" *SCB* 45 (January 1960), pp. 3, 4.

62. Siri, "Reflections," pp. 159–160, 281.

63. Wayburn, "Sierra Club Statesman," p. 59, 147.

64. Memorandum by David R. Brower to "Conservation Cooperators," November 23, 1962, *Sierra Club Archives*, Bradley papers, carton 114, file: Bodega Head.

65. Bradley to Brower, January 8, 1963, *Sierra Club Archives*, Bradley papers, carton 114, file: Bodega Head.

66. Minutes, BoD: May 4, 1963.

67. Minutes, BoD: June 9, 1963.

68. Minutes, BoD: July 27, 1963.

69. Minutes, BoD: September 7, 1963.

70. Ibid.

71. Brower, "Environmental Activist," p. 197.

72. Ibid., p. 200.

73. Author's interview with Litton, April 1985.

74. Brower, "Environmental Activist," p. 192.

75. Rachel Carson, *Silent Spring* (Boston: Houghton Mifflin, 1962).

76. Carson, *Silent Spring*, p. 261.

77. Ibid., p. 95.

78. Ibid., p. 23.

79. Minutes, BoD: November 20, 1955, May 3, 1958.

80. Minutes, BoD: July 4, 1959.

81. T[homas] H. Jukes, interviewed by Nadzan Haron, Sierra Club History Project, San Francisco, February 1981, pp. 3, 4. Shelved with the Oral Histories in the Sierra Club Library.

82. Quotations in this paragraph are from Alexander Hildebrand, "Sierra Club Leader and Critic," interview conducted by Ann Lage, Regional Oral History Office, the Bancroft Library, Berkeley, 1982, pp. 39, 40, unless otherwise noted.

83. Joel Hildebrand, "Sierra Club Leader and Ski-Mountaineer," interview conducted by Ann Lage, Sierra Club History Committee, San Francisco, 1974, pp. 31–34.

84. Siri, "Reflections," p. 36.

85. Clarence Cottam in *SCB* 48 (January 1963), pp. 4, 5, 13, 14.

86. The Leopold Report is reprinted as "A Vignette of Primitive America," *SCB* 48 (March 1963), pp. 4–11.

87. Bruce M. Kilgore, "'Above All . . . Naturalness': An Inspired Report on Parks," *SCB* 48 (March 1963), pp. 2, 3.

88. "A Vignette of Primitive America," p. 7. For a critique of the Leopold Report, see Alston Chase, *Playing God in Yellowstone: The Destruction of America's First National Park* (Boston: Atlantic Monthly Press, 1986), pp. 31–48.

89. Paul Brooks, "Wilderness in Western Culture," in Leydet, ed., *Tomorrow's Wilderness*, pp. 84–90.

90. Wallace Stegner in Leydet, ed., *Tomorrow's Wilderness*, p. 133.

91. Leydet, ed., *Tomorrow's Wilderness*, pp. 155, 156.

92. Udall in Leydet, ed., *Tomorrow's Wilderness*, pp. 211–213.

93. Gilligan in Leydet, ed., *Tomorrow's Wilderness*, pp. 51, 52.

94. Stephen H. Spurr, "The Value of Wilderness to Science," in Leydet, ed., *Tomorrow's Wilderness*, pp. 59–74.

95. Golden in Leydet, ed., *Tomorrow's Wilderness*, pp. 74, 75.

96. Wayburn to Brower, October 29, 1963, *Sierra Club Archives*, Brower papers, carton 225, file: S.C. Comm. Pub. Comm.

97. Michael McCloskey, "Wilderness Movement at the Crossroads, 1945–1970," *Pacific Historical Review* 41 (August 1972), p. 352.

98. Ibid.

99. For a complete list of Sierra Club *Exhibit Format* books, see Brower, "Environmental Activist," pp. 328, 329; for the proposed Sierra Club History, see the memorandum by Holway Jones, July 7, 1963, *Sierra Club Archives*, Wayburn papers, carton 184a, file: S.C. Comm. Pub. Comm.

100. Siri, "Reflections," pp. 121–125.

101. Wayburn, "Sierra Club Statesman," p. 191.

102. Brower to the author, February 20, 1987.

103. "Publications Policy," ca. 1952, *Sierra Club Archives*, Brower papers, carton 223, file: Pub. Comm.

104. Brower to Pete Van Gorp, May 23, 1963, *Sierra Club Archives*, Brower papers, carton 223, file: S.C. Comm. Pub. Comm..

105. N. Clark to August Frugé, October 3, 1960, Wayburn papers, carton 184a, file: S.C. Comm. Pub. Comm.

106. Minutes, BoD: December 15, 1962.

107. Wayburn, "Sierra Club Statesman," p. 192.

108. Ibid., p. 206.

109. Ibid., p. 194.

110. Statistical Comparisons, in Minutes, BoD: May 7–8, 1966.

111. Wayburn, "Sierra Club Statesman," p. 206.

112. Adams to Brower, September 30, 1962, *Sierra Club Archives*, Brower papers, carton 223, file: S.C. Comm. Pub. Comm.

113. August Frugé, Memorandum re: Publications Program of the Sierra Club, August 9, 1963, *Sierra Club Archives*, Wayburn papers, carton 184a, file: S.C. Comm. Pub. Comm.

114. Leonard to Honorary Officers et al., December 1, 1968, *Sierra Club Archives*, Adams papers, carton 111, file: Brower Controversy.

115. Memorandum re: Publications Program of the Sierra Club, August 9, 1963, *Sierra Club Archives*, Wayburn papers, carton 184a, file: S.C. Comm. Pub. Comm. Quotations from Frugé in this and the following two paragraphs are from the memorandum.

116. Adams memorandum, August 16, 1963, *Sierra Club Archives*, Wayburn papers, carton 184a, File: S.C. Comm. Pub. Comm.

117. Stegner to Brower, August 25, 1963, *Sierra Club Archives*, Brower papers, carton 223, file: S.C. Comm. Pub. Comm.

118. Farquhar to Van Gorp, May 2, 1963, *Sierra Club Archives*, Brower papers, carton 223, file: S.C. Comm. Pub. Comm.

119. Brower to Van Gorp, May 23, 1963, *Sierra Club Archives*, Brower papers, carton 223, file: S.C. Comm. Pub. Comm.

120. Wayburn, "Sierra Club Statesman," p. 205; Martin Litton, "Sierra Club Director and Uncompromising Preservationist, 1950s–1970s," interview conducted by Ann Lage, Regional Oral History Office, the Bancroft Library, Berkeley, 1982, p. 105.

121. Memorandum to the Publications Committee, October 9, 1963, *Sierra Club Archives*, Brower papers, carton 223, file: S.C. Comm. Pub. Comm.

122. Minutes, Ex Comm: November 23, 1963.

123. Peggy Wayburn, "The Tragedy of Bull Creek," *SCB* 54 (January 1960), reprinted in Phillip Hyde and François Leydet, *The Last Redwoods, Photographs and Story of a Vanishing Scenic Resource* (San Francisco: Sierra Club, 1963). The most complete history of the redwood campaigns is Susan R. Schrepfer, *The Fight to Save the Red-*

woods: A History of Environmental Reform 1917–1978 (Madison: University of Wisconsin Press, 1983).

124. Litton, "Sierra Club Director," pp. 25, 27.

125. Phillip Berry, "The Need to Revise California's Forest Practices Act," *SCB* 46 (October 1961), pp. 44–51.

126. Newton Drury, "He Left a Heritage of Beauty," *SCB* 45 (April–May 1960), p. 13.

127. "The Role of Private Philanthropy," in Leydet, ed., *Tomorrow's Wilderness*, pp. 157–167.

128. Wayburn, "Sierra Club Statesman," p. 63.

129. Litton, "Sierra Club Director," pp. 34, 35.

130. Wayburn, "Sierra Club Statesman," p. 64.

131. Litton, "Sierra Club Director," p. 35.

132. John Muir, *Our National Parks* (1901; repr., Madison: University of Wisconsin Press, 1981), pp. 364, 365.

133. Wayburn, "Sierra Club Statesman," p. 64.

134. Litton, "Sierra Club Director," p. 44.

135. Ibid., p. 46.

136. Schrepfer, *Fight to Save the Redwoods*, p. 117.

137. Quoted by Brower, "Environmental Activist," p. 159, and Litton, "Sierra Club Director," p. 37.

138. For maps of the location of proposed redwood parks, see Schrepfer, *Fight to Save the Redwoods*, pp. 114, 115.

139. Litton, "Sierra Club Director," p. 48.

140. Ibid., p. 44.

141. *National Geographic* 126 (July 1964), pp. 10–45; see also Schrepfer, *Fight to Save the Redwoods*, p. 120.

142. Brower, "Environmental Activist," p. 160.

143. Ibid.

144. Publisher's Note in Hyde and Leydet, *The Last Redwoods*, p. 12.

145. Acknowledgments in Hyde and Leydet, *The Last Redwoods*, p. 13.

146. Adams to Wayburn, Brower, Frugé, and Farquhar, February 11, 1964, *Sierra Club Archives*, Adams papers, carton 110, file: Brower.

147. Stewart L. Udall, Foreword to Hyde and Leydet, *The Last Redwoods*, p. 11.

148. Brower, "Environmental Activist," p. 160.

149. Hyde and Leydet, *The Last Redwoods*, pp. 92, 113.

150. Ibid., p. 110.

151. Ibid., p. 111.

152. Wayburn, "Sierra Club Statesman," p. 64.

153. Ibid., p. 88.

154. Ibid., pp. 67, 68.

155. Ibid., p. 90.

156. Litton, "Sierra Club Director," p. 37.

157. Leonard, "Mountaineer," p. 172.

158. Norman B. Livermore, Jr., "Man in the Middle: High Sierra Packer, Timberman, Conservationist, and California Resources Secretary," interview conducted by Ann Lage and Gabrielle Morris, Regional Oral History Office, the Bancroft Library, Berkeley, 1983, p. 68 and appendix E.

159. Leonard, "Mountaineer," p. 166.

160. President's Report, Minutes, BoD: May 2, 1964.

161. Wayburn to Edward A. Hummel, Regional Director, N.P.S., included in Minutes, Ex Comm, November 24, 1964; approved by Ex Comm: November 24, 1964.

162. Litton, "Sierra Club Director," p. 40.

163. Leonard, "Mountaineer," p. 168.

164. On the difference between the League and the Club, see Schrepfer, *Fight to Save the Redwoods*. See also her question in Leonard, "Mountaineer," p. 223.

165. McCloskey, "Sierra Club Executive Director," p. 6.

166. Ibid., pp. 17–22.

167. Brock Evans, "Environmental Campaigner: From the Northwest Forests to the Halls of Congress," interview conducted by Ann Lage, Regional Oral History Office, the Bancroft Library, Berkeley, 1985, p. 36; McCloskey, "Sierra Club Executive Director," pp. 20, 21.

168. "The North Cascades Wilderness—Almost Half Safe," *SCB* 45 (October 1960), p. 2.

169. Patrick Goldsworthy, quoted in "New Glacier Peak Wilderness Brings Both Commendation and Criticism," *SCB* 45 (October 1960), p. 3.

170. Minutes, BoD: October 15, 1961.

171. "The NCCC Proposes: A North Cascades National Park," *SCB* 48 (October 1963), pp. 7–13.

172. See Minutes, BoD: January 26, 1963.

173. Minutes, BoD: September 7, 1963.

174. Wayburn, "Sierra Club Statesman," p. 35.

175. McCloskey, "Sierra Club Executive Director," p. 21.

176. "The North Cascades on the Witness Stand," *SCB* 48 (November 1963), pp. 2, 18.

177. Ann Lage to the author, February 10, 1986.

178. Brower, "Environmental Activist," p. 95.

179. Harvey Manning, *The Wild Cascades: Forgotten Parkland*, with photographs by Ansel Adams, Phillip Hyde, David Simons, Bob Spring, Ira Spring, Clyde Thomas [Martin Litton], John Warth, and others, and with lines from Theodore Roethke, and Foreword by William O. Douglas (San Francisco: Sierra Club Books, 1965).

180. Brower, "Environmental Activist," p. 144.

181. Ibid., p. 138.

182. Ibid., p. 131.

183. Richard C. Bradley, "Grand Canyon of the Controversial Colorado," *SCB* 49 (December 1964), p. 77.

184. "Twilight for the Grand Canyon?" *SCB* 48 (October 1963), p. 5, quotes a report of August 27, 1963 by Stewart Udall.

185. Leonard, "Mountaineer," p. 137.

186. Brower, "Environmental Activist," p. 143.

187. Litton, "Sierra Club Director," p. 73.

188. Brower, "Environmental Activist," p. 143.

189. Bestor Robinson, "Thoughts on Conservation and the Sierra Club," interview conducted by Susan R. Schrepfer, Sierra Club History Committee, San Francisco, 1974, p. 24.

190. "Suggestions for Coordinating Grand Canyon National Park and Monument into Overall Plans for Colorado River," October 1948, *Sierra Club Archives*, Brower papers, carton 209, file: Grand Canyon, General.

191. Clyde Thomas [Martin Litton], "The Last Days of Grand Canyon Too?" *SCB* 48 (October 1963), pp. 4, 5.

192. Ibid.

193. Ibid.

194. Ibid.; Brower, "Environmental Activist," p. 143.

195. Minutes, BoD: May 2, 1963.

196. See Minutes, BoD: October 5, 1963.

197. Eliot Porter, *The Place No One Knew: Glen Canyon on the Colorado* (San Francisco: Sierra Club Books, 1963). The Foreword by David Brower is on pp. 7–8; the text "The Living Canyon" by Eliot Porter is on pp. 13–17.

198. Brower to Richard H. Ichord, June 27, 1963, including copies of letters from Brower to Udall, June 22, 1963 and June 24, 1963, and enclosures, *Sierra Club Archives*, Brower papers, carton 209, file: Glen Canyon Dam.

199. "Proposed Save the Grand Canyon Task Force," February 25, 1964, *Sierra Club Archives*, Brower papers, carton 211, file: Grand Canyon Task Force.

200. Brower, "Environmental Activist," p. 149.

201. Minutes, BoD: May 2, 1964.

202. "Our special Grand Canyon campaign needs . . . ," ca. 1963, 1964, *Sierra Club Archives*, Brower papers, carton 209, file: Grand Canyon, General.

203. "Foreword" by Stewart L. Udall, *Lake Powell: Jewel of the Colorado* (Washington, D.C.: G.P.O., 1965). It is generally conceded that Floyd Dominy wrote the whole book; see Mark Reisner, *Cadillac Desert*, p. 255.

204. *Lake Powell*, pp. ii, 13.

205. *Bridge and Marble Canyon Dams* (Washington, D.C.: U.S. Department of the Interior, 1964).

206. François Leydet, *Time and the River Flowing: Grand Canyon* (San Francisco: Sierra Club, 1964). Brower's Foreword is on pp. 5–10.

207. "Dear Friends of National Parks and Wilderness," March 18, 1958, *Sierra Club Archives*, Brower papers, carton 230, file: Wilderness Bill, 1959.

208. See interviewer's question in Wayburn, "Sierra Club Statesman," p. 31.

209. McCloskey, "The Wilderness Movement at the Crossroads," p. 354.

210. Michael McCloskey, "The Wilderness Act of 1964: Its Background and Meaning," *Oregon Law Review* 45 (1966), p. 298.

211. Wayburn, "Sierra Club Statesman," p. 36.

212. McCloskey, "The Wilderness Act of 1964," p. 298.

213. On the third wave, see McCloskey, "Sierra Club Executive Director," pp. 24, 25.

214. See *Sierra Club Archives*, Brower papers, carton 231.

215. Wayburn, "Sierra Club Statesman," p. 172.

216. Minutes, BoD: May 6, 1961.

217. McCloskey, "The Wilderness Act of 1964," p. 300.

218. Adams to Charles M. Teague, September 25, 1962, with Brower note, *Sierra Club Archives*, Brower papers, carton 231, file: Wilderness Bill 1962.

219. McCloskey, "Sierra Club Executive Director," pp. 30, 52.

220. "Politics and Conservation," in Leydet, ed., *Tomorrow's Wilderness*, p. 232.

221. Ibid., p. 234.

222. Ibid.

223. Minutes, BoD: December 14, 1963, May 2, 1964.

224. Minutes, BoD: March 2, 1964.

225. On the progress of the Wilderness Act, see Roderick Nash, *Wilderness and the American Mind*, 3d ed. (New Haven: Yale University Press, 1982), pp. 220–225.

226. John H. Hendee, George H. Stankey, and Robert Lucas, *Wilderness Management* (Washington, D.C.: U.S. Forest Service, 1978), pp. 64–75.

227. The Wilderness Act: Public Law 88–577, Eighty-eighth Congress, 1964.

228. McCloskey, "Sierra Club Executive Director," pp. 84, 85.

229. Brower, "Environmental Activist," p. 78.

230. Wayburn, "Sierra Club Statesman," p. 160.

231. McCloskey, "The Wilderness Movement at the Crossroads," pp. 354, 355.

232. McCloskey, "Sierra Club Executive Director," p. 82.

233. McCloskey, "The Wilderness Movement at the Crossroads," pp. 354, 355.

234. On facilitating, see McCloskey, "Sierra Club Executive Director," p. 107.

235. Siri, "Reflections," p. 29.

Chapter 7

1. William E. Siri, "Reflections on the Sierra Club, the Environment, and Mountaineering, 1950s–1970s," interview conducted by Ann Lage, Regional Oral History Office, the Bancroft Library, Berkeley, 1979, pp. 21, 22, 24, 32.

2. Minutes, BoD: September 11–12, 1965.

3. Siri, "Reflections," pp. 30, 33, 34.

4. Milton Hildebrand to David Brower, April 23, 1954, *Sierra Club Archives*, Leonard papers, box 1, file: Pesticides.

5. Leonard wire, June 10, 1963; Brower wire, June 30, 1963; Brower to Wirth, June 10 and June 30, 1963; and responses, in *Sierra Club Archives*, Leonard papers, box 1, file: Pesticides.

6. Minutes, BoD: September 7, 1963.

7. Brower to Milton Hildebrand, September 17, 1963, *Sierra Club Archives*, Leonard papers, box 1, file: Pesticides.

8. "Second Report of the *Natural Sciences Committee* Regarding the Aerial Application of Pesticides in Yosemite National Park," October 1, 1963, in Minutes, BoD: September 5–6, 1964, item 12.

9. "*Natural Sciences Committee*," August 26, 1964, in Minutes, BoD: September 5–6, 1964, item 7.

10. Siri, "Reflections," p. 35.

11. Minutes, BoD: March 13, 1965.

12. Minutes, BoD: May 1, 1965.

13. Martin Litton, "Sierra Club Director and Uncompromising Preservationist, 1950s–1970s," interview conducted by Ann Lage and Gabrielle Morris, Regional Oral History Office, the Bancroft Library, Berkeley, 1982, p. 74; Siri, "Reflections," pp. 34, 35, 39.

14. Minutes, BoD: May 1, 1965.

15. Thomas H. Jukes has written in correspondence to the author, October 23, 1987, "You have my permission to use the materials listed in your letter, provided that you include a statement by me as follows. About 15 or 20 years ago, I was criticised strongly in the Sierra Club 'Bulletin' for my defense of pesticides. I wrote a letter to the Sierra Club 'Bulletin' rebutting these statements, and the editor of the 'Bulletin' informed me that my letter would not be published because no space was available for material of this type, in view of the fact that the 'Bulletin' had to be devoted to defending

environmentalism. After this, I lost interest in attempting to communicate my dissenting views to the Sierra Club."

16. Minutes, BoD: June 12, 1965; Joel Hildebrand, "Sierra Club Leader and Ski-Mountaineer," interview conducted by Ann Lage, Sierra Club History Committee, San Francisco, 1974, p. 29.

17. Hildebrand, "Sierra Club Leader," p. 32.

18. Ibid., p. 31.

19. Siri, "Reflections," pp. 24, 121.

20. Michael McCloskey, "Sierra Club Executive Director: The Evolving Club and the Environmental Movement, 1961–1981," interview conducted by Susan R. Schrepfer, Regional Oral History Office, the Bancroft Library, Berkeley, 1983, pp. 88, 90, 91.

21. Minutes, BoD: September 7–8, 1963, March 3, 1964.

22. See enclosures, Minutes, Ex Comm: March 2, 1964.

23. John L. Harper, *Mineral King: Public Concern with Government Policy* (Arcata, Calif.: Pacifica Publishing, 1982), pp. 64–71.

24. Harper, *Mineral King*, p. 76.

25. Ibid., p. 78.

26. Ibid., pp. 80, 81.

27. Litton, "Sierra Club Director," p. 28.

28. Harper, *Mineral King*, p. 82.

29. Minutes, BoD: May 2, 1965.

30. Alexander Hildebrand, "Sierra Club Leader and Critic: Perspectives on Club Growth, Scope, and Tactics, 1950s–1970s," interview conducted by Ann Lage, Regional Oral History Office, the Bancroft Library, Berkeley, 1982, p. 36.

31. McCloskey, "Sierra Club Executive Director," p. 174.

32. Siri, "Reflections," p. 89.

33. Harper, *Mineral King*, p. 87.

34. McCloskey's response is in correspondence with the author, January 5, 1987.

35. McCloskey, "Sierra Club Executive Director," pp. 174, 175.

36. Minutes, BoD: September 11–12, 1965. See also Siri, "Reflections," p. 27. As Siri and Brower remember, Litton chuckled over the idea of establishing a department of conservation, because it seemed like bringing coals to Newcastle—conservation was what the Club did.

37. Minutes, BoD: September 11, 1964.

38. W. Lloyd Tupling, "Sierra Club Washington Representative," interview conducted by Ann Lage, Regional Oral History Office, the Bancroft Library, Berkeley, 1985, pp. 8, 9.

39. *Sierra Club Archives*, Publications, carton 23 and scrapbooks, v. 1–3.

40. David R. Brower, "Environmental Activist, Publicist, and Prophet," interview conducted by Susan R. Schrepfer, Regional Oral History Office, the Bancroft Library, Berkeley, 1980, p. 72.

41. Francis P. Farquhar, "Sierra Club Mountaineer and Editor," interview conducted by Ann Lage, Sierra Club History Committee, San Francisco, 1974, p. 72.

42. Memorandum, Adams to Wayburn, Brower, Frugé, and Farquhar, February 11, 1964, *Sierra Club Archives*, Adams papers, carton 110, file: S. C. Comm. Pub. Comm.

43. Brower to Adams, February 14, 1964, *Sierra Club Archives*, Adams papers, carton 110, file: S.C. Comm. Pub. Comm.

44. Adams to Brower, February 15, 1964, *Sierra Club Archives*, Adams papers, carton 110, file: S.C. Comm. Pub. Comm.

45. Adams to Wayburn, February 15, 1964, *Sierra Club Archives*, Adams papers, carton 110, file: S.C. Comm. Pub. Comm.

46. Edgar Wayburn, "Sierra Club Statesman, Leader of the Parks and Wilderness Movement," interview conducted by Ann Lage and Susan R. Schrepfer, Regional Oral History Office, the Bancroft Library, Berkeley, 1985, p. 216; Litton, "Sierra Club Director," p. 80. Brower's memory of Adams on color and on Porter is in correspondence with the author, February 17, 1987.

47. Marshall to Stegner, December 23, 1964, with copies to Brower, Siri, Adams, and Litton, in *Sierra Club Archives*, Adams papers, carton 111, file: S.C. Comm. Pub. Comm.

48. Adams to "Wally and all," December 28, 1964, *Sierra Club Archives*, Adams papers, carton 111, file: S.C. Comm. Pub. Comm.

49. Stegner to Adams, December 29, 1964, Stegner to Marshall, December 29, 1964, *Sierra Club Archives*, Adams papers, carton 111, file: S.C. Comm. Pub. Comm.

50. Krutch to Brower, October 3, 1968, *Sierra Club Archives*, Brower papers, carton 224, file: S.C. Comm. Pub. Comm.

51. See Susan R. Schrepfer, *The Fight to Save the Redwoods: A History of Environmental Reform 1917–1978* (Madison: University of Wis-

consin Press, 1983), pp. 90–91, 167–171. Brower hoped that Eiseley would play a much larger role in the Galapagos books, though he served only to introduce the first volume. See *Sierra Club Archives*, Brower papers, carton 224, file: S.C. Comm. Pub. Comm.

52. Adams to Brower and Marshall, July 1, 1966, July 2, 1966, *Sierra Club Archives*, Brower papers, carton 223, file: S.C. Comm. Pub. Comm.

53. Maxine E. McCloskey and James P. Gilligan, eds., *Wilderness and the Quality of Life*, Proceedings of the 10th Wilderness Conference, 1967 (San Francisco: Sierra Club, 1969), p. 13.

54. See Stephen C. Jett, *Navajo Wildlands: As Long as the Rivers Shall Run* (San Francisco: Sierra Club, 1967), p. 16; Richard Slotkin, *The Fatal Environment: The Myth of the Frontier in the Age of Industrialization, 1800–1890* (New York: Atheneum, 1985); resolution on Vietnam, submitted to Ex Comm June 4, 1970, and responses from chapters, in *Richard Sill Papers*, University of Nevada, Reno, box 14.

55. Terry Russell and Renny Russell, *On the Loose* (San Francisco: Sierra Club/Ballantine Books, 1967).

56. Ian Ballantine, Introduction to Brower, "Environmental Activist," p. vi.

57. See Minutes, BoD: March 5, 1966; President's Report, Minutes, BoD: May 7–8, 1966.

58. McCloskey to Brower, July 6, 1966, *Sierra Club Archives*, Publications, carton 23, file: Kauai.

59. Siri, "Reflections," pp. 128–130.

60. Figures are from the so-called Torre brief of May 22, 1967, prepared by Gary J. Torre of Lillick, McHose, Wheat, Adams & Charles of San Francisco, to appeal the IRS ruling on the Sierra Club's tax status. The Torre brief contains a history of the Sierra Club. Copy on loan to the author from Ann Lage.

61. McCloskey, "Sierra Club Executive Director," pp. 99–100.

62. President's Report, Minutes, BoD: May 6, 1967.

63. Minutes, BoD: May 6, 1967; Minutes, Ex Comm: June 18, 1967.

64. See Brower to Paul Brooks, October 21, 1968 (draft), *Sierra Club Archives*, Brower papers, carton 205, file: Brower Controversy, 1968.

65. McCloskey, "Sierra Club Executive Director," p. 43.

66. Brower, "Environmental Activist," p. 165.

67. Richard M. Leonard, "Mountaineer, Lawyer, Environmentalist," interview conducted by Susan R. Schrepfer, Regional Oral History Office, the Bancroft Library, Berkeley, 1975, p. 214.

68. McCloskey, "Sierra Club Executive Director," p. 37.

69. Ibid., p. 40.

70. Ibid., p. 38.

71. Ibid., p. 47.

72. Ibid., p. 41.

73. Schrepfer, *Fight to Save the Redwoods*, p. 289 and n. 64.

74. Brower, "Environmental Activist," p. 163.

75. Wayburn, "Sierra Club Statesman," pp. 163, 164.

76. Ibid., pp. 66–68.

77. Leonard, "Mountaineer," p. 170.

78. Brower, "Environmental Activist," p. 163.

79. Wayburn, "Sierra Club Statesman," pp. 77–79.

80. Leonard, "Mountaineer," pp. 144, 149.

81. Siri, "Reflections," p. 59.

82. Siri, "Reflections," pp. 47, 48; McCloskey, "Sierra Club Executive Director," p. 45; Brower, "Environmental Activist," p. 162.

83. Brower, "Environmental Activist," pp. 148, 164.

84. *New York Times*, December 17, 1965, reprinted in *SCB* 51 (January 1966), pp. 8, 9. See also Leonard, "Mountaineer," pp. 435–440.

85. Leonard, "Mountaineer," p. 170.

86. Schrepfer, *Fight to Save the Redwoods*, pp. 133, 134.

87. Siri, "Reflections," p. 47.

88. Minutes, BoD: January 22, 1966.

89. Minutes, Bod: September 17–18, 1966.

90. See "*Reader's Digest* Enlists in the Fight to Save Grand Canyon," *SCB* 51 (May 1966), pp. 6, 7.

91. Brower to Stewart Udall, April 29, 1966, *Sierra Club Archives*, Brower papers, carton 209, file: Grand Canyon.

92. Stewart Udall to David Brower, May 9, 1966, *Sierra Club Archives*, Brower papers, carton 209, file: Grand Canyon.

93. *SCB* 51 (May 1966).

94. Hugh Nash, "Grand Canyon Hearings," *SCB* 51 (July–August 1966), p. 2.

96. Roderick Nash, ed., *Grand Canyon of the Living Colorado* (New

York: Sierra Club/Ballantine Books, 1970). All of the Grand Canyon Battle ads are reproduced here: see pp. 132, passim.

97. Nash, ed., *Grand Canyon of the Living Colorado*, pp. 130–131.

98. The quote is from Wayburn, "Sierra Club Statesman," p. 293. See also Leonard "Mountaineer," pp. 145, 151; Siri, "Reflections," p. 57.

99. "President's Message: The Club Advertising Effort," *SCB* 53 (January 1968), p. 6.

100. McCloskey to the author, January 5, 1987. Brower believed that Morris Udall went to Assistant Commissioner Cohen of the IRS. Brower to the author, February 22, 1987.

101. Brower, "Environmental Activist," p. 151; McCloskey, "Sierra Club Executive Director," p. 183; Wayburn, "Sierra Club Statesman," p. 323.

102. Morris Udall, quoted in "Strong Words Betray a Weak Case," *SCB* (July–August 1966), p. 4.

103. Brower, "Environmental Activist," p. 151.

104. Roderick Nash, *Wilderness and the American Mind*, 3d ed. (New Haven: Yale University Press, 1982), pp. 230–231.

105. Siri, "Reflections," p. 57.

106. Nash, ed., *Grand Canyon of the Living Colorado*, p. 131.

107. William B. Devall, "The Governing of a Voluntary Organization: Oligarchy and Democracy in the Sierra Club" (Ph.D. diss., University of Oregon, 1970), pp. 181–192.

108. Leonard, "Mountaineer," pp. 140, 150.

109. Ad of March 16, 1967, reprinted in *SCB* 52 (August 1967), pp. 12, 13.

110. The "Sistine Chapel" ad was published after July 25, 1966, according to Nash, *Wilderness and the American Mind*, p. 231.

111. Nash, ed., *Grand Canyon of the Living Colorado*, p. 131; Brower, "Environmental Activist," p. 148.

112. Adams to Brower and Marshall, July 2, 1966, *Sierra Club Archives*, Brower papers, carton 223, file: S.C. Comm. Pub. Comm.

113. McCloskey, "Sierra Club Executive Director," p. 100.

114. Wayburn, "Sierra Club Statesman," p. 69; Brower, "Environmental Activist," p. 269.

115. Wayburn, "Sierra Club Statesman," pp. 206, 207.

116. *Congressional Record*, August 1, 1966.

117. Brower to Morris Udall, August 11, 1966, *Sierra Club Archives*, Brower papers, carton 210, file: Grand Canyon, Central Arizona Project.

118. "Dear Member," September 12, 1966, *Sierra Club Archives*, Brower papers, carton 210, file: Grand Canyon, Central Arizona Project.

119. Leonard, "Mountaineer," p. 174.

120. "To all members of the Board and Council of the Sierra Club," from Horace M. Albright, Phil S. Bernays, Harold C. Bradley, Harold E. Crowe, Francis P. Farquhar, Clifford Heimbucher, Alexander Hildebrand, Joel H. Hildebrand, Milton Hildebrand, Bestor Robinson, and Robert G. Sproul, April 28, 1967, reprinted in Leonard, "Mountaineer," pp. 446–448.

121. Leonard, "Mountaineer," p. 345.

122. Hildebrand, "Sierra Club Leader," p. 31.

123. Brower to the author, February 22, 1987. Brower believes that this letter was not occasioned by his ads or his use of the *Bulletin*, but by the "Half Bulletin" which Hugh Nash issued on Diablo Canyon in February 1967. Nevertheless, it called more than the issuance of the "Half Bulletin" into question. On the "Half Bulletin," see the next section of the text.

124. Siri, "Reflections," p. 126.

125. Phillip Berry, draft interview conducted by Ann Lage, Regional Oral History Office, the Bancroft Library, Berkeley, n.d., pp. 21–30.

126. Siri, "Reflections," p. 101. For a chronology of the Diablo campaign, see Leonard, "Mountaineer," p. 283–292.

127. Memorandum, Eissler to Siri, Brower, and the Club, February 23, 1965, Litton personal papers, in author's possession, file: Diablo.

128. McCloskey, "Sierra Club Executive Director," p. 93.

129. Siri, "Reflections," pp. 93–98.

130. Minutes, BoD: May 7–8, 1966. Material on discussions and resolutions of the board meeting of May 1966 are from this source except where otherwise noted.

131. Brower to the author, March 3, 1987.

132. See Minutes, BoD: September 7, 1963, for the official policy precedent.

133. Leonard to Sibley, July 4, 1966, *Sierra Club Archives*, Leonard papers, box 1, file: Diablo Canyon.

134. Litton, "To my fellow members of the Board of Directors," September 9, 1966, *Sierra Club Archives*, Leonard papers, box 1, file: Diablo Canyon.

135. Siri, "Reflections," pp. 103−105; Litton, "To my fellow members of the Board of Directors."

136. Leonard, "Mountaineer," p. 283.

137. Minutes, BoD: September 17−18, 1966.

138. Litton, quoted in Minutes, BoD: September 17−18, 1966.

139. Minutes, BoD: September 17−18, 1966.

140. Leonard's annotation to Litton, "To my fellow members of the Board of Directors," September 9, 1966, *Sierra Club Archives*, Leonard papers, box 1, file: Diablo Canyon.

141. Siri, "Reflections," p. 100.

142. "To my fellow members of the Board of Directors," September 9, 1966, *Sierra Club Archives*, Leonard Papers, box 1, file: Diablo Canyon.

143. Berry, draft interview, p. 24.

144. McCloskey, "Sierra Club Executive Director," p. 93.

145. Wallace Stegner, "The Artist as Environmental Advocate," interview conducted by Ann Lage, Regional Oral History Office, the Bancroft Library, Berkeley, 1982, p. 25.

146. Berry, draft interview, p. 26.

147. Minutes, BoD: December 10, 1966.

148. Brower to the author, February 19, 1987.

149. Minutes, BoD: January 7−8, 1967.

150. Ibid.

151. Draft [resolution], Sierra Club, January 7, 1967, *Sierra Club Archives*, Brower papers, carton 208, file: Diablo.

152. Memorandum, January 19, 1967, *Sierra Club Archives*, Brower papers, carton 205, file: Diablo.

153. Marshall to Porter, February 4, 1967, Porter to Marshall, January 20, 1967, *Sierra Club Archives*, Brower papers, carton 205, file: Brower Controversy.

154. Litton to Porter, January 26, 1967, *Sierra Club Archives*, Brower papers, carton 205, file: Brower Controversy.

155. Minutes, BoD: February 18, 1967.

156. Executive Director's Report, Minutes, BoD: February 18, 1967.

157. Hugh Nash to David Brower, January 19, 1967, *Sierra Club Archives*, Brower papers, carton 208, file: Diablo.

158. "For Immediate Release," January 9, 1967, *Sierra Club Archives*, Brower papers, carton 208, file: Diablo.

159. Siri to Marshall, January 11, 1967, *Sierra Club Archives*, Brower papers, carton 208, file: Diablo.

160. Sill memorandum, February 7, 1967, *Sierra Club Archives*, Brower papers, carton 208, file: Diablo.

161. Brower to Sill, with enclosure, February 9, 1967, *Sierra Club Archives*, Brower papers, carton 208, file: Diablo.

162. Brower to Marshall, March 2, 1967, *Sierra Club Archives*, Brower papers, carton 208, file: Diablo.

163. Litton, "To Directors and Chapter Chairmen of the Sierra Club," March 16, 1967, *Sierra Club Archives*, Leonard papers, box 1, file: Diablo.

164. Voter information sheet, n.d., *Sierra Club Archives*, Leonard papers, box 1, file: Diablo.

165. "Half Bulletin," published in 700 "preliminary" copies as *SCB* 52 (February 1967). Copies are in Litton personal papers, in author's possession, file: Diablo. For Siri's memory of the incident, see Siri, "Reflections," pp. 109−112.

166. Brower to Marshall, March 6, 1967 (drafted March 2, 1967), *Sierra Club Archives*, Brower papers, carton 208, file: Diablo.

167. Litton, "To Directors and Chapter Chairmen of the Sierra Club," March 16, 1967, and Marshall response, March 31, 1967, *Sierra Club Archives*, Leonard papers, box 1, file: Diablo.

168. Wayburn, "Sierra Club Statesman," p. 229.

169. President's Report, Minutes, BoD: May 6, 1967.

170. "Sierra Club Council Handbook and Appendices," Litton personal papers, in author's possession.

171. "Summary: The 6th Sierra Club Information and Education Conference, March 26−27, 1966," *Sierra Club Archives*, Charlotte Mauk papers, carton 145, file: Sierra Club, Misc.

172. Wayburn, "Sierra Club Statesman," p. 209.

173. See *Richard Sill Papers*, University of Nevada, Reno, box 8; Siri, "Reflections," pp. 150–152; President's Report, Minutes, BoD: May 6, 1967.

174. Siri, "Reflections," p. 151.

175. Wayburn, "Sierra Club Statesman," p. 209.

176. Albright and cosigners, "To all members of the Board and Council of the Sierra Club," March 28, 1967, in Leonard, "Mountaineer," pp. 436–438.

177. Minutes, BoD: May 6, 1967; *SCB* 52 (March 1967).

178. "To Sierra Club Leaders," June 5, 1967, October 5, 1967, November 22, 1967, *Sierra Club Archives*, Wayburn papers, carton 184b, file: Sierra Club President.

179. On the Torre brief of May 22, 1967, prepared by Gary J. Torre, see note 60 to this chapter.

180. Siri, "Reflections," p. 61; Wayburn, "Sierra Club Statesman," p. 41; Berry, draft interview, pp. 18–20.

181. Wayburn, "Sierra Club Statesman," p. 41; Berry, draft interview, pp. 18, 19.

182. Torre brief, pp. 10, 11.

183. Ibid., pp. 21, 22.

184. Ibid., pp. 29, 30.

185. *SCB* 51 (April 1966), pp. 10–13.

186. Grant McConnell, *Private Power and American Democracy* (New York: Knopf, 1966).

187. Ibid., p. 46.

188. "Quest for the Public Interest," McConnell, *Private Power and American Democracy*, pp. 336–368. On power, see ibid., pp. 29, 338.

189. McConnell, *Private Power and American Democracy*, pp. 295–296.

190. Ibid., p. 360.

191. Ibid., p. 368.

192. Ibid., pp. 150, 153, 154 (brackets mine).

193. "President's Message," *SCB* 52 (November 1967), p. 2.

194. Francis P. Farquhar, "Reminiscences of the Early Days," *SCB* 53 (January 1968), p. 8.

195. *SCB* 53 (January 1968), p. 15.

196. Letter, Directors to Mr. Shermer Sibley, June 22, 1968, *Sierra Club Archives*, Litton papers, carton 137, file: Diablo.

197. See Brower to Iva May Warner, October 22, 1968, *Sierra Club Archives*, Wayburn papers, carton 176, file: Diablo.

198. *San Francisco Examiner*, June 30, 1968, July 3, 1968, July 9, 1968. Copies in *Sierra Club Archives*, Leonard papers, box 1, file: Diablo.

199. Sibley to Wayburn, July 2, 1968, *Sierra Club Archives*, Wayburn papers, carton 176, file: Diablo.

200. Wayburn to Directors, July 9, 1968, *Sierra Club Archives*, Wayburn papers, carton 176, file: Diablo.

201. Berry, draft interview, p. 28.

202. Ibid., p. 27.

203. Minutes, BoD: September 14–15, 1968.

204. Phillip S. Berry, Secretary, Sierra Club, to S. L. Sibley, President, PG&E, September 16, 1968, in Minutes, BoD: September 14–15, 1968.

205. Litton to Sierra Club leaders, October 11, 1968, *Sierra Club Archives*, Litton papers, carton 137, file: Diablo.

206. Wayburn telegram of September 17, 1968, *Sierra Club Archives*, Wayburn papers, carton 176, file: Diablo.

207. Stewart L. Udall, "Shooting the Wild Colorado," *Venture, The Traveller's World* (February 1968), reprinted in Nash, ed., *Grand Canyon of the Living Colorado*, pp. 83–87; see also p. 104.

208. Edgar Wayburn, "Club Proposes Additions to Redwood National Park as Voted by Senate," *SCB* 53 (March 1968), pp. 14–16.

209. Brock Evans, "Showdown for the Wilderness Alps of Washington's North Cascades," *SCB* 53 (April 1968), pp. 7–16.

210. Michael McCloskey, Report of the Conservation Director, Minutes, BoD: September 14–15, 1968.

211. Ibid.

212. "Four Major New Conservation Laws: A Review and a Preview," *SCB* 53 (November 1968), pp. 4–10.

213. "Conservation Agenda for 1969," *SCB* 53 (December 1968), p. 5.

214. François Leydet, *The Last Redwoods and the Parkland of Redwood Creek* (New York: Sierra Club/Ballantine Books, 1969); Nash, ed., *Grand Canyon of the Living Colorado*.

215. See Schrepfer, *Fight to Save the Redwoods*, pp. 158, 186;

Nash, ed., *Grand Canyon of the Living Colorado*, pp. 106, 107; report by Jeffrey Ingram, Minutes, Ex Comm: July 29, 1969.

216. "How to Make a Wilderness Study," n.d., *Sierra Club Archives*, Wayburn papers, carton 189, file: Wilderness.

217. George Marshall to Wayburn, June 2, 1967, *Sierra Club Archives*, Wayburn papers, carton 189, file: Wilderness.

218. Mccloskey, "Sierra Club Executive Director," p. 55.

219. McCloskey to Club leaders, March 7, 1969, *Sierra Club Archives*, Adams papers, carton 111, file: S.C. Misc..

220. Davie Sive, "Natural Beauty and the Law," *SCB* 53 (May 1968), pp. 18–20.

221. Minutes, BoD: December 14–15, 1968; Harper, *Mineral King*, p. 161.

222. McCloskey, "Sierra Club Executive Director," p. 141.

223. Leonard, "Mountaineer," p. 426.

224. McCloskey, "Sierra Club Executive Director," p. 169.

225. Berry, draft interview, pp. 76–81.

226. Rice Odell, *Environmental Awakening* (New York: Conservation Foundation, 1980), pp. 4–5.

227. Brower, "Environmental Activist," pp. 170–171.

228. Minutes, BoD: December 14–15, 1968; Tupling, "Sierra Club Washington Representative," p. 14.

229. McCloskey to All Conservation Staff, December 20, 1968, *Sierra Club Archives*, Brower papers, carton 226, file: Department of Interior.

230. Minutes, Ex Comm: January 11, 1969.

231. "Statement of David R. Brower," January 16, 1969, *Sierra Club Archives*, Brower papers, carton 226, file: Department of Interior.

232. Minutes, BoD: February 8–9, 1969.

Chapter 8

1. Tom Turner, "A Perspective on David Brower and the Sierra Club, 1968–1969," interview conducted by Susan R. Schrepfer, Sierra Club History Committee, San Francisco, 1984, p. 9.

2. Wallace Stegner, "The Artist as Environmental Advocate," interview conducted by Ann Lage, Regional Oral History Office, the Bancroft Library, Berkeley, 1982, p. 28.

3. Adams to Brooks, December 31, 1968, *Sierra Club Archives*, Adams papers, carton 110, file: Diablo.

4. Alexander Hildebrand, "Sierra Club Leader and Critic: Perspectives on Club Growth, Scope, and Tactics, 1950s–1970s," interview conducted by Ann Lage, Regional Oral History Office, the Bancroft Library, Berkeley, 1982, pp. 33, 37.

5. Minutes, BoD: December 10, 1966.

6. Hildebrand to McCloskey, January 19, 1966, in Hildebrand, "Sierra Club Leader and Critic," pp. 55–57.

7. Martin Litton, "Sierra Club Director and Uncompromising Preservationist, 1950s–1970s," interview conducted by Ann Lage, Regional Oral History Office, the Bancroft Library, Berkeley, 1982, pp. 85, 87.

8. Foreword by David Brower in Joseph Wood Krutch, *Baja California and the Geography of Hope* (San Francisco: Sierra Club, 1967), pp. 7, 8.

9. Foreword by David Brower in Mireille Johnson, *Central Park Country: A Tune Within Us* (San Francisco: Sierra Club, 1968), p. 7.

10. Foreword by David Brower in Stephen C. Jett, *Navajo Wildlands: "As Long as the Rivers Shall Run"* (San Francisco: Sierra Club, 1967), p. 18.

11. Foreword by David Brower in Theodora Kroeber and Robert F. Heizer, *Almost Ancestors: The First Californians* (San Francisco: Sierra Club, 1968), p. 8.

12. Adams to Porter, January 24, 1967, *Sierra Club Archives*, Adams papers, carton 111, file: Brower Controversy.

13. Richard Hofstadter, *The Paranoid Style in American Politics and Other Essays* (New York: Knopf, 1965).

14. Porter to Adams, January 29, 1967, Adams to Porter, February 1, 1967, *Sierra Club Archives*, Adams papers, carton 111, file: Brower Controversy.

15. Marshall to Porter, with copies to the board and the executive director, February 4, 1967, *Sierra Club Archives*, Adams papers, carton 111, file: Brower Controversy.

16. Adams to the Directors of the Sierra Club, February 15, 1967, *Sierra Club Archives*, Adams papers, carton 111, file: Brower Controversy.

17. Adams to Frugé, December 6, 1968, *Sierra Club Archives*, Adams papers, carton 110, file: Brower Controversy.

18. Siri to Board of Directors, May 1, 1967, *Richard Sill Papers*, University of Nevada, Reno, box 11.

19. Edgar Wayburn, "Sierra Club Statesman, Leader of the Parks and Wilderness Movement," interview conducted by Ann Lage and Susan R. Schrepfer, Regional Oral History Office, the Bancroft Library, Berkeley, 1985, pp. 214–216.

20. Wayburn to Members of the Publications Reorganization Committee, July 15, 1967, in Minutes, BoD: September 14–15, 1967.

21. Minutes, BoD: May 6, 1967.

22. "Sierra Club to Reorganize Publishing Program," press release, May 9, 1967, *Sierra Club Archives*, Brower papers, carton 205, file: Brower Controversy, 1967.

23. Brower to Wayburn, June 6, 1967 ("Thought about until 6/14; by messenger"), *Sierra Club Archives*, Brower papers, carton 205, file: Brower Controversy, 1967.

24. Minutes, BoD: May 6, 1967. See also Turner, "A Perspective on David Brower," p. 17.

25. David Brower, "Environmental Activist, Publicist, and Prophet," interview conducted by Susan R. Schrepfer, Regional Oral History Office, the Bancroft Library, Berkeley, 1980, p. 238.

26. Brower to Brooks, October 21, 1968 (draft), *Sierra Club Archives*, Brower papers, carton 205, file: Brower Controversy, 1968.

27. Ibid.

28. "The Mad Hatter's Tea Party, or What Every Sierra Club Member Should Know," December 5, 1967, *Richard Sill Papers*, box 11.

29. Ibid.

30. Minutes, BoD: December 9, 1967.

31. Robert Marshall to David Pesonen, January 31, 1968, Robert Marshall to Board, Chapters, Group Chairmen, and Council, January 31, 1968, Marshall to Publications Reorganization Committee, January 17, 1968, *Sierra Club Archives*, Brower papers, carton 205, file: Brower Controversy, 1968.

32. Minutes, BoD: September 9, 1967, December 9–10, 1967.

33. Minutes, BoD: December 9–10, 1967.

34. Minutes, BoD: January 21, 1968.

35. Edgar Wayburn, "A Short Guide to Conservation Action in

the Sierra Club," March 25, 1968, in *Sierra Club Conservation Policy Guide: Abstracts of Directors Actions 1946–1968*, rev. ed. (July 1968). The author used the copy in the Sierra Club Offices, San Francisco.

36. Minutes, BoD: June 26–27, 1971. See also William E. Siri, "Reflections on the Sierra Club, the Environment, and Mountaineering, 1950s–1970s," interview conducted by Ann Lage, Regional Oral History Office, the Bancroft Library, Berkeley, 1979, p. 146.

37. Brower, "Environmental Activist," pp. 242–243.

38. Brower to George Marshall, February 1, 1968, *Richard Sill Papers*, University of Nevada, Reno, box 11.

39. George Marshall to Brower, February 12, 1968, *Richard Sill Papers*, University of Nevada, Reno, box 11.

40. Sill to Sierra Club members on lists 1–9 and 40, February 11, 1968, *Richard Sill Papers*, University of Nevada, Reno, box 11.

41. Siri, "Reflections," p. 151.

42. Sill to Council Organization Committee, February 29, 1968, Leonard to Sill, February 24, 1968, *Richard Sill Papers*, University of Nevada, Reno, box 11.

43. Minutes, Ex Comm: July 1967; Minutes, BoD: December 3, 1967; Siri, "Reflections," p. 134; Brower, "Environmental Activist," p. 227.

44. Minutes, BoD: February 3–4, 1968.

45. Siri, "Reflections," p. 135.

46. Minutes, BoD: February 3–4, 1968.

47. Sill to Wayburn, with attachments, February 29, 1968, *Richard Sill Papers*, University of Nevada, Reno, box 11.

48. Memorandum, Leonard to Board of Directors, April 24, 1968, *Sierra Club Archives*, Adams papers, carton 110, file: Brower Controversy.

49. Minutes, BoD: May 3, 1968.

50. Adams to Sill, September 29, 1968, *Richard Sill Papers*, University of Nevada, Reno, box 49.

51. See Ansel Adams to Board of Directors, Chapter Chairmen, Council Members, October 22, 1968, *Sierra Club Archives*, Adams papers, carton 110, file: Brower Controversy; Wayburn, "Sierra Club Statesman," p. 229.

52. Minutes, BoD: March 17, 1967. See also Phillip S. Berry, draft interview, conducted by Ann Lage, Regional Oral History

Office, the Bancroft Library, Berkeley, n.d., p. 18. See Siri, "Reflections," p. 140, for Brower's role in the IRS matter.

53. Minutes, BoD: May 6, 1967, September 9, 1967.

54. "Legislation by Chain-saw," *SCB* 53 (March 1968), pp. 12, 13.

55. Minutes, BoD: May 4, 1968.

56. Minutes, BoD: September 9, 1967.

57. See Wayburn comments in Minutes, BoD: September 14, 1967, December 14—15, 1968.

58. Michael McCloskey, "Sierra Club Executive Director: The Evolving Club and the Environmental Movement, 1961–1981," interview conducted by Susan R. Schrepfer, Regional Oral History Office, the Bancroft Library, Berkeley, 1983, p. 92.

59. See Susan R. Schrepfer, *The Fight to Save the Redwoods: A History of Environmental Reform 1917–1978* (Madison: University of Wisconsin Press, 1983), p. 180.

60. Martin Litton, "Sierra Club Director," p. 59. See also Martin Litton personal papers, in author's possession, file: PG&E.

61. "How Bold Shall We Be?" *SCB* 45 (January 1960), pp. 3, 4.

62. Stewart L. Udall, "David Brower and the Rise of the Sierra Club," a draft, September 28, 1986, intended for a new edition of *The Quiet Crisis*.

63. Katherine Barkley and Steve Weissman, "The Eco-Establishment," in *Eco-Catastrophe*, by the editors of *Ramparts* (San Francisco: Canfield Press, 1970); Paul R. Ehrlich, *The Population Bomb* (New York: Sierra Club/Ballantine Books, 1968); Garrett De Bell, Foreword to Garrett De Bell, ed., *The Environmental Handbook: Prepared for the First National Environmental Teach-In* (New York: Ballantine/Friends of the Earth, 1970), p. iii.

64. On political style, see Hofstadter, *Paranoid Style in American Politics*, pp. 5, 29–32. See also Michael Paul Rogin, *The Intellectuals and McCarthy: The Radical Specter* (Cambridge: MIT Press, 1967), pp. 2, 230.

65. McCloskey, "Sierra Club Executive Director," p. 90. In addition to Ansel Adams, both Edgar Wayburn and Richard Leonard use the term "paranoid" to describe David Brower's behavior in the late 1960s. See Edgar Wayburn, "Sierra Club Statesman," pp. 227, 237; Richard M. Leonard, *Mountaineer*, p. 394.

66. See *Southern Sierran* 25 (January–February 1969). Leonard praised the campaign conducted against Brower by the *Mugelnoos*, the newsletter of the Los Angeles Ski Mountaineering and Rock Climbing Section. He also provided the editor of this newsletter with a copy of an invoice for what he called Brower's "profligate expenditures" for restaurant bills. Leonard to *Mugelnoos*, March 20, 1969, in author's possession, on loan from Ruth D. Mendenhall.

67. Minutes, BoD: September 14–15, 1968, October 18–19, 1968.

68. "Statement of Eliot Porter at Board Meeting," September 15, 1968, *Sierra Club Archives*, Brower papers, carton 205, file: Brower Controversy, 1968. Excerpts from Porter in this paragraph are from this document.

69. For Brower's view of Robinson, see David R. Brower, "Environmental Activist," pp. 88, 90. On Jukes, see Gary Soucie, Eastern Representative, "Confidential Memo" and enclosures, May 8, 1969, *Sierra Club Archives*, Brower papers, carton 209, file: Grand Canyon.

70. Berry to Wayburn, n.d. (ca. September 1963), Litton personal papers, in author's possession, file: PG&E.

71. Leonard to Sibley, December 5, 1966, Litton personal papers, file: Diablo, on personal loan; Litton to the author, February 21, 1986.

72. Brower to Wayburn, June 6, 1967, *Sierra Club Archives*, Brower papers, carton 206, file: Brower Controversy, 1967.

73. "Report of the Sierra Club Publications Reorganization Committee," September 14, 1968, appendix to Minutes, BoD: September 14–15, 1968.

74. Ibid.

75. Brower to Brooks, October 21, 1968 (draft), *Sierra Club Archives*, Brower papers, carton 205, file: Brower Controversy, 1968.

76. Ibid.

77. See Kenneth Boulding, *The Organizational Revolution: A Study in the Ethics of Economic Organization* (1953; repr., Chicago: Quadrangle Books, 1968), p. 6.

78. Minutes, BoD: October 19, 1968; a complete transcript is in *Richard Sill Papers*, University of Nevada, Reno, box 5.

79. Richard M. Leonard, "Mountaineer, Lawyer, Environmen-

talist," interview conducted by Susan R. Schrepfer, Regional Oral History Office, the Bancroft Library, Berkeley, 1975, p. 349.

80. Adams to Jukes, October 6, 1968, *Richard Sill Papers*, University of Nevada, Reno, box 49.

81. Brower to members of Grand Canyon Task Force, November 25, 1968, *Sierra Club Archives*, Brower papers, carton 209, file: Grand Canyon, 1968.

82. On campaign slogans, see Sill's notes in *Richard Sill Papers*, box 5; on "High Noon," see Ruth D. Mendenhall to Sill, February 17, 1969, *Richard Sill Papers*, University of Nevada, Reno, box 5.

83. Brower to Adams, October 31, 1968, *Sierra Club Archives*, Brower papers, carton 205, file: Brower Controversy, 1968.

84. Brower to the Secretary, Sierra Club, December 31, 1968, *Sierra Club Archives*, Brower papers, carton 205, file: Brower Controversy, 1968.

85. "The Earth's Wild Places," *Sierra Club Archives*, Brower papers, carton 205, file: Brower Controversy, 1968.

86. *Sierra Club Explorer* 1 (Fall 1968).

87. Siri, "Reflections," p. 139.

88. "Earth National Park" advertisement, *New York Times*, January 14, 1969. A copy is in *Sierra Club Archives*, Adams papers, carton 111, file: Elections, 1969.

89. David Brower and Hugh Nash, "Stewart Ogilvy, 1914–1985," *Not Man Apart* 16 (January–February 1986), p. 8.

90. Minutes, BoD: February 8–9, 1969.

91. Brower, "Environmental Activist," p. 229.

92. Memorandum, Legal Committee to BoD, January 30, 1969, *Sierra Club Archives*, Adams papers, carton 111, file: Brower Controversy.

93. Minutes, BoD: February 8–9, 1969.

94. *Palo Alto Times*, February 11, 1969; a copy is in *Sierra Club Archives*, Adams papers, carton 111, file: Brower Controversy.

95. Stegner, "The Artist," p. 27.

96. "Elections and Electioneering," *SCB* 53 (December 1968), p. 2.

97. A.B.C. brochure in *Sierra Club Archives*, Adams papers, carton 111, file: Sierra Club Elections, 1969.

98. C.M.C. brochure in *Sierra Club Archives*, Adams papers, carton 111, file: Sierra Club Elections, 1969.

99. See Minutes, BoD: May 3–4, 1969, and Leonard, "Mountaineer," pp. 449–450.

100. Robert A. Jones, "Fratricide in the Sierra Club," *The Nation* (May 5, 1969). See also questions by Ann Lage in Siri, "Reflections," p. 66, and by Susan R. Schrepfer in Brower, "Environmental Activist," p. 246.

101. Michael Paul Rogin and John L. Shrover, *Political Change in California: Critical Elections and Social Movements, 1890–1966* (Westport, Conn.: Greenwood Publishing, 1970), p. 201.

102. Rogin and Shrover, *Political Change in California*, pp. xv–xvi. The Club election is analyzed in detail in William B. Devall, "The Governing of a Voluntary Organization: Oligarchy and Democracy in the Sierra Club" (Ph.D. diss., University of Oregon, 1970).

103. Devall, "The Governing of a Voluntary Organization," pp. 235–239.

104. Ibid., pp. 247, 248.

105. Ibid., pp. 305, 306.

106. As Michael McCloskey points out, within two years the C.M.C. did change the nominating procedures for candidates for the board so that they came from the chapters. McCloskey to the author, January 15, 1987.

107. Sill to C.M.C. leaders, April 10, 1969, *Richard Sill Papers*, University of Nevada, Reno, box 6.

108. Adams to Sill, April 18, 1969, Adams to Berry, September 25, 1969, *Sierra Club Archives*, Adams papers, carton 111, file: Election, 1969.

109. Minutes, Ex Comm: April 18, 1969, reading "No Minutes Ever Recorded."

110. Leonard to C.M.C. Directors, April 20, 1969, in Leonard, "Mountaineer," pp. 451–452.

111. "Thoughts and Recommendations on the Several Vice Presidents," May 1, 1969, *Richard Sill Papers*, University of Nevada, Reno, box 11.

112. Livermore to Leonard, April 29, 1969, with copy to Adams, *Sierra Club Archives*, Adams papers, carton 111, file: Sierra Club, misc.

113. Adams to Livermore, May 5, 1969, *Sierra Club Archives*, Adams papers, carton 111, file: Sierra Club, misc.

114. Minutes, BoD: May 3–4, 1969. These minutes document discussion of the May 3–4 meeting, except where otherwise noted.

115. For the eulogy passed by the board, see Minutes, BoD: May 3–4, 1969.

116. Siri, "Reflections," p. 144.

117. Minutes, BoD: May 3–4, 1969.

118. "Sierra Club Annual Organization Meeting May 3–4," *SCB* 54 (May 1969), p. 3.

Afterword

1. Michael McCloskey, "Sierra Club Executive Director, The Evolving Sierra Club and the Environmental Movement, 1961–1981," interview conducted by Susan R. Schrepfer, Regional Oral History Office, the Bancroft Library, Berkeley, 1983, p. 104.

2. McCloskey, "Sierra Club Executive Director," p. 122.

3. Ibid., p. 82.

4. Report of the Chief of Staff, Minutes, BoD: December 6–7, 1969, exhibit B. See also reports by Berry and McCloskey, Minutes, BoD: June 21–22, 1969, exhibits A and B.

5. Maxine E. McCloskey, ed., *Wilderness, the Edge of Knowledge*, Proceedings of the 11th Wilderness Conference, March 14–15, 1969 (San Francisco: Sierra Club, 1970), p. v.

6. See F. Fraser Darling and Noel D. Eichorn, *Man and Nature in the National Parks, Reflections on Policy*, 2d ed. (Washington, D.C.: Conservation Foundation, 1969), pp. 20, 22, 33.

7. Paul Ehrlich, "Population and Conservation: Two Sides of a Coin," in *Wilderness, the Edge of Knowledge*, ed. Maxine McCloskey, p. 3.

8. Kenneth E. Boulding, "The Economics of the Coming Spaceship Earth," in *Essays from the Sixth Resources for the Future Forum*, ed. Henry Jarrett (Baltimore: Johns Hopkins University Press, 1966); Adlai Stevenson, July 9, 1965, quoted in Jack Nease, ed., *Man's Control of the Environment* (Washington, D.C.: Congressional Quarterly, August 1970), p. iii.

9. Garrett Hardin, "The Tragedy of the Commons," *Science* 162 (1968), pp. 1243–1248, reprinted in Garrett Hardin and John

Baden, eds., *Managing the Commons* (San Francisco: W. H. Freeman, 1977), pp. 16–30.

10. Garrett Hardin, "Living in a Lifeboat," *Bioscience* 24 (October 1974), reprinted in Hardin and Baden, eds., *Managing the Commons*, pp. 261–279. This essay was abridged in *Psychology Today* as "Lifeboat Ethics: the Case Against Helping the Poor."

11. McCloskey, ed., *Wilderness, the Edge of Knowledge*, p. 204.

12. Brock Evans, "Environmental Campaigner: From the Northwest Forests to the Halls of Congress," interview conducted by Ann Lage, Regional Oral History Office, the Bancroft Library, Berkeley, 1985, pp. 165–167.

13. See *Beyond Repair, The Ecology of Capitalism* (Boston: Beacon Press, 1971), pp. 92, 93.

14. Minutes, BoD: May 3–4, 1969, appendix E, recommendations of the conservation department.

15. Phillip S. Berry, draft interview conducted by Ann Lage, Regional Oral History Office, the Bancroft Library, Berkeley, n.d., pp. 59–68.

16. Minutes, BoD: September 20–21, 1969, exhibit C.

17. Minutes, BoD: September 20–21, 1969.

18. Minutes, BoD: December 6–7, 1969.

19. Minutes, BoD: May 2–3, 1970.

20. Ibid.

21. On Club population concerns, see: Eissler to Siri and Brower, "Population Explosion," February 20, 1965, Litton personal papers, file: Population; Stewart Udall to Brower, letter and draft, "The Poverty of Overpopulation," January 3, 1967, Litton personal papers, file: Population; Marshall to Berry, November 29, 1969, in Minutes, BoD: December 6–7, 1969, exhibit I; Berry to Richard M. Nixon, April 9, 1970, Litton personal papers, file: Population.

22. Minutes, BoD: May 2–3, 1970.

23. Eugene Coan, "Oil Pollution and Marine Life: A Sierra Club In-House Document," February 23, 1971, Litton personal papers, file: Pollution; "Fill 'Er Up," August 1972, Litton personal papers, file: Pollution.

24. See "Sierra Club Mounts a New Campaign: Conservationist Group's Activism Is Clashing with Business Interests," *Business*

Week (May 23, 1970), pp. 64, 65; McCloskey to Board, "'Energy Crisis' Advertising Campaign by Industry," August 23, 1972, Litton personal papers, file: Power; "Report of the Electrical Power Task Force," January 9, 1972, Litton personal papers, file: Power; Minutes, BoD: October 25, 1972.

25. Minutes, BoD: January 12–13, 1974. See also William E. Siri, "Reflections on the Sierra Club, the Environment, and Mountaineering, 1950s–1970s," interview conducted by Ann Lage, Regional Oral History Office, the Bancroft Library, Berkeley, 1979, p. 166.

26. Raymond J. Sherwin, Editorial, *SCB* 56 (May 1971), p. 2; Raymond J. Sherwin, "Conservationist, Judge, and Sierra Club President," interview conducted by Ann Lage, Regional Oral History Office, the Bancroft Library, Berkeley, 1982, pp. 1–9, 83. See also Phillip S. Berry, "Corporate Responsibility and the Environment," *SCB* 55 (May 1970), p. 2.

27. Donella H. Meadows et al., *The Limits to Growth: A Report for the Club of Rome's Project on the Predicament of Mankind* (New York: University Books, 1974); E. F. Schumacher, *Small Is Beautiful: Economics as if People Mattered* (London: Blond & Briggs, 1973); Warren Johnson, *Muddling Toward Frugality* (San Francisco: Sierra Club Books, 1978); William Ophuls, *Ecology and the Politics of Scarcity* (San Francisco: W. H. Freeman, 1977); Richard Barnett and Ronald Muller, *Global Reach: The Power of the Multinational Corporations* (New York: Simon and Schuster, 1974).

28. Rice Odell, *Environmental Awakening: The New Revolution to Protect the Earth* (Cambridge, Mass.: Conservation Foundation, 1980).

29. Stephen Fox, *John Muir and His Legacy: The American Conservation Movement* (Boston: Little, Brown and Co., 1981), pp. 325, 326.

30. Minutes, BoD: February 14–15, 1970, exhibit A.

31. John G. Mitchell with Constance L. Stallings, eds., *Ecotactics, The Sierra Club Handbook for Environmental Activists* (New York: Pocket Books, 1970), p. 5.

32. Ibid., p. 12.

33. Adams in Minutes, BoD: September 20–21, 1969. See also *Sierra Club Archives*, Adams papers, carton 111, file: Elections 1970.

34. "Environmental Teach-In," *SCB* 55 (March 1970), pp. 14, 15. See also Minutes, BoD: February 14–15, 1970.

35. *SCB* 55 (March 1970), p. 2.

36. Minutes, Ex Comm: April 13, 1970.

37. Minutes, BoD: May 2–3, 1970, exhibit D, and in revised form; Editorial, *SCB* 55 (June 1970), p. 2.

38. McCloskey himself signed a letter to the board asking for some expression on the war in Indochina. See Minutes, BoD: May 14, 1970, exhibit A; Minutes, Ex Comm: June 4, 1970.

39. Minutes, BoD: February 8–9, 1969.

40. *SCB* 54 (July 1969), pp. 8, 9.

41. Gary Soucie, "The Everglades Jetport—One Hell of an Uproar," *SCB* 54 (July 1969), pp. 4–7.

42. Minutes, BoD: September 19, 1969.

43. George Cameron Coggins and Charles F. Wilkinson, *Federal Public Land and Resources Law* (Mineola, N.Y.: Foundation Press, 1981), pp. xx–xxvii.

44. For a summary, see Nease, ed., *Man's Control of the Environment*, pp. 1–8, 88–91.

45. Coggins and Wilkinson, *Federal Public Land and Resources Law*, pp. 599–602.

46. Ibid., pp. 260–274.

47. McCloskey, "Sierra Club Executive Director," pp. 70, 204, 205.

48. Michael McCloskey, Introduction to W. Lloyd Tupling, "Sierra Club Washington Representative," interview conducted by Ann Lage, Regional Oral History Office, the Bancroft Library, Berkeley, 1985, pp. i, ii.

49. Tupling, "Sierra Club Washington Representative," pp. 36–38.

50. Michael McCloskey, "Raiding the Forests," *New Republic* (December 13, 1969), pp. 10–11. See also Julie Cannon, "Timber Supply Act: Anatomy of a Battle," *SCB* 55 (March 1970), pp. 8–11.

51. See Nease, ed., *Man's Control of the Environment*, pp. 70–73; McCloskey to the author, January 15, 1987.

52. Evans, "Environmental Campaigner," pp. 109, 113.

53. Ibid., pp. 2, 3.

54. Ibid., p. 39.

55. Ibid., p. 151.

56. Public Land Law Review Commission, *One Third of the Nation's Land: A Report to the President and to the Congress* (Washington, D.C.: G.P.O., 1970).

57. Michael McCloskey, "The Environmental Implications of the Report of the Public Land Commission," *University of Wyoming Law Review* 6 (1970), pp. 350–368; Phillip Berry, "An Analysis: The Public Land Law Commission Report," *SCB* 55 (October 1970), pp. 21–30.

58. See Sidney Plotkin, "Policy Fragmentation and Capitalist Reform: The Defeat of National Land Use Policy," *Politics and Society* 9 (1980), p. 421.

59. Berry, "An Analysis: The Public Land Law Commission Report," *SCB* 55 (October 1970), pp. 19–20. See also Minutes, BoD: September 19–20, 1970.

60. Evans, "Environmental Campaigner," pp. 127, 162, 176–179.

61. McCloskey discussed the record of the environmental movement in the 1970s in "The Environmental Movement: Its Progress and Outlook," keynote address presented to the Environmental History Society, Duke University, April 30, 1987.

62. Michael McCloskey, "Wilderness Movement at the Crossroads," *Pacific Historical Review* 51 (August 1972), pp. 346–362.

63. Minutes, BoD: December 6–7, 1969.

64. Ibid. On the orientation of federal agencies, see Joseph Sax, *Mountains Without Handrails* (Ann Arbor: University of Michigan Press, 1980); McCloskey, "Wilderness Movement at the Crossroads," pp. 355–357; McCloskey, "Sierra Club Executive Director," pp. 66, 67.

65. John H. Hendee, George H. Stankey, and Robert C. Lucas, *Wilderness Management*, Miscellaneous Publication no. 1365 (Washington, D.C.: U.S. Forest Service, Department of Agriculture, October 1978), pp. 94, 95.

66. On RARE I and RARE II, see Hendee, Stankey, and Lucas, *Wilderness Management*, pp. 14, 101–105, 124; McCloskey, "Sierra Club Executive Director," pp. 187–188, 258.

67. Evans, "Environmental Campaigner," pp. 106–108.

68. Gary Soucie to David Brower, April 19, 1967, quoted in Su-

san R. Schrepfer, *The Fight to Save the Redwoods: A History of Environmental Reform, 1917–1978* (Madison: University of Wisconsin Press, 1983), p. 164.

69. Mitchell with Stallings, eds., *Ecotactics*, p. 11.

70. See Minutes, BoD: July 22, 1962, January 26–27, 1963, May 7, 1966; David Sive, "Natural Beauty and the Law," *SCB* (May 1968), pp. 18–20; Allan R. Talbot, *Power Along the Hudson: The Storm King Case and the Birth of Environmentalism* (New York: Dutton, 1972); Bestor Robinson, "Thoughts on Conservation and the Sierra Club," interview conducted by Susan R. Schrepfer, Sierra Club History Committee, San Francisco, 1974, p. 46; David R. Brower, "Environmental Activist, Publicist, and Prophet," interview conducted by Susan R. Schrepfer, Regional Oral History Office, the Bancroft Library, Berkeley, 1980, pp. 187–189.

71. Richard M. Leonard, "Mountaineer, Lawyer, Environmentalist," interview conducted by Susan R. Schrepfer, Regional Oral History Office, the Bancroft Library, Berkeley, 1975, p. 73.

72. John L. Harper, *Mineral King: Public Concern with Government Policy* (Arcata, Calif.: Pacifica Publishing, 1982), pp. 165–170.

73. Sherwin, "Conservationist," p. 110; Odell, *Environmental Awakening*, pp. 4–5. See also Susan R. Schrepfer, "Perspectives on Conservation: Sierra Club Strategies in Mineral King," *Journal of Forest History* 20 (October 1976), pp. 176–190.

74. "The Land Ethic," in Aldo Leopold, *A Sand County Almanac and Sketches Here and There* (New York: Oxford University Press, 1949), pp. 224, 225; Brower, "Environmental Activist," p. 189; Minutes, BoD: December 6–7, 1969; Roderick Nash, "American Environmental History: A New Teaching Frontier," *Pacific Historical Review* 41 (April 1972), pp. 363–372.

75. Harper, *Mineral King*, pp. 169–180. See also Christopher D. Stone, *Should Trees Have Standing? Toward Legal Rights for Natural Objects* (Los Altos, Calif.: William Kaufman, 1964), pp. 73–84; Berry, draft interview, pp. 76, 77; McCloskey, "Sierra Club Executive Director," pp. 167–173.

76. "Report of Legal Committee on Litigation," Minutes, BoD: July 19, 1969, exhibit A.

77. McCloskey, "Sierra Club Executive Director," pp. 153, 183.

78. McCloskey, "Sierra Club Executive Director," p. 158. See also

James W. Moorman, Editorial, *SCB* 57 (January 1972), p. 2; Fred Fisher, "Environmental Law," *SCB* 56 (January 1971), pp. 24–29.

79. Leonard, "Mountaineer," p. 144; Berry, draft interview, p. 51; Nathan C. Clark, "Sierra Club Leader, Outdoorsman, and Engineer," interview conducted by Richard Searle, Sierra Club History Committee, San Francisco, 1977, p. 44.

80. Berry, draft interview, pp. 81–83.

81. Minutes, BoD: June 21–22, 1969.

82. Minutes, BoD: June 26–27, 1971; Siri, "Reflections," p. 146.

83. Minutes, BoD: June 21–22, 1969.

84. "Bylaw changes for 1971" (for Sierra Club election, 1971), Richard A. Cellarius papers, on loan to the author.

85. Leonard, "Mountaineer," p. 399.

86. Minutes, BoD: May 1–2, 1971, appendix B.

87. See Nicholas Robinson, International Committee, Memo to List One, December 6, 1971, *Richard Sill Papers*, University of Nevada, Reno, box 12.

88. Sherwin, "Conservationist," pp. 87–92.

89. See Arne Naess, "The Shallow and Deep, Long-Range Ecology Movement. A Summary," *Inquiry* 16 (1973), p. 9; Bill Devall and George Sessions, *Deep Ecology* (Salt Lake City: Peregrine Smith Books, 1985).

90. Leonard to George Marshall, April 12, 1971, Leonard to Richard Cellarius, May 12, 1978, in Richard A. Cellarius personal papers.

91. Berry, draft interview, pp. 94–96; McCloskey, "Sierra Club Executive Director," p. 143, 144.

92. Evans, "Environmental Campaigner," p. 75; see also pp. 269, 289–290.

93. "Sierra Club Bylaws, 1981," pamphlet in the author's possession.

94. For the pamphlet Richard Sill sometimes in letters called "The Yellow Peril," see "The Future of the Sierra Club: A Paper for Discussion," January 31, 1971, *Richard Sill Papers*, University of Nevada, Reno, box 17.

95. See the so-called Two Term Memo, August 12, 1970, *Richard Sill Papers*, University of Nevada, Reno, box 12.

96. Adams to Leonard and the C.M.C. group, August 27, 1970,

Sierra Club Archives, Adams papers, carton 111, file: Sierra Club Elections.

97. Minutes, BoD: May 1–2, 1971, appendix B. See also Richard Sill, "By-Law Changes for 1971"; Richard Sill, "Clarifying Resolutions Bylaw Amendment in Article IV," for BoD: May 1, 1971, *Richard Sill Papers*, University of Nevada, Reno, box 11; Siri, "Reflections," pp. 146–152.

98. See Ruth Bradley, "Limitation of Terms for Elected Directors—Against," in "Bylaw Changes," 1971, in author's possession. See also Edgar Wayburn, "Sierra Club Statesman, Leader of the Parks and Wilderness Movement," interview conducted by Ann Lage and Susan R. Schrepfer, Regional Oral History Office, the Bancroft Library, Berkeley, 1985, pp. 273–277.

99. On the change in nominating procedures, see McCloskey to the author, January 15, 1987.

100. McCloskey, "The Environmental Movement: Its Progress and Outlook."

101. See Samuel Hays, *Beauty, Health, and Permanence: Environmental Politics in the United States, 1955–1985* (Cambridge: Cambridge University Press, 1987).

102. David R. Brower, Foreword to Eliot Porter, *The Place No One Knew: Glen Canyon on the Colorado* (San Francisco: Sierra Club Books, 1963), p. 7.

103. Linnie Marsh Wolfe, ed., *John of the Mountains: The Unpublished Journals of John Muir* (1938; repr., Madison: University of Wisconsin Press, 1978), p. 315.

104. Wolfe, ed., *John of the Mountains*, p. 353.

105. *SCB* 1 (January 1896), p. 271.

Index